Mobilizing Regions, Mobilizing Europe

Regional development strategies are becoming more similar all around Europe, even though regional differences are more pronounced than ever and many European regions have become more autonomous actors. This thesis of a peculiar standardized diversification of sub-national space in the modern European Union is the point of departure of this book.

Based upon analytical premises of Stanford School Sociological Institutionalism, Sebastian M. Büttner studies regional mobilization in contemporary Europe from a new and innovative perspective. He highlights the importance of scientific expertise and global scientific models in contemporary regional development practice, and exemplifies their significance with the example of region-building in Poland in the course of EU integration. This new wave of regional mobilization is not just conceived as an effect of local, national or European politics, but as an expression of a larger conceptual shift in governing society and space.

This well researched and clearly argued book not only provides fresh insights into region-building and regionalization in contemporary European space, but also contributes to the new sociology of Europeanization. It will be an illuminating read for scholars and students in Sociology, European and EU studies, International Relations, Cultural Studies, Geography, Regional Science, Polish Studies and related subject areas.

Sebastian M. Büttner is Lecturer in Social Theory and Cultural Sociology at the Institute of Sociology, University of Erlangen-Nuremberg, Germany. His research interests include sociology of knowledge and culture, theory of modernity, transnationalization and regionalization in contemporary Europe, theories and practice of social government and social mobilization.

Routledge/European Sociological Association Studies in European Societies
Series editors: Thomas P. Boje, Max Haller, Martin Kohli and Alison Woodward

Mobilizing Regions, Mobilizing Europe

Expert knowledge and scientific planning in European regional development

Sebastian M. Büttner

Zur Erinnerung

*an unsere Begegnung
in Paris und an
die Wohnung in der
Wolganter Str. in Berlin*

22. Jan. 2015

Routledge
Taylor & Francis Group

LONDON AND NEW YORK

First published 2012
by Routledge
2 Park Square, Milton Park, Abingdon, Oxon OX14 4RN

Simultaneously published in the USA and Canada
by Routledge
711 Third Avenue, New York, NY10017

Routledge is an imprint of the Taylor & Francis Group, an informa business

First issued in paperback 2014

British Library Cataloguing in Publication Data
A catalogue record for this book is available from the British Library

Library of Congress Cataloging-in-Publication Data
Büttner, Sebastian
    Mobilizing regions, mobilizing Europe: expert knowledge and scientific
    planning in European regional development/by Sebastian M. Büttner. –
    1st ed.
    p. cm. – (Routledge/European sociological association studies in
    European societies)
    1. Regional planning–Europe. 2. Regional planning–Poland–Case
    studies. 3. European Union countries–Economic integration. I. Title.
    HT395.E8.B88 2012
    307.1'2094–dc23

                                                            2011034953

ISBN: 978-0-415-67875-9 (hbk)
ISBN: 978-1-138-02001-6 (pbk)
ISBN: 978-0-203-09356-6 (ebk)

Typeset in Times New Roman
by Wearset Ltd, Boldon, Tyne and Wear

Contents

Illustrations

Figures

Tables

Maps

Preface

It is a common and indeed understandable tendency of people who are occupied with one topic for a long period of time to overestimate and overemphasize their particular field of interest, and to start seeing the world only from this particular point of view. After studying issues of region-building and regional development in contemporary Europe for some time, I do firmly believe, nonetheless, that it is not just my own selective bias that makes me quite bluntly assert here, right at the beginning of this book, that something is happening at the local and regional level in Europe – something that has never been so intense and all-embracing as it is today.

These days, regional symbols and idioms are with us in TV advertisements, in lifestyle magazines and even on large billboards at train stations, airports and bus stops. Sub-national areas and regions have become important reference points of both political participation and for sentiments of social belonging. They are celebrated as refuges for stable and authentic identities in an increasingly accelerating and globalizing world that no longer seems to provide stability and collective forms of belonging. And they have become important political actors even in countries without strong regional traditions or federalist systems of state government. Moreover, they have also become active promoters of global flows and market exchanges, vigorously promoting business development and outlining numerous programmes of economic stimulation and revitalizing local infrastructure, 'human capital' and all other resources required for favourable business development. More and more municipalities and regions all over Europe have started to create technology parks, business incubators and other types of knowledge-transfer centres in order to attract new investors and to reinforce the attractiveness, creativity and innovativeness of their local economy. And, against this backdrop, it is certainly more than just an astonishing coincidence that even this book was written to large extent in a science and technology park which is home to the campus of Bremen University and the Bremen International Graduate School of Social Sciences (BIGSSS) where I had the opportunity to conduct this research project and write my dissertation between autumn 2006 and autumn 2009.

Yet, this new upswing of sub-national regions in Europe today is not just driven by economic agents and anonymous market forces. When I first came across the topic of regionalization and regional development in the context of a research project, the so-called EUROCAP project at the University of Bamberg, which focused on capacities of economic revitalization in newly created regions in post-socialist Poland, I was impressed by the strong prevalence and involvement of professional and scientific expertise in practices of regional development. In fact, the newly created regions in Poland were ranked, measured and evaluated by numerous scientists, experts and professional organizations. A huge number of scientists as well as domestic and international professionals have explored the conditions of success and failure of development and promoted the most contemporary models of regional regeneration. The regional authorities naturally used the common jargon that can be found in current text books on regional development, and they published ambitious visions of future development in multi-annual development strategies designed to specify and justify the priorities of public development policy. Hence, I found a massive amount of expert knowledge and expert involvement in these newly created sub-national areas in Poland. And this observation was the point of departure of the study that is outlined in this book.

When I left my office in Bremen's technology park for a three-month research stay at the Institute of European Studies at the Jagiellonian University of Kraków in spring 2007, I travelled with one of the new European low-budget airlines from a newly created regional airport in Germany to an even smaller regional airport near Kraków in Poland. After my arrival I took a taxi to get from the airport to the students' dormitory at the Przegorzały hill, where the Institute of European Studies of the Jagiellonian University is located. The taxi driver was very eager to talk to me in English and practice his newly acquired English skills, although I also tried to impress him with my rudimentary Polish language skills. I was not successful, and he continued to talk with me in broken English and proudly told me that he recently finished an English class within the framework of a publicly financed job training course that was almost entirely funded by the European Social Fund (ESF) of the European Union. While he was telling me this, we drove on a new road that was co-funded by the European Regional Development Fund (ERDF) of the European Union. And on the way to the dormitory we passed some nice, newly refurbished churches and an old monastery that was being renovated. They had the familiar white information board with black lettering which I saw so often during my research stay in Poland, stating: 'This building is refurbished by the local authority with support from the Integrated Operational Programme for Regional Development of the Polish Ministry of Regional Development and co-financed by the European Regional Development Fund.'

On the way to the dormitory the taxi driver talked very enthusiastically about the positive changes in Kraków and its surrounding areas over the past decade and in particular since EU accession. The numbers of tourists were constantly rising each year, he said. He continued by stating that this was good for him and for his business, of course, but also for all people in the region. He also pointed out that the explosion of tourism had also brought about some ambiguous side-effects, such as exploding prices for food and housing in the city centre, mass movements of people both night and day looking for cheap drinks, fun and entertainment without taking much notice of the local people or local realities. But in general, he concluded, the expansion of tourism in and around Kraków was good for the future development of the region and for Poland in general. It was great, he conceded, that so many people from all over were coming to Kraków throughout the year, bringing with them new dynamics and of course money. He also said that he felt delighted that after the break-down of communism the city of Kraków finally got the international recognition it deserves and that so many people from all around the world were coming to visit his city. This was my first face-to-face contact during my research stay after having landed in Poland.

In the following weeks after arrival, I travelled throughout the country and had many conversations of this kind. But I was mainly talking to professionals, people who deal with regional policy and issues of regional development in their everyday professional lives. I met people in the national and regional ministries who are involved in the planning and implementation of regional development policies and, above all, the management of EU Structural Funds. They were talking about principles, practices and certain complex bureaucratic procedures which I had never heard of before, even though I had studied the major procedures and major regulations of the implementation system in preparing for these meetings. They were referring to indicators and standards of monitoring and evaluation that are common practice in the context of EU Structural Fund implementation, and they often referred to these as if they were common knowledge that is naturally shared amongst 'experts'. I met representatives of regional development agencies who proudly talked about the achievements of their institution and the future projects they are planning to realise and implement in the near future. Some of the interview partners also showed me maps, brochures, PowerPoint presentations and even miniature models of the science-and-technology-transfer centres they are about to build on the outskirts of their city which look similar to the technology park in Bremen that I came from. And I also met some employees of non-profit organizations who are involved in development programmes mainly co-funded by the European Social Fund (ESF) which focus on social problems and working with unemployed people, but also farmers and other actors in eco-farming and eco-tourism.

Thus, in short, I got impressions of a massive and multi-faceted mobilization of regional actors and institutions in Poland of today that strongly affects the transformation of sub-national lifeworlds. It can be seen, indeed, that this wave of mobilization is largely determined by EU funding and 'European' regional development policies, but it is mainly carried out by 'domestic' policy-makers and other professional agents of development. Hence, the language and practices the professionals used was strongly 'European'. But the models, concepts and recipes they apply can be found in similar ways in many places all around the world these days. And this is the main focus of the following study. It focuses on the particular *world-cultural* context in which the current wave of regional mobilization in contemporary Europe and Poland alike is being shaped.

Although writing and finishing this book has largely and ever more increasingly been an act of excessive individualization, the whole endeavour would not have been possible without the support of numerous friends, colleagues, my family and also a number of institutions. I would like to thank the Bremen International Graduate School of Social Sciences (BIGSSS) for hosting me in room W1050 of FVG-West in the middle of Bremen Technology Park and generously supporting me in many other ways and dimensions. I would like to say 'thank you' in particular to Werner Dressel, the executive secretary of BIGSSS, for always having his door, his eyes and his ears open to the needs of the research fellows. And I also thank all other members of the executive team of BIGSSS for their generous support and for contributing to create an extraordinary warm, uncomplicated and open working atmosphere. As regards official institutional support I am also grateful to the Heinrich Böll Foundation (HBS) for funding my research fellowship between 2005 and 2008 within the framework of the joint BIGSSS/HBS research group 'Risks of Exclusion and Strategies of Inclusion in an enlarged Europe', my research stay in Kraków in spring 2007, and, beyond that, giving me the opportunity to enjoy the entire 'Böll experience'. The Institute of European Studies of the Jagiellonian University hosted me for the duration of my research stay in spring 2007 and provided me with office space at the 'manorial' Przegorzały Castle. In this regard I would like to send a big *dzięki* to Monika Nowak, the head of administration of the Institute, and Magdalena Góra for welcoming and hosting me so openly and generously.

Furthermore, I am deeply grateful to my two supervisors Steffen Mau and Ulrike Liebert for providing me with all the essentials of good Ph.D. supervision: trust, patience, intellectual openness and an appropriate portion of severity. Moreover, my gratitude also goes to the other two members of my dissertation committee: Richard Münch and Stefan Garsztecki. Both of them were more than helpful at different stages of my Ph.D. project and decisively helped me to get started with my project and structure my thoughts. Special thanks also go to Ross McCalden for his accurate, super-punctual and diligent proofreading and Michael Woniarinski for helping me with the transcriptions of the Polish interviews. And there are many other people to whom I owe gratitude for their presence and their support. Among many others I would like to mention Jan Mewes and my former office mates Nadya Srur and Lars Viellechner, the BIGSSS lunch-time crew, the BIGSSS kicker team and many other colleagues from BIGSSS and the University of Bremen. Many special thanks go to Herwig Reiter, Stefan Bernhard, Arndt Wonka and Volker Balli for substantially commenting on several versions and parts of the book manuscript. Similarly, I would also like to thank Stefano Guzzini and John W. Meyer for comments on my research project and earlier drafts of the manuscript. Needless to say that the responsibility for all remaining mistakes and shortcomings lies with me. Finally, I would also like to express my gratitude to Marek Kozak and Grzegorz

Gorzelak from the Euroreg Institute, who gave valuable hints and insider views on regional development policy in Poland, and to all other interviewees I met during my research stay. They were all very helpful for my research project and generously ignored my rudimentary Polish language skills. The final 'thank you' goes to Tine, who supported and accompanied me throughout.

Abbreviations

CAP	Common Agricultural Policy
CEC	Commission of the European Communities
CEE	Central and Eastern Europe
CF	Cohesion Fund
CHF	Swiss Franc
CoE	Council of Europe
DG-Regio	Directorate General for Regional Policy
DIN	Deutsches Institut für Normung
EAFRD	European Agricultural Fund for Rural Development
EAGF	European Agricultural Guarantee Fund
EAGGF	European Agricultural Guidance and Guarantee Fund
EC	European Council
ECU	European Currency
EEA	European Economic Area
EFF	European Fisheries Fund
EIB	European Investment Bank
ENPI	European Neighbourhood Policy
ERDF	European Regional Development Fund
ERP	European Recovery Programme
ESDN	European Sustainable Development Network
ESDP	European Spatial Development Perspective
ESF	European Social Fund
ESPON	European Spatial Planning Observation Network
EU	European Union
EUR	Euro
EUSF	European Union Solidarity Fund
FDI	Foreign Direct Investment
FGI	Fisheries Guidance Instrument
GDP	Gross Domestic Product
GRIDS	Best Practice Guidelines for Regional Development Strategies
IPA	Instrument for Pre-Accession Assistance
IROP	Integrated Operational Programme for Regional Development
ISO	International Organization for Standardization

ISPA	Instrument for Structural Policies for Pre-Accession
IT	Information and Technology
LEED	Local Economic and Employment Development
LPR	Liga Polskich Rodzin
MDGs	Millenium Development Goals
MERCOSUR	Mercado comum do Cone Sul
M.I.T.	Massachusetts Institute for Technology
NDP	National Development Plan
NDS	National Development Strategy
NGO	Non-Governmental Organization
NSRF	National Strategic Reference Framework
NUTS	Nomenclature of Statistical Units
OCEI	Office of the Committee for European Integration
OECD	Organization for Economic Co-operation and Development
OP	Operational Programme
PAED	Polish Agency for Enterprise Development
PAIiIZ	Polish Information and Foreign Investment Agency
PARR	Polish Agency for Regional development
PHARE	Poland and Hungary Assistance for Restructuring their Economies
PiS	Prawo i Sprawiedliwość
PL	Poland
PLN	Polish Złoty
PO	Platforma Obywatelska
PPS	Standards of Purchasing Power
PSL	Polskie Stronnictwo Ludowe
R&TD	Research and Technology Development
RAPID	Rural Areas Programme for Infrastructure and Development
RDA	Regional Development Agency
RDS	Regional Development Strategy
RIS	Regional Innovation Strategy
RITTS	Regional Innovation and Technology Transfer Strategy
ROP	Regional Operational Programme
RSA	Regional Studies Association
RTP	Regional Technology Plan
SAPARD	Special Accession Programme for Agriculture and Rural Development
SDS	Sustainable Development Strategy
SERN	Sustainable European Regions Network
SEZ	Special Economic Zone
SLD	Sojusz Lewicy Demokratycznej
SME	Small and medium-sized enterprises
SOP	Sectoral Operational Programme
SWOT	Strenths, Weaknesses, Opportunities and Threats
TEN	Trans-European Networks

TP	Technology Park
U.N.	United Nations
UNDP	United Nations Development Programme
UNESCO	United Nations Educational, Scientific and Cultural Organization
UNIDO	United Nations Industrial Development Organization
USD	US-Dollar
WSSD	World Summit on Sustainable Development
ZPORR	Zanitegrowany Program Operacijne Rozwoju Regionalnego

1 Introduction

The study of the conditions of modern life has always been a key concern of sociological reflection. Even the rise and establishment of sociology as an independent scientific discipline is in itself a product of modernity. In fact, with the 'birth of the modern world' (Bayly 2004) by the end of the eighteenth century 'society' was discovered as a major *problematique* of social thought. Since then, the search for the driving forces of social change and development has been central to sociological analyses. Whether it be Auguste Comte's three-stages theory, Karl Marx's dialectical and materialist philosophy of social change, Herbert Spencer's utilitarian adaptation of Darwinian evolutionary theory, Emile Durkheim's functionalist analysis of the social division of labour, or Max Weber's conception of (occidental) rationalization, the 'founding fathers' of sociology were all concerned with the rise of modernity and its ambivalent consequences. Thus, even to this day, for better or worse, sociology is still strongly rooted in these initial foundations of sociological research (cf. Lefebvre 1962; Elias 1969, 1982; Habermas 1990; Schluchter 1996; Münch 2001; Wagner 2001a; Joas and Knöbl 2009).

Consequently, the emergence of sociology as an independent social-scientific discipline has brought about a broad strand of empirical research on social change under the 'grand narrative' of modernization which has dominated social thought in the post-war period (Alexander 2003). Modernization theories claim to describe more or less universal laws of change from 'traditional' to 'modern' society and the evolution of certain universal features of modern society, such as socio-economic progress, individualism, civil society, or the rule of law in all advanced and modernizing societies (cf. Lipset 1959; Rostow 1960; Deutsch 1961; Gerschenkron 1962; Zapf 1971; Parsons 1964 and 1967). However, after the 'golden age' of orthodox modernization theories during the 1960s the preoccupation with universal features of modern society or attempts to create a single narrative of social change were highly contested. Indeed, there is widespread agreement today that modernization theory is dead and that it rested on incorrect and misleading assumptions (Wallerstein 1974, 1980, 1989; Esteva 1985; Escobar 1995). More than ever before we are informed and enlightened about the errors and failures of all-too simplistic and optimistic beliefs in future progress and evolutionary models of civilization. First of all, so called 'postmodern theory' criticizes modernization theorists for their naïve belief in progress and civilization (for an overview: Delanty 2000; Wagner 2001b). The experience of two world wars, the cruel excesses of fascism and totalitarian communism and the threat of atomic war during the cold war between the Western and Eastern blocs were identified as clear indications of the huge barbarian potential of the modern era (cf. Bauman 1991). Second, postcolonial studies and the experiences of developing societies revealed that there is not just one path to modernity and that enforced modernization leads to negative social consequences and potentially even disasters, particularly in less industrialized societies (Chakrabarty 2000). Third, contemporary global history and globalization research have raised attention to the huge diversity and contingency of modernization processes (Appaduraj 1997; Eisenstadt 2000 and 2002a; Knöbl 2006). And last but not least we are also told that advanced modernity might be even more porous, transient and precarious than any epoch before (Giddens 1990; Beck *et al.* 1994). In sum, the assumption of the expansion of one (primarily occidental) modernity throughout the globe is largely dismissed; the belief in future progress is widely de-constructed as 'false consciousness'; even the very notion of modernity itself is considered as mere 'ideology' or 'myth'; and we have been enlightened that in fact 'we have never been modern', yet (Latour 1993).

However, if we look around, if we look in particular at what states, countless development agencies and professionals do and aspire to these days, we cannot avoid getting the impression that the spirit of modernization, the old belief in future progress and the governability of the fate of human development, is as vivid as ever. It even seems, in fact, that the decade of criticism and the 'legitimation crisis' (Habermas 1975) of highly industrialized Western modernity during the 1970s have been followed by an era of an ever more optimistic and radical belief in future progress (Alexander 2003). The revival of market liberalism and laissez-faire capitalism introduced and promoted by Anglo-Saxon governments at the beginning of the 1980s can be seen as a clear indication of this new paradigmatic shift. Fuelled by the break-down of communism we now, more than ever before, have the feeling that we live in 'one world' that is rapidly growing together through pragmatic and utilitarian interests and exchanges across former state borders (Fukuyama 1992). Beyond that state bureaucracies and ever more international organizations outline more and more programmes, strategies and funding schemes to foster socio-economic growth and human development. Apart from traditional state organizations all kinds of humanitarian organizations are constantly concerned with human aid and development. Indeed, the current wave of globalization is marked by a huge worldwide spread and expansion of modernist efforts and aspirations; and stronger than ever before modernist principles and practices are being institutionalized and enforced on a global scale (cf. Tenbruck 1990; Rosenau and Czempiel 1992; Meyer 2000; Lechner and Boli 2005).

Hence, there is a huge gap between the critical discourse of modernity and everyday aspirations and practices of social government and 'social mobilization' (Deutsch 1961). If we took the critics of modernity seriously, we would have to step back from forward-looking planning and attempts at changing and shaping the world – at least many development programmes would have to be enforced differently. It seems, however, as if the critical voices are not heard and regarded much in political practice and everyday life and that the modernist enthusiasm of actively shaping and engineering the conditions of human life is unbroken. This, in my opinion, needs more careful and more rigorous attention both in theoretical conceptions and empirical research of contemporary sociology.

Modernizing practices: intended projects of change and development

Certainly, a simple equation of the notion of 'development' with conceptions of some sort of linear and evolutionary 'progress' which is implicit in orthodox modernization theory is highly problematic and cannot be upheld (Nederveen Pieterse 2001; Long 2001; Ziai 2007). Paths of social change are discontinuous and contingent, and the question of appropriate means and ends of 'development' is a matter of constant competition and contestation both in political and intellectual discourses. Thus, we have to distinguish carefully between the overall modernist impetus of contemporary development thinking and practice, which perpetuates the belief in future progress and improvement, and the analytical concept of 'modernization' as a certain model of development.

In 1977, i.e. long before the rise of the postmodern critique of modernity and modernist theories of social change, but obviously in reaction to the then rising criticism of conventional modernization theories, the German sociologist M. Rainer Lepsius (1990b [1977]: 211ff.) acknowledged this tension and proposed a non-deterministic relational notion of modernization. Apart from the three conventional notions of 'modernity' and 'modernization' – i.e. 1) a mere Anglo-Americanization; 2) a teleological project resting on predefined patterns of change; and 3) an evolutionary process of convergence in social structures – he proposed a fourth, more mundane and practice-centred notion of modernization as a *process of planned and intended development*; a fairly 'political project' that aims to improve the performance of social systems deliberately:

> Modernization, as understood in these terms, is not predefined any more by constantly determined goals of development, but by standards of expectation that are politically relevant, which can be directed principally to all kinds of goals and emerge due to the experience of a relative backwardness in relation to certain reference groups, that is to say reference countries. Certainly, not all standards of expectation which are prevalent within a certain population become relevant, but only those with the power to assert themselves at the political level. This can be achieved by elites in all possible variants (above all, political elites or military elites, of course), but it can also be caused by horizons of expectations that are carried by non-elite groups, who address certain demands to the ruling elites and sanction non-achievement by deprivation of legitimacy.
>
> (Lepsius 1990b [1977]: 224, translated from German by S.B.)

Whilst the first three notions of modernization are highly contested and have been discredited by the critics of the modernization theory, it is this latter notion proposed by Lepsius which helps to capture the spirit of active intervention that remains vivid to this day, and it is this notion that is at the heart of the study at hand. This notion unhinges the concept of modernization from predefined and evolutionary notions of social change. Modernization is no longer regarded as a teleological process, but an intended project of change that is highly dependent on contingent goals and intentions, on the ability to mobilize respective resources that are regarded as necessary to achieve these aims and on the abilities of development agents to enforce their modernizing agenda. According to Lepsius, such a 'relative' and 'relational' conception of modernization was open to failure and non-intended consequences. Thus, everything is possible and conceivable depending on contingent social, political, economic and cultural conditions and on respective historical constellations of social forces within a certain society. Some projects of modernization may be quite limited in scope and remain incomplete. The intended effects may not appear, or the intended projects of modernization may get out of control and transcend the confined areas of planned intervention. However – and this is decisive for an understanding of all of the subject matter of this book – these intended processes of change are decisively and predominantly shaped by 'cultural' factors and standards: namely, by prevailing expectations of 'development', prevailing notions of 'modernity', prevailing conceptions of how to achieve future goals and aspirations, and on the imitation and adaptation of successful role models.

Transnationalization and amplification of modernizing practices

When Lepsius introduced his relational and practice-centred notion of modernization, he was mainly referring to the world of nation-states during the era of 'organized modernity' (Wagner 1994). He referred to large-scale 'modernization offensives' of nation-state governments and national elites in the period between the mid-nineteenth century and the era of postcolonial nation-building after the Second World War. However, in the second half of the twentieth century we have witnessed the emergence of a whole range of new development actors and agents of change and future progress. Over the past decades, the efforts made on the development front have become both more globalized and more localized simultaneously. In fact, the focal points of development, the centres of authority and the places of planning and determining modernizing projects have become increasingly dispersed (Nederveen Pietersee 2001; Hwang 2006). Hence, the agendas of development are increasingly determined beyond and across the level of nation-state governments, such as international organizations, international expert circles and even non-governmental organizations (cf. Evers and Gerke 2005; Deacon 2007); and they are also increasingly determined at the sub-national level by the municipalities and regions that implement development interventions on the ground.

This shift is particularly visible on the European continent, which has experienced substantial supra- and transnational integration and the emergence of a European authority with its own and distinct competences and policy measures over the past 50 years (Green Cowles *et al.* 2001; Rumford 2002; Featherstone and Raedelli 2003; Zürn and Joerges 2005; Bartolini 2005; Liebert *et al.* 2006). At the same time, we can observe a more pronounced role for sub-national regions as focal points of policy intervention and a more powerful role for sub-national regions as development agents outlining and implementing their own development agendas (Hooghe 1996; Keating 1998; Le Galès and Lequesne 1998).

Consequently, this book is concerned with the amplified diffusion of both development thinking and practice in contemporary Europe and the expansion and perpetuation of the 'spirit' of *instrumental activism* and *social mobilization* all around the European continent.[1] More particularly, it is concerned with the massive expansion of standardized practices of social mobilization to sub-national spaces over the past decade and the emergence of regions as 'strategic' development actors that are proactively planning and implementing their own agendas of development. This process certainly correlates strongly with the intensification of European integration and the creation of a common European Single Market during the 1990s and an increasing Europeanization of regional policy agendas during the past two decades (cf. Keating 1994; Hooghe 1996; Leonardi 1995, 2005; Stone Sweet *et al.* 2001; Bache 2008). However, this more recent upswing of regional mobilization is not just an effect of 'national' or 'European' political activities. Rather it must be seen as an expression of a more general and global transformation of modernity and of a broader conceptual shift in governing society and space.

It can be observed, moreover, that the *more visible and pronounced* the differences amongst sub-national areas have become over the past decades, the *more similar and homogenous* also the activities and structures of European regions have become. In fact, the strategies of development the regions choose and implement are based on relatively similar principles and models of regional mobilization that are widely shared and taken for granted amongst both experts and policy-makers alike. This paradox of an increasing *standardized diversification* of sub-national areas all around Europe is at the centre of this study, and it is analysed on the basis of an analytical perspective which deliberately focuses on the macro-structural contexts and the transnational conditions of region-building in contemporary times rather than on local institutions, traditions and actors.

Mobilizing regions, mobilizing Europe: the main research focus

The study which is outlined in this book departs from classical assumptions of sociological neo-institutionalism – more particularly, the so called 'world-polity approach' as it was proposed by John W. Meyer and his collaborators at Stanford

University – and develops a particular *macro-phenomenological perspective* on the emergence of distinct sub-national regional 'actors' with pronounced agendas of social mobilization. It is argued that over the past 20–30 years a robust common sense on the necessity of regional development and on some of the fundamentals of 'prudent' regional development practice has emerged among experts from many parts of the world fuelled both by academic discourse and political initiatives. In the framework of European regional development policies – above all, the so-called 'EU Cohesion Policy' – some models and practices of regional mobilization have been strongly promoted and institutionalized, fostering the diffusion of highly generalized development standards to localities and local lifeworlds all around Europe.

Hence, from this particular analytical perspective 'Europeanization' is considered, first and foremost, as a modernizing project that mobilizes society – i.e. individuals, (political) actors, organizations, nation-states, and even the most 'peripheral' and 'outermost' localities and regions of the European Union (EU) – on the basis of relatively similar models, standards and aspirations of future development. It will be shown that the all-encompassing mobilization of sub-national units in contemporary is largely embedded in a highly rationalized 'culture' of professionals and expertise, the so-called 'world culture' (Meyer), which is considered to be the primary cultural account of what is commonly referred to as 'modernity' and fosters the diffusion of rationally justified and often scientifically approved 'world-cultural' models and practices. The more highly generalized and scientifically approved justifications of development gain 'practical validity' (e.g. by way of institutionalization), the more the modernist ethos of 'instrumental activism' becomes the driving force of social change which is the prerequisite, in turn, for further expansion of rationalized structures (Meyer *et al.* 1997; Münch 2001).

Having said this, it is one of the major aims of this book to show how and to what extent both the rather general and global process of world-cultural diffusion and the more particular process of Europeanization are interrelated and interwoven. It is the aim to show that EU policy programmes, such as the EU Cohesion Policy, are strongly 'world-cultural' in itself *reinforcing, accelerating* and *specifying* the diffusion of 'world-cultural models', and thus fostering the expansion of certain expert practices and agency-based developmental imperatives all around the territory of the European Union. Hence, in line with new sociological approaches in EU and Europeanization studies (cf. Delanty and Rumford 2005; Favell and Guiraudon 2009; Münch 2010) this book provides an account of Europeanization which situates the particular social and cultural dynamics of policy-making and institution-building in the European Union within the broader picture of globalization. However, this analysis is not limited to the study of transnational discourses and overarching institutional structures. It also further elaborates and specifies the thesis of a reinforcing world-cultural mobilization of sub-national territories in contemporary Europe by means of a comparative analysis of regional development strategies in three selected Polish 'regions', namely the Voivodships of Lower Silesia, Lublin and Sub-Carpathia

(Dolnośląskie, Lubelskie and Podkarpackie in Polish). These regions were newly created in 1999 in the course of Poland's impending accession to the EU and integration into the European regional development framework. While one of the three selected regions (Dolnośląskie) is regarded as a relatively prosperous 'up-and-coming' region, the other two regions (Lubelskie and Podkarpackie) are widely conceived to be amongst the 'most remote' and 'least developed' regions of the enlarged European Union. Hence, the empirical analysis which is outlined in Chapters 6, 7 and 8 of this book is also meant to be a critical study of 'unequal development' in contemporary EU territory and of the eastward enlargement of the European Union, the largest modernizing project in more recent European history.

Regions as sites of social mobilization

Europe has always been a continent of extraordinary regional diversity with pronounced regional traditions. During medieval times the European continent was mainly shaped by smaller territories, small independent cities and a multitude of smaller counties and duchies inhabited by a huge variety of different tribes and ethnicities (Braudel 1996). Yet with the expansion of central state administrations and the rise of the modern nation-state model during the eighteenth and nineteenth century, many counties and independent regional territories lost their autonomy and distinctiveness and were incorporated into the larger territory of nation-states or degraded to the status of provinces of larger empires. During the era of nation-building, 'national identity' was vigorously promoted and strongly fostered in opposition to persisting regional identities and political movements (Rokkan 1975; Anderson 1983; Therborn 1995; Poulantzas 2003; Taylor 2003; Bartolini 2005).

Although overcoming internal territorial barriers and taming particularistic regional assertiveness was one of the primary aims of emerging European nation-states, the transformative and all-encompassing force of nation-building has not led to an entire abolishment of regional structures or loss of regional identities anywhere in Europe. In fact, many regions and provinces managed to preserve some degree of political autonomy and assertiveness, though in varying degrees from one European country to another, mainly depending on particular regional traditions and the ethnic composition of the population.[2] Thus, each country has its own history of regionalization, and the reasons for the persistence of regional traditions, regional cultures and regional political institutions are manifold. In some cases regionalization constitutes an expression of regional assertiveness and strong regional identification, and in other cases regional structures were introduced in order to make state administration more efficient and to strengthen the authority of nation-state rule (cf. Paasi 1986, 2003; Keating *et al.* 2003). Accordingly, political scientists usually distinguish between *bottom-up* and *top-down* regionalization (cf. Keating 1998 and 2003).

Yet, except for some traditionally strong bottom-up regional movements, 'regionalization' has been an important measure of top-down policy-making during the twentieth century – a deliberate 'development strategy' of modern state governments and an integral part of national projects of 'planned modernization'. During the peak of large-scale Keynesian state planning in the 1950s and 1960s regions have become a focal point of state intervention and an important object of redistributing public funds from richer to poorer regions (cf. Keynes 1997 [1936]; Keating *et al.* 2003; Hwang 2006). However, along with the crises of Fordism at the beginning of 1970s, the initial euphoria of spatial planning and intensive investments in regional development policy began to cool down considerably in European countries. Therefore, for a certain period of time in the 1970s and 1980s regional development policies remained a minor or secondary issue on the European continent.

This has changed markedly during the past two decades. Since the beginning of the 1990s a new wave of regionalism and regionalization has spread all over Europe (cf. Le Galès and Lequesne 1998). Over the past two decades many regions have gained more political authority in increasing numbers of policy areas ranging from economic policies, cultural-educational policies to welfare policies, sometimes even including distinct immigration and citizenship policies (Marks *et al.* 2008a and 2008b). Moreover, regional governments have become proactive 'development planners' through multi-annual programming (Nanetti 1996). It has been observed by analysts of the more recent upswing of regionalization in today's Europe that a new 'model' of regional development policy has started to take shape. Regions are no longer 'spectators' in policy processes, as Robert Leonardi (2005: 6f.) claimed. '[Today,] European regions are increasingly able to acquire administrative, legislative, and even fiscal competences that enable them to increase their own capacities of governing major social and economic functions.' (Mau 2006: 129f., translated from German by S.B.).

Indeed, the old paradigm of 'regional policy *for* the regions' has been replaced by the principle of 'regional development *by* the regions' (Leonardi 2005). These days regional development policies in Europe tend to be 'more decentralized' than ever before, extending both to regional and local levels. There is a strong drive towards 'institution- and capacity-building' at sub-national levels of government, with a new emphasis on 'multi-annual' and 'strategic' development planning. Both national and regional governments try to foster 'close linkages' and 'cross-fertilization' amongst various business sectors as well as between science and business by promoting the establishment of 'clusters' and other sites of knowledge-intensive economic value creation. Thus, all over Europe, 'science and technology parks', 'science-business-transfer centres', and 'business incubators' have been set up in order to foster innovation. (Keating (2001: 218f.).

From existing approaches to a macro-phenomenological account of regionalization in contemporary Europe

The driving forces of a stronger political and economic mobilization of regions in contemporary Europe, and in particular the rise of regions as distinct and increasingly empowered development actors, have mainly been studied on the basis of two major analytical frameworks: (international) political economy and multilevel governance approaches. The first strand of literature addresses the globalization of market competition, and especially the new economic geography (cf. Krugman 1991) and international division of labour amongst regions brought about by the intensifying integration of markets in the past few decades (cf. Taylor 1993; Keating and Loughlin 1996; Hudson 2001). With the rise of post-industrial society economists, economic geographers and economic sociologists discovered localities, regions and regional regimes of production to be critical factors for the success or failure of business activities and economic development (Piore and Sabel 1984). It has been observed that the increasing globalization of economic activities and chains of production has by no means led to the disappearance of 'place'. On the contrary, places, local conditions of production, and, above all, local institutions and social structures were considered as decisive factors for successful (economic) development (cf. Saxanian 1994; Storper and Salais 1997; Ohmae 1995; Keating and Loughlin 1997; Ashheim 1997; Cooke and Morgan 1998; Cooke *et al.* 2004).

The latter strand of research, the multilevel governance approaches, aim to account for the peculiar nature of government in times of increasing transnationalization of political decision-making and the emergence of new political actors, new political arenas and new fields of interest formation at various levels of society and their complex interplay (cf. Marks *et al.* 1996; Boyer and Hollingsworth 1997; Scharpf 1999; Hooghe and Marks 2001). In this context, an increasing 'Europeanization' of regional policy in the area of the EU Cohesion Policy has been observed (Leonardi 1993, 1995, 2005; Keating and Hooghe 1994; Hooghe 1996; Benz and Eberlein 1999). It has been explored how and to what extent new European institutional rules and regulations contributed to the empowerment of sub-national actors alongside national and European actors and institutions (Kohler-Koch 1999; Börzel 2001; Conzelmann and Knodt 2002). And it was shown, accordingly, that the EU Cohesion Policy fostered the emergence of decentralized structures of regional government and governance even in countries and contexts without stronger regionalist or even federalist traditions, such as Ireland or Great Britain, and especially in the post-socialist countries of Central and Eastern Europe (Gorzelak 1996; Brusis 1999 and 2005; Gualini 2004; Keating and Hughes 2003; Pieper 2006; Bache 2008).

Both research strands have definitely contributed to a deeper understanding of the politico-economic conditions of regional mobilization over the past decade and the dispersion of state authority and governance capacity across various spatial levels in contemporary Europe. Politico-economic perspectives mainly point to greater diversification and an increasing inequality between – if not to say polarization of – regions in times of intensifying economic integration. The multilevel accounts of Europeanization also rather emphasize the differences amongst regions in terms of their competencies and their endowment with resources. Yet none of the existing approaches accounts for the great structural homology of regional development practice across the regions against the backdrop of increasing diversification and socio-economic inequality of European regions (cf. Dunford 1996; Heidenreich 1998; Duro 2001; Castro 2003).[3]

From a sociological point of view, however, which aims to account for the social implications of contemporary transformations in Europe, the prevailing perspective on multiple levels of 'society' and 'government' – or concrete institutional arrangements and actor-constellations within existing regional units – is not sufficient. First and foremost, the identification of fixed and homogenous (political) actor-interests and identities on various spatial layers and even in opposition to one another is by no means self-evident. If we take the more recent insights of research on globalization and transnationalization really seriously, and in particular the idea of the spatial transcendence of ideas, artifacts, exchanges and interactions (Giddens 1984, 1990; Hannerz 1996; Appaduraj 1997; Urry 2007; Mau 2010; Mau and Büttner 2010), we cannot adhere to the idea of static spatial distinctions and territorial arrangements. 'Ideas associated with discrete "levels" need to be replaced by a notion of spaces interpenetrated by the global, local and national, in the context of which the conventional idea of inside and outside, domestic and international, no longer holds.' This was vigorously pointed out by Gerard Delanty and Chris Rumford (2005: 136) in *Rethinking Europe*, their ground-breaking plea for a new sociology of Europeanization. Thus, instead of reifying clear-cut distinctions between inside and outside, above and below, we need to get an idea of the extent to which 'global' processes interact with more static territorial arrangements constituting new social spaces of local, global and transnational exchange and interaction.

Second, region-building and regional mobilization are usually considered and explored as processes of endogenous development and incremental interest formation on the part of regional actors. However, there is no approach that captures extra-regional, transnational and largely 'non-governmental' institutional factors. It is acknowledged in existing research, indeed, that practices, institutional principles and models of regional development '(...) have been diffused through EU Structural Funds programmes, academic publication, consultancy and interregional cooperation' (Keating 2001: 219). But there is no account of this particular trans-regional institutional context.

Certainly, from a sociological point of view this cannot just be solved by making the existing state-centred and governance-centred accounts on regional mobilization in Europe more 'sociological' (cf. Christiansen *et al.* 2001; Green Cowles *et al.* 2001; Checkel 2005; Risse 2010). Sociological accounts must transcend the prevailing government- and governance-centred perspectives and take the macro-sociological institutional conditions of the transformations in contemporary Europe into account more systematically. Yet until recently sociology did not pay much attention to the process of European integration. It was mainly cast in the description of a comparison of national societies, and, unlike political scientists, sociologists had huge difficulties with conceptualizing increasing integration of European nations beyond national borders (Therborn 1995; Delanty and Rumford 2005; Favell 2006; Beck and Grande 2007; Favell and Guiraudon 2009). In the past few years this has definitely changed, for a huge variety of social areas and phenomena have been studied and theorized from a distinctly transnational sociological perspective (cf. Fligstein and Stone Sweet 2002; Boje *et al.* 2007; Gerhards 2007; Fligstein 2008; Outhwaite 2008; Rumford 2009; Immerfall and Therborn 2010; Mau and Verwiebe 2010; Münch 2010), but empirically grounded distinctly macro-sociological accounts of Europeanization are still rare.[4]

This study aims to contribute to these new and intensifying sociological reflections on Europeanization by adding a 'macro-phenomenological' account of regional mobilization in contemporary Europe. On the basis of this particular analytical perspective the current phase of regional mobilization in Europe is conceived as an expression of a broader transformation of (European) modernity and not 'just' an outcome of EU policy agendas.[5] And instead of assuming fixed actor-identities, and interest-formation on various spatial levels and even in opposition to one another, it focuses on the cultural and institutional context that is shared by actors, organizations, groups and all various social entities *across* different territories and strongly contributes to the formation of interests, expectations, perceptions and images of actors. Consequently, from this perspective 'Europeanization' does not necessarily appear as a process that runs counter to 'domestic' interests, but as a project that is jointly carried out by different actors from various backgrounds both within and outside 'domestic' contexts.

The macro-phenomenological research perspective which is taken in this study has been introduced and shaped by John Meyer and colleagues under the label of 'world-polity theory'. It is 'macro-phenomenological' in that it builds on both the classical phenomenological assumption of an all encompassing *social construction* of reality (cf. Berger and Luckmann 1966) and on Max Weber's (1976) famous macro-sociological assumption of an increasing *cultural significance and legitimacy* of formal-rational models of social organization with the breakthrough of modernity (cf. Meyer and Rowan 1977; Thomas *et al.* 1987; Meyer *et al.* 1997). At the centre of this perspective is the concern with the worldwide expansion and diffusion of 'world culture', the highly rationalized and overarching cultural umbrella of (global) modernity. Accordingly, all modern purposeful actors are seen as being constitutively shaped by 'world culture' which significantly determines and pre-defines what modern, purposeful social actors think, aspire and believe in (Meyer and Jepperson 2000).

In marked contrast to orthodox modernization theory and popular notions of modernity, however, the expansion of modern structures is not conceptualized as a teleological project that is automatically heading towards certain pre-determined goals. In explicit reference to classical sociological accounts of religion it conceives of modernity as a quasi-religious 'cultural system' (cf. Durkheim 1915; Bellah 1970; Geertz 1973). Thus, the huge expansion of rationalized structures in contemporary times is not just explained by the factual supremacy of 'rationality', or rather 'rational reasoning' (cf. Habermas 1985), but by its quasi-religious status that – as religion did in former times – mobilizes society around transcendent goals and aspirations of human development.

In other words, sociological neo-institutionalism conceives of the evolving modern society as accumulated with alleged purposive actors and actions;

yet the whole scene rather looks like a cultural or religious drama. The phenomena remind us of rational and efficient structuration – the reality, however, has more in common with a religious ceremony.

(John Meyer in: Hasse and Krücken 2005: 11, translated from German by S.B.)[6]

Yet according to the proponents of the world-polity perspective 'world culture' does not and has never developed outside of society. On the contrary, it is vivid and constantly reproduced in the institutional structures and practices of modern sciences and professions. Consequently, scientists, professionals, specialized bureaucrats, and many other groups of people which can be grouped together under the term of 'knowledgeable expert' are considered as the major social carriers of the expansion of rational structures.

The new religious elites are the professionals, researchers, scientists, and intellectuals who write secularized and unconditionally universalistic versions of the salvation story, along with managers, legislators, and policymakers who believe the story fervently and pursue it relentlessly. This belief is worldwide and structures the organization of social life almost everywhere.

(Meyer *et al.* 1997: 174)[7]

In a short and in an admittedly slightly stylized way this is the essence of the macro-phenomenological account of modernity as it was put forward by John W. Meyer and his collaborators. During the past two or three decades Meyer and many other proponents of the 'world-polity approach' have mainly specified their thesis of an exponential worldwide expansion of rationalized structures ('diffusion of world culture') by large-scale quantitative analyses of nation-states, professional organizations, individual life-courses as well as major organizing principles of modernity. This book contributes to this literature by adding a more in-depth qualitative analysis of 'world-cultural diffusion' which emphasizes the constructionist element of this particular theoretical model.[8] Moreover, it adds an account of the 'world-cultural' construction and constitution of a social category that was not studied yet in macro-phenomenological research: the 'world-cultural' constitution of sub-national regions and the huge cultural significance of 'world-cultural' principles and practices of development at local and regional levels of society.

Implications for the analysis of Europeanization

It is a widespread conviction in modern social thought to conceive of all highly rationalized realms of modern society in marked distinction from one another. In fact, it is regarded as one of the major characteristics, often even as *the* 'accomplishment' of modernity, that highly rationalized spheres or realms of society, such as the economy, politics, jurisprudence, the sciences and even such spheres as religion, community or civil society have separated from one another and have developed their own internal functional principles and logics (cf. Parsons 1967 and 1971; Habermas 1985; Luhmann 1982 and 1997a). However, if we understand 'rationalization' in modernity as a simultaneous process of both stronger 'purification' of rationalized social spheres *and* stronger 'mediation' (cf. Latour 1993) or 'interpenetration' (Münch 2001 and 2011) of these spheres, we get to a fairly different image of the characteristics of modernity. Then we start to realize that contemporary modernity constitutively rests on particular combinations and re-combinations of highly rationalized social spheres, such as, for example, the 'scientization' of economic development or modern politics, or the 'commoditization' of non-economic spheres (cf. Illouz 1997 and 2008). Moreover, we come to realize that modern politics, modern capitalism, modern jurisprudence or even modern civic community would not be existent without categories and practices developing by and largely within modern sciences. In fact, much of contemporary political practice is carried out in collaboration of politicians, bureaucrats, lawyers, scientific experts of various kind, and even more so, almost all of the practical or technical work – the 'construction of the nature of things' – is primarily done by scientifically trained experts and all sorts of technically educated 'hybrids' (Latour 1993).

These kinds of insights we also gain from a rigorous macro-phenomenological analysis of contemporary society. In fact, the thesis of massive and rapid world-cultural diffusion in contemporary times suggested by the 'word-polity theory' is not only a broad analytical and methodological conception, but also provides us with an account and interpretation of most current developments in society in the sense of sociological *Zeitdiagnose*. It is the diagnosis of a fundamental shift in long-existing modes of social reproduction in modern society which has been described by analysts of our contemporary knowledge society as the all-encompassing 'scientization of society' (cf. Weingart 2001). It is the thesis that current social transformations are constitutively linked with the expansion of scientific knowledge and practice to all areas of human life and that these days scientifically-grounded rationality has become the primary source of 'cultural legitimacy' (Drori *et al.* 2003). In fact, in the absence of former political restrictions the 'scientific method' has become the standard routine of our times, expanding ever more pervasively in our new digital era. More and more social and factual entities – subjects, objects, ideas, values and many other aspects of reality – are structured, assessed and legitimated on the basis of rational principles.

Hence, in contrast to more affirmative analysts of the rise of a new 'knowledge society' (cf. Bell 1973; Stehr 1994; Florida 2002) it is not only the thesis of an increasing significance of 'knowledge' in *economic* production, or a transformation of capitalism due to an increase in academically-educated knowledge workers and symbolic analysts, but of overall and all-encompassing *cultural* significance of scientific reflection and expertise (Latour 1993; Knorr-Cetina 1999; Nowotny *et al.* 2001; Weingart 2001; Drori *et al.* 2003). And this shift has huge repercussions on the nature of entrenched modes of (political) steering and governance of society which is becoming manifest at least in the following four dimensions: first, an increasing generalization and institutionalization of 'reflexive mechanisms' in social government bringing about a huge expansion of scientific reflexivity and a shift to pro-active learning and reflection in all areas of human life, and especially in political practice (Giddens 1990; Weingart 2001: 17f.); second, a paradigmatic shift in the prevailing mode of social government from more hierarchical and mechanical top-down steering to social (or individual) 'self regulation', e.g. expressed in an increasing 'social participation' in planning processes and implementation of political projects This is also often described as a shift from 'government' to 'governance', or from traditional 'state government' to more liberal techniques of 'social regulation' (cf. Rose and Miller 2008); third, a fundamental reorganization of existing relations between knowledge, space and government; and, fourth, an increasing 'reflexive self-application' of the concept of 'knowledge-based society' by the rising European 'knowledge society' itself.[9]

It is exactly this fundamental transformation in today's European modernity which is the focal point of the following macro-phenomenological analysis of regional mobilization in contemporary Europe. Sub-national spaces (local communities, cities, regions) are strongly affected by the new imperatives of prospective planning and pro-active agency. They are strongly mobilized (and mobilize themselves) as 'strategic', 'future-oriented' and 'prudent' development actors in the name of 'participation', 'capacity-building' and 'cooperative governance'. Sub-national governments aim to create and institutionalize new networks, business cluster and milieus of learning and innovation in order to be able to constantly adapt to the changes and demands of 'modern times'. Accordingly, cities and regions (mainly larger agglomerations and metropolitan 'city-regions', in fact) are seen as the natural source of innovation and knowledge production, the motors of the imagined and politically-desired 'knowledge society'. At the same time, sub-national areas are also increasingly promoted as the primary pre-servers of 'sustainable development', 'cohesion' and 'local traditions', since sub-national local and regional territories are considered as a 'natural refuge' for social cohesion and social traditions. Consequently, more and more sub-national governments start to rediscover and promote the distinct local traditions and cultural heritage of their territory and express it in marked distinction to others.

It will be shown in the subsequent chapters that the current phase of regionalization and somewhat epidemic spread of a 'new regionalism' to all areas of Europe is primarily driven by 'world-cultural' principles, standard practices and models of development. These principles, standard practices and models are increasingly institutionalized and promoted by international agents of development, such as the European Union. Since in contrast with traditions-based, primordial and collectivist myths of social mobilization (as was the case in the era of nation-building during the nineteenth and twentieth century), the cultural ethos of the project of European integration essentially rests upon highly rationalized 'myths' of future development (Meyer 2001; Münch 2010). Yet the question is whether all regions (or just the city-regions?) are able to fulfil all these demands and expectations? This question guides the comparative empirical case study of three newly created regions in contemporary Poland in Chapters 6, 7 and 8 of this book.

Structure and content of the book

This book is divided into three major parts. In the first part the analytical categories and concepts that were briefly introduced above will be sketched in more detail (Chapters 2 and 3). As already pointed out, the macro-phenomenological world-polity approach was first outlined more than 30 years ago. Obviously, some notions and categories have reasonably changed over time. Notions, such as 'institution', 'culture' or 'institutional diffusion' have been used differently from time to time, which has led to misinterpretations and misconceptions of the major argument and analytical scope of this approach. Therefore, the world-polity perspective has also been highly criticized and contested by other analysts and perspectives of modernity and globalization. Based on this observation, in the subsequent chapter the classical foundations of the macro-phenomenological research perspective will briefly be reconstructed in light of this criticism. Moreover, at the end of this chapter the strong culturalist and phenomenological impetus of world-polity thinking will be highlighted, including some of the implications for research projects concerning social mobilization in contemporary times. These implications will be further explained and outlined in Chapter 3.

The second major part of this book is concerned with the world-cultural underpinnings of regionalization and regional development in contemporary Europe, which is mainly based on content analyses of the scientific debate on regional mobilization and policy papers (Chapters 4 and 5). Accordingly, Chapter 4 starts with an introduction to the scientific discourse and debate on globalization and regionalization. It is the aim of this content analysis of scientific concepts to show that with the increasing globalization of social activities and particularly the increasing observation of the crisis of nationally entrenched Fordist production, a new scientific discourse on fixed territorial space and the role of regions was breaking into the scientific discourse on 'development'. The 'region' was discovered by economists, by geographers and by other social scientists as a key source of value-creation in an allegedly new post-industrial era. In marked contrast to the declining industrial cities and regions by the end of the 1970s, regional research identified the renaissance of so-called 'new industrial districts' based on unique local or regional institutional settings. The notions of highly adaptive and innovative 'regional cluster economies' and 'learning regions' were born, and the observation of new role models of successful regional development has inspired a whole range of social scientists (human geographers, sociologists, economists and political scientists alike) to reflect upon the conditions of favourable regional development in contemporary times.

It is indeed one of the major advantages of a macro-phenomenological research perspective to be able to account for the strong inter-linkage between scientific discourse, political practice and everyday life. Accordingly, the massive spread of scientific interpretations of 'good' regional development practice is strongly associated with newly emerging political efforts to institutionalize and implement new principles, practices and models of regional development in everyday life. In this context, we can observe that international organizations and international agents of development such as some U.N. organizations, the OECD and the European Union were especially receptive to the scientific discourse of regional development and started to promote respective principles in their policy programmes about 20 to 25 years ago. The emergence and institutionalization of a new multilevel system of regional mobilization under the umbrella of 'Cohesion Policy' strongly fosters the diffusion of world-cultural models, principles and practices of regional development in EU member states and beyond.

Based on this observation the structure of the current 'world-cultural script' of regional mobilization in Europe is depicted in Chapter 5. It is argued that regional development practice in contemporary Europe is fundamentally based upon five central developmental 'myths' – four 'substantial myths' (*innovation, competition, sustainability* and *cohesion*) and one 'constitutive myth' (*regional agency*) – which have become focal points of development thinking in reference to regions over the past decades. This should not imply that the European Union promotes one particular model of regional development, or that all five institutional myths are implemented in equal ways. Rather, the distinction between five different myths of development should show that regional development policies are based on various antagonist principles which are more or less routinely implemented in European regions these days. The implementation of these principles, however, always depends on particular historical situations and contexts and respective political forces and interest constellations and therefore requires more careful and closer attention.

This is the major concern of the last part of this study which contains an empirical case study of region-building in Poland, one of the newer EU member states from Central and Eastern Europe which joined the European Union in May 2004 (Chapters 6, 7 and 8). This research context is distinctly fruitful for a macro-phenomenological analysis of regional mobilization in contemporary Europe. On the one hand, Poland constitutes a strong affirmative example of world-cultural diffusion since it has witnessed a massive transformation of society from Soviet state communism to democracy and capitalism within a short period of time. Moreover, it could be noticed in Poland that regionalization and regional policy programmes were strongly initiated by the efforts of European integration. On the other hand, however, the three Polish regions which are presented in Chapters 6, 7 and 8 in a more in-depth comparative analysis – the Dolnośląskie Voivodship (western Poland), the Lubelskie Voivodship and the Podkarpackie Voivodship (both located in eastern Poland) – are also hard cases for the assumption of a massive world-cultural thrust for regional mobilization. At least two of them, the two eastern regions, do not seem to match with the new knowledge-intensive and scientifically driven development agenda in contemporary Europe at first sight.

2 A critical introduction to world-polity research

Introduction

What would happen if an unknown society on an unknown island was suddenly discovered these days? This is the classical thought experiment which the proponents of the world-polity approach use to introduce their research perspective to a wider audience (cf. Meyer *et al.* 1997: 145f.). It was most likely, they then further contend, that highly standardized, rationalized and formalized structures of social organization would rapidly be implemented on this island, based on existing prototypes of 'modern' nation-states. Moreover, globally recognized models of social development would immediately spread to the unknown island via associational processes, provoking substantial restructuring of existing institutions, cultural practices and traditions in accordance with these models. Consequently, 'modern' citizenship principles, 'modern' educational programmes and other development programmes would be enforced and all types of standard data on the socio-economic, or the ecological, development of this island would be collected. In short, the unknown island would immediately become the object of constant assessments and concerted international efforts of 'planned intervention' in order to integrate this unknown territory as quickly as possible into the existing 'community' of modern nation-states.

This thought experiment is indeed an extraordinarily illustrative and convincing description of the major analytical scope of the world-polity perspective. But at the same time it is also highly problematic, and a gateway to misunderstandings and misinterpretations of world-polity research. For on the one hand this thought experiment certainly illustrates well the huge prevalence and nearly irresistible worldwide expansion of modern rationalized structures both in politics and everyday life, and particularly the great extent of standardization and routinization of development practices and 'active intervention'. In this way, the world-polity perspective raises important questions and emphasizes a dimension which is often taken for granted in social sciences. On the other hand, however, the highly stylized island-metaphor obscures concrete logics and powers which are at the heart of world-polity analyses, i.e. the massive and coercive institutional powers behind these changes. The simple island-metaphor can in fact give one the impression of a completely inevitable logic of change that comes about naturally all by itself. While this impression is certainly intended by the proponents of the world-polity perspective, since they aim to account for the self-reinforcing forces of modernization, over-simplified depictions such as the island-metaphor have contributed to misunderstandings of the strong constructionist foundations of their research perspective and provoked strong opposition. In fact, world-polity research has been strongly criticized for its vague and simplistic 'actorless' or 'agentless' conception of institutional change. Critics have put forward that world-polity analysts would obscure the 'real' forces and interests behind the world's development and world politics. And it is also accused of reifying an old, out-dated and overly problematic functionalist theory of (Western) modernization.

The following discussion will counter misleading interpretations of the world-polity perspective as a 'functionalist' and 'teleological' model of social change. And it spells out a more adequate reading of the world-polity research approach, whose empirical yardstick is not a monolithic and uniform global society, but a cultural project that establishes agency and rational planning. Hence, the culturalist (or rather phenomenological) argument of the world-polity perspective is not its weakness, but the great asset of the world-polity approach when compared to other takes on current transformations of modern society. It enables us to look at accustomed frames and conceptions of reality from another perspective and challenges familiar beliefs and epistemic foundations of our modern 'enlightened' and 'developed' world.

In the following, I will first of all briefly situate the macro-phenomenological research perspective as proposed by the proponents of the world-polity approach within the existing multi-faceted interdisciplinary branch of (neo-)institutional research (1). I will then briefly outline some of the key concepts and notions of the world-polity perspective (2). This will be further spelled out by a short overview of the wide range of empirical accounts that the proponents of the macro-phenomenological world-polity perspective have used in an attempt to 'prove' their supposition of an increasing and ever more rapidly expanding 'world culture' (3). Since this is highly contested, I will then present some major criticisms of macro-sociological accounts of globalization, followed by alternative perspectives as well as more recent accounts of development studies. This section ends with a short discussion of the major logical inconsistencies within the world-polity approach, which in my opinion is the main reason for the misunderstandings briefly addressed above (4). I will finally plead for a strengthening and a more rigorous unfolding of the social-constructionist foundations of this approach which enables us to study the translation of broader cultural scripts and models into concrete social practice (5).

1 World-polity research – an offspring of sociological institutionalism

The macro-phenomenological world-polity approach belongs to the broad strand of neo-institutionalist research, or rather 'new institutional theories', in sociology (for an overview, see: Thomas *et al.* 1987; Powell and DiMaggio 1990; Scott 2001; Senge and Hellmann 2006; Powell 2008). Over the past 30 years, institutionalism has become popular in sociology and many other disciplines of social science as well, namely in economics, political science, and especially in the interdisciplinary field of organizational studies (cf. Coase 1937; Meyer and Rowan 1977; Williamson 1985; March and Olsen 1989; North 1990; Scott and Meyer 1994; Smelser and Swedberg 1994; Scharpf 1997). All these different institutionalisms share a degree of scepticism with regard to reductionist micro-analytical research perspectives giving exclusive explanatory power to individualist models of social behaviour solely focusing on the (rational) motifs and purposes of both individual and collective social actors. Thus, in one way or the other, all existing institutionalisms challenge this assumption by pointing to the importance of 'structural categories' and more inter-subjective 'institutional effects'.

Yet this more recent interdisciplinary upswing of institutionalist thinking and research neither follows a common theoretical tradition nor a coherent school of social thought. The notions of the term 'institution', even the basic understandings of what institutions are and how they affect social life, vary tremendously across research traditions, and even within disciplines. The same applies to variations in the explanatory strategies amongst different institutionalist traditions and disciplines – i.e. in claims regarding the strength and scope of the alleged institutional effects. Hence, while most institutionalist approaches in economics and in political science still give a strong role to 'real actors' (Scharpf 1997) – to educable interests, purposes and individual choices – sociological institutionalist approaches are usually less focused on micro-analytical, actor-centred explanations (cf. Thomas *et al.* 1987).[1] In fact, new institutional approaches in sociology often strive to completely overcome the prevailing 'methodological individualism' in the social sciences by stressing the primacy of relatively persistent *institutional* logics and rules. This ranges to rules which have emerged over long periods of time out of everyday social practice up to more complex social, political or juridical regulations. And it applies to rules which are mostly implicit and commonly shared as well as rules which are explicit and largely ignored.

The world-polity approach goes farthest in this direction. It is based upon the assumption of an all encompassing *cultural construction* of social actors in phenomenological tradition (Berger and Luckmann 1966; Schütz 1973); and, secondly, on Max Weber's (1976) classical assumption of a growing *cultural significance* and *legitimacy* of formal-rational models of social organization (cf. Meyer and Rowan 1977). Against this backdrop the world-polity perspective was deliberately developed as a 'macro-phenomenological' approach to state formation and societal development in the new global era (cf. Thomas *et al.* 1987; Meyer *et al.* 1997; Boli and Thomas 1997; Drori *et al.* 2003; Lechner and Boli 2005). Accordingly, the world-polity approach questions the assumption of independent and autonomous actorhood and considers both individual and collective interests as being structured by overarching institutional environments and cultural rules. By spelling out such a strong culturalist conception of institutions, the proponents of the world-polity approach aim to draw attention to something which is disregarded in all actor-centred approaches, namely that the 'purposes' they mainly focus on – the 'means' and 'ends' of actorhood, and even the shape of their dramaturgical performances – are constantly shaped and enacted within overarching cultural contexts: 'Actors are not treated as unanalysed "givens" but as entities constructed and motivated by enveloping frames.' (Boli and Thomas 1997: 172). However, in marked contrast to most other institutionalist approaches, which apportion a great deal of influence to 'culture', the world-polity approach does not focus on structural differences in world society, i.e. on different paths of social development or unique institutional settings shaped by particular historical patterns of interaction (cf. Hall and Soskice 2001; Eisenstadt 2002; Pierson 2004). Instead, it mainly focuses on the formation of structural similarities across the globe that can be recognized in many different realms of contemporary society despite all existing local cultural variations:

> Worldwide models define and legitimate agendas for local action, shaping the structures and policies of nation-states and other national and local actors in virtually all of the domains of rationalized social life – business, politics, education, medicine, science, even the family and religion.
>
> (Meyer *et al.* 1997: 145)

2 Key concepts of world-polity research

Based upon the premises presented above the world-polity perspective has been outlined in numerous articles and books over the past 30 years; and depending on the publication in question and the time it was published, different notions and terms have been set out and emphasized as the approach's key concepts, such as 'institutional change', 'polity', 'culture' or 'institutional diffusion'.[2] As an introduction, and in order to avoid misunderstandings, some of the key concepts will briefly be described below.

World polity – a conception of worldwide institutional coherence of modern society

The term 'polity' is one of the central classical notions of political philosophy. It is a constitutive element of the famous triad of policy, politics and polity in modern political thought that – based on its etymological origin, the Greek word *polis* – signifies the principal political coherence and identity of particular (local or national) political communities. Accordingly, in contemporary political thought the notion of 'polity' is usually used to characterize the overall (formal-institutional) constitution and the democratic quality of spatially confined political units. Until now world society has certainly neither developed common political goals or visions, nor coherent political procedures and state structures; and there are even doubts as to whether the supranational political structures of the European Union, which are built on certain common principles, can really be called a 'polity' in the strict sense of the word (cf. Scharpf 1999; Friese and Wagner 2002; Bartolini 2005). Nevertheless, the proponents of the world-polity approach deliberately chose this notion in order to characterise the distinctive institutional cohesiveness of contemporary world society:

> *Polity* is here defined as the system of creating value through the collective conferral of authority. Our term *polity* is used in the broad cultural sense that we have described: It includes state action, as is conventional, but also other forms of collective action that might in the modern social scientific lexicon be dismissed as merely 'cultural'.
>
> (Meyer 1987: 44, emphasis as original)

Hence, the proponents of world-polity thinking seek for a direct link to the debate on transnational and global integration of world society which has been dominated for a long time by the fields of International Relations and international political economy (cf. Wallerstein 1974; Waltz 1979; Krasner 1983; Jacobson 1984; Keohane 1986; Finnemore 1996a; Wendt 1999). But in marked contrast to common conceptions of 'polity' in the political sciences the notion of 'world polity' is not just meant in political terms, i.e. as an emerging system of government, a certain (hegemonic) political regime, or even a common '(U.N.) state' on a global scale (cf. Rosenau and Czempiel 1992; Katzenstein 2005; Jessop and Sum 2006). Rather, it is a conceptual vision of 'world society' as a highly interdependent, but independent and self-sustaining, social system, which encompasses '(...) all aspects of human activities in extensive webs of social interaction and flows of goods, ideas, money, values (...)' (Boli and Lechner 2005: 20), and not just networks of political interaction or economic exchange.

Based on this broader sociological notion of 'social authority' (Weber) the 'world polity' is conceived of as a distinct social system which is largely exogenous to individual (local) societies, but increasingly institutionalized on a global scale, and continually reified in many different kinds of human activities and by all different kinds of social units (individuals, ethnic groups, companies, associations, states etc.).

> World society has increasingly taken on a life of its own, transcending even the level of social organization of the dominant national societies, and it enjoys rather strong legitimacy, in part because of the formal equality among all nation-states in the present world.
>
> (Boli-Bennett and Meyer 1980: 525)

Thus, from the point of view of world-polity analysts the 'world polity' is not just driven by organized interests, such as those of national governments and other official political institutions, but by 'word culture', the overarching cultural core of the world polity, which increasingly structures and shapes the performances and actions of contemporary social entities, such as individuals, organizations, and even nation-states, as 'modern' purposeful actors.

World culture – the 'sacred canopy' of globalizing modernity

The macro-phenomenological research perspective rests on a very broad, almost monolithic and all-embracing conception of 'culture'. From this perspective all elements of social life are shaped and structured by culture, even those aspects which are often regarded as distinct, autonomous and largely non-cultural, namely individual purposes and rational interests. Accordingly, 'culture' as proposed by proponents of world-polity thinking is *constitutive* in the sense that it assigns reality to actors and actions as well as to means and ends; and it exhibits a certain *signifying* function in that it endows actors and actions, as well as means and ends, with constitutive meaning and legitimacy (Thomas *et al.* 1987: 21). However, in marked contrast to reigning micro-phenomenological or interactionist accounts of culture (cf. Berger and Luckmann 1966; Goffman 1959 and 1967; Swidler 1986), the world-polity perspective largely focuses on broader cultural rules and conceptions of 'legitimate' and 'appropriate' actorhood:

> The local interplay between interaction and its meaning, whereby actors (...) continually discover and construct who they are through looking-glass feedback processes, allows for no level of reality external to the phenomenological situation itself. This tradition of research ignores the extraordinary power of exogenous institutionalized definitions of reality.
>
> (Meyer *et al.* 1987: 23)[3]

And in a world that has increasingly become a common, yet still loosely integrated, 'polity' over the past centuries, the cultural context which constitutes and structures actions and actors is seen as a *sui generis* reality on a global scale. Consequently, in explicit reference to the classical phenomenological research tradition (cf. Berger 1967), the particular cultural account of the 'world polity' – the modern 'world culture' – is considered to be the 'sacred canopy' of contemporary world society.[4]

On the basis of this particular macro-phenomenological conception of culture, 'world culture' is not just a generic term for all expressive cultures of contemporary world society. Thus, it is not just conceived as a collection of all local cultures and ethnic traditions that are preserved and presented these days in museums of national and world cultures as well as in history books, or defined by international organizations such as UNESCO as the common 'cultural heritage' of world society (cf. UNESCO 2000). Instead, 'world culture' is conceived as a set of highly generalized and rationalized cultural models, rules and practices which might just contribute to the very emergence of 'authoritative preservers' of local traditions and cultural diversity, such as UNESCO and other concerned agents of 'responsible' and 'prudent' actorhood. Thus, drawing on classical culturalist accounts (cf. Geertz 1973; Bellah 1970), the world-polity approach claims that 'world culture' exhibits a similar cultural impact in secular societies as religion did in religious societies: It provides (ultimate) truths and meaning to all constituents of society and all areas of social life (cf. Meyer 1997: 148). And just as traditional religious societies were based upon clear-cut religious prescriptions, routines and transcendent goals, 'world culture' also provides contemporary society with numerous standardized rules and routines, transcendent myths and ultimate beliefs (Meyer and Rowan 1977).

In accordance with classical theories of modernity the proponents of the world-polity approach allege that in marked contrast to people shaped by religion, who see the fate of human being essentially lying in the hands of God, people who are shaped by 'world culture' would always believe that fate can be influenced through 'active' and 'rational' intervention. It is in fact this ethos of 'instrumental activism' (cf. Münch 2001), which is considered to be the overarching principle of modernity by world-polity analysts, and the driving force of modernizing projects in the contemporary world polity. Consequently, world-polity analysts claim – again in analogy to sociological analysis of religion – that rational principles and rationalized structures and practices shaped by cool-headed scientific reflection have attained the status of 'sacred goods' of modernity and are widely regarded as the central means to 'salvation' (Meyer *et al.* 1997).

Scientization – the underlying logic of world-cultural diffusion

In order to understand how (modern) rational principles become relevant and how diffusion of world-cultural models takes place from a macro-phenomenological perspective, one has to acknowledge the huge practical repercussions and implications of both scientific knowledge and practice. Although 'world culture' is conceptualized as a cultural system that is mainly external to local contexts, it does not develop outside the social domain. On the contrary, it develops and expands within society, namely within the expanding institutions of (modern) society, and, in particular, in connection with all types of scientific practice (see also: Giddens 1990; Beck *et al.* 1994). Hence, from a world-polity perspective 'authoritative scientization' is seen as the hallmark of our contemporary global modernity, and it is spreading particularly due to the absence of other strong regulatory systems (Drori and Meyer 2006: 31). Following Max Weber's (1976) notion of inevitable 'disenchantment with the world' [*Entzauberung der Welt*] since the rise of (occidental) modernity through permanent exploration and scrutiny of all aspects of reality, the proponents of the world-culture approach see the sciences and the professions as the major generators of world-cultural diffusion (cf. Strang and Meyer 1993; Meyer *et al.* 1997; Drori *et al.* 2003; Drori and Meyer 2006; Scott 2008).

According to Gili S. Drori and John W. Meyer, 'scientization' would transform uncertainties from mystery into risks that can be managed rationally. It would stimulate the constitution of organized rule-making, and empower actors gaining authority in strong reference to scientifically-based 'expertise' and professional ethics of science and similar institutions of higher education. In this way, 'scientization' creates both the demand for and the supply of ever more 'rationalization' and 'rule-making' in everyday life. And it is regarded as the main force behind the extraordinary global expansion of rationalized organizational structures and purposeful actorhood (Drori and Meyer 2006: 31). Yet, in line with major analytical assumptions of new cultural sociology the proponents of the world-polity approach point out that scientific knowledge has not just become so pervasive these days due to its mere functionality and factual superiority in relation to other forms of knowledge, as is usually assumed, or because it is often closely linked with political power (cf. Foucault 1991; Gordon 1991; Haas 1990; Bauman 1991; Wagner *et al.* 1991; Carroll 2006). In contrast, Meyer and his colleagues stress that rationalized structures often expand far beyond necessity and functionality just because rationality and scientific knowledge are highly valued and highly endorsed culturally in our time. And due to this huge 'cultural significance' (in the sense of Max Weber's classical notion of *Kulturbedeutung*) of modern science and scientifically-proven knowledge 'world culture' has expanded largely detached from concrete needs and functions, and ever more rapidly during the past 30 to 50 years (Drori *et al.* 2003: 25ff.; Drori and Meyer 2006: 44ff.).[5]

Moreover, apart from rationalization and rule-making in the narrow sense, 'authoritative scientization' is considered to be central to the production and pervasive spread of formal-rational models of social organization, so-called *world-cultural models* (Meyer *et al.* 1997: 162), in contemporary social practice. According to Meyer and colleagues world-cultural models were 'relatively stylized', but often 'well-known theories' on how society and certain actors function, or should function, in a proper way. Often they directly derive from reflections on everyday practice, but they are mainly produced by scientists and other scientifically-based agents of social development, such as think tanks and different types of consultancies. They are usually formulated and expressed as general principles and functional requirements which are in principle applicable everywhere. They then take the form of relatively standardized 'institutional scripts' of social conduct and other rationally specified models of best practice. This inherent claim of 'universal applicability' provides world-cultural models with a high level of authority and bestows them with a tremendous suggestive power to structure social life. Thus, the more highly world-cultural models gain universal validity on a world scale, the less alternative modes and scripts are able to maintain their legitimacy.[6]

3 Empirical accounts of world-cultural diffusion

World-polity researchers have not just elaborated an analytical account of the worldwide diffusion and expansion of 'world culture', but also provided massive and multi-faceted empirical indications of their major arguments and assumptions. This empirical evidence is based on both widely backward-looking historical analyses and extensive quantitative data sets of present-day expansion of world culture. Thus, the material produced by world-polity research has mostly been quantitative, descriptive longitudinal data on the growing worldwide expansion of various world-cultural standards, principles, models and practices, such as modern educational systems, standardized organizational procedures, or fundamental rights and even standardized models of how to conduct one's own life.[7] Most of these quantitative empirical accounts show almost identical images of the expansion of world culture during the history of modernity. First, a very low and slow increase of diffusion during the nineteenth century, a significant increase at the beginning of the twentieth century before and after the First World War, and an exponential worldwide diffusion of relatively similar world-cultural models and practices since the mid-twentieth century after Second World War and ever more extensively during the past three decades.

In the following, we will take a brief look at the major empirical areas where 'world-cultural diffusion' was explored and observed by world-polity analysts. The discussion is structured by the distinction of two different dimensions of knowledge: 'technical' and 'existential' knowledge. This should help to identify the major features of existing empirical accounts of world-polity research.[8]

The increasing global homogeneity of technical knowledge

There is wide-spread consensus in social sciences these days that technical know-how, standards and artefacts – in short, *technical knowledge* – has become ever more widespread around the world since the emergence of modern times (cf. Bayly 2004). This increasing structural homogenization of technical standards and knowledge constitutes a major dimension of the diffusion of world culture (cf. Lechner and Boli 2005). This, above all, concerns a whole variety of aspects of the multi-faceted material world of contemporary global modernity, ranging from the construction of machines, automobiles or tooth brushes, to certain DIN or ISO standards for universal global production, and even to global regulations for money circulation or air traffic control (Brunsson and Jacobsson 2000). Moreover, there is also a multitude of other aspects and dimensions of world culture which are not economic and material in the narrow sense. One only has to think of the many standard procedures and working assumptions of modern organizations, or the globally standardized regulations for sports like football, athletics or chess which are administered and enforced by transnational, national and local sports associations in similar ways.[9] Thus, the world-polity perspective does not only capture the shared standards and culture of highly spe-cialized technicians and experts that have become more homogenous interna-tionally, but also the increasing structural homogenization of the practices and techniques in our everyday lives. In fact, driving cars, communicating with mobile phones, using electronic kitchen equipment and the like are forming a normal and natural part of life for more and more people all around the world (cf. Urry 2007). And with the global expansion of modern technology and modern communication infrastructure, the speed of the worldwide diffusion of technical knowledge is increasing at an ever faster rate.

Certainly, this assumption of an increasing structural approximation and homogenization of technical standards in contemporary global society might seem intuitively plausible. However, if we look at other areas and major trends in modern society, such as the individual conduct of social life or the increasing de-legitimation of long-lasting traditions and collectively binding institutions, this supposition seems to be utterly misleading. In fact, with the rise of modern times, universal structural elements have lost their prevalence, while individualism and subjectivity have gained more importance than ever before. Today, people are less restricted by social obligations, they are much less predefined by birth, ancestry, or rigid class or family structures than they were in pre-modern times, and they are free to choose their own favoured social relations, social contexts and spatial environments (cf. Giddens 1990; Beck *et al.* 1994) – or as Peter Wagner (1994: 6) has put it at the outset of his *Sociology of Modernity*:

> [M]odernity is about the increase of individualism and individuality. In an early phase, few may have benefited at the expense of many. In a second era, differentiation may have occurred group- and role-wise, but not really on the level of the individual. Nowadays, however, modernity's achievements allow the development of a great plurality and variety of individual life-styles and life-projects.

The worldwide approximation of existential knowledge

Against the backdrop of what is just been said it is the somewhat provocative assumption of world-polity research to conceive of 'world culture' not only in terms of globally shared technical standards and practices, but also in terms of an increasing global homology of *existential knowledge*. In fact, the proponents of the world-polity perspective claim a worldwide diffusion of similar cognitive frames containing similar 'modern' beliefs and expectations of progress, justice, instrumental activism and (rational) purposeful modern actorhood and increasingly replacing other, more primordial beliefs and patterns of social organization, such as clan structures, patronage dependencies, local rules and belief systems (cf. Meyer *et al.* 1987 and 1997; Meyer and Jepperson 2000). And they emphasize that the reflexive impact of world culture on existential definitions of social actor identities would widely exceed the confined realm of instrumental rationality, and also involves other dimensions of 'appropriate' and rationally justified behaviour.

Thus, according to John Meyer and his colleagues, 'world culture' is not just the source of increasing instrumental rationalization in modern times, but also the source of the ever increasing social validity of such moral claims and standards of 'good' and 'appropriate' social conduct which are usually highly contested and not equally accepted around the world, such as human rights, notions of citizenship, democratic principles, definitions of human development and so forth (Meyer *et al.* 1997). In fact, the world-polity analysts have provided massive empirical evidence for this argument, which ranges from the worldwide spread of standardized models of modern organizations, state bureaucracies and non-governmental organizations to the diffusion of standard models of national constitutions, national educational systems, and even to the standardization of the routes that individuals take in their lives, a creeping global standardization of life-courses (cf. Thomas and Meyer 1984; Thomas *et al.* 1987, Meyer *et al.*

1992 and 1997b; Scott and Meyer 1994; Boli and Thomas 1997, 1999; Lee and Strang 2003; Drori *et al.* 2003, 2006; Lechner and Boli 2005; Schofer and Meyer 2005). Many other scholars have studied the diffusion of new principles such as corporate social responsibility, universal citizenship and human rights as well as social policies in the tradition of world-polity research (Soysal 1994; Ramirez *et al.* 1997; Finnemore and Sikkink 1998; Hasse 2003; Hiß 2006; Koenig 2008). And they have explored the scientific construction of new 'world-cultural' standards such as environmentalism and sustainable development as well as the spread of new management standards, liberal economic ideas, and models of professional organizations around the world (cf. Fourcade-Gourinchas 2002; Hironka 2003; Drori 2005, 2006; Djelic 2006, Fourcade 2006; Hwang 2006; Mendel 2006; Ramirez 2006).

Hence, the numerous research endeavours conducted by world-polity analysts add up to an impressively multi-faceted picture of the pervasive worldwide diffusion of relatively similar world-cultural standards, models and practices. However, empirical analyses of the world-cultural make-up of 'modern' actors and actor-identities have mainly centred on the construction of modern nation-states, all types of (modern) organizations, and individuals. The world-cultural construction of regions, or rather 'modern' regional actor-identities has not been explored from a world-polity perspective, yet. Moreover, world-polity research does not say much about the 'moral content' of world culture itself. Although world-polity analysis has been such a vital field of empirical research, the underlying cultural principles of modernity have remained underspecified. The proponents of world-polity research presuppose a strong modernizing impetus and the compelling force of world-cultural diffusion, and they also point to the importance of abstract transcendental goals like progress and justice for world-cultural diffusion (cf. Thomas *et al.* 1987; Meyer *et al.* 1997). But the substance of world culture, the material 'content', remains largely underspecified in the existing empirical accounts of world culture.[10]

4 Contestations of the world-polity perspective

Despite numerous and extensive empirical evidence produced by world-polity research the assumption of an increasing homology and diffusion of 'world culture', and even the fundamental methodological assumption of a 'cultural' force of diffusion, are highly contested. In fact, the world-polity perspective has been criticized by many different researchers of various theoretical backgrounds for putting forward an all-too simplistic narration of globalization. Critiques and contestations of the world-polity approach are manifold and multi-faceted. Sometimes criticism has been raised in clear contrast and opposition to the world-polity approach, sometimes it has been brought forward to complement the assumptions of John Meyer and his colleagues. Furthermore, there is also a huge amount of 'indirect' criticism which is not brought forward with respect to the world-polity perspective itself, but simply by the outline of alternative conceptions and narrations of globalization and development. This will be briefly outlined in the following, before I present both my major criticism of the existing world-polity research and my plea for more rigorous macro-phenomenological research on the transnational diffusion of modernizing projects that arise as a result of global interconnectedness.

Popular criticisms and challenges of world-polity research

Most fundamentally, John Meyer and his followers have been criticized for putting huge efforts into analysing the outcome of world-cultural diffusion, i.e. the structural similarities across national borders and political demarcations, while being much less specific in elaborating the content and the concrete institutional logics and forces behind this process. This has been put forward, for example, in a famous review article by Martha Finnemore (1996b). In this article Finnemore in particular criticizes the world-polity researchers for not specifying the enormous tensions in all the processes of change and the unavoidable contradictions inherent to the transcendent goals of modernity.

> Indeed, there are good reasons to believe that the elements of world culture, even as the institutionalists have specified it, contain deep tensions and contradictions that constrain isomorphism and limit the stability of behavioural convergence. Most obvious is the tension between the two 'ends' of Western world culture – progress, defined as economic accumulation, and justice, defined as equality.
>
> (Finnemore 1996b: 341)

Thus, the world polity school is accused of depicting an overly harmonious and conflict-free project of modernization; a criticism which also resonates with suspicions that world-polity scholars put forward an overly positive account of modern culture, while obscuring its 'dark sides' (cf. Chase-Dunn 1989). Moreover, Martha Finnemore also bewails a systematic 'inattention' to agency, which, as she contends, would lead to an underspecification of both the mechanisms through which social structures produce change and the content of the social structures:

> Institutionalist models imply a world social structure made up of norms that are largely congruent. Their emphasis is on the mutually reinforcing and expansive nature of these norms. They stress the consensus that arises around various cultural models – of citizenship, of statehood, of education, of individual rights – to the point that these norms are taken for granted in contemporary life. The implication is that the spread of world culture is relatively peaceful. Institutionalists specify no sources of instability, conflict, or opposition to the progressive expansion of world culture.
>
> (Finnemore 1996b: 343)

In the same vein, but from a different theoretical angle, it is argued that the assumption of a cultural force of both modernization and globalization entirely obscures and neglects the 'real' forces of social change and socio-economic development, i.e. material interests, power asymmetries, and the capitalist mode of production (cf. Wallerstein 1991 and 2006). In fact, from a distinctly materialist perspective, world-cultural diffusion would be induced primarily by the worldwide expansion of the mode of production of Western capitalism, the triumphant worldwide procession of 'Western bourgeois culture' that was ebulliently described by Karl Marx and Friedrich Engels in 1848 in their famous *Manifesto of the Communist Party*.[11] Thus, on the basis of this perspective, it is argued in marked opposition to world-polity researchers that the worldwide expansion of an all-encompassing world culture is nothing more than the outcome of the worldwide expansion of modern capitalism. Accordingly, Chase-Dunn (1989: 99ff.) conceives of 'world culture' not as a neutral and ideology-free project of rationalization, but as the central legitimizing structure of the worldwide hegemony of Western capitalism:

> I agree that normative and value-based consensus has increased at the global level, and that world culture is evolving as a differentiated complex system of institutionalized values. But I also contend that these emergent features do not yet play a strong role in the dynamics of the contemporary world-system. System integration is primarily mediated by markets, and this is backed up by the functioning of the interstate system, a political-military balance of coercive power which regularly (but not randomly) employs warfare as a means of competition. World culture operates to legitimate commodifying production and the interstate system, but is not an important determinant of the dynamics of our world system.
>
> (Chase-Dunn 1989: 104)

Apart from this criticism several alternative views of globalization also seem to challenge the assumption of a rationalizing and homogenizing cultural force, such as Shmuel Eisenstadt's proposal of 'multiple modernity', and Roland Robertson's thesis of 'glocalization'. For Eisenstadt (2000, 2002a, 2002b) there has never been one single cultural model of modernity which has spread all over the world, but different versions of modernity that emerged quite independently and sometimes even in marked distinction to the Western archetype. Robertson (1995), in turn, claims that globalization was not just a source of growing homogeneity, but also divergent (local) paths of change. From his point of view, the culture of modernity spreads highly selectively, depending on the given local conditions. Similarly, contemporary macro-anthropologists have asserted a trend towards greater diversity and cultural complexity in a globalizing world (cf. Hannerz 1992 and 1996; Appadurai 1997). In detailed case studies, anthropologists have analysed how localities and individuals are being transformed by forces of globalization. They have also shown to what extent global models have become 'indigenized' and 'creolized' once they are adopted in particular local contexts. As a result, it is not only the local adaptations of world culture that constitute variations of similar cultural models, since the logic potentially works the other way round as well (see also: Urry 2003).

Some clarifications and specifications

Without doubt, an all-too simplistic and superficial reading of the world-polity perspective would confirm many of the problems, contractions and ambiguities outlined above. And it is true that the proponents of the world-polity perspective have often not been very accurate with their specifications of concrete processes, contexts and logics of diffusion. They pointed to the importance of 'cultural' processes through which world culture would 'authorize' and 'fashion' the constitution of actors: a) the cultural construction of actor identities and purposes, b) the strong coercive force of systemic maintenance of actor identities, and c) the strong cultural legitimation of rationalized models of 'modern' actorhood (Meyer *et al.* 1997: 157ff.). However, the micro-sociological conditions by which highly rationalized world-cultural models gain validity remain largely underspecified.

Nevertheless, apart from this particular and certainly intended 'shortcoming', much of the criticism which has been put forward is simply wrong and misleading. It is based on misunderstandings and misconceptions of the macro-phenomenological research perspective and its empirical specifications, to which the proponents of the world-polity approach have admittedly also contributed, since they have not been consistent with their own outline of a distinctly constructionist research perspective. In fact, they have proposed a macro-phenomenological perspective without being very 'phenomenological' in the large-scale quantitative empirical specifications of their argument. This is my major criticism of most existing world-polity research, which I will briefly outline in the following. However, this criticism aside, I will argue in subsequent sections that much of the popular criticism presented above is based on misunderstandings of the constructionist thrust of macro-phenomenological sociology.

a) Contradictions in the empirical specifications of the world-polity perspective

It is certainly true that in empirical accounts of the world-polity approach it is often not clear whether John Meyer and his colleagues claim an actual increase in similarities across the globe, or whether they assert that the diffusion of 'world culture' proceeds largely detached from concrete local and social contexts. On the one hand, the proponents of the world-polity approach make strong functionalist statements regarding the major direction of the driving force behind world-cultural diffusion leading to the conclusion that the world *is* in fact becoming ever more similar. Worldwide models of development, it is argued, increasingly determine the construction of ever more social entities – from individuals to organizations and even political entities like states. It is contended that individuals, states and even whole societies are increasingly structured around the same 'modern' (originally Western!) principles. In empirical accounts, this process of diffusion often looks like an inevitable, linear and even exponentially rising process, and, accordingly, in numerous studies and articles the many followers of world-polity research have measured these structural homologies.

On the other hand, however, as highlighted above already, the world-polity approach stands in a constructionist tradition of social thought, i.e. phenomenological sociology which does not primarily aim at 'explaining' social effects, but rather at interpreting and making sense of the nature of social phenomena in classical hermeneutic tradition. This does not exclude explanations, but these explanations tend to take the shape of interpretations rather than simple causal models. On the basis of this tradition of thought, the proponents of the world-polity approach withhold from making strong essentializing statements about universalizing cultural forces that would make the world ever more homogenous. Instead, they highlight the huge constructive character of world culture that might also lead to huge contradictory results and diverse effects of world-cultural diffusion. In the tradition of culturalist sociology, they always point to the huge importance and independent relevance of cultural principles, beliefs and symbolic dimensions of interaction – in short: the pre-rational dimensions of norm diffusion. Accordingly, they highlight the often blind, routine-like and unconsciously mimetic forms of diffusion that might lead to a huge *decoupling* of rationalized models and social practice, as well as the *expansive structuration* of rational actor models far in excess of what is necessary or instrumentally rational (cf. Meyer *et al.* 1997: 154ff.):

> World culture contains a good many variants of the dominant models, which leads to the eclectic adoption of conflicting principles. Diffusion processes work at several levels and through a variety of linkages, yielding incoherence. Some external elements are easier to copy than others, and many external elements are inconsistent with local practices, requirements, and cost structures. Even more problematic, world cultural models are highly idealized and internally inconsistent, making them in principle impossible to actualize (...).
>
> (Meyer *et al.* 1997: 154)

b) Macro-phenomenology: a non-deterministic account of modernity and global change

Having stressed this, it would be completely misleading to allege that the world-polity approach retains old orthodox narrations of 'modernization' of the Parsonsian kind. In fact, the whole research programme has been set in motion in order to overcome overly simplistic assumptions of modernization. For this reason, 'world culture' should by no means be understood as a westernizing monoculture, since it always incorporates contradictory claims, controversies as well as counter-arguments. And the notion of 'world-cultural diffusion' does not claim a coherent and harmonious package of Western values coming into force everywhere in the world in similar ways and the same degree. From a world-polity perspective the world is much too interconnected and multi-polar for one single state or 'civilization' to be the leader of world development once and forever. This has been vigorously stressed many times by John Meyer and his colleagues (cf. Boli and Thomas 1997; Meyer *et al.* 1997: 169f.). Consequently, world culture is conceived as the cultural core of a polycentric world polity (cf. Lechner and Boli 2005: 25ff.), and this is alleged to have strong repercussions on the dynamic construction and reconstruction of the cultural core itself:[12]

> The forces motivating local actors (including states) to incorporate, employ, and legitimate world theorists and theories thereby strengthen the authoritative worldwide network of sciences, professions, and consultants. They also reinforce and modify, in continuing contest, the elements of world culture that undergird them. Global discourse intensifies and becomes ever more complex as the world-societal arena of interaction is ever more routinely activated.
>
> (Meyer *et al.* 1997: 171)

Thus, controversy, contradiction and constant contestation are seen as the major driving forces of world development. Indeed, according to John Meyer and his colleagues (Meyer *et al.* 1997: 170f.) the irony of world-cultural diffusion was that the perception of the 'problems', 'contradictions' and 'backlashes' it provokes would often stimulate ever more efforts to achieve a more effective and rigorous implementation of world-cultural models. This is a strongly relativist and constructionist point of view. And against this backdrop, it is simply wrong to assert that world-cultural diffusion is conceptualized as a smooth and peaceful process without internal contradictions and inconsistencies. In fact, many proponents of the world-polity approach acknowledge themselves that world culture is complex, and most of the values and goals of world culture are highly contradictory and a matter of ongoing contestation and conflict (cf. Lechner and Boli 2005). It is even one of the major aims of the world-polity approach to point to the ambivalent and contradictory effects of world-cultural diffusion:

> What critics of cultural analysis overlook is the dynamism that is generated by the rampant inconsistencies and conflicts within world culture itself. Beyond conflicts of interests among individuals or among states, beyond the dualistic inconsistencies between individuals and organizations or groups and national collectives, there are also contradictions inherent in widely valued cultural goods: equality versus liberty, progress versus justice, standardization versus diversity, efficiency versus individuality.
>
> (Meyer *et al.* 1997: 172)

Last but not least, although the world-polity perspective mainly emphasizes growing worldwide approximation of cultural frames this does not mean that it is not sensitive to the huge 'diversities' produced by an expansive diffusion of world-cultural models. Rather the argument is that the expansion of 'rationality' and the pervasive diffusion of world-cultural models and rationalized organizational procedures constitute the condition for the strong evocation of 'diversity' in contemporary times. And while structural homologies are growing on the level of cultural models and expectations, the concrete realization of these models in concrete local contexts are always local variants and variations of the same cultural models. In this sense, the world-polity approach is closer to Roland Robertson's (1995) account of 'glocalization' than to any theory of worldwide homogenization, or rather 'McDonaldization' (Ritzer 1997), of social structures.

World-polity research accounts in fact for the very phenomenon that Robertson has called 'glocalization', the huge 'legitimated diversity' of expressive culture (Meyer and Ramirez 2005: 231f.), or rather the 'standardization of diversity' under conditions of 'modernity'. This conceptual link between the world-polity approach and Robertson's notion of 'glocalization' is also highlighted and further explained by Lechner and Boli (2005: 51f.). Yet in contrast to the approaches of Eisenstadt, Robertson and the macro-anthropologists mentioned above the world-polity perspective accounts for the increasing worldwide significance and cultural validity of (modern) rationalized structures and principles. It accounts for the significance of a global cultural force that must be adhered to – at least in symbolic terms – and de-legitimizes alternative modes of interaction and social organization if social entities are part of the (modern) world polity. Hence, the world-polity perspective is not blind to 'existing' structural imbalances or social inequality at all. As the following quote shows, the proponents of the world-polity approach have even put forward strong (quasi-deterministic) assumptions regarding the unequal effects of world-cultural diffusion in different social contexts:

> Any rationalized 'actor', whether an individual, organization, or nation-state, reveals much decoupling between formal models and observable practices (...). Resource-rich 'actors' facing exogenous pressures to assume a given posture may be able to do so convincingly (...). Weaker actors, faced with the same imperative, may emphasize formal structuration instead. Peripheral nation-states do a good deal of symbolic educational reform via national policies and control systems (...), but they have more difficulty bringing change into the classroom.
>
> (Meyer *et al.* 1997: 155)

Conclusions

After a brief depiction of major concepts and elements of world-polity research it should be clearer what the shortcomings and pitfalls of this particular account of contemporary modernity and globalization are. But it should also have become much clearer that macro-phenomenological research begins at the very point where many micro-analytical and actor-centred analyses usually end. It helps to describe the culture of 'late' modernity in which 'purposeful actorhood' and 'scientific' (or somewhat 'scientized') knowledge has become a natural part

✳ contadt

of our daily life and gained widespread cultural significance (*Kulturbedeutung*) on a global scale. It accounts for the cultural dynamics of world development beyond rational actorhood by conceptualizing the rationalized core of contemporary modernity as a distinct cultural system that is often routinely actualized and ceremonially evoked (cf. Meyer and Rowan 1977). Based on Weber's thesis of rationalization it asserts the cultural logic of world-cultural diffusion but it does not simply reify the often alleged and taken-for-granted pre-eminence of 'occidental' (instrumental) rationality. And it is open to the highly ambiguous and contradictory 'effects' of world-cultural diffusion. Hence, a macro-phenomenological research perspective can account for both the homogenizing force of world-cultural diffusion and its diversities, its inevitability and at the same time its discontinuity. Moreover, it helps us with grasping the central myths and beliefs on which contemporary projects of change are based without making claims about the functionality of these projects. This is, in my opinion, the great strength and indeed the main thrust of a macro-phenomenological analysis of the expansion of modernity, and therefore it can constitute a good starting point for an empirical sociological analysis of projects of social mobilization and regional mobilization in Europe.

Based on the wide range of empirical accounts provided by world-polity analysts we can assume that 'world culture' is significant to the identity formation of social entities (individuals, organizations, states etc.) all over the world these days. World cultural models and normative world-cultural claims have been institutionalized in loosely integrated systems, but they multiply interconnected authority structures on a world scale. More than ever before, standard recipes, standard procedures and standard practices for all types of situations are available and applied by professionals, experts and consultants to all aspects of social life. Often elements of this highly rationalized world culture are just taken for granted, since they seem to offer the most suitable, most practicable and most efficient solution to certain organizational problems. The more the world-cultural elements gain the status of universal applicability, the less other alternatives, even long-existing 'traditional' solutions to the same 'problems' are able to sustain their validity. And even if people are opposed to certain world-cultural principles such as commoditization, human rights or individual autonomy, they often conceive of these principles as givens with claims of universal applicability and position themselves in relation to these principles. In this sense, 'world culture', as the rationalized and rationalizing cultural core of contemporary modernity, can certainly be regarded as 'inevitable', 'globally significant' and 'commonly shared' (cf. Lechner and Boli 2005).

However, in order to turn the analytical perspective outlined by the proponents of world-polity research into a fruitful phenomenological account of social transformations in contemporary modernity, some theoretical assumptions and empirical implications have to be specified in more detail. Hence, first and foremost, the notion of 'institutional diffusion' through, 'rationalization', or rather 'scientization', must be specified. It has been highlighted that we have to acknowledge the huge 'practical' implications of all sorts of social-scientific models and reflections if we want to understand how world-cultural diffusion takes place and the way in which 'rational' principles have become increasingly relevant in modern times. Theoretical knowledge, theorization and scientific reasoning are seen as the major driving forces behind the rapid diffusion of world-cultural principles in contemporary world society. But it is not sufficient to highlight the inherent universalism of scientific knowledge and 'authoritative scientization' (Drori and Meyer 2003). The alleged universalism that is inherent in world-cultural diffusion is as much a matter of construction, evocation and belief as it is a matter of mimetic adoption or 'unconscious' social acceptance. These are different institutional logics and these different logics must be specified in more detail.

It is not sufficient, beyond that, to highlight the prevalence and increasing global relevance of distinctly 'modern' notions and principles, such as 'progress', 'justice', 'equality' and 'self-realization'. Surely, modern technology, artefacts and even some allegedly 'modern' values and practices have emerged throughout the globe largely independent of existing political restrictions and boundaries. However, an empirical account of world-cultural diffusion that approaches (global) society at this level of abstraction remains pretty vague and is empirically empty. And, in fact, although world-polity analysts have been reluctant to specify the 'content' of world culture, we have seen that they presuppose the assertiveness of some world-cultural models which are first and foremost associated with (Western) liberalism such as modern individualism, modern citizenship, human rights, purposeful actorhood, or instrumental activism (cf. Meyer and Jepperson 2000; Boli and Lechner 2005; Boli 2006). Hence, the empirical account of world culture is not completely arbitrary, as there seem to be 'elective affinities' (Weber 1980) between certain (allegedly Western) models and principles of social conduct and organization. This must be addressed more explicitly and explored empirically and not hidden behind a vague notion of 'world culture'.

Consequently, macro-phenomenological analyses should not end with the quantitative measurement of structural similarities between formal organizations around the globe. Instead, the 'content' of particular world-cultural models gaining cultural significance in particular social contexts – in our case the area of the European Union – must be empirically further specified. This can be achieved by a closer interlinking of the world-polity perspective with prevailing discourses and practices of 'development' (cf. Escobar 1995; Nederveen Pieterse 2001). Based on these desiderata, major assumptions of an empirically grounded macro-phenomenological research perspective will be outlined in the following chapter.

3 Outline of a phenomenology of late modernity

Macro-phenomenological institutionalism enables us to gain deeper insights into fundamental institutional changes and transformations of contemporary society. However, in order to be applicable in qualitative research some analytical presumptions and features of macro-phenomenological institutionalism must be specified in more detail than has thus far been done by the proponents of world-polity research. This requires, first and foremost, a more differentiated definition and a clearer conception of one of its central analytical concepts, namely the notion of 'institutional diffusion' (1). Second, it requires a more specific and detailed elaboration of the assumption of an endemic global diffusion of 'world culture' in relation to an increasing 'cultural significance' of scientific knowledge in contemporary society (2). Third, it requires a clearer outline of the link between the notion of world-cultural diffusion and the spread of development, or rather development practice, all around the world (3). And before these analytical presumptions are sketched out in more detail in the two subsequent empirical parts of this book, some major methodological implications of a macro-phenomenological research perspective will be briefly summarized in the final sub-section of this chapter (4).

1 Logics and carriers of world-cultural diffusion

In empirical research processes of diffusion are often studied and explained on the basis of relational interactionist accounts. In this context, researchers usually focus on the invention of a certain policy or social practice by a certain actor at time t and observe the adoption, adaptation, or imitation of the same practice by other actors at time t+1. The process of diffusion is then explained in terms of exchanges and interrelations between these two parties, and the transfer of institutional elements is usually described as a more or less intended process of emulation (cf. Westney 1987; Rogers 1995; Valente 1995; Czarniawska and Sevón 1996). From the perspective of macro-phenomenological institutionalism, however, interactionist models of diffusion are not sufficient to explain the speed and pervasiveness of the diffusion of many world-cultural models and principles in contemporary society, since diffusion often proceeds more immediately and on a more unstructured basis than predicted in interactionist accounts.

The proponents of the world-polity approach have therefore pointed out that the decisive factor of the pervasive transnational diffusion of 'world culture' in contemporary times is not the growing interconnectedness of the world per se, or the more recent tremendous growth of exchange between actors across borders. First and foremost, it is the worldwide expansion of 'modern' perceptions and interpretations of social situations ('existential knowledge') (see Chapter 2). In an article on the cultural conditions of diffusion David Strang and John W. Meyer (1993: 487ff.) have bluntly stated that relational and interactionist models might be appropriate for explaining the diffusion of non-social elements such as viruses or infectious diseases. However, where diffusion would essentially involve the identity formation and constitution of 'social actors', it was the increasing approximation of cultural definitions and culturally framed actor-identities amongst different and largely disconnected social entities in the first place that would create a tie between them and a common sense of belonging to the same social category. 'Clearly the prediction of simple relational models will go astray if they are not made conditional on the larger cultural context.' (ibid.: 504). Hence, according to Strang and Meyer, increasing *relational* interconnections amongst nation-states might indeed foster a substantial increase in structural similarities or even cross-border solidarity. Yet this tendency is not self-evident as long as it is not framed and flanked by respective cultural definitions of alignment, for it might also simply lead to greater differentiation and boundary formations. Thus, the decisive element for the massive worldwide diffusion, transfer and adoption of similar patterns of social organization is the (relatively independent) worldwide expansion and approximation of general interpretations of social situation and models of social organization. This is what Strang and Meyer consider as the defining momentum, the constitutive phenomenological condition, of worldwide endemic and isomorphic diffusion in contemporary society: 'We argue that diffusion is importantly shaped and accelerated by culturally analyzed similarities among actors, and by theorized accounts of actors and practices. These institutional conditions are argued to be especially rife in "modern" social systems' (ibid.: 487).

In a more recent review of institutionalist approaches to diffusion Marie-Laure Djelic (2008) has distinguished three major types of diffusion studies reflecting different epistemological traditions. First, diffusion as *epidemiology*, which conceives of diffusion as the spread of norms, ideas or practices across large populations and boundaries in the tradition of classical 'population ecology' and early neo-institutionalist approaches. Second, diffusion as an *encounter with embeddedness*, in which the contextual reception of institutional models is largely addressed rather than the substance or elements of diffusion itself. And third, diffusion as *mediation and construction*, which focuses on the institutional conditions, the carriers and the effects of diffusion. Against the backdrop of this tripartite categorization it becomes obvious that the macro-phenomenological approach to diffusion incorporates elements of all three perspectives on diffusion in one way or the other, but it mainly represents the first and the latter type of the above-mentioned types of approaches to diffusion.

In fact, the second dimension remains largely underspecified in world-polity research. While Strang, Meyer and others have stressed that cultural construction and the availability of similar interpretations of the situation were essential, there is hardly any study that has defined or differentiated between different institutional logics of diffusion in world-polity research. This specification, however, would be a decisive step towards a more precise qualitative account of diffusion within the framework of macro-phenomenological research. This will be done in the following sections, where we refer to distinctions of different logics and carriers of institutional diffusion which have been put forward and discussed during the past decades in the wider field of new institutional research.

Three different logics of institutional diffusion

Over the past three decades, sociological neo-institutionalism and students of organizational change have provided extensive accounts of, and revealing insights into, the nature of institutions. Indeed, institutionalist researchers have determined a whole range of macro-structural conditions of institutional change, but they have also integrated ever more micro-sociological relational categories into their institutional models, such as agency, conflict or coercion (cf. Meyer and Rowan 1977; Zucker 1983; Meyer and Scott 1983; DiMaggio and Powell 1983; Douglas 1986; Powell and DiMaggio 1991). In this context, W. Richard Scott (2001) has proposed a convincing summary of the major assumptions and insights of neo-institutionalist research endeavours of the past three decades and proposed a definition of institutions which integrates different strands of research: '*Institutions are social structures that have attained a high degree of resilience. They are composed of cultural-cognitive, normative, and regulative elements that, together with associated activities and resources, provide stability and meaning to social life.*' (ibid.: 48, emphasis by S.B.). On the basis of this definition we can distinguish three dimensions of institutions, or rather three different institutional logics, which together reflect the complexity and analytical depth of new institutionalist research and its different institutionalist conceptions of institutional order, compliance and legitimacy (see Table 3.1).

As can be seen in Table 3.1, many terms and notions summarized by Scott represent well-known and well-established concepts of neo-institutional analyses, such as the distinction between instrumental logics of institutions and the logic of appropriateness (March and Olsen 1989), or the distinction between coercive, normative and mimetic types of diffusion (DiMaggio and Powell 1983). Moreover, each of the three pillars outlined in Table 3.1 also reflects three different strands of institutionalist research traditions, or rather different types of 'institutionalisms': The first pillar contains the *regulative* dimension of institutions, such as explicit rules, laws and sanctions. This has usually been the domain of institutional economics and policy analyses that focus on the compliance (or non-compliance) of social actors in relation to given rules and regulations (cf. Williamson 1985; North 1990; Scharpf 1997; Falkner *et al.* 2005). The second pillar, the realm of more or less implicit *norms* and *standards*, in turn,

Table 3.1 The three logics of institutional diffusion

	Regulative	*Normative*	*Cultural-cognitive*
Basis of order	Regulative rules	Binding expectations	Constitutive schema
Basis of compliance	Expedience	Social obligation	Taken-for-grantedness/ shared understanding
Basis of legitimacy	Legally sanctioned	Morally governed	Comprehensible/ recognizable/ culturally supported
Institutional logic	Instrumentality	Appropriateness	Orthodoxy
Diffusion mechanism	Coercive	Normative	Mimetic
Indicators	Explicit rules, laws, sanctions	More or less explicit normative standards or expectations/ officially certified or accredited	Common beliefs, shared logics of action

Source: Scott (2001: table 3–1, p. 52), slightly adapted.

this distinction is unclear

has mainly been the domain of classical institutional sociologists and so called 'constructivist' analyses of policy change (cf. Alexander *et al.* 1987; Finnemore and Sikkink 1998; March and Olsen 1998; Green Cowles *et al.* 2001; Checkel 2005). The third pillar, the *cultural-cognitive* pillar, is the institutional logic which has gained the most attention within the recent surge in new institutionalist thinking and new culturalist conceptions of social and political change (cf. Meyer and Rowan 1977; DiMaggio and Powell 1983; Thomas *et al.* 1987; Steinmo *et al.* 1992; Rotstein 1999; Thelen 1999; Steinmetz 1999). Therefore, it is often regarded as *the* intrinsic and central dimension of sociological institutionalisms.

Certainly, all the different concepts and notions depicted in Table 3.1 have also been addressed by proponents of the world-polity approach, but they have not been differentiated explicitly.[1] In this way, W. Richard Scott's differentiation brings some conceptual clarity to the language of macro-phenomenological institutionalism. Based on the preceding explanations it should become clearer that the third pillar is the institutional logic that is closest to conceptions of macro-phenomenological accounts of institutional diffusion. Macro-phenomenological institutionalism claims pre-eminence of the cultural-cognitive domain. If there were no cultural-cognitive 'apriorities', then legal rules, explicit normative standards and implicit expectations would not exist and they would not have coercive effects on everyday social life in their capacity as institutions. However, when we speak of 'institutional diffusion', all three different logics must always be considered together and in close connection to one another, and it is the task of qualitative empirical analyses to grasp these different institutional logics and their social effects.

Institutional carriers of diffusion

Apart from differentiating various conceptions and logics of institutional diffusion, it is also important to acknowledge that the spread of ideas, principles or institutional models can take place via a multitude of different 'institutional carriers'. As pointed out already, in most of the relational and rationalist conceptions of diffusion the major carriers are 'real actors'. However, from a phenomenological perspective, carriers of diffusion are as diverse and impersonal as the various institutional logics outlined above in Table 3.1. Potential institutional carriers of diffusion range from more concrete legal rules, obligations and standards to more abstract and less explicit interpretative schemas or institutional scripts. Accordingly, W. Richard Scott (2001) has also proposed to distinguish a whole range of different 'institutional carriers' of diffusion which he tentatively groups in the following four classes: 1) symbolic systems, 2) relational systems, 3) routines and 4) artefacts (see also: Scott 2003). This broad distinction of four classes of institutional carriers brings about a complex understanding of institutional diffusion and opens up a multi-faceted 'universe' of potential carriers of institutional diffusion in addition to interactionist cause-and-effect models (see Table 3.2 below).

This shows, for one, that many aspects and elements of institutional diffusion, such as social practices, routines, cultural schemas, which are now vigorously promoted as new and major objects of research by theorists of a new cultural sociology (cf. Latour 1993; Lamont and Thévenot 2000; Reckwitz 2002), have always been part of institutional analyses of diffusion. Moreover, such a multi-faceted universe of institutional carriers gives way to a multi-dimensional understanding

Table 3.2 The universe of institutional carriers of diffusion

Institutional carriers	Pillars		
	Regulative	*Normative*	*Cultural-cognitive*
Symbolic systems	Rules, laws	Values, expectations, standards	Categories, typifications, schema
Relational systems	Governance systems, power systems	Regimes, multiple authority systems	Structural isomorphism, identities
Routines	Protocols, standard operating procedures	Jobs, roles, obedience to duty	Scripts
Artifacts	Objects complying with mandated specifications	Objects meeting conventions, standards	Objects possessing symbolic value

Source: Scott (2001: table 4–1, p. 77), slightly adapted.

of the social meaning or social significance of the same institutional features. From a *cultural-cognitive* point of view, for example, habitual institutional routines are understood as 'institutional scripts' (Powell 2008), and institutional researchers often reconstruct the emergence of these scripts and the processes contributing to their cultural validity or de-legitimation. Moreover, routines may also occur in stronger *regulative* terms, for example in terms of standard operating procedures for businesses or bureaucratic organizations, contemporary standards of customer relations management, or certain rules and standards of project management that have to be followed in order to fulfil the criteria of a successful project manager. Moreover, routines may also have a *normative* connotation implying a fixed set of tasks, roles or duties which are not explicitly codified but which are somehow known to all who are enacting them. The same applies to the other three groups of carriers: symbolic systems, relational systems and artefacts. They may all convey, in one way or the other, both regulative, normative and/or cultural-cognitive institutional logics and principles. Their concrete forms and their interplay in a given situation and at a certain point of time have to be explored and made explicit by way of detailed qualitative analyses.

Theorization – the fundamental condition of endemic diffusion

It has been pointed out already that the diffusion of world-cultural models, which today is considered to be rapid and on a massive scale, is mainly associated with the 'cultural construction' of social ties and similarities amongst various social entities, even amongst entities which are not connected in relational terms. According to Strang and Meyer (1993), in modern society this cultural construction is mainly provided by 'theorization' and the circulation of theoretical knowledge in scientific and semi-scientific expert discourses. Hence, from the point of view of macro-phenomenological institutionalism, scientific exploration and abstraction – which are core activities and products of modern science – constitute fundamental conditions for the rapid and extensive diffusion of (modern) world culture in contemporary society. Theoretical generalization facilitates meaningful communication and interdependence amongst social entities which are not very related to each other in everyday life. It enables the perception of similarities between different social settings and situations, and it provides people with standard reflections and standard techniques which can be applied and adapted rather easily to local contexts and particular local requirements. Thus, for Strang and Meyer it was the 'theoretical specification' of welfare policies, environmental issues and educational institutions, for instance, or the 'theorization of problems of organizational control and communication', that would above all foster the rapid diffusion of similar institutional structures across different countries. And it was not just the mutual perception of best practices as usually asserted in diffusion research.

> Standardized categories make it plausible for organizational analysts to provide recipes for successful management and motivate public authorities

to dictate or provide incentives for approved forms. As these models gain a taken-for-granted or rule-like status, it becomes advantageous for organizations to comply in at least symbolic ways.

(Strang and Meyer 1993: 491)

Consequently, Strang and Meyer define 'theorization' as the '(...) self-conscious development and specification of abstract categories and the formulation of patterned relationships such as chains of cause and effect' (ibid. 492). Theoretical models which were subject to rapid diffusion range from simple concepts and typologies to quite abstract and complex systems, and they enter into diffusion processes in at least three different ways: First, they represent a knowledge base for potential adopters, identifying and interpreting general regularities and conditions for adoption. Second, they provide adopters with simplified and highly generalized accounts of practices, and specify the outcomes they produce, e.g. in terms of more or less efficiency, justice or progress. And, third, theoretical models can also constitute the mechanisms of diffusion themselves. 'Where potential adopters internally reproduce and act on the basis of the theoretical model, we might describe theorization itself as the diffusion mechanism' (ibid. 499). This is the inherent compelling and self-propelling logic of theorization and scientific reasoning which gains huge diffusion-generating power in itself. And it is important to acknowledge this compelling institutional logic of theorization which enhances the diffusion of world-cultural models and institutional scripts in contemporary society: Theoretical models specify the subjects, the objects and the mechanisms of diffusion. They provide adopters with scientifically approved justifications for institutional change and often even specify the potential outcomes of adoption. And in modern times, when social entities are increasingly constructed and legitimated as 'modern' entities, or in particular as 'modern' actors, we can expect a huge circulation of social material among these actors. Thus, the more that scientific explanations, models and principles become prevalent around the world, providing the most appropriate and legitimate answers to the existential challenges of our time, the more rapid and endemic the diffusion of scientifically rationalized models of development is likely to take place (ibid. 500ff.)

Although the major proponents of the world-polity approach have not mentioned and elaborated on this link systematically (for an exemption: Drori *et al.* 2003), it seems obvious that this argument is built upon a broad strand of social-scientific research that came up by the end of the 1960s. It is the research which predicted *The Coming of Post-Industrial Society* (Bell 1973) and its diverse social repercussions, namely the emergence of a 'new class' of knowledge workers and the rise of a 'knowledge society' (Lane 1966; Parkin 1971; Bell 1979; Gouldner 1979; Bruce-Briggs 1979; Weingart 1983, 2001; Freidson 1986; Beck *et al.* 1994; Stehr 1994). Thus, for a deeper understanding of the assumption of a pervasive diffusion of 'world culture' as put forward by the major proponents of macro-phenomenological institutionalism, it is worthwhile to present at least some aspects of this debate in more detail.

2 The advent of 'knowledge society'

The proponents of the world-polity perspective were certainly strongly influenced and inspired by Robert K. Merton's sociology of knowledge and, above all, Merton's structural-functionalist outline of a sociology of sciences (cf. Merton 1973). Moreover, it has been particularly inspired by the discussion on the new role of sciences and academic education in modern society that evolved in the U.S. social sciences at the end of 1960s. Daniel Bell (1973), one of the figureheads of this debate, considered the transition from industrial to post-industrial society as a fundamental break in modernity, for he observed a fundamental transformation of the character of knowledge-production and a new role of knowledge in society. Though he pointed out that the use of scripted and codified knowledge is nothing new and nothing exceptional for contemporary times, the unique and distinctive feature of 'post-industrial society' was the new prevalence and more direct adaptation and implementation of theoretical knowledge in economic production and political planning.

The extension of practical rationality throughout modernity

In his famous book *The Coming of Post-Industrial Society* Bell asserts a qualitative shift in Max Weber's classical interpretation of the nature of (occidental) rationality and his famous prediction of an undamped disenchantment with the world through ongoing (scientific) reflection and rationalization. Whilst at the beginning of the twentieth century Weber described 'rationalization' mainly as the expansion of instrumental knowledge or functional rationality, Bell points at a fundamental qualitative change in the logic of rationalization in the late twentieth century that is even more comprehensive than Weber's thesis of inevitable instrumental rationalization.

> What has become decisive for the organization of decisions and the direction of change is the centrality of theoretical knowledge – the primacy of theory over empiricism and the codification of knowledge into abstract systems of symbols that, as in any axiomatic system, can be used to illuminate many different and varied areas of experiences.
>
> (Bell 1973: 20)

Bell's thesis of the 'coming of post-industrial society' was first and foremost taken up and vividly discussed by industrial and economic researchers. However, his prediction of the 'coming of post-industrial society' was not just confined to the area of economic production. He pointed to path-breaking changes of social reproduction in a much broader sense. Since the beginning of 1970s many theorists of modernity have asserted a fundamental break in the nature of knowledge production and the rise of a 'knowledge-based society'. In his classic critique of contemporary 'practical rationality' the German sociologist Friedrich Tenbruck (1972), for instance, also forcefully pointed to fundamental qualitative changes in the logics and character of 'rationalization'. Tenbruck conceded that in earlier stages during the nineteenth century and the beginning of the twentieth century modernity was indeed mainly shaped by an instrumental logic of 'rationaliza-tion' in the old Weberian sense. During that period of time the practical imple-mentation of advances in science was mainly limited to the areas of economics, labour and organizational advancement. With the growth of scientific knowledge and the awareness of the limits and narrow-mindedness of instrumental rational-ity, however, new theoretical knowledge (especially knowledge from social and human sciences) and other dimensions of rationality have increasingly become part of 'practical rationalization' as well. Thus, according to Tenbruck the quali-tative shift of knowledge production in the second half of the twentieth century is, above all, shaped by the extension of dimensions of practical rationality and the expansion of applications of scientific methods and techniques.[2]

Accordingly, it is widely acknowledged these days that almost all human activities, almost all processes of life, are mediated by expert knowledge provid-ing socially approved problem-specific solutions to almost all imaginable and unimaginable situations in life (cf. Stehr and Ericson 1992; Latour 1993; Beck *et al.* 1994; Urry 2003). Every realm of society and every aspect of reality are put into question and become subject to comprehensive (scientific) reflection. Exper-tise and expert knowledge has increasingly substituted personal skills and experi-ences as well as traditional knowledge – or as Zygmunt Bauman (1991: 214) put it: 'It is now the expert-produced and managed technique that constitutes the true environment of individual life'. And in his book *Consequences of Modernity* Anthony Giddens (1990: 39) stated astutely:

> It is often said that modernity is marked by an appetite for the new, but this is not perhaps completely accurate. What is characteristic of modernity is not an embracing of the new for its own sake, but the presumption of whole-sale reflexivity – which of course includes reflection upon the nature of reflection itself. Probably we are only now, in the late twentieth century, beginning to realize in a full sense how deeply unsettling this outlook is.

Increased and accelerated 'reflexivity' of institutional change

According to more recent theorists of contemporary 'knowledge society', the main characteristic of the rise of the contemporary knowledge society was the 'generalization' of scientific reflection and the 'expansion' of scientific methods of exploration to all areas of social life (Stehr 1994). It is said that over the past 30 years the traditional social distance between science and society has decreased markedly, and that all areas of social life are affected and governed by all-embracing (scientific) reflection. Consequently, scientific methods, reflection and expertise have been linked much more closely with modern politics, economics and the mass media than ever before (Weingart 2001; Weingart *et al.* 2007). The extraordinary expansion of scientific reflection has made 'reflexive loops' and 'reflexive mechanisms' (Weingart), such as organizational procedures, routines of learning and constant scrutiny common practice in all areas of human life. Thus, in marked contrast to all societies that existed before the rise of the contemporary 'knowledge society', as Peter Weingart (2001) has pointed out, knowledge and experiences are now not only 'internalized' and 'processed' passively, but are constantly *explored, reflected on* and *re-interpreted* through procedures of 'prospective' and 'active' learning:

> Social innovations in all functional realms of society are increasingly governed by the imperative of learning through active reflection. In order to be able to act strategically, the future is seen through hypothetical concepts, simulations and models. The causes of deviations in factual outcomes from expected events are constantly explored on a systematic basis. The data produced in this way are saved and further processed – which means they are once again put back into the process of reflection. In this way, both the speed and the capacity of information processing changes markedly. This is accompanied by an increasing establishment of respective institutional infrastructures.
>
> (Weingart 2001: 18; translated from German by S.B.)

[handwritten margin note: ✳ (but not a "phenomenology"?)]

This is exactly what the proponents of the world-polity approach and other macro-phenomenological sociologists consider as 'all-embracing scientization' in contemporary world polity (cf. Meyer and Drori 2006).³ It must be noted, however, that the relation between scientific expertise and more mundane realms of social practice is not a one-way street. Scientific knowledge is received and adapted in many different ways, and its practical implementation always feeds back to science and expertise, conversely (cf. Bell 1973; Beck and Bonß 1989; Stehr and Ericson 1992; Latour 1993; Gibbons *et al.* 1995; Knorr-Cetina 1999). Moreover, it has been ascertained that the flipside of an increasing 'scientization' of society is a reverse increase of 'socialization' (*Vergesellschaftung*) and 'trivialization' (*Trivialisierung*) of scientific practice (Weingart 2001 and 2007). Thus, the more that scientific reflexivity gains cultural significance, the more scientific knowledge becomes precarious and the more it loses its 'sacrosanct' authority. This seems to be the major paradox of contemporary 'knowledge society', and therefore we cannot simply assume the universality and unchallenged 'authority' of scientific knowledge.

However, it has been observed that the growing uncertainty of scientific knowledge does not lead to the de-legitimation of scientific expertise, but to the expansion of new authority structures and new rationalized structures of 'cultural legitimation'. Since expert authority is no longer sacrosanct and self-evident in itself, it is increasingly co-produced by new 'external' and 'independent' structures of control and legitimation. Therefore, transparency, accountability and certified reputation are increasingly becoming important currencies of expert authority. Expertise and scientific authority are increasingly assessed, examined and certified by 'independent' auditing experts and certifying authorities. This was most insistently (and paradigmatically) described by *[handwritten margin mark: ✳]*

Michael Power (1997) as the expansion of an *Audit Society* during the past two decades. This macro-phenomenological institutionalists consider as the self-propelling logic of diffusion of rationalized structures that goes beyond mere efficiency and functionality (see also: Rose and Miller 2008; Le Galès and Scott 2008; Münch 2009a).

'Knowledgeable experts' – the major social carriers of world-cultural diffusion

Although the rise of a 'knowledge society' during the 1970s is often considered and depicted as a fairly unleashed, self-propelling institutional process, it has also manifested in remarkable ways in the social structure of advanced modern societies. In fact, the rise of the 'knowledge society' was accompanied by the emergence and the massive expansion of new industries and sectors of employment, new professions, and new types of employees. Accordingly, social scientists discovered the expansion of professional and technical strata of society and the emergence of a 'new class' of post-industrial knowledge workers (Gouldner 1979; Bruce-Briggs 1979; Freidson 1986; Heuberger 1992). This new 'knowledge class' (Bell 1979) is alleged to consist mainly of people with some sort of academic background who have managed to obtain positions in the variously expanding knowledge fields in both public and private domains. In short, it is alleged to constitute a societal stratum of scientifically trained professionals that mainly deal with the production and distribution of non-material goods and services. Thus, a huge part of the so-called 'knowledge class' is alleged to be employed in state bureaucracies in areas like planning and administration, or in research, education and training. An ever increasing amount of knowledge workers are also employed in private businesses, e.g. as engineers, consultants, freelancing advisors, journalists or publicists.

However, one should be careful not to understand the notion of 'class' in the literal and conventional sense of the term. First, the so-called 'knowledge class' neither represents a homogenous socio-economic group, nor one particular type of 'profession' or one particular occupational group. In fact, it consists of people from very diverse professional as well as social backgrounds. Second, we must acknowledge that the 'knowledge class' does not usually constitute a homogenous caste of political or functional elites. Although the intersection between knowledge workers and professional politics is often blurred – since, for instance, many members of the knowledge class serve as civil servants in state bureaucracies or as public officials – the knowledge class does not just represent a functional or political elite. In fact, the knowledge class is much too big and diverse to be confined to the political domain and the state sector, and, moreover, it is one of the typical characteristics of the members of these (new) professions that they tend to serve as experts, consultants and advisors to decision-makers rather than act as decision-makers themselves (cf. Freidson 1986; Abbott 1988; Meyer and Jepperson 2000).

Nonetheless, the new knowledge workers exhibit some common features which make it possible to highlight major commonalities between them, and not just assign them to various professional groups or fields of activity. Thus, it has been put forward that the knowledge class represents a 'reflective elite' (*Reflexionselite*) (Schelsky 1975), rather than some sort of functional or political elite in the narrow sense; and that it obtains its distinctiveness and (discursive) authority through the symbolic representation of practical rationality. According to Heuberger (1992), the members of this new reflective elite gain their relative discursive power through their distinctive ability to interpret and explain ideas to others. Their typical self-image was fundamentally based on 'rational principles' and on the ability to represent an unbiased moral universalism, convincingly.

> The key argument to be made is that the New Class – regardless of its professional location in the private or public sector – succeeds most easily in the seemingly unselfish enforcement of the rational discourse of permanent justification that is grounded in moral universalism.
>
> (Heuberger 1992: 46)

This particular attitude of the new reflective elite is personified in an ideal-typical way by the social figures of the 'rational' (business) consultant or the 'prudent' lifestyle engineer (Kellner and Berger 1992) that have evolved just recently with the rise of the knowledge society and increasingly became the primary professional authorities of contemporary society.[4] While the taken-for-granted social status of established professional authorities such as priests, lawyers, politicians and public officials has decisively decreased these days, professional authorities must prove their authority through the continuous provision and symbolic representation of 'superior' (scientific) knowledge or 'superior' (academic) reflexivity. Today, it is the role of all types of scientific experts and lifestyle consultants to tell individuals, groups, organizations and society as a whole what is best for them and what should be done. They provide society with all different kinds of advice on all aspects of social life and human behaviour, and they define the standards of normality, acceptable deviations, and respective problem-solving.

> All sorts of 'how-to' instructions, advice, and counselling are available. Almost no area of life seems to be left out; apparently nothing exists for which some 'expert' has not claimed competence. (...) The massive spread of rational advice offered by what has been called 'service industry' is a hallmark of our time.
>
> (Kellner and Heuberger 1992: 49f.)

It is this assumption of an inherent 'rationalizing imperialism' (Berger and Heuberger 1992) of the new professions that Meyer and his colleagues have in mind when they see the sciences and the professions at the centre of world-cultural diffusion (cf. Strang and Meyer 1993; Meyer *et al.* 1997; Meyer and Jepperson 2000). According to macro-phenomenological institutionalists rapid diffusion of world-cultural models and principles is grounded in the 'epistemic cultures' (Knorr-Cetina 1999) of contemporary world society. This global prevalence and fluidity of scientific models and expertise is a central feature of contemporary world society. The various professions, professionals and experts, who are quite vaguely grouped together under the broad and obscure label of the 'knowledge class', constitute the major social carriers of world-cultural diffusion and expansion of 'knowledge society' (Scott 2008).[5] This is visible, not least, in the wider field of development practice. With regard to current activities in development practice it has been observed that it is mainly professionals and scientifically trained experts who define the dividing lines of wealth and poverty, of development and underdevelopment, based on highly generalized and standardized indicators and models of development. Today, scientific models and scientific experts are central to all efforts of institutional change, political reform and human development. Almost all concepts and practices of contemporary development policy originally emanated from academic research. They were discussed at countless academic symposia and semi-academic conferences before they found their way into official documents and practices of development planning (cf. Evers 2000).[6] After assessing the social situation and the major problems of 'underperformance', experts often immediately propose the appropriate 'treatment' – this was at least the usual practice of big international development agencies such as the IMF and the World Bank in many Latin American and African countries as well as in East Asia and Russia during the 1990s (cf. Sachs 1992a; Chossudovsky 1997; Stiglitz 2003).

3 Intellectual underpinnings of the spirit of 'active intervention'

The problem of development and underdevelopment and the exploration of factors determining the wealth of states and regions have instigated dozens of research endeavours in the social sciences over the past centuries. Indeed, a wide range of assumptions and hypotheses has been brought forward which highlights all different kinds of factors that potentially determine the social, economic and political well-being of society. Classical economists, for example, highlighted the importance of free market competition, unhindered economic activity, and international trade for overall societal prosperity (cf. Smith 2007 [1776]; Ricardo 1996 [1817]). Classical sociologists and historians tended to point to so-called 'ideational' or 'cultural' factors, such as religious orientations, occupational lifestyles and structures of *longue durée* which shape the respective attitudes or behavioural patterns that are decisive for favourable socio-economic development (cf. Weber 1976; Braudel 1996; Landes 1998). Political economists and political scientists, in turn, have stressed the role of power relations and the interplay of political institutions as the most decisive developmental factors (Lipset 1959; Hirschman 1977; Skocpol 1979; Wallerstein 1984; Scharpf 1984; Putnam 1993; Rogowski 1995).

All these various aspects of social life, and many more, have been put forward in endless academic debates. Some scholars have even stressed the importance of purely natural or geographical factors to human development, such as the influence of the climate or the availability of natural resources (Huntington 1915; Karmack 1976). It has often been the case that various explanatory factors have been put forward in marked contrast to one another, reflecting the multiple disciplinary orientations which have evolved in the realm of the social sciences. Sometimes various factors have been seen as related and closely linked to one another. However, regardless of the multiple disciplinary approaches, from a phenomenological institutionalist perspective all these different research endeavours and attempts to theorize 'development' have one thing in common: They are offshoots of 'enlightened' modern social thought and uphold in one way or another secularized belief in societal progress. They uphold the belief in improvement through active intervention and in this way contribute to the diffusion of world culture around the globe.

This argument might sound quite polemic and inappropriate at first glance, since the vast majority of research endeavours are not explicitly set in motion to solve practical problems or to instruct processes of development. However, in order to understand how the diffusion of world-cultural models takes place, we have to understand the 'practical' implications of all sorts of social-scientific models and reflections on the 'problem' of development. Hence, I will briefly present some major assumptions of a macro-phenomenological approach to development in the following sections.

The mythical element in theories of development

Long before the recent upswing of new institutionalist thinking in sociology, social theorists and intellectuals repeatedly highlighted the close relationship between social-scientific research and practice as well as the political – or even 'ideological' – implications of theories of social change and development (cf. Mannheim 1936; Myrdal 1969). In fact, it is one of the central theses of the 'old institutionalist' Karl Polanyi (2001), if I may call him so, in his classic masterpiece *The Great Transformation: The Political and Economic Origins of Our Times* that the modern aspiration of 'development', the idea that society can be changed through rational intervention, has been deeply inherent in the history of modern social thought since its very beginnings. Polanyi asserts that the intellectual preoccupation with society and social issues changed decisively when the industrial mode of production emerged in the late eighteenth century. Politicians and intellectuals were increasingly confronted with new social ruptures such as mass poverty, unemployment and 'social disembedding', and many new intellectual enterprises of that time were dedicated to theorizing the causes and effects of societal challenges as well as respective measures to tame or overcome them.[7] Beyond that, Polanyi (2001: 136ff.) has described the history of human development since the rise of industrial society during the nineteenth century as a 'double movement' of two antithetic 'organizational principles' determining to a large extent the political struggle throughout the nineteenth century. The principle of *economic liberalism* was aimed at establishing a self-regulating market by enforcing laissez-faire beliefs and free trade, and the principle of *social protection* was aimed at the conservation of nature and society through protective legislation, restrictive regulatory frameworks and other instruments of targeted intervention. According to Polanyi, both principles have been carried and supported by social forces and gained social and political significance during the nineteenth century, though to various degrees at various points in time. Thus, the central methodological elements of his research approach included the question of what kind of principles gain social support and political backing, what provides this support, under what conditions and in which period of time.

In principle, macro-phenomenological institutionalism takes a similar stance. Yet in contrast to Polanyi, who mainly emphasized the role of political assertiveness and power relations in Marxist tradition, it primarily stresses the inherent transformative logics and cultural force of development knowledge itself, and the conditions of its diffusions. Thus, macro-phenomenological institutionalism first and foremost points to the extra-scientific 'mythical' elements which are inherent in all theories of social change and development and bestow them with a powerful practical impact. In fact, it is one of the major concerns of macro-phenomenological institutionalism to stress the persistence of pre-rational 'cultural' functions of scientific rationality against the predominating 'enlightened' belief that mythology or metaphysics have faded away in the modern scientific era. It is pointed out, in this regard, that theorizing is by no means merely a neutral and unbiased exercise of knowledge production; it is also always a strategy of making sense of the world (Strang and Meyer 1993: 493). Hence, social theories are always more than sterile objective reflections on the nature and coherence of social life. They constitute a whole universe of symbols, meanings and constitutive schemas which suggest a particular view of the world, and they provide people with existential truths and meaningful 'narrations' (cf. Lakatos 1976 and Alexander 2003). In this way, social theories and social scientific models can become powerful 'myths' of social mobilization and change.[8]

With the rise of secular modernity, in which traditional wisdom and ultimate truths have become highly suspect and the speed of societal change is confronting people with growing instabilities and insecurities, the myth of 'forward progress' through rational planning and intervention has become the most powerful idea of social change (cf. Rapp 1992). This myth is implicit in many social-scientific theories, and especially in those accounts which explicitly put the question of 'modernization' front and centre. According to Alexander (2003), the notion of modernization constitutes the predominating narrative of modern times. It functions as a 'metalanguage', as Alexander puts it, telling people how to live. And it was the particular mythical function of modernization theories '(...) to divide the "known world" into the *sacred* and the *profane* and to provide a clear-cut picture of how to act in order manoeuvre the space in between' (ibid.: 195f.). This was, according to Alexander and other students of modernization, the powerful suggestive force of modernization theories and all scientific models relating to them. They provide people with interpretations, motives and sometimes even with instructive knowledge of how to accomplish a better future and, above all, how to get on the path to future well-being. Thus, the idea of 'development' is closely related to the notion of 'future progress'. In this way, development thinking constitutes an essential part of the modernizing project, and it is deeply inherent in the broad explanatory frameworks of the 'metalanguage' of modernization. Development thinking suggests that the improvement of living conditions is feasible, and respective theories or research endeavours often aim at specifying the 'problems' of development as well as the appropriate means of how to overcome them. Future progress, socio-economic well-being and universal justice are often more or less explicitly proclaimed as the 'sacred' goals of development in this context. Rational reasoning, 'prudent' (scientific) knowledge and the rational application of methods are embraced as the 'sacred' means of achieving success. In contrast, standing still, or even going backwards, are characterized in an unambiguously negative way. And the belief that controlling and converting of the existential conditions of human life was possible, constitutes the all-encompassing 'illusion' of modern times (Tenbruck 1990).

Yet contemporary theorists of development have vigorously pointed to the ambiguity of development, and they have emphasized that the equation of development, progress and modernization is highly problematic. In fact, the 'myth' of future progress and the 'grand narration' of modernization have been eyed with a good portion of suspicion in development thinking in the past few decades. Contemporary development analysts have widely deconstructed almost all mythical elements of development thinking and theories of modernity.

Pluralism, ideology and self-criticism in contemporary development thinking

'Grand narrations' of development and macro-sociological conceptions of world development are largely dismissed in contemporary development studies (cf. Escobar 1995; Long 2001; Nederveen Pieterse 2001; Ziai 2007). It is pointed out that the substance of development, i.e. the very meaning of what is considered as improvement and as appropriate intervention, is highly contextual and largely depends on class, culture, historical contexts, prevailing power relations and so forth. Besides that, it is highlighted that the meanings of progress and development have changed markedly over time depending on major paradigmatic shifts in the field of social theory and on broader hegemonic politico-economic constellations in the international system. This makes a clear-cut determination of the very notion of development far more complex and broadens the picture of the 'grand narration' of modernization. In short, these days it is widely acknowledged in development studies that knowledge is always political in the way it shapes perceptions, political agendas and policies. And this is especially true of development theory, which is always policy-oriented and problem-driven to certain extent – or as the development theorist Jan Nederveen Pieterse (2001: 3) has put it:

For a development theory to be significant, social forces must carry it. To be carried by social forces it must match their worldview and articulate their interests; it must serve an ideological function. However, to serve their interests, it must also make sense and be able to explain things.

In fact, it is one of the major concerns of contemporary (critical) development theorists to emphasize the huge political implications of all scientific preoccupations with issues of development (cf. Esteva 1985; Sachs 1992b; Escobar 1995). Development analysts have also made in-depth analyses of the 'battlefields of knowledge' (Long and Long 1992) at the interface of development theory and local practice. However, as Nederveen Pieterse also points out, contemporary development theorists have completely different views on the degree of autonomy that development theory has in relation to politics. Some would treat development thinking primarily as part of the social sciences. Others, in turn, would see development theories as pure expressions of prevailing political ideologies. He himself takes a middle position in this regard: 'It doesn't make sense to isolate development theories from political processes and treat it as an ivory-tower intellectual enterprise; but neither can one simply reduce it to ideology or political propaganda.' (Nederveen Pieterse 2001: 3). Against this background, he identifies six major 'discourses' of development that have evolved since the advent of modern social thought in the nineteenth century, depending on both prevailing power relations in international politics and predominating theoretical conceptions in the realm of science: progress/evolutionism during the nineteenth century, and classical development, orthodox modernization, dependency, neo-liberalism and human development as the major discourses of development during the twentieth century (see Table 3.3).

This rough categorization is neither complete nor sufficient. It could be complemented, on the one hand, by a seventh discourse: the discourse of 'sustainable development', which is increasingly gaining momentum in global politics (cf. OECD 1997; World Bank 2005; Baker 2006; Strange and Bayley 2008). On the other hand, it could also be complemented by a new type of 'anti-hegemonic' discourse that has increasingly gained significance both in development thinking and practice since the mid-1980s: the discourse of post-development (cf. Escobar 1995), which deliberately aims to abolish completely the whole notion and concept of development in reaction to the reinforced neo-liberal turn in development practice and the failures of (Western) development policy in Latin America (for an overview see Ziai 2007). Beyond that, it could also be criticized for its Western bias, since the big development projects based on communist ideas are not mentioned at all (Arnason 1993). Nevertheless, at the example of Nederveen Pieterse's discursive approach to development it becomes clear that notions such as development, progress or justice which are put forward by the proponents of the world-polity perspective as the central 'sacred' goals of contemporary globalizing modernity are strongly challenged and constantly shaped and reshaped discursively. Therefore, macro-phenomenological analyses must be open to discursive accounts of development in order to avoid proposing overly simplistic

Table 3.3 Major discourses of development since the nineteenth century

Development thinking	Historical context	Hegemony	Explanation
Progress, evolutionism	19th century	British Empire	Colonial anthropology, Social Darwinism
Classical development	1890–1930s	Latecomers, colonialism	Classical political economy
Modernization	Post-war boom	US hegemony	Growth theory, structural functionalism
Dependency	Decolonization	Third World, nationalism, NAM, G77	Neomarxism
Neoliberalism	1980s >	Globalization: international finance and corporate capital	Neoclassical economics, monetarism
Human development	1980s >	Rise of Asian and Pacific Rim, big emerging markets	Capabilities, Developmental state

Source: Nederveen Pieterse (2001: 9), slightly adapted.

and monolithic notions of 'development' as 'modernization'. At the same time, however, there are good reasons to assert that the 'modernizing' and, in particular, 'mobilizing' impact of world-cultural diffusion has reinforced transnationally with the rise of 'knowledge society'. Therefore, a macro-phenomenological research perspective seems to be suitable for a more in-depth analysis of the major institutional dynamics and logics of regional mobilization in contemporary Europe.

Hence, in sum, contemporary development studies reflect a fundamental contradiction (or paradox) of contemporary development thinking: On the one hand, it is widely accepted today that development thinking has largely resigned from universal claims and from the 'grand narrative' of modernization (Sachs 1992b; Nederven Pieterse 2001; Long 2001). According to current development studies, the classic aim of development, such as 'modernization' or 'catching-up' in accordance with advanced (Western) societies, no longer seems attractive. This no longer seems appropriate in times in which 'diversity' and 'local cultures' are given more attention. And with the proclamation of a post-development agenda, development theorists have fully abandoned all existing notions and sentiments of development in general (cf. Ziai 2007). On the other hand, however, we can see that the neo-liberal paradigm which has dominated development practice since the 1980s represents nothing less than an all-embracing universalizing force of world development. In fact, neo-liberalism has successfully revived beliefs in universal applicability and future progress.[9] Beyond that, it seems that in the era of an alleged 'decay' or 'crisis' of development, many principles and concepts of development have never been so commonly accepted, so widely shared and so largely institutionalized as they are today. Development analysts have observed the emergence of new global standards and the establishment of a huge consensus on the common future challenges of development on a global scale (Evers 2000). It even seems, in fact, that the field of development policy has never been as large and extensive as it is today. In the past two decades a whole industry of both governmental and non-governmental development agencies has emerged on a global scale promoting countless ideas, concepts and approaches to development (Nederveen Pieterse 2001). International, national and local non-governmental organizations, international organization, business actors, regions and local governments are increasingly overtaking the conventional tasks of national development agents.

Thus, despite the alleged crisis of development thinking, and despite the rise of the anti-developmental neo-liberal agenda, the notion of 'development' has actually witnessed a significant boost in the past two decades rather than a decline.[10] And it is this change which is at the centre of the following macro-phenomenological study of diffusion of world-cultural models and practices of development to areas and regions all over the territory of the European Union and beyond.

Conclusions

It was shown in the previous discussion that a macro-phenomenological institutionalist research perspective offers a good approach to the transnational expansion and diffusion of standards and practices of development in contemporary society. In contrast to ethnographic and discursive approaches in contemporary development studies (cf. Escobar 1995; Long 2001), it sticks to a distinct macro-sociological conception of social change and transnational diffusion of development practices. At the same time, however, it is not entirely detached from social structure or 'actorless' in the literal sense. On the one hand, it presupposes a wide array of different 'institutional carriers' of world-cultural diffusion. World-cultural diffusion is mainly put forward and carried by 'knowledge experts' and many different types of scientifically-based 'professions'. It is inherent in the practices and routines of experts and professionals and it is often scripted and enforced in explicit organizational rules, standards and policy prescriptions. On the other hand, the macro-phenomenological research perspective presumes a certain degree of self-reinforcement within the logic of world-cultural diffusion itself. The more scientific concepts, scientific knowledge and respective practices gain social relevance and cultural significance within a certain social context, the more we can assume an 'epidemic' spread of ever more scientific practices. As the more recent accounts of contemporary 'knowledge society' have shown, the 'scientization' of society (Weingart 2001; Dori et al. 2003) is usually accompanied by the 'generalization' of explorative reflection in many areas of social life, the 'institutionalization of reflexive mechanisms' that foster pro-active, future-oriented learning, and the expansion of new rationalized structures for monitoring auditing, control and certification.

We have also learnt from the previous discussion that one of the major assets of macro-phenomenological approaches to contemporary society is the way it conceives of world-cultural diffusion as a project of rationalization that mobilizes social entities around highly generalized, scientifically-sanctified principles of progress and future development without presuming these principles to be efficient, functional and eternally valid. Indeed, in analogy to religious societies, macro-phenomenological sociology conceptualizes these rational principles as transcendent myths around which the strongly scientized and widely de-mystified 'modern society' is centred (Krücken 2005). In contrast to religious myths, however, we should not conceive of these 'sacred' myths of modernity as god-given eternal truths that make social entities reifying the sacred traditions once and for all, but as discursively constructed and in principle modifiable 'paradigms' (Kuhn 1962) of development. This was not pointed out enough by the proponents of the world-polity perspective, and requires particular attention in empirical macro-phenomenological accounts of world-cultural diffusion. In addition to this, apart from the *cultural-cognitive* logic of institutional diffusion, macro-phenomenological analyses must also take the *regulative* and *normative* dimensions into consideration more systematically and more seriously than has thus far been the case in world-polity research. This gives us the opportunity to explore both processes of cultural construction *and* institutionalization, the discursive construction of world-cultural models *and* their transformation into standard practices, institutional routines, organizing principles, or even clearly legally codified prescriptions.

Against this backdrop, it is the major aim of the following macro-phenomenological study of region-building and regional mobilization in contemporary Europe to explore and elaborate the cultural conditions that contribute to the construction of regions as pro-active and forward-looking 'world-cultural actors' (cf. Meyer and Jepperson 2000). It focuses on the emergence of the new notions and images of regions as generic spatial units and active agents of change, which has fundamentally changed former conceptions of governing social and spatial development. Such a research perspective is geographically confined and context-specific (Chapters 4 and 5 of this book will focus on the territory of the European Union, while Chapters 6, 7 and 8 will focus on contemporary Poland). It does not claim that this process marks a global and world-wide phenomenon. However, the conditions under which this process is taking place are principally 'global' (and not just 'local' or 'regional'). In this way, the empirical case studies of region-building and regional mobilization in Poland under world-cultural conditions (as outlined in Chapters 6, 7 and 8) reflect global (world-cultural) tendencies under particular historical, political and social conditions.

4 A phenomenology of the rise of a 'new regionalism'

Introduction

It has been pointed out in the previous chapter that the most fundamental condition for extensive and rapid diffusion of world-cultural models and principles is the prevalence of theoretical knowledge which creates cultural linkages amongst distinct and disconnected social entities (Strang and Meyer 1993). The sciences constantly analyse social reality and produce interpretations and social imaginaries on the nature and coherence of social life. Some of these scientific interpretations gain broader political and cultural significance. They are taken up by influential political actors, and often they are even institutionalized as standard knowledge in official political programmes. Hence, a macro-phenomenological institutional analysis which aims at reconstructing the increasing cultural significance of regions and regional tiers of government in contemporary times must start with a reconstruction of the scientific discourse and the broader theoretical models which fundamentally shape spatial perceptions and conceptions on the role of regions in human development. This requires more than simply exploring the interests and ideas of powerful actors which promote certain 'political ideas' or 'policy paradigms' (cf. Blyth 2002); it also involves the reconstruction of larger conceptual shifts in intellectual discourses beyond and across concrete interest constellations. For, as has been shown above, prevailing interpretations and conceptions of reality in everyday life are largely mediated through scientific discourse – particularly in contemporary times (Foucault 1965; Stehr 1994; Drori *et al.* 2003).

Accordingly, the first part of this chapter is concerned with an exploration of conceptions of 'space' and 'place' in contemporary scientific research and the major shifts in scientific discourse which have contributed to a new awareness of sub-national territories. However, as already pointed out, this scientific discourse is not detached from everyday social life and political structures. Indeed, for a theoretical model to be socially significant it must be established within authoritative interpretations and schemata and also requires the support of powerful social forces: 'In some way, models must make the transition from theoretical formulation to social movement to institutional imperative.' (Strang and Meyer 1993: 495). Hence, apart from the exploration of abstract scientific interpretations, taken-for-granted models and principles, formal and informal rules as well as processes of routinization, a macro-phenomenological institutional analysis must also be sensitive to processes of 'authoritative institutionalization', especially if it is dealing with highly politicized issues such as the determination of future paths of social development. Therefore, this chapter also deals with the question of how sub-national regions became politically relevant in the European context and what kind of 'authoritative forces' led to this larger developmental shift at local and regional levels.[1]

It is argued in the following sections that the innumerable and multi-faceted research endeavours that have extensively explored the geographical conditions and the spatial consequences of post-industrialization – above all since the end of the 1970s and beginning of the 1980s – have profoundly changed the common understanding of regional development. Regions were no longer considered to be the mere backdrops or passive contexts for economic production and business activities. Instead, they were increasingly considered as the 'generic' loci of economic value-creation; as 'key sources of development' (Storper 1995) in post-industrial times and as the 'motors' (Scott 1996) of vivid economic production. Over the past three decades the scientific preoccupation with regions and regional questions of development has increased massively, and this has contributed to the emergence of an enormous stock of knowledge on the regional conditions of development and causes and effects as well as pitfalls and opportunities. Some assumptions have become widely accepted and taken for granted, some have even acquired the status of quasi-universal knowledge in terms of contemporary regional development and have been institutionalized in mainstream political programmes (1). In fact, regional development policy and mobilization of development forces at the regional level have witnessed growing importance and significance in political practice over recent decades, especially in the European context. By the end of the 1980s, the European Union (EU) established a new framework of structural policy with a strong regional scope of activity. This brought new significance to the spatial – and especially the regional – dimension of government in Europe and gave impetus to a strong drive for regional mobilization (2). This increase in the status of regions both in scientific discourse and political practice has been accompanied by a huge extension of the aims, objectives and aspirations of regional development. Sub-national territorial units and regions are increasingly becoming the central places of large-scale development interventions in today's Europe. Regional development is widely considered as the solution to many of the pressing problems of our times. This marks a fundamental shift in common governmental practices in contemporary Europe which have been shaped by the massive diffusion of world-cultural principles and practices to the regional and local levels (3 and 4).

1 A new awareness of 'space' in the social sciences

The observation of intensifying globalization which has flourished in the social sciences since 1970s – and with increasing intensity since the 1990s – constitutes a fundamental shift in the socio-scientific discourse of recent decades. Indeed, it is widely acknowledged these days that both processes of globalization and localization are leading to an increasing fragmentation of nation-state authority and national social integration. This has brought about a new awareness for the spatial dimensions of social life, and in particular the multi-scalar dimensions of the social interactions within the sphere of political authority (cf. Boyer and Hollingsworth 1997; Brenner *et al.* 2003; Taylor 2004). Analysts of changes in contemporary state authority have identified certain policy areas where requirements of political problem-solving widely transcend territorial borders of nation-states (Held *et al.* 1999; Shaw 2003; Rieger and Leibfried 2003; Zürn and Leibfried 2005; Heintz *et al.* 2005). Moreover, there has been a vivid debate on the huge transformative impact of globalization on established modes of social integration and on the political sovereignty of nation-states. Some observers have detected the emergence of new multi-ethnic and multicultural assemblages of society due to increasing trans-border exchanges and movements of people (Hannerz 1992, 1996; Appadurai 1997; Beck 2000; Mau *et al.* 2008; Favell 2008; Mau 2010). Others have pointed to the huge impact of the worldwide expansion of mass communication and the global presence of mass media as a catalyst for changes within nation-state societies and local social contexts (Urry 1995, 2003, 2007; Lechner and Boli 2005; Larsen *et al.* 2006; Cohen and Kennedy 2007). Thus, theorists and analysts from various schools and disciplinary backgrounds of social sciences have shifted their attention to changes in various realms of society by exploring the dimensions and driving forces of current 'global transformations' (Held *et al.* 1999). Decreasing national containment and multiple dispersal of national sovereignty and territorial authority are widely seen hallmarks of our time.

Most of the analyses and interpretations of the transformation of contemporary modernity are based on materialist politico-economic accounts of social change and start with the assumption of a fundamental shift in the economic reproduction of social and political life in most advanced industrial societies between the 1970s and the 1980s (Wallerstein 1974, 1980, 1989; Knox and Agnew 1989; Giddens 1990; Sklair 1991; Featherstone and Lash 1995; Thurow 1996; Held *et al.* 1999; Hirst and Thompson 1999; Stiglitz 2003). It is widely acknowledged that the prevailing mode of Fordist industrial mass-production came to an abrupt end with the rise of 'post-industrial society' (Bell 1973) during the 1970s. Social-scientific analysts widely agree that the breakthrough of post-industrialism marks a new surge of economic liberalization and political deregulation, bringing about a new international division of labour, new rules for the economic game, and, above all, a new level of economic competition on a global scale (cf. Piore and Sabel 1984; Lash and Urry 1987; Amin 1994; Porter 1998b). While the previous Fordist mode of production was mainly based on integrated mass production and Keynesian interventionist economic policy within nation-state structures, economic activities are now increasingly uncoupled from national markets and former territorial restrictions. Globally active companies are able to relocate their production to those places which seem most favourable and profitable to them – and they are also able to leave these places much faster and with greater ease when favourable circumstances change (cf. Bartlett and Goshall 1989, 1999; Dicken 2003). The international trade and exchange of commodities, and above all the trade of semi-finished goods, has risen tremendously as large-scale linear chains of production have increasingly been broken down and re-allocated in different places around the world. Moreover, post-industrial value creation no longer solely depends on 'real' production in 'concrete' places. It is increasingly shaped by intangible and placeless assets such as trade in financial products on capital markets, revenues from franchises, patent protection or brand-selling in global (often virtual) 'spaces of flows' (cf. Lash and Urry 1994; Knorr-Cetina and Preda 2004; Sud de Surie 2008).

Divergent interpretations: decreasing or increasing importance of fixed space?

These observations of new virtual social spaces have provoked some theorists of the new global era to predict a growing devaluation and disappearance of 'fixed' physical space; of distinct local or regional places and the emergence of spatially de-coupled and de-territorialized 'network society' (Castells). They claim that the more symbols, signs, commodities, information and even people transcend certain places at an ever faster rate, the more 'global spaces of flows' will substitute and transform the existing 'spaces of place' (cf. Bauman 2000; Castells 2002; Urry 2003, 2007). Yet, at the same time, in marked opposition to this assumption other observers contend that the significance of local and regional places has become even more visible and important in the new global era. In fact, a whole range of researchers have asserted a new upsurge of local and regional identities and even a new trend of 're-territorialization' of both the economy and society in the face of decreasing nation-state integrity (cf. Porter 1990; Krugman 1991; Taylor 1993; Hall and Soskice 2001; Brenner *et al.* 2003). It has been observed that globalization not only leads to institution-building on the supranational level and the unhinging of social space from (national) territorial boundaries, but also to the emergence of new territory-based regulatory structures and an increase in the status of the sub-national level (cf. Storper and Scott 1992; Amin and Thrift 1994; Ohmae 1995; Scott 1998; Storper and Salais 1997; Porter 2003; Cox 1997; Smith 2003; Lipietz 2003; Taylor 2003).[2]

Hence, there is no essential contradiction or opposition between globalization, the process of an increasing 'time-space compression' (Robertson 1995), on the one hand, and the revaluation of local and regional space on the other. It seems that increasing globalization constitutes the condition for the intensified perception of new spatial variations within, beyond and independent of segmented nation-state differentiation (Luhmann 1997; Stichweh 2000). Indeed, analysts of the newly emerging post-industrial geographies have observed a diffusion of spatial units within the political domain and the emergence of new spaces, geographies and new spatial delineations within and beyond nation-state territories (Soja 1989; Harvey 1989; Massey *et al.* 1999). Accordingly, in marked opposition to simplistic one-dimensional accounts of globalization (cf. Ritzer 1997) the notions of 'glocalization' (cf. Robertson 1995; Swyngedouw 1997) and 'multi-level governance' have gained huge prominence (cf. Marks *et al.* 1996; Boyer and Hollingsworth 1997).

Thus, alongside the academic discussion on post-Fordism and globalization, academics have (re-)discovered the region as a major object of research. By the end of the 1970s and the beginning of the 1980s a new wave of research on the role of regions in the new post-industrial era had broken its way into the social sciences. Geographers, economists and other social scientists have increasingly started to explore the spatial, geographical, and especially the local and regional features of post-industrial change. This new regional research marks a paradigmatic shift in prevailing perceptions of sub-national space largely transcending the realms of geography and economics while radiating into other social scientific disciplines and everyday life.[3]

The discovery of 'local institutions' by the new regional research

The first generation of new regional research was mainly concerned with exploring the challenges posed by the transition from integrated mass production to more mobile and flexible forms of economic production in existing business locations (cf. Bagnasco 1977; Piore and Sabel 1984; Storper and Walker 1984; Hall and Markusen 1985). Yet, in contrast to prevailing neo-classical economic theorists who predicted a universal trend of de-industrialization and economic restructuring on a global scale, these new regional researchers asserted that there was no single model of post-industrial change – but rather a huge number of individual responses due to the plethora of unique regional histories and contexts. The economic revival of some traditional industrial agglomerations and the rise of 'new industrial districts', larger industrial agglomerations, and so called 'world cities' has inspired a whole range of researchers to explore and outline the particular features of these multi-faceted 'regional worlds of production' (cf. Scott 1988; Goodman and Bamford 1989; Zeitlin 1990; Sassen 1991; Storper and Scott 1992; Saxenian 1994).

In fact, new regional researchers have observed a huge geographical divergence in coping with post-industrial change. One dominant interpretation put forward by economic geographers to account for the growing importance of agglomeration in the post-industrial era was the rationale of *transaction costs* (Scott and Storper 1987; Porter 2003). It contends that geographic proximity, intensified exchange and cooperation, and access to privileged channels of information were decisive factors of production especially in times of rapid technological change and accelerating competition. Consequently, businesses from different sectors would tend to cluster together in order to minimize transaction costs by concentrating complementary functions and tasks at certain places and establishing stable inter-firm relations. Moreover, in addition to cost-efficiency arguments, economic geographers and regional researchers from other disciplines also stressed the importance and intrinsic value of so called *untraded interdependencies* (Storper 1995), which businesses have established at certain places over time. These are non-commodifiable factors of production, such as particular social relations, locally entrenched forms of exchange and cooperation, local attitudes and conventions, local institutional arrangements or peculiar local milieus, which are unique to certain places and neither easy to reproduce nor easy to transfer from one place to another (cf. Maillat 1995; Amin and Thrift 1995; Storper and Salais, 1997; Keating *et al.* 2003).

Indeed, this new awareness of local and regional peculiarities and 'intangible' social conditions has decidedly changed current reflections on economic value-creation and business development.[4] The view that business activities and (global) economic flows are always 'embedded' in particular spatially entrenched (local, regional, national) contexts has received wide recognition in recent years. Thus, despite the trend towards reductionist neo-classical models of universal change in economics and business studies, economic geography has become more sensitive to social, cultural and geographical variation than ever before (cf. North 1990; Krugman 1991; Porter 1990, 1998b; Boyer and Hollingsworth 1998).

The discovery of institutional learning and flexible adaptation in the social sciences

The new academic interest in regions, regional social practices and regional institutions has also widely transcended the narrow disciplinary focus on business activities and enterprise strategies. Increasingly, researchers have started to address questions of regional innovation and socio-economic development from a broader sociological, political and politico-economic perspective. These days it is widely acknowledged in regional research and beyond that (regional) innovativeness and overall socio-economic well-being is decisively determined by certain relational, institutional or cultural factors. In particular, 'flexible adaptation' and 'regional learning' entrenched in unique local systems of production were identified as the major sources of successful economic value-creation and social well-being (Piore and Sabel 1984; Amin 1999; Cooke *et al.* 2004).

Consequently, throughout the 1990s the 'innovativeness of regions' and capacities of 'institutional learning' became major subjects of regional research. After economists and economic geographers started to explore the broader socio-spatial underpinnings of economic regeneration and innovation at the beginning of the 1990s (cf. Lundvall 1992; Edquist 1997), a whole range of regional geographers, economists and social scientists from other disciplines studied the innovative potential of local and regional networks of production. Many researchers have deduced theoretical assumptions on the relationship between regional institutional structures and innovativeness from empirical case studies of some extraordinarily successful regions such as Silicon Valley in Northern California, and some urban areas in Southern Germany, Northern Italy and France (Scott 1993; Maillat 1995; Cooke *et al.* 2004). Other researchers, in turn, have focused on the peculiarities of regions that have suffered particularly badly from post-industrialization, such as old-industrial areas and less urbanized rural regions (Grabher 1993).

This new branch of innovation research has rejected former atomistic and linear notions of innovation and emphasized the broader systemic character and the role of particular social or institutional environments which support creativity, openness and constant organizational change and learning. The future potential of regions, it is claimed, depends largely on endogenous capacities for constant learning and creativity which derive from interactions between actors from different areas of society, such as the sciences, politics and business (cf. Camagni 1991; Ashheim 1997; Cooke and Morgan 1998; Lawson and Lorenz 1999; Scott and Storper 2003; Porter 2003; Keating *et al.* 2004; Cooke *et al.* 2004).[5] In this context, the notions of 'trust' and 'social capital' have gained huge prominence in contemporary academic debates on regional development. In fact, open-minded and inclusive attitudes based on generalized forms of trust and interactions rather than bonding types of social capital are widely seen as decisive elements of favourable socio-economic development (Gambetta 1988; Putnam 1993; Trigilia 2001).

The growing political promotion of regional mobilization in Western Europe

Alongside the growing preoccupation with regional features of production, regional conditions of innovativeness and regional economic regeneration, regional researchers have also extensively surveyed the political dimensions of regional development in the past two decades. Policy researchers have observed a trend towards growing administrative decentralization and a relocation of structural and regional policies from the central state to sub-national levels, especially in Western European countries (cf. Bennett 1990; Keating and Loughlin 1996; Deacon 1998). Therefore, the rise of a 'new regionalism' in scientific debates and surrounding areas since the 1980s has been accompanied by an increase in the status of regions and a new wave of regionalization in political practice, especially in Europe (cf. Keating 2003). Over the past two decades the creation of 'functional' intermediate administrative structures, the implementation of 'effective' structures of regional governance and the promotion of 'vital' regional development have become political priorities in more and more European countries. Today, regions are widely considered as important political actors in multi-level systems of modern government and an 'appropriate' spatial unit of both effective and democratic governance. After a cooling down period of regionalization at the end of the 1960s and the beginning of the 1970s, old territorial and cultural identities have been revived, and in some countries new identities have even been created (Paasi 1986; Le Galès and Lequesne 1998; Keating 1998a; Keating 2003). In addition, researchers have observed the emergence of new political actors, new corporatist arrangements and new forms of policy experimentation at local and regional levels (Voelzkow 1997; Martin 2000; Benz and Fürst 2002; Crouch *et al.* 2004; Morgan 2004; Bruszt 2005).

This increased importance of regions in political practice, the drive towards regional mobilization and the greater self-determination of regions in Western countries has by far not just been a matter of domestic politics and bottom-up mobilization, as is often alleged in discourses on regionalization. It is also closely linked to the increasing attention given to regions and sub-national processes of development in international politics. In fact, the idea of local and regional self-determination and mobilization of political actors and resources on local and regional levels has been promoted vigorously by various inter- and supranational political agents. In Europe, the European Union – above all – has established a comprehensive policy approach to regional mobilization over the past two decades. It has institutionalized a whole range of standards, principles, procedures and practices of regional mobilization and development on local and regional levels, and this has significantly changed both the political and material landscape of European territory (Barry 1993; Leonardi 1993, 1995; Hooghe and Keating 1994; Hooghe 1996). This will be depicted in more detail in the following.

2 The growing relevance of sub-national government in international politics

By the end of the 1980s and the beginning of the 1990s a number of international organizations and international development agents started to launch distinct local and regional development programmes. On the global level, some U.N. agencies, such as above all the UNDP, or loan-giving institutions, such as the World Bank, now actively support administrative devolution and political self-determination at local and regional levels. In the European context regional mobilization or local and regional reforms have been encouraged, in particular, by the Council of Europe (CoE) and the European Union since the beginning of the 1990s. Furthermore, the OECD has also become a vigorous promoter of regional development approaches and regional policy reforms, especially during the past decade.

Undoubtedly, the motifs and policy priorities of promoting regional reforms differ significantly amongst these different organizations, depending on their respective policy agendas.[6] However, what all these international organizations have in common is their role as transnational diffusers of policy knowledge. They contribute to the establishment of transnational 'organizational fields' (DiMaggio and Powell 1983) of world-cultural diffusion, in which knowledge, experts, practices and even financial resources on regional mobilization permeate rapidly and massively across national borders. By outlining common standards for regional reform, institutionalizing transnational channels of exchange or publishing reports, rankings and huge amounts of statistical material on regional development, they create transnational linkages and new discursive fields in which states and – with ever more frequency – regions and other sub-state units can locate themselves and compare their own situation in relation to other similar political units. This facilitates the mutual perception of similarities and differences amongst similar social entities from formerly rather un-connected social environments, which is one of the most important conditions for the rapid and massive transnational diffusion of world-cultural models.[7]

By far the most comprehensive and most influential policy agenda of regional mobilization was developed and established by the European Union about two decades ago. In fact, by the end of the 1980s, the EU had developed a distinct approach to regional development with co-ordinated EU-wide aims and objectives. The territorial and, in particular, the regional scope of policy-making was always highlighted as an important element of the common European project since the beginning of the process of European integration.[8] However, for decades there was no distinct European approach to regional mobilization and regional development policy. Some European funds supporting structural policies in problem areas – the so called 'Structural Funds' – were introduced during the first decades of the existence of the European Economic Community: at first, the 'European Social Fund' (ESF) which was established in 1958. In 1962 the 'European Agriculture Guidance and Guarantee Fund' (EAGGF) followed. And, in 1975, after the accession of Ireland, Great Britain and Denmark, the 'European Regional Development Fund' (ERDF) was set up. The Structural Funds were initially introduced to compensate individual member states for the collective costs of economic integration, reimbursing certain member states for the additional costs of structural interventions on an annual basis. However, all these funds were quite limited both in terms of budget and scope, and there was no explicit regional policy component attached to this.

In the 1970s, furthermore, the European Commission introduced a European database of regional statistics with a uniform European classification of territorial units, the so called 'Nomenclature of Statistical Units' (NUTS), in order to provide uniform regional statistics on the territory of the European Union.[9] But in general, all these measures did not much contribute to an increasing significance of the regions in European policy-making, not to mention a distinct European regional policy approach. This changed significantly, however, with the creation of the common European market in mid-1980s, which was blueprinted by the Single European Act in 1986 and finally introduced with the enforcement of the Treaty of Maastricht in January 1993. With the establishment of a common European regional policy agenda under the umbrella of 'Cohesion Policy', the use of the Structural Funds was made conditional to common European policy aims and objectives including incentives for increasing regional mobilization and self-organization.

The institutionalization of a multi-level system of regional mobilization in Europe

The efforts to establish a common European Single Market led to a strong reinforcement of the territorial or geographical levels of European government (cf. Barry 1993; Hooghe 1996; Marks *et al.* 1996). In the Single European Act of 1986 the goal of reducing imbalances between the most advanced regions and those areas which are 'most lagging behind' (measured in terms of GDP per capita), was put forward as a fundamental condition for the functioning of the European Common Market. Consequently, the goal of promoting 'economic and social cohesion' amongst different sub-national areas of the European Union became legally binding for the first time, and the regional level has become the focal point for the perception and management of territorial disparities in contemporary EU policy-making (cf. Rumford 2002; Molle 2007; Mau and Büttner 2008).

This also laid the ground for a new system of regionally-targeted structural policies at the European level. In the course of a larger reform of the financial budget of the European Community in 1988, which introduced new budgetary priorities and the principle of multi-annual financial perspectives, the existing European Structural funds – the ERDF, the ESF, the EAGGF and the so-called 'Fisheries Guidance Instrument' (FGI) – were integrated under the umbrella of the Cohesion Policy. This was accompanied by a substantial increase in financial resources and the introduction of a new multi-level system of regional development planning. Based on the experience of some former experimental attempts at local and regional mobilization in Southern Europe during the 1980s, the 1988 reform of structural policies also brought about a range of new standards and practices in policy-making: firstly, the *multi-annual programming* of policy interventions; secondly, the *concentration* of European funds on a limited number of objectives with a particular focus on the least developed regions; thirdly, the principle of *additionality* of European funding to ensure that national expenditures on structural policy are not merely substituted by European grants; and, fourthly, the principle of *partnership* to ensure cooperation amongst different (national, sub-national and European) policy-makers who are involved in the programming and implementation of European structural policies and, in particular, the inclusion of social partners and non-governmental organizations in the policy process.

These are some of the fundamental organizing principles and standard procedures of the EU Cohesion Policy, which were introduced in 1988 and are still in place today; though, some institutional procedures and policy instruments have changed over the past two decades. The policy process is organized in terms of multi-annual programming periods which are synchronized with the overall EU 'financial perspective' – the major multi-annual budgetary plan of the European Union. In each transition from one programming period to another the programmes, initiatives and institutional procedures have been slightly changed and adapted according to new policy conditions and challenges. Yet the overall structure, the scope and major principles of the Cohesion Policy have more or less remained the same.[10]

What has changed significantly over the past decades, nonetheless, is the total allocation of funds for the EU Cohesion Policy. In fact, the Cohesion Policy witnessed a significant increase in budget since its official introduction in 1989 – not least due to the tremendous territorial increase of the European Union and the inclusion of ever more member states in recent times.[11] Thus, between 1989 and 2007 the number of EU member states increased from 12 to 27, and the total allocation per programming period has increased almost six-fold (see Table 4.1). Between 1989 and 2007 more than EUR400 billion were spent on measures funded by Structural and Cohesion funds, supporting numerous development projects in municipalities and regions all over the EU. In the current fourth programming period from 2007 to 2013 another EUR347 billion have been allocated for the Cohesion Policy, of which more than 80 per cent goes to least developed territories (GDP per capita less than 75 per cent of the EU average).

Against this backdrop we can therefore see that unlike other international agents which mainly promote smaller projects of regionalization with small amounts of funds, the European Union has established a large-scale and comprehensive approach to regional development supported by substantial amounts of financial resources. In fact, the support for regional development policies in contemporary Europe is exceptional. The European Union is by far the biggest supporter of regional reforms. The expenditures for the Cohesion Policy since the beginning of the 1990s have already exceeded the grants and loans provided by the famous 'Marshall plan' – which supported the reconstruction of industries and infrastructures in post-war Western Europe – several times over.[12]

The regional level as a focal point of social government in contemporary Europe

The introduction of the EU Cohesion Policy in the late 1980s entailed a tremendous increase in the significance of sub-national levels of government in contemporary European politics. In 1993 the Treaty of Maastricht officially introduced and anchored the principle of *subsidiarity* into EU policy-making. This step not only met the interests and expectations of national governments, but also clearly marks an increase in the significance of sub-national levels of governance and the multi-level structure of European policy-making (Hooghe 1996; Marks *et al.* 1996). Furthermore, the 'Committee of the Regions' was established by the Maastricht Treaty, the first official representation of regions at the European level giving sub-national regions an independent voice in European policy debates.[13] In addition, the regional level was also given stronger attention and significance in policy assessments, socio-economic reporting, and political strategies. Hence, in 1996 the European Commission launched the first 'Report on Economic and Social Cohesion', which assessed the socio-economic disparities amongst member states and regions of the European Union as well as the impact of Structural Funds in the municipalities and regions that benefited

Table 4.1 Financial allocation for EU Cohesion Policy 1989–2013 by programming period

	1989–93	1994–1	2000–6	2007–13
Number of member states	12	12 + 3 (1995)[+]	15 + 10 (2004)[+]	27
Total EU population in millions (approx.)	342 (1990)	364 (1995)	455 (2005)	500 (2009)
Total spending in billions	ECU69[a,b]	ECU168[a,b] (of which ECU15 from Cohesion Fund)	EUR34.7[b] (of which EUR213 for EU-15 and EUR21,7 for 10 NMS in 2004–6)	EUR347[c,d] (of which EUR69,7 from Cohesion Fund)
Share of total EU budget (%)	25	approx. 30	approx. 30	35
Share of total GDP of EU (%)	0.3	0.4	0.4	0.4
Total spending for the 'least developed' territories (GDP/cap. < 75%/EU av.)	ECU43.8[a,b] (64% of total budget) (25% of EU pop.)	ECU91.7[a,b] (68% of total budget) (25% of EU pop.)	EUR173.6[b] (71.6% of total bud.) (37% of EU pop.)	EUR282.8[c,d,e] (8.5% of total bud.) (35% of EU pop.)

Sources: Eurostat and CEC (2008b).

Notes

+ accession of new member states in the programming period.

a ECU (European Currency Unit) was the arithmetic predecessor of the Euro. It was transferred 1:1 into Euro in 1999.

b at former prices.

c at current prices (as of July 2008).

d estimated total spending as allocated in 2006, real allocation can change until 2013.

e another amount of approx. EUR70 billion is allocated for rural development under the Common Agricultural Policy (CAP).

from them (CEC 1996). This has since been repeated every few years (CEC 2001a, 2004, 2007d, 2010) and complemented by the publication of annual progress reports and other periodic reports.

In 2003 the EU classification of statistical units, the so called NUTS classification, was given legal status, and it was officially introduced as the standard classification of data collection in the statistical offices of all EU member states. This has increased the availability of European regional statistics and the comparability of regional statistics across EU countries. Furthermore, the European Council officially adopted a comprehensive and long-term spatial development plan for the territory of the European Union in May 1999, the 'European Spatial Development Perspective' (ESDP). Though this document has remained non-binding in legal terms, it sketched for the first time a common European vision of spatial development planning. It indicates all envisaged projects of territorial integration, such as cross-border infrastructure projects, and provides an integrated policy framework for all sectoral policies with a territorial focus on all territorial levels (cf. CEC 1999). The creation of the ESDP also led to the establishment a new pan-European programme of spatial analysis and planning, the so-called 'European Spatial Planning Observation Network' (ESPON). Since its introduction in 2004, this programme, which is mainly funded by the European Regional Development Fund, has produced a huge amount of new data, images and spatial representations on the development of territory in Europe, and in particular the regional dimension of development.[14]

In all these different ways and in all these various dimensions the establishment of the Cohesion Policy has fostered an increase in the status of the regional level in European policy-making. Thus, regional policy has become a vital and important element of contemporary policy-making in the EU over the past two decades. Moreover, it has even become a role model for administrative reform and regional development policy in other areas and regions of the world as well.[15] However, the huge popularity and increasing significance of the Cohesion Policy cannot be explained by its extraordinary effectiveness or successful goal-attainment. In fact, in the past two decades the EU Cohesion Policy has not contributed much to achieving the major goal for which it was initially introduced, namely: reducing economic and social disparities amongst the regions. It is widely acknowledged – even by the Commission itself – that the Cohesion Policy is far from achieving its official objective of generating stronger 'cohesion' amongst European states and regions and reducing inequalities between the least and the most developed areas of the European Union (cf. Sapir *et al.* 2004; Rodríguez-Pose and Fratesi 2004; CEC 2007d). And some authors even claim that the Cohesion Policy would actually reinforce the processes it officially aims to tackle (cf. Amin and Tomaney 1995; Rumford 2000: 2f. and 6ff.).[16]

In a small assessment of the impact of the EU Cohesion Policy in the 'least developed' EU regions Leonardi (2005) comes to relatively positive conclusions. According to his assessment 15 out of 59 of the 'least developed' regions in 1988 had moved above the threshold of 75 per cent of the EU average in GDP per capita. However, this also means that the remaining three quarters have more or less remained where they were before. Other assessments have shown that 45 per cent of the least developed regions (with less than 60 per cent of EU average GDP) of the former EU-15 moved up in their level of GDP per capita between 1995 and 2005, whereas 55 per cent remained at the same level (CEC 2008b: back page). Thus, in sum, one can conclude that the significance of the EU Cohesion Policy has not increased due to its mere efficacy and effect, but because it transfers substantial amounts of financial assistance to sub-national regions and municipalities. It constitutes, in this sense, one of the few redistributive measures of European politics (Delhey 2004; Mau and Büttner 2008). Moreover, the Cohesion Policy also exhibits the important governmental function of inducing policy changes within its member states and bringing the aims and objectives of European integration to municipalities and regions all across Europe (cf. Rumford 2000; Mairate 2006; Varró 2008). Due to its elaborate system of planning and funding and the strong conditionality which is built into the funding system, the European Union – or more precisely the European Commission – is able to wield far-reaching influence on the domestic policies of the member states (Hughes *et al.* 2004; Brusis 2005). As a result, the importance of the regional dimension of policy-making increased substantially with the 'Eastern Enlargements' of the European Union in 2004 and 2007. In fact, the standards and regulations of the EU Cohesion Policy constituted the central means for preparing the so-called CEE candidate countries for EU accession. By way of targeted pre-accession programmes and cross-border projects funded under the Cohesion Policy's objective of 'European Territorial Cooperation', the aims, objectives, rules and procedures of the Cohesion Policy are even transferred beyond the borders of the current EU member states (cf. CEC 2007b and 2008d).

Moreover, with the transition to the current programming period 2007 to 2013, the EU Cohesion Policy witnessed another significant increase in its status, since it has been linked more closely with the renewed Lisbon Strategy for Jobs and Growth, the common development vision of the European Union (cf. CEC 2005a). In the current programming period the EU Cohesion Policy is even considered as one of the central means for implementing Lisbon goals and priorities in municipalities and regions all over Europe. Accordingly, all regions receive some sort of EU funding from Structural and Cohesion Funds in the current programming period, and the national and regional authorities are obliged to allocate certain proportions of the Cohesion Policy measures in accordance with the priorities of the renewed Lisbon strategy.[17] Table 4.2 outlines the basic organizational structure and major objectives of the EU Cohesion Policy in the current programming period as well as the other major structural policies of the European Union. It should give an impression of the plurality of different EU structural policies and an overview of the major areas of activity and priorities and how they relate to regional policies in the broader sense. One of the most important changes the new programming period has brought about is the stricter separation of the Cohesion Policy funding on the one hand, and the 'Common Agricultural Policy' (CAP) funding on the other. The former 'European Agricultural Guidance and

Table 4.2 Overview of major EU Structural Policies 2007–13

Cohesion Policy

European Regional Development Fund (ERDF) (since 1975)	European Social Fund (ESF) (since 1958)	Cohesion Fund (CF) (established in 1993 as an independent fund providing assistance to member states; since 2007 same rules and admin. procedures as Structural Funds)

Structural Funds

Objectives 2007–13:

Convergence
(allocation: EUR282.8 billion)

– Least developed territories (NUTS-2) of the European Union
Criterion: regional GDP/capita lower than 75% of the EU-27 average;
– Slowly decreasing funding for regions at the edge of 75% (phasing-out)

Regional Competitiveness and Employment (EUR54.9 billion)

– all other EU regions not eligible for 'convergence' objective or 'phasing-out'

Territorial Cooperation
(former INTERREG-programme)
(EUR8.7 billion)

– cross-border cooperation of all border regions (NUTS-3-level)
– trans-national cooperation, all regions eligible
– interregional cooperation, networking and exchange

Common Agricultural Policy (CAP)

European Agricultural Guarantee Fund (EAGF)	European Agricultural Fund for Rural Development (EAFRD)	European Fisheries Fund (EFF)
Direct subsidy payments to farmers/ funding of price support mechanisms (incl. guaranteed minimum prices, import tariffs, and quotas on certain goods from outside the EU)	Funding of rural development activities in addition and parallel to Structural and Cohesion Funds according to new European Strategic Guidelines for Rural Development (2007–2013)	Granting financial support to the European fishing industry (sea and inland fisheries, aquaculture businesses, producer organisations as well as fisheries areas)

EAGF and EAFRD replaced the former EAGGF (from 1962) and Leader + programmes replaced the former FIFG

Financial allocation: about EUR55 billion/per year (=45% of total EU budget), but progressively decreasing until 2013 (80% of total allocation for EAGF and EFF/ 20% for EAFRD – [total allocation for EFF: EUR3.8 billion])

Structural aid for accession candidates

Programmes before 2007:
PHARE: provided assistance to strengthen economy, administrative capacity and social cohesion
ISPA: provided assistance for transport and environment projects along the lines of Cohesion Policy regulations
SAPARD: provided assistance to prepare accession countries for the structures of the CAP
CARDS: development assistance specifically targeted to the countries of former Yugoslavia in the Western Balkans
Pre-accession financial assistance for Turkey

Since 2007:
Instrument for Pre-Accession Assistance (IPA): replaced all former pre-accession programmes and instruments; provides financial aid to *candidate countries* (Croatia, Turkey, and the Former Yugoslav Republic of Macedonia) and *potential candidate countries* (Albania, Bosnia and Herzegovina, Montenegro, Serbia and Kosovo); major components of funding: a) transition assistance and institution-building; b) cross-border cooperation; c) regional development (transport, environment, economic development); d) human resources development (strengthening human capital and combating exclusion); e) rural development – with an annual budget of more than EUR1 billion

European Union Solidarity Fund (EUSF) (since 2002)

Providing special aid for areas affected by certain exceptional circumstances (e.g. big natural disasters) in order to support the reconstruction of infrastructure and local economies, with an annual budget of about EUR 1 billion

Source: Commission of European Communities 2009, own depiction.

Guarantee Fund' (EAGGFF) was replaced by two new funds: the 'European Agricultural Guarantee Fund' (EAGF) and the 'European Agricultural Fund for Rural Development' (EAFRD). This brought about a new and independent funding scheme for the development of rural areas under CAP in additional to Cohesion Policy measures. Moreover, the different programmes and measures for pre-accession assistance were restructured and integrated into one programme, the 'Instrument for Pre-Accession Assistance' (IPA). It is structured in close accordance with the rules, regulations and procedures of the Cohesion Policy and mainly targets the current and potential candidate countries in South Eastern Europe.

3 The twofold extension of regional development agendas

The growing significance of regions in scientific debates and the increase in the importance of the regional level of government in European politics have brought about an enormous extension of the aspirations of regional development and, at the same time, a huge standardization of regional development practices all over Europe. In fact, over the past two or three decades, regional policies have shifted from confined interventions in certain business areas or industrial sectors to more comprehensive and all-encompassing strategies of moderniza-tion. More and more issues and activities have been integrated into regional development programmes and regional policy agendas. Today regional develop-ment is therefore no longer merely an afterthought to large-scale central plan-ning, or a minor issue of extensive industrial policy interventions of a Keynesian kind (cf. Hoover and Fisher 1949; North 1955; Myrdal 1957; Perloff *et al.* 1960; Richardson 1969). It now constitutes a central component of structural policy interventions in European policy-making, and an integral element of common European efforts to govern desirable future development.

Consequently, we can observe a peculiar simultaneous increase and intermin-gling of two contradictory, or even opposing, aspirations of development in con-temporary regional development practice. In fact, with the rise of sub-national regions both as objects and as subjects of development interventions, regional policy agendas and regional development have been refocused more forcefully both in *economic* and *non-economic* terms. Thus, on the one hand regional development policies are – as they have always been – strongly driven by eco-nomic rationales. Issues such as 'economic growth', 'productivity' and 'employ-ment', as well as questions concerning the 'revitalization' of existing regional industries and the 'stimulation' of economic forces are still at the top of regional policy agendas. This tendency has been reinforced significantly since the crises of old-industrial areas and the emergence of post-industrial economies during the 1970s. Today there is an even stronger drive of economic mobilization in regional development, often referred to as 'neo-liberal' strategies of economic revitalization based on renewed neo-classical concepts of economic develop-ment, such as new growth theories, theories of human capital development, and new concepts of regional competitiveness (cf. Freeman 1982; Romer 1990;

Porter 1990, 1998, 2003; Krugman 1991; Feldman 1994; Barro and Sala-i-Martin 1995; Ohmae 1995).

On the other hand, however, the scope of local and regional development aspirations has broadened extensively during the same period of time. In the past decades in particular, more and more 'holistic', 'sustainable' and 'progressive' approaches to local and regional development have begun to flourish in regional policy debates (cf. Pike *et al.* 2006). Thus, in addition to reinforced neo-liberal strategies regional development accounts increasingly cluster around numerous normative notions such as 'justice', 'equality', 'equity', 'democracy', 'unity', 'cohesion', 'solidarity', or 'sustainability' (cf. Amin 1999; Bianchini 2002; Bollman 2004; Miller 2005; Salais and Villeneuve 2005; Morgan 2004; Hadjimichalis and Hudson 2007). The new approaches to regional development often aim at transcending the narrow focus on economic development by encouraging broader multi-dimensional conceptions of wellbeing and quality of life as well as long-term thinking in development strategies. Some approaches are even highly critical of the destructive effects of one-dimensional capitalist development strategies and the social injustices, environmental damage and cultural atrophy it produces – thus espousing strong interventionist and regulative measures. These tendencies in the contemporary discourse of regional development were appositely summarized as following:

> Building upon the pioneering experimentalism of the 1980s and stimulated by growing concerns about the character, quality and sustainability of local and regional 'development', the often dominant economic focus has broadened in recent years in an attempt to address social, ecological, political and cultural concerns. (…). Unequal experiences of living standards and wellbeing between places even at equal or comparable income levels has fuelled dissatisfaction with conventional economic indicators of 'development' (…). Reducing social inequality, promoting environmental sustainability, encouraging inclusive government and governance and recognizing cultural diversity have been emphasized to varying degrees within broadened definitions of local and regional development (…). Often uncertain moves toward notions of quality of life, social cohesion and wellbeing are being integrated or balanced, sometimes uneasily, with continued concerns about economic competitiveness and growth.
>
> (Pike *et al.* 2007: 1254f.)

If we look at the various priorities and objectives of the contemporary EU Cohesion Policy, we can directly grasp this extension in the aspirations of regional development policies. In the new programming period 2007 to 2013, for example, we can see *classical structural policies* such as investment in local, regional and trans-regional transport infrastructure (motorways, airports, high-speed rail links) as well as infrastructure development in deprived areas; *new activating employment policies* such as the development of 'human capital', the promotion of entrepreneurship, and new knowledge-based businesses; not to mention measures *enhancing environmental protection, energy efficiency* and *sustainable development*, as well as *intra-* and *interregional cooperation* and *cohesion* (CEC 2005; CEC 2007a; 2008a). Regional development policy is not just presented as a means of overcoming the economic and social disparities between 'the wealthiest' and 'least developed' sub-national territories in Europe, but as a response to pressing contemporary challenges such as '(...) globalization, climate change, population ageing, external immigration and the need for sustainable energy supply.' (CEC 2008a: 1). The Cohesion Policy is also expected to contribute strongly to the overall EU agenda of promoting economic growth and job creation. And, beyond that, it is presented as a means of supporting a wide range of other EU policies, such as state aid, transport, the promotion of innovation and the information society, and 'improving' and 'modernizing' public administrations to enhance 'transparency' and 'good governance' (ibid.).[18]

This multiple extension to aspirations of regional development in contemporary Europe seems to reflect a larger and more general shift of governmental rationalities in advanced modern societies which has been widely interpreted as a reinforcement of the liberal practices of state government (cf.; Foucault 1989; Gordon 1991; Painter 2002; Jessop 2007; Drori 2006; Rose and Miller 2008; Münch 2010). However, from the macro-phenomenological research perspective which is outlined in this study it is important to note that this shift is not only the outcome of 'raw' material interests or shifts in contemporary regimes of capitalist accumulation, as is usually suggested by materialist or econo-centric accounts of regional development.[19] Thus, from a macro-phenomenological perspective the current extension of development aspirations in Europe does not necessarily represent the result of 'strategic discursive moves' on the part of the European Union, the Commission or other strategic groups to gain more power or reinforce the hegemonic forces of capitalist accumulation (cf. Lagendijk 2007; Paasi 2009). Rather, it should be seen as the expression of larger changes and transformations of the intellectual discourse of development, as was described above in Chapter 3, and the way this shift becomes manifest in everyday political practice. The discovery of the region as the 'appropriate' spatial unit for development intervention and the activities of international agents, such as the European Union, have contributed to a massive expansion of world culture (rationalized models, principles, practices etc.) at the local and regional levels. This entails the constitution of sub-national regions as world-cultural actors and fosters the ever more far-reaching extension of modernist aspirations and the expansion of highly rationalized organizational structures to govern and manage 'good' or 'favourable' development.[20]

Certainly, as pointed out already, the rise of the 'new regionalism' is strongly motivated by an exploration of new conditions of value creation under post-industrial conditions. Moreover, there is no doubt about the reinforcement of neo-classical economic models of development since the 1980s. This indicates that economic concerns still enjoy a high reputation in contemporary development politics, as always in the history of modernity (cf. Polanyi 2001 [1944];

Fourcade-Gourinchas 2002). But this is just one side of the current development *problematique*. The other side is shaped by increasing moral concerns about the appropriate standards, means and ends of development, the shift towards alternative, multi-dimensional, and post-economic notions of regional development and the rediscovery of regions as objects of projection for new communitarian or environmental sentiments. In fact, there is a strong movement of both common people and professional organizations alike vigorously advocating for the improvement of living conditions on non-economic grounds, the promotion of solidarity, the establishment of equality and justice in all possible dimensions, and the protection of nature, community, traditions and culture. These aspirations are usually backed – just as economic concerns are – by strong scientific support and highly rationalized justifications. They are also supported by other social actors and are brought into the political arena with strong and emphatic argumentation. All these various aspects are part of the current reinforced diffusion of world-cultural models and practices to the local and regional levels. It is highly questionable, indeed, whether all this can be placed under the heading of economic neoliberalism and capitalist hegemony.[21]

Thus, instead of presupposing the constant discursive expansion of capitalism, the crucial question is which conceptions, principles and justifications gain political and practical validity and become part of the mainstream regional development agenda in contemporary Europe. Before we judge political actors it is important to explore what type of concepts find their way into political practice, as well as how they are applied and adopted by important political actors. We must focus on the interplay between science and politics and explore what kind of theoretical models are actually translated in common political practice, i.e. what has actually become mainstream development practice. This is the major concern of a macro-phenomenological exploration of prevailing standards and practices of regional development in contemporary Europe which will be undertaken in the following chapter. It should give us a more detailed picture of the multi-faceted paths of world-cultural diffusion and the extensiveness and complexities of (regional) development governance.

Conclusions: the world-cultural mobilization of regions in contemporary Europe

It has been shown in the previous sections that with the crisis of integrated Fordist production and the increasing break-up of nation-state integration, 'the region' was discovered by economic geographers and other social scientists at the end of the 1970s as a new object of research and a new 'laboratory' for extensive scientific reflection on the conditions of future development. Regions have been subject to countless research projects and scientific debates, and it has become the object of new experiments of development and local revitalizations often initiated and accompanied by sound scientific expertise. This new scientific discourse of regionalism has strongly fostered the *discursive* construction of new regional-level social imaginaries, new notions of regional development and the revaluation of regions in political terms, especially in the European context. The new concepts, vocabularies and quasi-analytical models of regional development produced by scientists have been taken up by other scholars, scientifically-trained practitioners and all kinds of 'hybrids' (Latour 1993) between science and everyday practice, further promoting the ideas of regional development and experimentation. However, a clear distinction between the realm of 'pure' scientific reflection and the sphere of practice is hardly possible, since the link between the scientific production of practical knowledge and political practice is not a one-way street. Sometimes researchers and scientists directly participate in projects of regional experimentation by acting as policy advisors. Often, however, scholars neither leave their ivory towers nor participate in any kind of practical discourse or implementation directly. Nonetheless, their models and reflections can be widely received and taken up by practitioners, political actors and decision makers.[22]

Moreover, since sub-national regions are considered as an important – if not *the* central – units of contemporary development intervention, 'regional development' has witnessed a huge increase in its status in political practice, and especially in policy agendas of influential international agents of development, such as the UN, the OECD or the EU. In fact, these international agencies are a central element of the rapid and massive diffusion of world-cultural models amongst and beyond confined nation-states. They are catalysts of both the massive production and dissemination of scientific 'informational capital' (Bernhard 2009) on development policies, since they were founded as the diligent custodians of the project of Western modernity and as 'keepers of the flame' for future progress and development (cf. Meyer 2001; Hopgood 2006). In this sense, international political agents such as the OECD or the EU are indeed an integral part of the diffusion of world-cultural models, standards and practices of regional development at the interface of scientific discourse and political practice. They *reinforce, specify* and *accelerate* the diffusion of certain world-cultural models of regional development, perpetuating modernist projects of all-encompassing social mobilization all around the EU territory.

In fact, the European Union exhibits an extraordinarily important position, since it not only produces and disseminates abstract world-cultural models of regional development; it has the legislative power and the financial means to institutionalize certain world-cultural principles and practices of regional development as standard principles and procedures for regional policy interventions in Europe. With the establishment of the Cohesion Policy in the late 1980s it has institutionalized a whole range of principles and practices which have become 'social facts' and absolute conditions of development practice. This institutional framework of the EU Cohesion Policy turns abstract and unspecific world-cultural models into concrete organizational principles and standard procedures, and it makes the loose scientific approaches of development coercive, at least to a certain extent. It constitutes a relatively comprehensive institutional framework fostering the rapid diffusion of world-cultural principles and practices and the huge standardization of regional development agendas all around Europe.

How these European standards, principles and practices are institutionalized at a local and regional level will be shown in more detail in the case study that follows. But before we turn to this more in-depth case study we will have a closer look at the central 'myths', the fundamental 'norms', the major 'organizing principles' and the 'standard procedures' which together make up the 'world-cultural script of regional development' in contemporary Europe. In this way, the following chapter interlinks more closely the two areas which have been presented separately in the previous section: the intellectual discourse producing the major interpretative schemata of regional development (4.2) and the political process which takes up scientific notions, contributes to the dissemination of certain concepts and standards, and institutionalizes them extensively (4.3). On the basis of this account it is possible to capture both the complexities of development strategies as well as the growing isomorphism of regional development practice in contemporary Europe. Although there is certainly no single model of regional development, I contend that contemporary regional development policies cluster around a limited number of rationalized standards and myths that have mainly been established by scientists or quasi-scientific experts and adopted by various political actors and institutionalized in political practice.

5 The European script of regional mobilization

Introduction

Despite constant dispute and vital discourse on the 'dos' and 'don'ts' of regional development as well as a permanent quarrel over the most effective measures and strategies there is nevertheless a certain degree of tacit agreement on some of the major ingredients of successful regional development. Indeed, some models, concepts and notions are widely accepted – at least for some time – in circles of both academics and practitioners and unremittingly evoked in countless how-to handbooks, policy papers and political programmes. Some models have even become role models and iconic examples of 'good practice' informing practitioners about the most appropriate and successful ways of carrying out regional development. Some have been directly transformed into policy prescriptions and built into political agendas. And once they are taken up by powerful political actors and built into official political programmes they acquire the status of undoubted social facts and common knowledge.

Accordingly, this chapter introduces the world-cultural script of regional mobilization in contemporary Europe. It is the aim of this chapter to demonstrate the distinctive world-cultural nature of contemporary regional development policies and the scientific underpinnings of mainstream regional development practice. This should give us a comprehensive overview of which theoretical notions and models are important today and a deeper understanding of how they are translated into political practice. As pointed out in the previous chapter, the discourse on regional development circulates around an enormous and ever increasing number of well-known socio-scientific notions such as innovation, economic growth, good governance, transparency, accountability, cohesion, strategic planning, entrepreneurship, sustainability, creativity, cultural diversity, active citizenship, social, human and cultural capital, and many more. So far, the different aspects implied by these notions have largely been discussed and studied separately from one another. Regional researchers have either focused on economic development and regional economic innovation – and therefore they have mainly discussed questions concerning the innovativeness of regional economies; or they have focused on issues of sustainable regional development and discussed issues of regional development or regional economic growth from the perspective of sustainability. In fact, there is no account in the existing literature on regional development which captures the broader picture and the coherence and interrelation of these different notions.[1] Yet, as we already know from previous discussions, there is a certain logic and rationale behind the massive diffusion of these conceptions and notions in contemporary development discourse. Most of them did not just come about randomly or arbitrarily, but witnessed a certain evolutionary history. The cultural script of regional mobilization which is depicted in the following sub-sections in more detail should bring to light the coherence of these different and seemingly conflicting notions and make some sense of the massive spread of world-cultural models in contemporary regional development practice.

The following discussion starts with an overview and a rough sketch of the major elements of the world-cultural script of regional mobilization (1) before it goes into a more detailed discussion of the central 'myths' of regional mobilization and their way into political practice in contemporary Europe (2). These insights are drawn from the analysis of the discourse of regional development in Europe outlined in the previous chapter and on content analysis of major publications, policy papers, and statements of important (political) actors in the field of regional development in Europe. This includes, in particular, the publications of the European Union on the rules and regulations of the EU Cohesion Policy; and, where suitable and illuminating, publications and statements from other relevant actors, such as the OECD, UN organizations, or expert statements in mass media.

1 The European script of regional mobilization: an overview

The script of regional mobilization, which will be sketched subsequently, is just a snapshot of most prevailing notions, principles and practices of regional development in contemporary Europe. Nonetheless, it is the outcome of an intensive exploration and interpretation of existing policy regulations, policy papers and policy proposals against the backdrop of the macro-phenomenological premises, which were outlined and introduced in previous chapters.[2] Based on these analytical premises it is assumed that regional mobilization in Europe clusters around a bundle of *world-cultural myths* which largely determine both the basic structure and the concrete substance of current development efforts in the sphere of regional development. Although the notion of 'myth' is usually associated with signifiers of 'wrong knowledge' or 'false consciousness' in the tradition of ideological critique (cf. Barthes 1957; Elias 1978: 50–70), I deliberately use this notion here. For I insist on the old assumption of the sociology of knowledge that scientific knowledge is not just a neutral body of certainties and truths, but also an important device of sense-making which also always contains some traits of myth and quasi-religious beliefs (cf. Mannheim 1936; Foucault 1972; Geertz 1973; Meyer and Rowan 1977; Alexander 2003). Certainly, scientific knowledge mainly derives from highly standardized and rationalized processes of knowledge production, and it is often tested, refined and also contested. Therefore it is usually regarded as knowledge of 'higher quality' or 'validity' (cf. Habermas 1985). Yet the notion of a strong 'mythical thrust' in world-cultural diffusion reminds us that there is still an element of belief involved in highly rationalized and highly contested theoretical notions and models. Often this belief is evoked by acts of official sanctification through 'authoritative scientization' and public ceremonial acts. Thus, from the perspective of phenomenological sociology 'scientific myths' are not necessarily considered as 'false consciousness', but relatively fundamental and widely shared representations of reality, without which concerted and projected action would hardly be possible.[3] And they have a strong inherent mobilizing force, mobilizing peoples' motives, intentions, and in particular their inner contentions in accordance with these fundamental 'mythical' narrations.

If we look more closely at prevailing discourses and existing practices of regional development in Europe, I contend that we can identify at least five highly rationalized and scientifically sanctified myths which largely structure and determine current practices of regional development in Europe. To be even more precise, there is one central and fundamental 'constitutive' myth of regional development, the *myth of regional agency*, and four material, or rather 'substantial', world-cultural myths which determine the qualitative shape of development activities, namely the *myths of regional innovation, regional competition, sustainability* and *cohesion*. These five myths together constitute the fundamental intellectual cosmos, the overall 'epistemic field' so to speak, within which contemporary development practice takes shape. The most fundamental and constitutive myth of regional agency is characterized by the strong common belief and institutional imperative that regional development can be rationally mastered and planned; and that contemporary regions must be capable of governing their development in a highly professional and rational way. This cultural construction of rational agency underlies all processes of world-cultural diffusion. Indeed, it is the major assumption of macro-phenomenological institutionalism that as much as world-cultural diffusion proceeds, it brings about ever more rational actors and highly structured and rationalized (or rather: 'professionalized') actor identities (cf. Meyer and Jepperson 2000).

The *four substantial myths* of regional development, in turn, mirror in an ideal-typical way the various aspirations and taken-for-granted concepts of contemporary regional development practice; they mainly contain the various categories and paradigms of the prevailing (scientific) regional development discourse. In line with Karl Polanyi's observation of two fundamentally opposing principles and aspirations of development in modern society also mentioned in Chapter 3 – economic liberalism and social protection (cf. Polanyi 2001: 136ff.) – the four substantial myths can be divided analytically into two pairs of antagonistic streams: *two myths of economic activation*, namely the myths of regional innovation and competition; and *two myths of social and ecological protection*, namely the myths of sustainability and territorial cohesion. Certainly, these myths are strongly interwoven and intersected in everyday discourses and practices of development. They are not confined and reduced to a certain role or function, and often they are just used superficially, as 'empty signifiers' (Laclau 1996: 36–46) that have largely become detached from their discursive origin or meaning. The protecting myth of sustainability, for instance, is often linked discursively with notions of sustainable economic growth and innovation. Conversely, the activating myths of innovation or competition are often associated discursively with the imageries of innovative environmental planning or new measures of social protection. However, all four substantial myths are representations of different and largely antagonistic orientations of human development deriving from distinct intellectual backgrounds and discourses, and therefore they affect the constitution of development policies in different ways.

Moreover, the five 'sacred' myths of regional development are linked to 'fundamental norms' of contemporary world-cultural modernity, and implicit as well as explicit 'meta-norms' (Wiener) of the common European project of European integration. These fundamental norms and meta-norms have developed and have become culturally significant largely independent of the discourse of regional development. In fact, they are outcomes of larger intellectual discourses of modernity, and they are constantly evoked by political discourse and authoritative scientization. Nonetheless, once codified they constitute fundamental norms of common European development aspirations, and in this way regional development practice in Europe is also largely structured by such multi-faceted and often contradictory norms such as economic growth, equality, justice and so forth.

The *fundamental norms* of European modernity and the *five world-cultural myths* of regional development have largely been institutionalized in form of relatively authoritative 'organizing principles' and 'standard procedures' with the enforcement and extension of the EU Cohesion Policy over the past 20 years.[4] They are legally codified and binding to certain extent, and they become manifest in numerous publications on 'good' regional development practice and models of 'best practice'. All these elements are summarized in an admittedly highly stylized and provisional way in Figure 5.1. Of course, this is just a first modest attempt to put together all these different issues into one broader overview. It should be clear that this attempt of a graphical representation of the cultural script of regional mobilization is fairly schematic and does not fully capture the complex, multi-faceted and dynamic nature of world-cultural regional mobilization.

Moreover, this script does not contain one particular model of European regionalism, but it constitutes the major discursive field (or corridor) in which regions and regional development actors (must) accommodate themselves and justify their actions. And it is a framework for massive institutional diffusion of standard knowledge, methods, strategies and techniques on how to govern, manage, and design the future of individual regional lifeworlds. Thus, in sum the European script of regional mobilization is by far more than just a set of abstract discursive objectives and general institutional principles. It is in fact an entire 'ecology' (Fourcade 2006) consisting of world views, institutional principles, policy tools, and organizational arrangements that are highly rationalized and

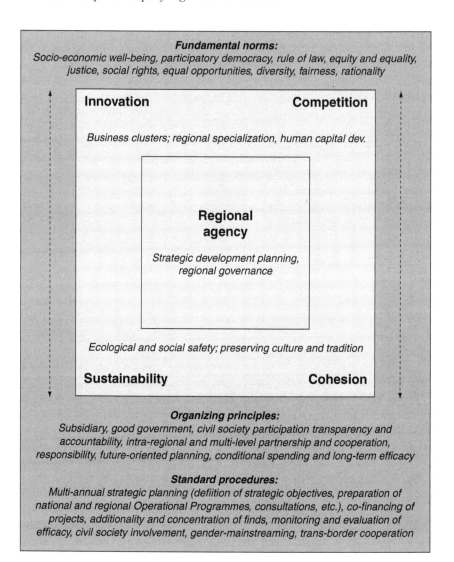

Figure 5.1 The script of regional mobilization in contemporary Europe.

codified by scientific authority, institutionalized in official political programmes, and more or less routinely applied in everyday (political) practice. But it is a 'cultural' *and* 'institutional' script in the literal sense: it structures, first and foremost, development programmes and development agendas in a quite fundamental and substantial sense; secondly, it provides regional development actors and policy-makers with codified conceptions and meaningful justifications for implementing policies and initiating development processes; and, thirdly, it constitutes a scientific knowledge base or a 'tool-box' of scientific standards, methods and techniques endowing development actors and organizations with the means to enact and rationalize development.

2 The five central myths of regional mobilization

In the following sub-sections the cultural core of this script, the epistemic and conceptual foundations of regional mobilization in contemporary Europe, will be illuminated in more detail. The sub-sections are sub-divided according to the analytical division of the five central myths of regional mobilization I have presented above. This means that the presentation of the emergence and evolutionary history of the five myths will start at first with an illustration of the emergence of the two economically activating myths. It will then continue with a depiction of the intellectual origins of the two substantial myths of protection. And, finally, it will conclude with a more detailed description of the current elements of the constitutive myth of regional agency, and in particular the evolution of the standards of regional governance and strategic regional development planning. The following depiction of the conceptual history of the respective concepts and notions and concepts is phenomenological in the literal sense, rather than strictly 'genealogical' or 'historical' (cf. Djelic and Quack 2007). Thus, it focused on what is most relevant and on what has become standard practice in everyday regional development programmes, not on the complete history of emergence of a certain notion, or single controversies and political struggles which might have contributed to this. Nonetheless, it should give an impression on the current standards of regional development in Europe and the complex nature of world-cultural diffusion.

The activating myths of 'regional competition' and 'innovation'

> There is a growing awareness among regional authorities that the economic growth and competitiveness of their regions depend largely on the capacity of indigenous firms to innovate. Offering the appropriate support to indigenous firms to become more competitive through innovation is a rising star on the regional policy agenda. Policy-makers at local and regional levels are formulating regional technology strategies, which sometimes is embedded in their economic development policies, and sometimes is separate from other policy domains. There is a clear need for support in the design of regional innovation policies, both from an analytical perspective and based on experiences and best practices in regions around the world.
>
> (Philip Cooke 2003: 8)

The above quote comprises a number of widely shared assumptions on the ingredients of the successful mobilization of regional economies. It is just an individual quote taken out of a single policy paper on regional development. Yet it is not just an exceptional individual opinion, but largely reflects the essence of the new regional research on *regional competitiveness* and *regional innovation* in post-industrial times that has flourished during the past two or three decades (cf. Keating and Loughlin 1996; Lovering 1999; Morgan 2004). And there is a huge number of policy papers and prescriptive articles of this kind written by other authoritative 'knowledgeable experts' as well. Nonetheless, this quote was selected here as an introductory statement because it represents 'world culture' and world-cultural diffusion in the field of regional development in an almost ideal-typical way. The quote derives from a well-known and well-established scientist of 'new regionalism'. It is not taken from an academic textbook, but from a policy paper of the United Nations Industrial Development Organization (UNIDO) published in 2003, which aims to inform practitioners and policy makers about current academic standard knowledge and trigger institutional learning and reflection in regional development practice. Hence, these two central assumptions of the econo-centric strand of new regional research were directly transferred into key assumptions and key principles of current regional development practice. Though it is acknowledged that each region is different and that all regions must find their own unique way into the post-industrial era, the necessity to promote regional *competitiveness* and to stimulate the capacities of regional *innovation* is commonly accepted and almost universally put into practice. Today, regions all over Europe put a great deal of effort into forming networks and linkages among firms, universities, research centres and public institutions. Science and technology parks, research and technology centres and special areas are set up to foster research-business linkages. Contemporary regional policy places huge emphasis on the stimulation of innovative business activities and not just on the provision of technical infrastructure. They increasingly promote training activities and other activities in human resource development. They vigorously foster entrepreneurship and small business initiatives, and they increasingly try to stimulate the settlement of new 'innovative' industries through active promotion of outside investments (Keating 2001, 2003).[5]

The scientific underpinnings of regional economic mobilization

This policy shift has taken place on the basis of a few concepts and models of regional research that have become standard assumptions of regional development practice in recent times. One standard assumption of contemporary regional development practice is the notion of *flexible specialization* that derived from the research on 'new industrial districts' at the beginning of the 1980s (cf. Piore and Sabel 1984). Although new regional researchers initially addressed the question of regional adaptation in the post-industrial era in marked opposition to neo-classical assumptions of the universal law of economic change, the notion of 'flexible specialization' has become a quasi-universal model of contemporary development practice. Thus, it is not only an outstanding world-cultural model of regional development, but also a good example of the often intricate, sometimes even dialectical paths taken by world-cultural diffusion. In fact, the pioneers of the 'new regional research' did not aim to define a common, simple and universally applicable formula of regional development. On the contrary, they claimed that place makes a difference and that some regions are more able to keep pace with the changes of post-industrialism than others. Accordingly, they pointed to very few successful examples with very distinct and peculiar local circumstances, such as Silicon Valley in Northern California, Route 129 in Boston (Massachusetts), or some more traditional, but highly specialized and innovative, industrial districts in northern Italy and southern Germany. Moreover, they described the economic structure of larger urban agglomerations and metropolises domiciling huge amounts of financial services, consulting businesses, media and communication industries, and company headquarters. However, drawing on insights of these various research endeavours the notion of 'flexible specialization' has turned during the past three decades into a practical quasi-universal dictum implying that all municipalities and regions must specialize and redefine their distinctive 'core competences' in order to find their niche in the global economy. And some of the few successful regions and new industrial districts have become the role models and prototypes of successful regional economic mobilization and regeneration, promoted massively in numerous studies and collections of 'good practice'.[6] Indeed, the most prominent new industrial district, Silicon Valley, has even become the iconic idol of contemporary regional development practice and subject of massive emulation. Consequently, most of the business activities all around the world take place in some sort of 'valley' these days, whether there is an actual valley or not.

Closely linked with the notion of 'flexible specialization' and concentration of business activities in certain business agglomerations the assumption that the innovativeness of regions can be increased through clustering productive forces in regional *business clusters* has become very popular. Initially deriving from economic geography, and vigorously promoted in a very stylized and easy-applicable way by Michael E. Porter, a widely known figurehead of business studies from Harvard Business School, the concept of bundling and clustering producers and suppliers as well as research and production geographically definitely constitutes one of the most prominent world-cultural models of economic mobilization of recent times (cf. Porter 1990). Without doubt, the assumption that innovation evolves out of intensified, multi-faceted and fruitful interlinkages between science and businesses is widely accepted these days. It has been supported by an interdisciplinary consensus and complemented by similar models and modified versions of other geographers, sociologists and political scientists such the model of 'learning regions' (Asheim 1997), the notion of 'associational economies' (Cooke and Morgan 1998), or the concept of 'regional innovation systems' (cf. Lundvall 1992; Cooke *et al.* 2004). Thus, contemporary regional development practice is largely based on a few models and concepts,[7] and the idea of 'boosting innovations' in 'regional systems of innovation' have become typical policy proposals of policy actors such as the OECD or the European Union these days.

The OECD's policy agenda in the field of regional development

Indeed, the OECD has extensively and fairly successfully evoked the myths of regional competition and innovation and promoted in particular the model of cluster economies in recent times. It has published numerous studies, policy-papers, and 'how-to' reports on the implementation of cluster economies and on the importance of regional innovation in contemporary politics, and it has pro-duced detailed assessments and reviews of existing regional innovation strat-egies both in OECD countries and non-OECD countries such as China and Brazil.[8] Moreover, for more than 25 years the OECD has also fostered innova-tion and new modes of governance at the local level, in particular within the framework of the so called 'Local Economic and Employment Development Programmes' (LEED), and it promotes new innovative policies and practices of economic restructuring in rural areas.[9] Last but not least, in 2005 the OECD has started to produce its own statistical database on regional development in order to 'overcome the national bias' in assessments of economic performance and to 'better identify' the 'outperforming regions' of the OECD and those regions that are 'lagging behind' (cf. OECD 2005c, 2007c, 2009).

Obviously, OECD publications and reports do not constitute neutral scientific assessments and reflections on issues of regional development and innovation; they vigorously promote a very limited number of notions and key concepts and pursue a distinctive policy agenda. One of the most recent publications of regional statistics from 2009, for example, is mainly structured around the fol-lowing themes: 'regional innovation', 'regions as actors of national growth', 'making the most of regional assets', 'key drivers of regional growth', 'competi-tion on the basis of regional well-being' (OECD 2009: 5f.). This gives an impression and an overview of the major themes and policy priorities of the OECD. In fact, regional competition and innovation are mainly promoted to foster economic revitalization in times of intensifying globalization and the devaluation of nation-state policy. Beyond that, the OECD aims to stimulate administrative devolution and new regional innovation policies in its member states as a means of reducing public costs and shifting away from traditional redistributive public policies. This is clearly stated as a key rationale of the OECD's regional policy agenda in the introductory statement to its policy field 'regional development':

> (...) OECD work on regional development recognises that a new approach to regional development is emerging; one that promises more effective use of public resources and significantly better policy outcomes. This involves a shift away from redistribution and subsidies for lagging regions in favour of measures to increase the competitiveness of all regions.[10]

*The promotion of 'regional innovation' by the European Union over
the past 15 years*

Apart from the OECD, the European Union has certainly been the largest promoter of 'regional learning', 'regional innovation' and 'regional experimentation' at the regional level in Europe over the past 10 to 15 years. Similar to the OECD, the European Union also primarily promotes an economic definition of regional development, which is highly influenced by the prevailing academic discourse of regional innovation:

> Regions can be key players in the global economy: they are the first to be affected by economic changes and they represent the right 'critical mass' to manage them. They have to build on their unique characteristics, their people, and their cultural and environmental assets. To attract companies and well-trained people, to improve their competitive edge, each region needs to capitalise on its knowledge base and to develop its capacity to innovate.
>
> (European Commission, DG-Regio)[11]

In fact, the European Union strongly promotes the prevailing academic ideas and models of regional innovation in its reports, assessments, and policies. In a more recent policy paper called *Innovative Strategies and Action. Results from 15 years of Regional Experimentation* which addresses regional and national decision makers responsible for public policies in the area of regional development, the European Commission explicitly refers to Michael E. Porter's concept of 'regional cluster economies' and his notion of 'regional competitiveness'. It is presented as a background assumption of contemporary development thinking which is simply taken for granted as common knowledge and conventional wisdom (cf. CEC 2007b: 3). In addition, it introduces the 'systemic approach' to regional innovation mentioned above and summarizes the major assumptions and elements of the concept of 'regional innovation systems' in well-arranged and easy-to read paragraphs.

> The understanding of innovation has developed much over the last fifteen years. First viewed in a linear fashion (innovation comes from research laboratories and is exploited by an enterprise or a community), the vision has become systemic. Innovation comes above all from the quality of interactions between producers, users and mediators of knowledge in the regions: local authorities, companies, centres of production or of transfer of knowledge, local coordination institutions, bodies providing financing for SMEs or research, collective foresight systems, etc. (…).The regional level is particularly appropriate for such interactions. Sharing a territory, culture, values and common references facilitates exchanges and joint projects and allows the development of clusters, as described by Michael Porter.
>
> (CEC 2007b: 3)

This non-binding document is a good example of the kind of publications and material published by organizations such as the OECD and the EU. It is supposed to inform policy-makers and practitioners all around Europe about 'valuable experiences' and 'good practice' in regional experimentation and to give some hints and policy advice to policy-makers on how these experiences may be put into practice in their own environment. However, the European Union has not merely produced reports and policy papers, it has vigorously promoted the concept of regional innovation through several policies and programmes set out within the framework of the EU Cohesion Policy.

It started out in 1994 with the introduction of so called 'Regional Technology Plans' (RTP) in eight pilot regions. In 1997 it significantly expanded the support of innovative actions on regional levels and fostered the implementation of 'Regional Innovation Strategies' (RIS) and 'Regional Innovation and Technology Transfer Strategies' (RITTS) in 101 regions from all former member states (EU-15).[12] By the year 2006 more than 150 RIS were put in place in regions from all member states of the enlarged EU-25. This process of implementation was accompanied by 145 so-called 'Regional Programmes of Innovative Actions' co-financed by the European Regional Development Fund (ERDF), the creation of 13 pan-European thematic innovation networks, and numerous parallel activities and projects on innovation funded by other programmes of the Structural or Cohesion Funds between 2002 and 2006.

As already pointed out in the previous chapter, however, regional policy is not the only policy area where the European Union puts special emphasis and attention on the issue of innovation. With the launch of the Lisbon strategy in the year 2000, the concept of innovation became one of the key objectives of EU policy-making. In the aftermath of re-focusing the Lisbon strategy in 2005 the European Commission outlined a 'new broad-based innovation strategy' (cf. CEC: 2006a) officially adopted by the European Council in December 2006 which was a new roadmap to a 'more innovative Europe' that proposed ten concrete actions of particularly high political priority.[13] In this context, the regional level is highlighted as an important level of policy intervention, and the EU Cohesion Policy is linked more closely with the Lisbon goals between 2007 and 2013 (action 5). Moreover, most of the current world-cultural standards, models and assumptions on the successful stipulation of development in regions are reaffirmed and put together in one policy paper. And the myth of innovation is evoked extensively as the following quote shows:

> The EU can only become comprehensively innovative if all actors become involved and in particular if there is market demand for innovative products. This broad strategy needs to engage all parties – business, public sector and consumers. This is because the innovation process involves not only the business sector, but also public authorities at national, regional and local level, civil society organisations, trade unions and consumers. Such a wide partnership for innovation will create a virtuous circle, where supply of new ideas and demand for new solutions both push and pull innovation.
>
> (CEC 2006a: 2f.)

This quote derives from the introductory statement of the renewed EU Innovation Strategy, which was largely penned by the European Commission. It clearly indicates the way in which the notion of partnership and cooperation and the concept of innovation through cross-fertilization of different realms of society are directly translated into institutional imperatives of contemporary policy-making. It is promoted as a means of fostering the mobilization of all resources for new economic value creation. Thus, the EU innovation strategy constitutes a pertinent example of the mobilizing force of world-cultural myths: while acknowledging previous actions and efforts aimed at development, it is concluded that these were insufficient and even more concerted efforts are needed to assure favourable development and economic well-being in the future. However, as pointed out already, economic mobilization is just one side of the coin in terms of the diffusion of world culture in contemporary Europe; the other side is formed by myths of protection. In fact, apart from regional innovation and competition, sustainability and cohesion have also been promoted vigorously in the past decade.

The protecting myths of 'cohesion' and 'sustainability'

Sustainable development is a powerful, innovative and effective guiding aim for policy at all tiers of government. Sustainable development is in many ways a natural base for regional policy, with the potential to provide an overarching long-term vision for the region, its people and businesses. Our view of sustainable development (…) incorporates the economic, the social, and the environmental, it incorporates openness and equal opportunities and it is an effective tool for integration. Sustainable development, as we see it, is fundamentally good governance.

(SERN 2004: 7)[14]

Just as *competition* and *innovation*, so too *cohesion* and *sustainability* have become key notions in regional development practice in contemporary Europe, and they have also been subject to massive scientific reflection and discussion. However, in contrast to the two former notions, the economically activating world-cultural myths of regional mobilization, the two latter notions were not at the centre of the new regional research and the regional development discourse in the early 1980s. Certainly, both notions were often implicit in studies of innovation (cf. Storper and Salais 1997; Amin 1999; Trigilia 2001; Cooke *et al.* 2004), but they have largely been at the margins of interest of mainstream regional research for a longer period of time. This has changed substantially with the massive expansion of regional research over the past two decades. Today, notions of social cohesion, environmental protection, and, in particular, the concept of sustainable development are at the centre of the discourse of regional development. Regions are widely considered to be refuges of social stability and cohesion in times of intensifying globalization, and, as also expressed in the introductory quote at the beginning of this paragraph, they are considered a 'natural base' for the governance of sustainable development. In fact, the well known slogan *think globally, act locally*, which has become popular with the environmentalist movement in past decades, is directly applied in current conceptions of regional governance and development. In this way, sub-national tiers of government have been given special attention in discourses on the protection of society.

The rise of 'cohesion' in socio-scientific discourse

As with many other notions in social sciences the term 'cohesion' originates from the natural sciences, namely physics and chemistry, where it designates the degree of 'interconnectedness' and 'intermolecular attraction' between elementary particles. The notion of 'cohesion' was primarily introduced to social sciences by social psychologists to signify the social and material fabric of smaller groups and associations, or the density and intensity of interconnections between group members (for an overview, see Friedkin 2004). In the meantime, the notion of 'cohesion' has gained huge attention both in empirical research on socio-economic well-being and in philosophical debates on the shrinking social and moral fabric of advanced modern societies. Thus, on the one hand the growing significance of 'cohesion' in contemporary development practice derives from attempts in social research to enrich the prevailing structural measurements of living conditions by less tangible, more 'qualitative' dimensions of social well-being, such as 'social integration' or 'subjective well-being' measured in terms of trust, social capital, civic engagement and other qualitative indicators (cf. Diener and Suh 1997; Portes 1998; Putnam 2001; Delhey *et al.* 2002; Fahey *et al.* 2003). On the other hand, the increasing significance of 'cohesion' is certainly linked with growing concerns of social scientists and intellectuals with the 'stability' and the 'coherence' of (national) societies in times of intensifying globalization and economic liberalization. In fact, both distinctly leftist and conservative thinkers have expressed their concern with growing tendencies of 'social fragmentation' and the consequences of 'excessive individualism' (cf. Habermas 1985; Walzer 1992, 1999; Etzioni 1993; Putnam 2000). By the end of the twentieth century when inequalities, unemployment rates and indicators of 'social exclusion' were on the rise even in the most affluent Western welfare states, the discourse of decreasing social cohesion also entered political practice. New policy approaches aiming at fostering the cohesiveness of society against the backdrop of increasing globalization were introduced, the 'fight against tendencies of social exclusion' and the promotion of 'social inclusion' have become central policy goals of Western governments, particularly in Europe (cf. Münch and Büttner 2006; Bernhard 2006; Rose and Miller 2008: 88ff.). And again, these policy shifts have been strongly promoted by the major international agents of policy reform such as the World Bank, the OECD, and, first and foremost, the European Union.

'Territorial cohesion': the new focus of the EU Cohesion Policy

As briefly mentioned above in Chapter 4, 'cohesion' received a special status in European politics from the very beginning of European integration. With the adoption of the Single European Act and the establishment of the Cohesion Policy from the mid-1980s, it finally made its way into the treaties of the European Union.[15] Today, 'strengthening economic and social cohesion' is anchored in Article 2 of the Treaty on European Union as one of the major policy goals of the European Union.[16] And it is specified in Article 158 of the Treaty establishing the European Community as the aim of promoting an

> overall harmonious development of the territory of the European Union' through actions aiming at the reduction of '(...) disparities between the levels of development of the various regions and the backwardness of the least favoured regions or islands, including rural areas.[17]

Hence, in the context of EU politics the meaning of 'cohesion' is primarily territorial rather than linked with the notion of cohesion or cohesiveness of individuals. It is based on the normative ideal that the European Union should be more than just an ever-enlarging market place, but also a territory in which the vision of harmonious territorial development and equal levels of wealth and living conditions is pursued (Rumford 2000: 19ff.). Huge territorial socio-economic disparities and imbalances of living conditions amongst member states or sub-national regions are considered as an expression of social imbalance and a source of instability, conflict and social rupture. In this sense, the EU Cohesion Policy is only indirectly concerned with 'cohesion' in the strict socio-scientific sense of the term, but rather with the 'convergence' of living conditions and opportunities all over the territory of the European Union as a means of taming or even resolving potential risks of instability.[18]

Beyond that, researchers have observed another fundamental contradiction in the territorial strategies of EU policies: One part of the measures deals with the development of functional and self-organized *sub-national* regions, another part aims at refocusing policies of social inclusion and strengthening social cohesion at the *member-state level*. Thus, in the first case the European Union promotes regional differentiation as a means of fostering 'European cohesion', which may run counter to the second bundle of policy proposals aimed at strengthening social inclusion and cohesion at the national level (cf. Delhey 2004: 9).[19] However, regardless of inherent potential contradictions, lacunae and shortcomings, the aim of 'increasing cohesion' in Europe, has been further reaffirmed in European politics in recent times. In Article 3 of the newly adopted 'Lisbon Treaty', the notions of 'solidarity' and 'territorial cohesion' are explicitly set out in addition to the usual references to economic and social cohesion.[20] Moreover, most recent policy proposals on the future shape of the EU Cohesion Policy are increasingly directed towards the notion of 'territorial cohesion'. The European Commission recently published a Green Paper on 'Territorial Cohesion' under the bold title *Turning Diversity into Strength* (cf. CEC 2008c). This proposal reaffirms the sub-national dimension of policy interventions, but it is no longer solely concerned with enhancing socio-economic convergence amongst territories. It proposes measures that strengthen the connectivity amongst places and regions all over Europe more explicitly and foster new forms of inter-regional partnerships and cooperation.[21] Moreover, territorial cohesion is proposed as a means of '(...) transforming diversity into an asset that contributes to sustainable development of the entire EU' (ibid.: 3), and it is linked to a wide range of policy areas. In this way, as was the case with the proposal to enhance the 'innovativeness' of European regions, the aim of strengthening 'territorial cohesion' in sub-national regions is introduced as a means of comprehensively restructuring the European territory.

> Issues such as coordinating policy in large areas such as the Baltic Sea region, improving conditions along the Eastern external border, promoting globally competitive and sustainable cities, addressing social exclusion in parts of a larger region and in deprived urban neighbourhoods, improving access to education, health care and energy in remote regions and the difficulties of some regions with specific geographic features are all associated with the pursuit of territorial cohesion.
>
> Increasingly, competitiveness and prosperity depend on the capacity of the people and businesses located there to make the best use of all of territorial assets. In a globalising and interrelated world economy, however, competitiveness also depends on building links with other territories to ensure that common assets are used in a coordinated and sustainable way (...).
>
> (CEC 2008c: 3)

The rise of the awareness of 'sustainability'

The notion of 'sustainability' has followed a similar route from intellectual discourses to political practice as the notions of 'competition', 'innovation' and 'cohesion'. Thus, like innovation and cohesion, 'sustainability' is understood in different ways and propagated by various political actors as well. There is huge disagreement on the exact meaning of sustainable development and what is required to actually 'achieve' sustainability. Proposals range from economic solutions to distinctly anti-economic or even non-economic notions. All sentiments of prudent, progressive, holistic, inclusive, participatory modes of governance are usually associated with sustainability (cf. Gladwin *et al.* 1995; Baker 2006). Nonetheless, there is a broad consensus on the importance and its core meaning: sustainability is usually seen as the opposite of short-sighted and narrow-minded thinking and behaviour (cf. OECD 1997).

Indeed, the current notion of 'sustainability', the initial idea and the concern that human development should be processed in a 'sustainable' way mainly derived from environmental research, and in particular the new strands of scientific research which discovered the negative impact of industrial production on the environment during the 1960s (cf. Hironaka 2003). Moreover, by the beginning of the 1970s an international group of scientists and intellectuals from different subject areas, the famous Club of Rome, reflected on the future prospects of human development. This group coined the formula of the 'limits of growth' and advocated an alternative, multi-dimensional and more sustainable notion of progress and human development (Meadows 1972 and 1992). These are only two outstanding examples of the discursive climate that evolved at the interface of science, public discourse and political engagement during the 1960s and the 1970s. In fact, the global environmental movement that evolved during the 1970s was largely informed by new scientific reflections on the threats to natural life and future development posed by excessive industrial modernization.

During the 1980s the new environmentalist awareness and the notion of sustainable development was brought to the table of mainstream development discourses. The notion of 'sustainable development' received official political sanctifications and huge public recognition with the appointment of the so called 'Brundtland Commission' (1984–7) by the United Nations and the publication of its famous report *Our Common Future* in 1987.[22] Moreover, the United Nations organized several World Summits on environmental protection such as the Rio Earth Summit in 1992 which adopted the famous Agenda 21 Action Plan, and, more recently, the World Summit on Sustainable Development (WSSD) held in Johannesburg in 2002.[23] Due to these high-profile political initiatives the notion of 'sustainable development', and in particular the concept and definition proposed by the Brundtland Commission, has gained worldwide recognition and authoritative status. The World Bank, the OECD and the EU also took up this notion of sustainable development and outlined their own models, policy recommendations and political programmes (cf. OECD 1997; CEC 2001, World Bank 2005). Hence, it is widely acknowledged by the majority of political actors that promoting sustainable development is about steering societal change at the interface between the socio-cultural realm (human needs and values, traditions and culture, institutions etc.), the economy (concerns about allocation and distribution of scarce resources), and the environment (respect for the sensitivity of ecological systems, protection of threatened species and landscapes etc.) (cf. Baker 2006; Strange and Bayley 2008). Accordingly, the 'sustainable development triangle', which is depicted in the following, has attained the status of a widely-shared world-cultural model; i.e. it has become a standard conceptual framework for sustainable policy-making and a popular image of the different concerns and the trade-offs of development (see Figure 5.2).[24]

The institutionalization of 'sustainable development' in EU governance

While 'environmental protection' and 'sustainable development' gained a foothold at the global level in the 1980s, they have also gradually entered the EU regional policy agenda during the 1990s. They received strong support and official recognition with the adoption of the European Spatial Development Perspective (ESDP) in May 1999 (CEC 1999).[25] Moreover, 'sustainable development' is also anchored as one of the major principles of the Cohesion Policy in Article 17

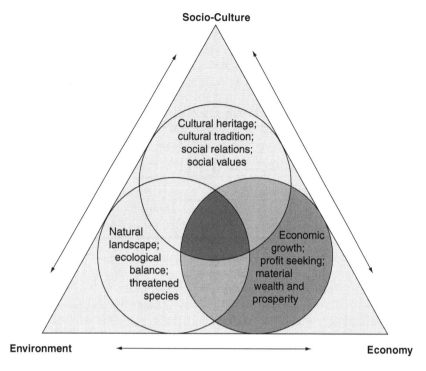

Figure 5.2 The Sustainable Development Triangle.

of the official Council Regulation laying down all general provisions on the management and implementation of policies funded by the ERDF, ESF and CF.[26] Apart from promoting environmental protection, energy efficiency and renewable energy sources the European Commission placed special emphasis on the promotion of sustainable urban development within the framework of the so-called URBAN Community Initiative (cf. CEC 2009). And the EU also co-funded the creation of transnational networks of experts and regions to exchange ideas and 'best practices' in sustainable development, such as the 'Sustainable European Regions Network' (SERN), which was the source of the introductory quote to this section above, or the 'European Sustainable Development Network'.[27] Moreover, in 2001 the European Union officially adopted a common European Sustainability Development Strategy (SDS) at the EU summit in Gothenburg 2001, which was renewed at the European Summit in June 2006.

The overall aim of the renewed EU Sustainable Development Strategy is '(…) to identify and develop actions to enable the EU to achieve a continuous long-term improvement of quality of life through the creation of sustainable communities able to manage and use resources efficiently, able to tap the ecological and social innovation potential of the economy and in the end able to ensure prosperity, environmental protection and social cohesion.'[28] The renewed

EU Sustainable Development Strategy set out a number of concrete actions to be undertaken by 2010 in the following seven key priorities: (1) climate change and clean energy; (2) sustainable transport; (3) sustainable consumption and production; (4) conservation and management of natural resources; (5) public health; (6) social inclusion, demography and migration; (7) global poverty and other sustainable development challenges. Certainly, in the current programming period from 2007 to 2013 regional policy is one of the central policy areas in which measures serving these priorities are implemented at the local and regional level. This entails an enormous expansion of policy aims and objectives of regional policy, an even stronger emphasis on the control and government of lifestyles and behaviour of individual citizens, and reaffirms the commitment to local and regional agency as well as citizenship involvement in the policy process:

> Sustainable Development stands for meeting the needs of present generations without jeopardizing the ability of future generations to meet their own needs – in other words, a better quality of life for everyone, now and for generations to come. It offers a vision of progress that integrates immediate and longer-term objectives, local and global action, and regards social, economic and environmental issues as inseparable and interdependent components of human progress.
>
> Sustainable development will not be brought about by policies only: it must be taken up by society at large as a principle guiding the many choices each citizen makes every day, as well as the big political and economic decisions that have [sic.]. This requires profound changes in thinking, in economic and social structures and in consumption and production patterns.[29]

These far-reaching ambitions of the EU Sustainable Development Strategy are, at least to some extent, in marked contradiction to the Lisbon Strategy, the meta-strategy of the European Union, aiming in the first place at the promotion of 'sustainable' *economic* growth and development. Therefore, we can retain that EU regional policy is influenced by different notions of sustainability and different strategic visions, and regional development practices in Europe are always shaped within the discursive field of the four formerly discussed substantial myths of regional development. It is not clear which notion and what kind of approach of 'sustainability' prevails in political practice, since notions and approaches change dynamically. At the beginning of this century, when the EU launched its Sustainable Development Strategy, many European policy-makers were quite optimistic about meeting the goal of a multi-dimensional and balanced development agenda and EU institutions. In light of massive economic downturn all around Europe, in turn, ambitious aims of 'sustainable development' were dropped in 2005 with the renewed Lisbon strategy. Yet in the face of larger, more devastating natural catastrophes, such as floods and landslides, and also under the threat of economic shocks, such as the financial crisis of 2008, calls for extensive 'sustainability' are always high on the policy agenda – at least for a certain period of time. However, it is not certain and indeed hardly easy to assess how 'sustainable' these efforts are.

The constitutive myth of 'regional agency'

> Perhaps one of the most obvious traits of human beings that distinguishes them from other animals is the desire to influence their own destinies. Rather than accept the notion of social Darwinism, they try to twist or control the way the world works. Of course whether this is ultimately for their own good is not always certain, but nevertheless the instinct to control or 'plan' seems to be ingrained. (…) Planning is concerned with a rational and systematic analysis of alternative courses of action, and with ways of implementing an appropriate course of action to meet relevant aims, goals and objectives. It has gained a particularly important place in the public domain, although it continually enters private decision-making from the level of individuals deciding on how to plan family activities to large multinational companies seeking to deal with uncertainty.
>
> (Plane *et al.* 2006: xi)

The idea that that the human species is able to plan and master future development, and the institutional imperative that development interventions should be structured as rationally as possible, is not confined to policy-making in late modernity. From ancient times to the rise of modernity human beings and political leaders always aimed at planning and projecting future developments. However, the conceptions of how development can and should be planned and the techniques of forecasting, planning and implementation have been markedly different over time. Today, the proactive approach of regional development and the institutional cooperation of regional key actors are standard principles in development practice. Regions, or rather actors within regions, are endowed with a huge amount of prescriptive knowledge and techniques of 'rational' development planning (in the sense of both efficiency and prudence) as well as standards of 'good' regional governance (in terms of efficacy and legitimacy). Thus, the belief that regions must be active and innovative is widely shared these days and has encouraged massive efforts of 'planned intervention' and institution-building in sub-national areas. This strong evocation of *regional agency*, however – i.e. the strong conviction that development can and should be fostered endogenously and through comprehensive strategic regional planning – is relatively new. It emerged over the past 30 years through an extensive expansion of world-cultural models and practices in regional development planning before it was institutionalized and promoted as standard practice in EU governance. This development will briefly be explained in the following section.

The scientific underpinnings of regional planning

It is certainly true that systematic, scientifically-grounded spatial planning and regional intervention have a long tradition in the modern history of many European nation-states. However, from the end of nineteenth century until the 1950s and the 1960s, territorial planning was mainly conceived as part of national industrial policies pursued by specialized civil servants of the central state administration. Accordingly, regional development policy was mainly planned and put forward by the policy-makers and planning units of central governments. If there were some systematic approaches of planned intervention at local and regional levels, they were largely reactive and part of the crisis management of Keynesian industrial policies. And there was also almost no awareness of regions and regional economies in developmental economics and the related social sciences.[30]

With the expansion of expertise in regional development planning at the beginning of the 1970s the character of regional development planning and regional development practice changed tremendously. As highlighted in the literature, both regional development planning and practice has undergone an era of substantial 'professionalization' (cf. Heintel 2001). Thus, during the 1970s the concept of project-based regional development slowly entered the regional arena. These new project-based approaches of regional development were rather experimental and incremental. However, they have brought about new actors of development, such as semi-public or private regional development agencies (RDAs) and regional planning offices and a whole array of new methods and techniques of systematic regional development planning and management. This was largely determined by regional development practitioners and planning experts 'on the ground', but also accompanied by extensive scientific reflection on new practices of regional development as well as ever more 'innovative', 'effective' and 'practical' techniques of regional development planning (cf. Hall 1970, 1982; Cooke 1983; Friedmann 2001; Plane *et al.* 2006). Consequently, the emergence of new standards and principles of regional development can be seen as a highly reflective process, bringing about an increasing 'rationalization' and 'scientization' of regional development practices and the emergence of new occupations and educational programmes, such as regional planning, city management, or the management of tourism in cities and regions.

The new prevailing models: 'regional governance' and 'strategic planning'

Indeed, contemporary regional development practice is highly reflexive in terms of the 'appropriate' objectives, purposes and means of development. All models, principles and techniques are subject of constant reflection, challenges and refinement. They are future-oriented and focused on managing processes and change as well as bringing together actors from different realms of society in common projects rather than simply achieving abstractly determined outcomes (Benz and Fürst 2002). Key notions of contemporary regional development practice are all-encompassing 'regional governance' and 'self-regulation': Regional governance is defined as a mode of collective self-regulation on regional levels which includes various strategic actors from different realms of society, such as political-administrative actors, business actors, trade unions, other interest-based alliances and representatives of civic organizations (Fürst 2004). Hence, the actor-capacity of regions, or rather the capacity of 'regional agency', is considered to be dependent on the institutional structure of regions and on the capacity of regions to mobilize broad-based consensus on the strategic goals and aims of future development.

This discussion on regional self-regulation and 'good' or 'rational' regional governance goes hand in hand with references to concepts of holistic and long-term *strategic* regional planning. In fact, strategy-building is one of the key principles of 'modern' regional and urban planning, which has become widespread in cities and regions all over Europe in the past two decades (cf. Salet and Faludi 2000; Adams and Harris 2005; Dimitriou and Thompson 2007). The new strategic approaches in contemporary local and regional development practice are reminiscent of the older approaches to urban and industrial planning during the 1960s (cf. Hall 1970). Yet in contrast to former approaches of development planning the new strategic approaches mark a radical change in planning culture. The new approaches are strongly influenced by models of strategic management as proposed by managerial economics, which have become the major producers of easily-applicable models of the 'rational' management of organizations and individuals in the past three or four decades (cf. Chandler 1962; Mintzberg 1994; Montgomery and Porter 1996; Grant 2008). They are more holistic and focus on the integration of different policy fields, issue areas and responsibilities. They put more emphasis on the inclusion of private actors into the planning process, both business actors and representatives of civil society. Accordingly, 'good governance', 'long-term-orientation' and 'sustainability' are as much key words and institutional imperatives of the new strategic approaches as 'output-orientation', 'effectiveness' and 'resource efficiency'.

One of the standard models of strategic development planning is the processing of planning into a compact *Strategic Management Cycle* which is known from project management (see Figure 5.3). In principle, but certainly in slightly stylized terms, the Strategic Management Cycle comprises the following elements: (1) the creation of a common *development vision* for the region; (2) a *SWOT-analysis*, which is a comprehensive analysis and interpretation of the strengths, weaknesses, opportunities and threats of a region; (3) the determination of concrete aims, objectives and measures of development; (4) *implementation* and *change management*, which is accompanied by constant *monitoring*; (5) careful *auditing* of the costs and benefits as well as an *evaluation* of the measures and their implementation; (6) *re-thinking* and *re-adjustment* of the strategy on the basis of assessments and measurements and potentially the start of a new round of planning and implementation.

The whole planning process can certainly be more elaborate than described in this simplified and stylized depiction of the cycle of strategic regional

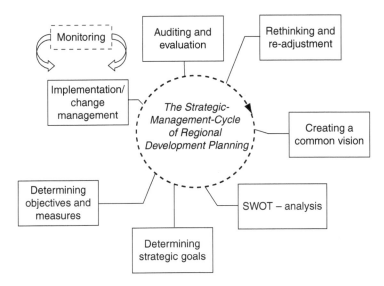

Figure 5.3 The Strategic Management Cycle of Regional Development Planning.

development. Indeed, each of the tasks can be executed with ever more complex measures and techniques of rational planning such as sophisticated forecasts and computer-based simulations, elaborate techniques of monitoring and evaluation, or more contemporary procedures of decision-making and issue management. Moreover, the planning process may also include in various degrees the involvement of citizens and important 'stakeholders'. According to contemporary imperatives as well as standards of good governance and participatory democracy, a broad consultation of the public is usually obligatory in contemporary planning processes. However, the Strategic Management Cycle constitutes a powerful world-cultural model of contemporary development planning, and a huge part of political planning processes are processed along the lines of this model. The inherent norm that a planning process is only complete if all steps of the cycle are completed and executed deliberately contains a strong institutional imperative constitutively shaping and structuring respective actions and interactions in distinct ways.

The promotion of 'regional agency' by the EU Cohesion Policy

The shift from traditional planning to regional self-regulation and strategic management is often seen as a direct consequence of the introduction of New Public Management techniques and the increasing 'privatization' of public policies in many countries around the world (cf. Lane 2000). However, the transfer of management knowledge is not just a process of economizing public policy, but mirrors a more general trend for an all-embracing rationalization and re-organization of social life. It also corresponds to more general changes in governmental rationalities and prevailing standards of social control and social self-regulation (cf. Power 1997; Sahlin-Andersson and Engwall 2002; Schimank 2005; Djelic and Sahlin-Andersson 2006; Dori 2006; Rose and Miller 2008; Le Galés and Scott 2008). In this context, international political agents such as the European Union also play a crucial role. They foster the diffusion of new techniques and methods of political planning.

In fact, the trend towards strategic planning in urban and regional development has been strongly influenced by the increasing Europeanization of territorial planning and regional development policies since the beginning of the 1990s (Healey 1997; Salet and Faludi 2000; Faludi 2008).[31] With the establishment of the Cohesion Policy in 1989 the European Union institutionalized a whole range of principles, standards, and techniques of transnational (multi-level) governance, regional mobilization and strategic development planning. The participation of regions and regional actors in planning processes has become a common standard in modern state governance across the European Union. World-cultural principles and practices such as 'multi-annual programming', 'partnership', 'good governance', 'gender-mainstreaming', 'non-discrimination', 'accountability', 'responsibility', 'scientific evaluation' and 'monitoring', 'transparency' and 'publicity management' are obligatory standards of European regional development policy. All these elements are outlined in official regulations as conditions *sine qua non* of EU regional policy implementation.[32]

Most strikingly, the organizational structure of the programming and implementation of the EU Cohesion Policy is largely structured along the lines of the model of strategic development planning that was described above (see Figure 5.3). Both national governments and regional administrations are obliged to participate in the programming process and to draft 'National Strategic Reference Frameworks' (NSRFs) in accordance with the official *Community Strategic Guidelines On Cohesion* (CEC 2005b). After the official approval of the strategic priorities, objectives and measures indicated in the Strategic Reference Framework, national governments and regional administrations then draft individual 'Operational Programmes' (OPs) comprising a consistent set of priorities and multi-annual measures which may be implemented with resources of one or more of the Structural Funds. The OPs are the official planning documents of European regional policy indicating all important information and details relevant for policy implementation. They are also approved officially by the European Commission, and the creation of these documents is based on a set of mandatory standard tasks set out by the Commission. These are: a detailed diagnosis of the object of planning by way of comprehensive SWOT-analyses; an outline of an official explanatory statement on the selection of priorities; an indication of a detailed funding plan; a designation of the official management, auditing and certification authorities; an indicative list of envisaged large-scale projects (environment projects exceeding EUR25 million and other projects exceeding EUR50 million) and a detailed description of the envisaged evaluation and follow-up systems (cf. CEC 2007: 27ff.).

By issuing rules and regulations on the programming and implementation of European regional polices, the European Union fosters the *normative* and *coercive* diffusion of 'European' standards of regional planning and structural funds management to municipalities and regions all across Europe. In addition, it also publishes numerous guidance and working documents, sourcebooks and databases with easy-to-apply methods and methodologies of evaluation. It also provides guidance on how to prepare planning and programming documents properly.[33] Moreover, the EU has also co-funded thousands of international conferences, meetings and consultations for scientists and public officials, not to mention trans-European projects. In each programming period each EU member state eligible for structural funds receives a certain amount of money for workshops, training courses and exchanges between their local, regional and national levels. Beyond that, the INTERREG Programme (before 2007) and the new programme 'European Territorial Co-operation' (since 2007) are specifically dedicated to promoting cross-border exchanges and activities for experts, public officials, scientists, NGOs and all other types of 'active citizens'.[34]

Thus, in all these different ways, the European Union promotes the 'professionalization' of national, regional and local agents ('knowledgeable experts') who are concerned with planning and evaluation, and contributes to the *cultural* construction of regional agency. This entails the massive spread of highly stylized and standardized models and techniques and fosters the structural assimilation of planning and auditing cultures in regional development.[35] One impressive example of the many world-cultural by-products of EU funding is the online and interactive database for the evaluation of socio-economic development called EVALSED, which was developed by independent evaluation experts in order to promote and improve the practice of evaluation in the European Union.[36] Another example of a project co-funded within the INTERREG-framework is the so-called GRIDS-project, which focused on the development of best practice guidelines for regional development and spatial planning.[37]

3 Conclusions

The previous portrayal of the world-cultural script and the central myths of regional mobilization have indeed unearthed a huge amount of models, principles and standard techniques and practice of regional development in Europe. It has been shown to what extent the process of institutionalization is underpinned by scientific discourse and quasi-scientific 'hybrids' (Latour) at the interface of science and political practice. It has been demonstrated that many of the world-cultural elements presented above are even institutionalized in formal rules and standard procedures in mainstream development programmes. An explanation has also been provided for the way in which the major international agents of policy change and development, the World Bank, the OECD, and in the European context, above all, the European Union, *reinforce*, *specify* and *accelerate* the diffusion of world-cultural models, principles and practices. Thus, the world-cultural script of regional mobilization is truly 'world-cultural', indeed. It is largely determined by highly rationalized assumptions on the appropriate means of development practice and promoted on a transnational scale through 'authoritative scientization' and other types of expert authority (legal expertise, auditing expertise, management expertise, etc.).

Yet, when we look at the intellectual discourse around the four substantial myths of contemporary development practice – competition, innovation, sustainability and cohesion – we notice that there is huge disagreement concerning the fundamental ideas and conceptions of 'good' development and that there is also some latitude in determining concrete paths of development. We have seen that development increasingly oscillates between both reinforced aspirations of *economic activation* and ever more and louder claims of 'alternative', 'more prudent', 'tamed', *sustainable* and *cohesive* versions of development. All these different demands and aspirations are representations of distinct scientific discourses, and they are brought into political practice by various powerful political actors with a massive amount of rational, scientifically-based justifications. Consequently, all these different claims and aspirations are politically significant and gain practical validity, and therefore contemporary development practice is determined in one way or the other by *all* four substantial myths.

Nonetheless, despite all contradictions, it is clear that the four substantial myths share some common ground. They coincide in that they all imply that intensive interactions and cooperation amongst different actors and a certain amount of intermingling between different spheres of society is fruitful and advantageous for development. In fact, the *myth of competition* entails the institutional imperative that regions and all other types of collective actors 'exposed' to competition must be deliberately constituted as competitive actors by the collective act of determining distinctive competitive advantages. The *myth of innovation* is based on the assumption that innovativeness is the key to favourable development and that the spirit of innovation emerges from an open discursive climate and inter-disciplinary thinking. The *myth of sustainability*, in turn, is based on the conception that development can and must be mastered by a prudent balancing of different economic, socio-cultural, and environmental issues and aspirations. And, similarly, the *myth of cohesion* urges that fundamental socio-cultural norms and traditions and a sense of cohesiveness amongst individuals and actors from different areas of society must be preserved against reinforcing 'economic', 'libertarian' or 'modernist' forces.

Thus, the four substantial myths of regional development promote a strong impetus to think and act across boundaries and reconcile different institutional goals and requirements reflexively – something which is considered to be typical for our advanced modern era, as opposed to the era of 'organized modernity' between 1890 and 1970 (Wagner 1994). Moreover, all the four different world-cultural myths convey the old modernist belief that society can be changed and that the fate of human development must be mastered by means of active and rational intervention. The *myth of rational agency*, the assumption that social entities – and in our concrete example: regions – should develop and improve their capacity of rational agency in order to succeed is fundamental to all efforts and aspirations of development. Hence, the four substantial myths of regional development mobilize regions in terms of certain aspirations (ends), but they all convey certain assumptions of self-reflection and rational mastery (means). Highly rationalized practices and techniques, such as rational planning, or carrying out SWOT-analyses, evaluations and constant monitoring should ensure and enhance the capacity of agency. This brings about an increasing amount of self-reflection regarding the conditions of development and mobilizes actors to carry out constant reform and re-invention. It fosters the constant challenging and questioning of existing structures on the basis of different indicators, standards and further reaffirms the world-cultural spirit of rationalization.

With these remarks and conclusions this chapter which introduced the world-cultural underpinnings of regional mobilization in Europe of today has now come to an end. The case study in the subsequent chapters will illustrate in more detail how the cultural script of regional mobilization finds its way into concrete regions and localities in Europe of today. The case study includes the description of three relatively newly established regions in Poland – one of the new EU member states in Central and Eastern Europe, which was exposed to a completely different project of modernity until the end of the 1980s: the project of state communism under Soviet hegemony (cf. Arnason 1993). Poland has since then changed at tremendous speed to adapt to the model of Western modernity, and this has entailed a massive diffusion of 'world culture'. Hence, the study of the process of regionalization in Poland will reveal some of the logics and driving forces in world-cultural diffusion.

As noted above in Chapter 2, macro-phenomenological institutional analyses have tended to be quantitative and focus on the depiction of the worldwide prevalence of certain world-cultural principles, models or scripts in contemporary times. Qualitative analysis specifying particular contextual conditions and the concrete logic of world-cultural diffusion are still rare. Thus, the following empirical analysis contributes to the existing body of literature in a three-fold way: first, it adds a more qualitative, more in-depth phenomenological analysis of world-cultural diffusion to the existing body of literature; second, it sheds light on the world-cultural construction of regions – social entities which have thus far been disregarded in world-polity analyses; and, third, it further specifies local contextual conditions of world-cultural diffusion.

6 Region-building and regional mobilization in Poland

Introduction

It is the overall aim of this study to explore the diffusion of highly rationalized principles and practices of regional development to sub-national areas in contemporary Europe. Accordingly, we will explore and specify the enormous (world-)cultural drive of regional mobilization in the following on the basis of a comparative case study of sub-national regions. The regions that were selected for this analysis – Lower Silesia (*Dolnośląskie*), the Lublin region (*Lubelskie*) and the Sub-Carpathian region (*Podkarpackie*) – are 3 of 16 administrative regions of the Republic of Poland (see Map 6.1).[1] These 'voivodships' (*województwa,* in Polish

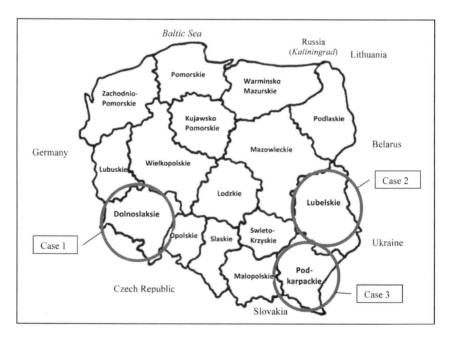

Map 6.1 Territory of contemporary Poland and geographic location of the three selected cases.

diction) were only created about a decade ago, in January 1999, as part of a larger administrative reform. Hence, the following analysis provides a good opportunity to study the construction and constitution of 'regional agency' and new world-cultural regional actor-identities in Europe of today almost in 'real time'. In fact, the study of regions which only came into existence about a decade ago should contribute to a more detailed exploration of both the intellectual underpinnings as well as the institutional logics of diffusion.

With a size of $312,679 \text{ km}^2$ and a population of approximately 38 million inhabitants, Poland is certainly a special representative of the EU member states from Central and Eastern Europe (CEE) which entered the European Union in the past few years. It is by far the biggest of all these post-communist states, and therefore it is not just dominated by one single centre–periphery divide between the capital city and the rest of the country, which is the case for most of the other eastern EU member states. In fact, it has a more diverse and polycentric regional structure with a number of larger agglomerations and urban growth poles apart from Warsaw, the outstanding and yet still uncontested political and economic centre of Poland. In this sense it exhibits favourable conditions for the creation of a pronounced regional structure. Moreover, due to its sheer size and population Poland is by far the biggest receiver of external financial resources that are targeted at regional development in European policy-making. In the current programming period of the EU Cohesion Policy between 2007 and 2013, Poland alone receives about EUR67 billion from the EU Structural Funds and the Cohesion Fund, which is about one quarter of all funds assigned by the European Union to regional policy. It is the largest amount of structural aid ever paid to a single EU member state by the European Union. This huge amount of EU funding for local and regional initiatives constitutes a big push towards a comprehensive 'modernization offensive' (Wagner 1994) of the country and a stimulus to change and overcome persistent structural problems and imbalances. Therefore, Poland is particularly interesting for an analysis of regional mobilization within the European institutional framework of regional development.

Indeed, there are huge structural differences amongst the three selected regions, which reflect a deeply-rooted and historically persisting 'developmental gap' in Polish space. The three selected regions are located at different borders of Poland (see Map 6.1). While one region, Dolnośląskie, is located in the west of the country and shares a border with the region of Saxony in eastern Germany and with the Czech Republic along the Sudeten mountain area, the other two, Lubelskie and Podkarpackie, are both located in the eastern part of Poland and at the external border of the European Union to Belarus and Ukraine (in the case of Lubelskie) and to Ukraine and Slovakia (in the case of Podkarpackie). The different geographic location of the regions, especially the distinction between western and eastern Poland, is usually regarded as a major determinant of the socio-economic situation of Polish regions, and it is even considered as the major determinant of their future prospects. In fact, the two selected eastern regions, Lubelskie and Podkarpackie, are considered to be the two 'poorest' regions of Poland in terms of GDP per capita, and they can also be found on the list of the ten regions with the lowest GDP per capita of the present-day European Union (EU-27). Hence, the following analysis explores how and in which way even the 'outermost' European regions are affected and shaped by world-cultural diffusion.[2]

The method of contrasting either the most dissimilar or the most similar regions is quite common in regional studies (cf. Rodriguez-Pose 2000; Tatur 2004a, 2004b; Keating *et al.* 2003). However, the research design that is chosen here should not be seen as a 'clinical', experimental setting for testing or refining theory (cf. Gerring 2004; George and Bennett 2005). Rather, it should be seen as an interpretative framework for exploring in more detail if, and in what way, the new Polish regions (or rather the respective authorities and decision-makers in the regions) are actually able to create and stipulate their own and distinct path of favourable future development. Since the developmental levels and the structural conditions between regions in western and eastern Poland are so different, we should rather expect different interpretations of development and different measures and strategies to cope with the situation within the same institutional framework of policy-making. In comparing the regions which are most different, we can address these differences and explore how world-cultural (re-)invention of the regions has taken place over the past decade. By selecting two similar economically 'low-performing' regions with almost identical development indicators and economic structures, but with different historical determinants, we can analyse potential traces of regional differentiation amongst governmental bodies of relatively identical areas.

Yet, before we go deeper into the comparative analysis of the developmental challenges and the development strategies of the three selected regions (Chapters 7 and 8), the particular research context 'Central and Eastern Europe' (1) and the 'prehistory' of region-building before 1999 will be depicted in the following two sections (2). This rough sketch should provide an overview of the construction of the current regional structure in Poland and it should give an impression of the manifold efforts of social mobilization at the local and regional level over the past two decades. After this short introduction to measures and initiatives of regional mobilization, the major patterns of regional inequalities in Poland will be outlined in more detail. This will reveal some of the structural imbalances in contemporary Poland that motivated the comparative case study (3). At the end of this chapter major characteristics – some structural indicators and some qualitative differences of the three regions are depicted schematically (Figure 6.2). If the reader wants to skip the subsequent discussion of the major steps of region-building in Poland over the past two decades this overview should directly provide a rough sketch of the major characteristics of the three selected cases.

1 A new breakup: regime change in central and eastern Europe

The area of contemporary Central and Eastern Europe constitutes a unique and exceptional research context for the study of world-cultural diffusion. On the one hand, this area is an outstanding example of the huge varieties and contingencies of projects of modernization. In historical terms the area is regarded as the traditional 'periphery' of the European continent – at least since the onset of industrialization in the core countries of Western Europe.[3] Moreover, for about four decades after the end of the Second World War the area was under the hegemony of the Soviet Empire, the communist antagonist of the Western model of society (Sztompka 1993; Arnason 1993; Watson 1998). Thus, for almost half a century of communist rule all countries and regions from Central and Eastern Europe were shaped in one way or another by an alternative project of 'modernization', namely the model of totalitarian state socialism. This was radically different to the Western project of modernity that is usually referred to as the normative core of contemporary world society by the proponents of the world-polity perspective (cf. Boli 2006). On the other hand, nonetheless, after the end of the Cold War in 1989 a whole range of countries from Central and Eastern Europe radically broke with their communist past, rapidly and enthusiastically taking over core institutions of the Western model of society into their new state structures and transforming themselves into democratic market societies (Przeworski 1991; Offe 1994; Beyme 1994; Grabher and Stark 1997; Merkel 1999; Hann 2002; Outhwaite 2005).

Certainly, the process of transformation proceeded relatively similarly to the stylized image of the 'world-cultural discovery' of an 'unknown island', as described by the proponents of the world-polity perspective to account for the strong pervasive force of world-cultural diffusion (see Chapter 2 above). Undoubtedly, in the early 1990s the area of Central and Eastern Europe had become one of the largest laboratories for world-cultural diffusion in contemporary history – a project of planned, steered and massively rationalized institutional change (Elster *et al.* 1998; Stark and Bruszt 1998; Balcerowicz 1999; Bohle 2000; Bönker *et al.* 2002). From the very beginning of state transformation, external consultants and advisors were involved in the reform processes, 'teaching' the new political elites how to implement most contemporary models of economic policy and accompanying the first steps of state reform (cf. Sachs 1992a). During the 1990s a whole industry of both governmental and non-governmental development agencies entered the arena, promoting economic, democratic, administrative and cultural change at all levels of society. Accordingly, the process of transformation was widely considered as a condensed reification of processes of state-building and societal modernization in Western European countries. And it was also celebrated enthusiastically as a 'return to Europe' (cf. Sztompka 1993; Balcerowicz 1999; Adamski *et al.* 2002; Reiter 2007).

However, it must be noted that regime changes and processes of system transformation in post-Soviet Europe proceeded quite differently from country to country (Hellman 1998; Stark and Bruszt 1998). And by no means all post-Soviet countries were able to transform into liberal democracies or receive support in taking part in the process of European integration. The 'return to Europe', materializing in far-reaching European integration and EU membership, has become real only for a very limited number of post-socialist states. This includes Poland and nine other countries from Central and Eastern Europe (cf. Schimmelfennig and Sedelmeier 2005).[4] Consequently, since the Eastern Enlargement of the EU there is a new demarcation in the European territory that goes through the former Soviet bloc (Hann 2002; Burawoy and Verdery 1999; Vobruba 2005). Hence, the transformation of Central and Eastern Europe is not just a process of natural self-realization of Western models and principles of state-building. It has a distinctive geographical and temporal dimension, and it is also shaped by concrete political interests that become manifest in formal political institutions and state borders. Yet once world-cultural standards gain ground and get support by authoritative institutions and numerous 'institutional carriers', they exhibit a strong force for social change and transformation which mobilizes all social entities around prevailing standards of 'development'.

It is a common feature of all post-socialist countries in Central and Eastern Europe that they do not have pronounced regional and federal traditions.[5] In fact, the significance of regions and the awareness of regional specificity and regional diversity only returned to the spotlight after 1989 (Gorzelak 1996). And the 'making of regions' (Tatur) only became a focal point of policy-making and institution-building in Central and Eastern Europe after almost a decade of centrally steered state reforms (Bachtler and Downes 2000; Bachtler *et al.* 2000; Keating and Hughes 2003). In fact, during the first phase of state transformation, when new governments were mainly concerned with large-scale economic and state reforms, the drive towards political decentralization and governmental devolution was not very pronounced (Baldersheim *et al.* 1996). After the first round of large-scale societal transformations, regional traits were rediscovered and some historical regions were able to re-invent and mobilize their socio-cultural heritage (cf. Tatur 2004a, 2004b; Heidenreich 2008). In this context, the process of European integration that intensified with the official beginning of the accession process in 1997 played a major role indeed (cf. Brusis 1999; Bachtler *et al.* 2000; Pieper 2006). Accordingly, there has been a big debate in the academic literature on role of the European Union in the process of region-building in Central and Eastern Europe. Some authors saw the EU as the major driving force of administrative decentralization and regionalization in the former candidate countries (cf. Grabbe 2001; Radaelli 2003; Schimmelfennig and Sedelmeier 2005). The coercive force of the 'conditionality' of EU membership was put forward as the decisive factor for administrative reforms, particularly the requirement of EU candidate countries to develop the necessary institutional framework and capacities for adopting the *acquis communautaire* and administering pre-accession funds. Other researchers, however, have strongly questioned the role of EU conditionality (cf. Hughes *et al.* 2005) and have highlighted the importance of the interplay of internal and external political forces on region-building in CEE EU member states (Ferry 2003; Brusis 2002 and 2005).

However, independent of the debate on the concrete influences of political actors and the concrete constellation of actors involved, we can ascertain that decentralization and region-building in Central and Eastern Europe tended to be a top-down process. It was mainly driven by specialized work force of the central-state administration and groups of distinguished domestic and international experts rather than by strong regional advocacy and mobilization from the bottom-up. Thus, region-building does not take place in local vacuums but is always influenced by massive expert involvement and prevailing standards of 'modern' statehood in an increasingly interconnected 'world-polity'. This will be discussed and depicted in the following sections in more detail with the example of the emergence of a new regional structure after regime change in Poland.

2 The revitalization of sub-national territories in Poland after 1989

The current regional structure of Poland was created on 1 January 1999 by a larger administrative reform (adopted by the Polish Parliament in July 1998). This reform replaced the former two-tier administrative system of 49 smaller voivodships and approximately 2,400 municipalities (*gminy*) that had been in place since 1974. In its place came a three-tier system of 16 new voivodships, 373 counties (*powiaty*) including 65 larger cities and urban municipalities with a county status, and 2,489 local municipalities.[6] Indeed, the administrative reform from 1998/9 marks an important milestone in the transition of the country from a centralized socialist state to a more diversified form of state authority in the course of European integration. It put an end to the endless and heated political debates on the role of the state in post-communist Poland and the necessity of creating a new territorial division. It also represents a certain degree of state decentralization, since it created the principle of regional self-government on the intermediate administrative level. In this sense, just like the other voivodships of contemporary Poland, the three selected regions represent relatively newly constructed sub-national territories and, at the same time, a new intermediate level of government that integrated the existing urban and rural municipalities into a newly structured regional administrative system (see Maps 6.2 and 6.3).

Local reform and international development aid: the first approaches of regional mobilization after 1990

As Map 6.2 shows, the communist government had created a distinct subnational administrative structure in 1974, already. Yet the idea of regional self-government was strongly rejected by the communist ideology, and as a result the administrative structure that was established in 1974 did not aim to strengthen the local or regional level of government, but instead sought to abandon former historical regions and foster the authority of the ruling communist party. Right after the fall of communism in 1990 the first Polish government rapidly passed legal acts to foster local democracy and to strengthen the local level of self-government in Polish communities (Swianiewicz 2002; Baldersheim *et al.* 2003; Regulski 2003; Swianiewicz *et al.* 2005). However, region-building, the establishment of

Map 6.2 Regional structure of Poland 1974–98.

Map 6.3 Regional structure of Poland since 1999.

self-governing administrations at the intermediate level, and a distinct regional policy approach on the part of the central state, were not high on the agenda during the first years of state transformation. If regional policy initiatives were undertaken at all they were nothing more than ad hoc interventions in areas with high unemployment and areas particularly affected by socio-economic decay. And reforms that were only undertaken when social order and political stability were seriously threatened, e.g. in response to workers' protests (Yoder 2003).

However, from the early 1990s onwards Poland received special financial support for administrative and economic capacity-building at the local and regional levels from other European countries. In 1989 the 'Poland and Hungary Assistance for Restructuring their Economies Programme' (PHARE) was established by Western European countries to support the processes of economic restructuring in the neighbouring CEE countries. After the official invitation of Poland and other CEE countries to join the European Union at the Copenhagen Summit in 1993, this programme was integrated into the structures of EU structural policies and refocused to support the process of European integration. Beyond that, in 2000 new instruments of pre-accession assistance were introduced – the ISPA and SAPARD programmes – which added further financial and institutional support to the existing structures of the PHARE programmes.[7]

In fact, the influence of the European Union and EU funding played a vital role right from the very beginning of regional policy-making (Pieper 2006). Accordingly, the first national institution with an explicit regional-policy approach, the Polish Agency for Regional Development (PARR), was set up by the Polish government in 1993. It was mainly responsible for the management and implementation of several PHARE programmes such as the 'Structural Development in Regions Programme' (STRUDER), the 'Rural Areas Programme for Infrastructure and Development' (RAPID) and the CROSS-BORDER programme. These programmes constituted the first coordinated initiatives of a distinctive regional development policy in Poland (Kozak 2000; Kosarczyn 2001). During the 1990s the European Union strongly promoted the idea of decentralization and institution-building at local and regional levels, and it funded projects to foster the self-organization of local actors and institutions. The major focus of the pre-accession assistance provided by the European Union and other European countries was on restructuring the economy of the country, particularly in problem areas, for example by promoting entrepreneurship, development of small-medium-sized businesses (SMEs), and stipulating new economic initiatives. Other priorities of pre-accession assistance were the development of transport and technical infrastructure including measures to improve environmental protection and strengthen the capacities of administrative personnel. Hence, in short, from the early 1990s many of the common world-cultural standards of regional development were promoted in Poland with external financial support.

With the beginning of the accession process in 1997 the PHARE programme was officially turned from a programme that supports the process of political and economic changes in Poland and other CEE countries into an instrument preparing the candidate countries for EU accession. Thus, between 1997 and 2003, PHARE funding and other pre-accession programmes were mainly driven by the aims of ensuring the 'functioning' of governmental bodies at all tiers of government and 'reducing' structural socio-economic imbalances as much as possible before the official date of EU enlargement. Apart from investments in technical infrastructure and economic restructuring, innumerable workshops, training courses, study tours, conferences, and the introduction of new study programmes were financed by the pre-accession funds under the heading of 'technical assistance' in order to foster 'capacity-building' in accordance with 'European' rules and standards of policy-making (see also Table 4.2 above).

The European Commission also introduced new practices of exchange and cooperation amongst practitioners and experts from Western European EU member states and CEE accession countries. Amongst other initiatives, the concept of 'twinning' was particularly promoted and supported as a new practice of international exchange and as a new distinctly non-hierarchical form of advisory support provided by experts from the EU member states to so-called 'candidate countries'. Just like all the other measures of training, exchange and knowledge transfer, it can be regarded as a vehicle of world-cultural diffusion. It has contributed to the massive and rapid diffusion of world-cultural standards and practices and the emergence and institutionalization of expertise in the field of EU policy-making.[8] The concept of twinning and the way it was applied in the pre-accession process in Poland is briefly described in Figure 6.1. The excerpt is taken from an official description of the pre-accession process from the Polish state agency responsible for the management of the accession process. Moreover, the major funding priorities of PHARE and ISPA are also outlined in Figure 6.1.

Endemic diffusion of new local institutions of economic mobilization during the 1990s: a short period of 'free experimentation'

As stated above, there was no 'functional' intermediate regional system and almost no coordinated and coherent regional policy approach in Poland and most other CEE countries during the first years of transition. However, this should not lead to the conclusion that there was no drive towards regional development in Poland before the administrative reform in 1998/9 and that the former local administrations and voivodships have been inactive or non-functioning. On the contrary, in the midst of large-scale macro-economic reforms and reorganization of state structures a whole range of new initiatives and activities of local and regional revitalization were flourishing all around the country. Though many of these initiatives were funded by PHARE programmes and pre-accession assistance from the European Union, many of these new activities were initiated bottom-up by proactive local authorities, city mayors, industrious business people, representatives of labour and employers' organizations and other private and civil society actors. Therefore, this period of local and regional mobilization before 1999 is also celebrated as a short 'golden age' of vivid

---

'Twinning'

'Projects supporting public administration in order to bring it in line with the requirements of the EU membership are carried out under the Institution Building
Programme. The most widely used instrument of this programme is twinning, which
involves support of the EU Member States for beneficiaries from Candidate
Countries. A twinning partner is selected prior to the execution of an institution
building project. It is usually an institution from an EU Member State with a similar
scope of responsibilities to its Polish counterpart and which wishes to share its
experience with a Polish partner. This type of assistance focuses mainly on public
administration responsible for aligning Polish legislation with the EU requirements
and controlling its enforcement (among others a small part of assistance is
addressed to the Non-governmental Organisations – NGOs). (...) Each twinning
project involves a Pre-accession Advisor (occasionally supported by a long-term
expert as well as medium- and short-term experts). The PAA is selected by the
partner from a Candidate Country based on offers collected and delivered by the
European Commission. The PAA remains in a country applying for the EU membership for a period of 12 – 36 months. The PAA cooperates closely with the Project
Leader supervising the project, who resides in his country of residence.
Counselling under a twinning covenant was first introduced in 1998. Seventy out of
all projects financed with Phare funds (ca. 19%) in Poland in the period 1998 – 2000
were carried out with the assistance of PAAs, which is the highest number among all
Candidate Countries. In 2003 the European Commission offered a new three-year
post-accession financial programme to promote activities aimed at strengthening the
administration and the judiciary as well as implementing the legislation of the
European Union the Transition Facility. (...)' (OCEI 2004: 6).

**Other measures and initiatives funded by PHARE and ISPA in particular
between 2000 and 2003:**

- improving business-related infrastructure: support for infrastructural
  projects targeted directly at increasing the activity of the productive sector
  and improving the conditions for business activities on a local level;
- increasing the activity of the productive sector (activities directed at
  assistance for diversification of the economy, development of the private
  sector, restructuring and modernization of industry and the services
  sector);
- human resources development (support for an increase in the employment
  level, the development of entrepreneurship, the improvement of adaptation
  capacity on the part of companies and their employees and the promotion
  of equal opportunities for women in the labour market);
- improving environmental protection.

Source: OECI (2004).

Figure 6.1 Vehicles of world-cultural diffusion in EU pre-accession programmes.

bottom-up regionalism in Poland (cf. Kozak 2000; Hardy 2004; Bruszt 2005; Woodward *et al.* 2005).[9]

One of the outstanding examples of new bottom-up initiatives of local and regional economic revitalization in Poland during the 1990s is the widespread establishment of private, semi-private or publicly run 'regional development agencies' (RDAs). They were established in all 49 then existing voivodships and they played a vital role in mobilizing the economic structure of the former voivodships (cf. Ferry 2007). The first RDA was founded in 1993 in Rzeszów, which since 1999 constitutes the capital city of the Podkarpackie Voivodship. By the year 1996, there were more than 60 RDAs spread all over the country and most of them are still in place today. Furthermore, the former voivodships and local governments introduced numerous self-administered 'business incubators', such as 'technology transfer centres', 'centres for enterprise support', as well as 'technology parks' (TPs), in order to stimulate new economic activities. During the 1990s many such initiatives of local and regional development were set up in Poland, but they were not part of a deliberate governmental strategy of regional development. The organizational structures of RDAs and business incubators were taken directly from Western European countries and transferred to Poland, often with support of external experts and partners from outside – mainly from Ireland, Scotland, France and Germany.[10] In this context, the support of pre-accession funds, the twinning programmes and the funding of exchanges played a vital role indeed. However, the diffusion of RDAs and business incubators was also proceeding independently in private circles and networks of associations, partnerships and businesses support relations. By the mid-1990s the central government also started to promote the 'cluster-approach' of economic regeneration more systematically and increasingly shifted its strategy of economic restructuring from sectoral interventions to more locally-targeted strategies of economic revitalization. Above all, it started to support the establishment of so-called 'special economic zones' (SEZs) both in areas with high unemployment and in areas with favourable conditions for investment. SEZs are specifically demarcated in areas in which tax incentives are given to investors. They are initially financed publicly in terms of kick-off funding provided by the government, but they are mainly privately run and profit-seeking, particularly in the Polish context.[11] The first Polish SEZ was created in 1995 on the outskirts of the old-industrial agglomeration of Mielec (again located in the current Podkarpackie Voivodship). By the end of the 1990s there were 17 such zones, which attracted on average about ten investors each.

All these new actors and institutions of local and regional regeneration – the RDAs, TPs and SEZs which were established on a massive scale during the 1990s – have been major vehicles for the rapid and often mimetic diffusion of 'best practice' models both within and independent of official state structures. In fact, they are still the major vehicles and fundamental elements of the economic restructuring of sub-national areas all around Poland. A huge part of business activities in Poland and almost all foreign direct investments (FDIs) are concentrated in SEZs, TPs, and other types of business clusters, not least due to the special support provided to respective entrepreneurs and investors. Consequently, the number of SEZs, TPs, and new science and technology transfer centres is still growing. Today, there are more than 40 business clusters and 14 SEZs in Poland with an increasing number of sub-zones.[12] However, due to the socio-geographical path-dependencies and contingencies of regional policy-making during the 1990s, the SEZs and business clusters are spread une-qually around the country. There are areas and voivodships with numerous SEZs and business clusters, and there are areas without any SEZs and just a small number of business clusters.[13]

Moreover, most of the initiatives promoting entrepreneurship and small and medium-sized business activities are conducted by the numerous local and regional Polish RDAs and other organizations of this kind. They consult poten-tial entrepreneurs on how to write business plans, how to finance their business ideas, and how to put these ideas into practice. They train and 're-educate' people whose skills no longer match the 'new requirements' of the job market and support potential investors in embedding their enterprise into the new local environment. They often plan, establish and run TPs and other business incuba-tors in their local environment and establish new trans-border cooperation for regional businesses and organizations and their counterparts in other regions. Thus, the RDAs play an important role in the diffusion of new principles and practices of economic restructuring at local and regional level. They often serve as the 'right hand man' of local and regional authorities and as major promoters of world-cultural diffusion. They are also important multipliers of European practices and principles, since they often serve as managing authorities of pro-grammes funded by Pre-Accession and EU Structural Funds, for a huge part of their activities is now financed by EU funds in one way or another.

In Table 6.1 the current RDAs, SEZs, TPs, and new Science and Technology Parks (STPs) of the three selected regions Dolnośląskie, Lubelskie and Podkar-packie are listed in detail. It shows that the spread of RDAs and SEZs in Dolnośląskie and Podkarpackie is relatively similar. We can also see, moreover, that in Lubelskie no SEZ was established over the past 15 years. This definitely constitutes a disadvantage in the competition for potential investors. However, in the past few years some sub-zones of SEZs from other areas have been estab-lished in Lubelskie as well.

The administrative reform and the new administrative structure in Poland

From the mid-1990s onwards the questions of administrative devolution, the establishment of 'functional' self-governed regions, and at the same time a stronger central co-ordination of regional policies had been high on the policy agenda. Certainly, the need to restructure the administrative system in light of EU accession and to create functional regions which were eligible for the struc-tural funds was a crucial element in this regard. There is therefore no doubt that the creation of a new administrative structure on the meso-level was compelled by standard requirements of EU structural policies and urged by the recommen-dations of the European Commission (Ferry 2003). In 1995 the Polish govern-ment set up a task force on regional policy in order to drive forward the process of regionalization and political decentralization, and one year later a joint task force of the Polish government and the Directorate of the European Commission

Table 6.1 Major institutions of economic activation in the selected regions (2009)

	Dolnośląskie	*Lubelskie*	*Podkarpackie*
Regional Development Agencies (RDAs)	6 RDAs located in Wrocław, Wałbrzych, Legnica, Jelenia Góra, Głogów, Nowa Ruda	3 RDAs (two located in Lublin, one located Biłgoraj) + local branches	6 RDAs located in Rzeszów, Mielec, Tarnobrzeg, Krosno, Przemyśl, and Ustrzyki Dolne
Special Economic Zones (SEZs)	3 SEZs: Legnica SEZ; SEZ for Medium Business (Kamenia Góra) and INVEST PARK (Wałbrzych) + various subzones at other locations	No SEZs; but sub-zones of other SEZs in Lublin, Puławy, Tomaszów, Janów Lubelski, Łuków	2 SEZs: EURO-PARK (Mielec, the first Polish SEZ funded in 1995) and EURO-PARK WISŁOSAN (Tarnobrzeg) + various subzones at other locations
Industrial Parks (IPs) and Science and Technology Parks (STPs)	3 IPs in Legnica, Nowa Ruda, and Bukovice 3 STPs in Wrocław, Szcza-wno Zdrój and Brzeg Dolny	2 IPs in Świdnic and Puławy 1 STP in Lublin	2 IPs in Mielec and Jasło 1 STP 'Aeropolis' in Rzeszów

Note
Based upon own research (last update: 11 November 2009).

responsible for Regional Policy (DG Regio) were established. Many elements of these recommendations were taken over into the law on the major administrative reform which was adopted by the Polish Parliament, the Sejm, in July 1998 (Garsztecki 2001; Zientara 2008).

However, although the whole process was mainly initiated top-down and driven forward by selective domestic and foreign experts the political process which led to the administrative reform was by far without political conflict. In fact, the decentralization of state government as well as the structure, size and demarcation of the newly created regional territories was a matter of heated political debates. Even the number of administrative regions was unclear until the very end of the debate. The proposals ranged from having twelve larger regions, 25 to 31 smaller regions, or even preserving the former system of 49 smaller regions. Finally, the current regional structure of 16 voivodships was pushed forward and decided politically, which are markedly smaller than the initially proposed models of EU-NUTS-2 regions (Ferry 2003: 1105ff.). In this sense, the administrative reform of 1998 can be seen as a compromise of 'etatists', who feared a loss of the newly acquired national sovereignty and stability through excessive decentralization, and 'reformers' who aimed for an increase in administrative, economic and democratic capacity by strengthening local and regional self-determination (Ferry 2003; Hughes *et al.* 2005: 118ff.).

This compromise has also become manifest in the new administrative structure and division of competences between the new regional governments and the central government that was introduced by the administrative reform. As in other more centralist states, such as France for instance, there is a dual structure of government on the regional level with bodies of regional self-government on the one hand, and a parallel governmental structure acting at the local and regional level on behalf of the central state on the other. In fact, the model of federal systems with relatively independent and strong regions such as in Germany had never been a realistic choice for Polish policy-makers (cf. Regulski 2003). Thus, compared to federal states, the newly created regions are relatively weak and relatively dependent on central directives.[14] In principle the division of labour amongst different the governmental bodies on the sub-national level and between the sub-national self-governing authorities and the central state is as following: There are elected sub-national governments at the local level (*gmina*), the county level (*powiat*) and the regional level (*województwo*), each with its own legislative and administrative functions. The regional self-government is constituted by the directly elected regional council (*Sejmik*) and the regional executive board (*Zarząd Województwa*), which is chaired by the region's marshall (*marszałek*). On the other hand, the central state is represented by the governor, called the *wojewoda*, who has his or her own administrative apparatus (*Urząd Województwa*) that has the task of controlling and monitoring the conformity of all decisions at local and regional level with national legislation. He or she is also responsible for supervising the execution of central government tasks, such as policing, sanitary and epidemiological inspections, environmental protection and so forth. The *wojewoda* is directly nominated and appointed by the Prime Minister.

Certainly, one of the main goals of the 1999 administrative reform was to establish a clearer separation of functions and policy areas between tiers of government and to eliminate vertical (hierarchical) dependency of lower tiers of government upon the higher ones (Swianiewicz *et al.* 2005). This has been achieved formally by enforcing the administrative reform. The *marszałek* and the *wojewoda* are by definition completely independent of each other; both are assigned to distinct areas of competence. Most of the regional executive competences are in the hands of the *marszałek* and his or her executive board, whereas the *wojewoda* holds a monitoring role, a representative and safeguard of the interests of central government at sub-national levels. The local and regional self-governing authorities are responsible for the governance of all policy issues at local and regional level and for conducting their own independent development policies. The representative of the central government, in turn, is not supposed to interfere in this business and merely carries out its monitoring tasks. In practice, however, certain ambiguities remain within the dual structure of regional government. One ambiguity concerns the relationship between the two administrative bodies. Since the *wojewoda* has the final say in the implementation of regional policies, the divisions of tasks are not fully separate; and there is the tendency for the *wojewoda* to interfere and actively intervene in regional politics (Ferry 2003: 1104). Moreover, another critical aspect that is also always highlighted in public and scientific debates on regional policy is the financial dependency of the regions on the central state and the low level of financial resources that the regions are endowed with. Therefore, some authors speak of a semi-reform, regret that decentralization stopped at the half-way mark, and doubt that the (self-governing) regional authorities will be able to pursue their tasks properly (cf. Zientara 2008).

The tentative revitalization of historical regions in Poland

Alongside the remaining lacunae in the existing division of tasks between the central level and the sub-national governments, criticism has also been voiced that the administrative reform established new demarcations within and amongst former historical regions, which prohibits strong regional identifications and the emergence of distinct regional identities (Zientara 2008). In some cases historical regions and historical regional demarcations that already existed centuries earlier were re-established – or at least the old names of historical regions were revived such as Lesser Poland (Małopolskie), Greater Poland (Wielkopolskie), Pomerania (Pomorskie), or Mazuria (Warmińsko-Mazurskie). In other cases the region-building entailed merging some of the former smaller voivodships that were created by the communist government in 1974 into bigger regions. Sometimes, in turn, new regional demarcations were established by splitting the former regional territories of the previous system into different parts and adding them to various new voivodships.

It can be questioned, however, whether a clear-cut determination of stable demarcations between historical regions would have been possible at all. Although there are historical regional traits, the historical basis for the articulation of distinct regional identities is relatively weak in Poland. In the past century the political map of Poland frequently changed, as did the regional division of the country (cf. Davies 1981a, 1981b; Zukowski 2004). Besides that, it was not just the territorial structure of the country that changed substantially, but also the population. Due to the partition of the territory and foreign rule during the 'long nineteenth century', as well as the two world wars, the Polish population has witnessed extraordinary suppression, displacement, and forced migration.

This can be seen in the example of the three selected regions as well. It is true that contemporary Dolnośląskie is just one part of a larger historical area of Silesia (in Polish: Śląsk) which used to be one of the richest and most developed areas of Europe during the eighteenth and nineteenth centuries.[15] In 1918, after the First World War the eastern part of the Silesian province was transferred to the Second Polish Republic and governed as the 'Autonomous Voivodship of Silesia'. With the agreements of the Treaty of Yalta that sealed the 'westward shift' of Polish territory in 1945, a large part of the western area of Silesia was given to Poland after the Second World War. The historical region of Silesia is therefore now spread over four different voivodships of Poland's current regional administrative structure: the voivodships of Silesia and Opole (former Upper Silesia), Lower Silesia and even some parts of Lubuskie (cf. Figures 6.2 and 6.3 above).[16]

In fact, the historical traits of the other two selected voivodships, Lubelskie and Podkarpackie, are relatively similar. They also witnessed a dramatic and changeful history. Both the long-lasting period of the partition of the Polish territory between 1795 and 1918 and the re-determination of the eastern border of the Polish state in 1945 decisively affected the current shape of these Voivodships (see Figure 6.5). The area of Lubelskie once constituted the core area of the Polish-Lithuanian Commonwealth (*Unia Lubelska*) and during the period of partition it was part of the Russian Empire. The area of contemporary Podkarpackie, in turn, belonged to the historical region of Galicia during the partition (cf. Hann 2000; Hann and Magosci 2005; Buzalka 2007). This region once used to be the most eastward region of the former Habsburg-Hungarian Empire in the nineteenth century which at the time stretched from the area south of Kraków – which now constitutes the territory of Małopolskie – to the area between the cities of L'viv and Czernivtsi in the western part of the present-day Ukraine (see Hann 2000: 4). These days, the external EU border constrains historical connections of people from both Lubelskie and Podkarpackie to the more Eastern areas and countries much more than it ever used to be in former times.

Hence, the example of the three selected Polish regions impressively illustrates the huge contingencies of region-building. Nonetheless, the administrative reform of 1998/9 has brought about a certain consolidation of older regional structures and a revival of regionalism in Poland (cf. Tatur 2004a, 2004b;

Source: Zarycki (2007: 488).

Map 6.4 Changing territorial demarcations on the Polish territory 1795–1945.

Zientara 2008). After the establishment of 16 administrative regions, both the new regional structures and the shape of the regions were largely accepted by the population. There were at least no big protests or distinct political mobilization against the new demarcations after the regional structure was decided and put in place.

3 A tremendous inflow of European funds since 2000

Despite all remaining weaknesses and ambiguities of the current regional structure in Poland, the administrative reform of 1998/99 marks a starting point for the upswing of a new coordinated approach of regional policy-making in Poland. Since then, the balanced development of the Polish territory, and regional development in particular, has become the focal point of policy interventions (cf. Grosse 2006). Along with the introduction of a new system of administrative regions, the preparation of a national strategy for regional development was initiated in 1999, which constituted an integral part of the country's overall National Development Plan 2001–2006 (cf. Garsztecki 2003 and 2005). The national development plan (NDP) was the central tool of the Polish government for spatial and regional development planning at that time being, and it was concerned, first and foremost, with the allocation of EU pre-accession funds designated for regional development as well as the allocation of the EU Structural and Cohesion Funds that were earmarked for the period after EU accession in 2004. Beyond that, important legal and organizational steps were undertaken to strengthen the regional focus of policy-making: In the year 2000 the newly created voivodships drafted and adopted their first multi-annual development strategies according to certain principles set out in the legal act adopted in July 1998 that outlined the major administrative reform. Moreover, the adoption of the Laws on the Rules of Regional Development in May 2000 entailed a more accurate determination of the major principles of the Polish regional policy system, in particular those passages which specify the relationship between the central and regional tiers of government as well as the programming, management and instruments of regional development (cf. Grosse 2006: 152f.).

Finally, in October 2005 the task of planning spatial, and in particular, regional development as well as coordinating the implementation of the EU Cohesion Policy, which till then used to be in responsibility of the Ministry of Economy and Employment, was fully transferred to the newly created Ministry of Regional Development. This indicates that regional policy and spatial development have reached the top of the political agenda in Poland over the past few years – not least because of the huge amount of EU support provided for regional development in the period between 2004 and 2006 and especially in the new programming period between 2007 and 2013. In the first period after EU accession between 2004 and 2006 all operational programmes (OPs) that were put in place in order to absorb EU funds were drafted and managed at the national level by the administration of the Ministry of Economy and Employment until October

2005, and subsequently by the Ministry of Regional Development. This has contributed to huge concentration of coordinated activities regarding all major regional development initiatives at the central state level.

Allocation of EU funds in the post-accession period from 2004 to 2006

After an inflow of about EUR 5.9 billion of EU pre-accession funding between 1990 and 2003 the accession of Poland to the EU in 2004 certainly brought about a significant increase in financial support for local and regional development initiatives under the EU Structural Funds and the Cohesion Fund. Between 2004 and 2006 EUR11.3 billion of EU funds (EUR7.6 billion of Structural Funds and EUR3.7 billion of the Cohesion Fund) were allocated to Poland. Together with the contribution of national funds (EUR37 billion) and private sources of co-financing (EUR1.8 billion) the total amount of financial allocation for EU Structural policies between 2004 and 2006 amounted to EUR16.7 billion. This amount of money was distributed to different national and sectoral OPs in accordance with the guidelines of the EU Community Support Framework and the specifications of the national development plan 2001–6. It was distributed to municipalities, counties, voivodships, and individual beneficiaries who applied for funds; and it has been invested in numerous projects of national, regional and local development ranging from small infrastructure projects on the community level to large-scale investments in innovative business environments and the construction of motorways, railway tracks, airports and so forth.

The overall distribution of the Structural Funds is indicated in Table 6.2, as well as the additional financial allocation of the Cohesion Fund for the period 2004 to 2006. It can be seen that the largest portion of financial resources provided by the Structural Funds (about 39 per cent of total Structural Funds) was allocated to the 'Integrated Operational Programme for Regional Development' (IROP). It was dedicated to supporting projects of social and economic revitalization within the 16 voivodships. It was managed by central government, but the money was given to these self-governing regional authorities responsible for the selection of potential beneficiaries and project partners. The other major portions of the Structural Funds were allocated to economic revitalization (about 18 per cent of the total) and human resource development (mainly occupational re-training, about 17 per cent of the total). However, by far the largest share of financial contributions under the Cohesion Policy between 2004 and 2006 was provided by the Cohesion Fund (about EUR4.1 billion in total). It constituted an additional source of funding for the EU member states which are most 'lagging behind' mainly dedicated to the development and modernization of transport infrastructure and measures to improve the protection of the environment.

Table 6.2 Implementation of EU Cohesion Policy in Poland 2004–6

	EU funding in EUR (million)	Share of total SF (%)
SOP increasing competitiveness of Polish economy	1,300 (ERDF)	17.8
SOP transport	627 (ERDF)	8.6
SOP human resources development	1,270 (ESF)	17.3
IOP regional development (IROP)	2,870 (ERDF)	39
SOP restructuring the food sector and rural development	1,055 (EAGGF)	14.4
SOP fisheries and fish processing	179 (FIFG)	2.4
OP technical assistance	20 (ERDF)	0.3
Community initiatives INTERREG and EQUAL	310 (ERDF + ESF)	4
+ national contribution to structural funds	2,864 (27.3 of total)	
Cohesion fund (additional investments in transport and environment)	3,733 + 661.5 of national contribution	

Source: Grosse (2007), Ministry of Regional Development, Poland.

An enormous inflow of EU funds between 2007 and 2013

In the new programming period from 2007 and 2013 Poland receives approximately EUR67 billion from the Structural Funds and the Cohesion Fund. In addition, Poland receives another EUR14 billion of financial resources from the European Union for rural development from EAFRD and FIGF for the restructuring of agricultural production under the reformed Common Agricultural Policy (CAP). Consequently, the financial allocation of EU funding for structural policies, and in particular policies of local and regional revitalization, amounts to EUR81 billion between 2007 and 2013. Moreover, apart from EU funding there is also a reasonable contribution provided by the so-called 'EEA and Norwegian Financial Mechanisms' 2004–9 (EUR553.5 million) and the 'Swiss–Polish Co-operation Programme' 2007–12 (CHF489 million).[17] Hence, it is estimated that the total allocation of financial resources for initiatives of local and regional development between 2007 and 2013 exceeds over EUR100 billion if one also takes into account the financial resources of co-financing from the national budget and private contributions. This brings about an additional increase in the importance of EU structural policies and EU regional development initiatives in Poland.

The financial contribution of the European Union provided by the Structural Funds, the Cohesion Fund and the EAFRD between 2007 and 2013 is considered to be the largest and most comprehensive development programme in the history of the country. Consequently, the Act on the National Development Plan which came into force in June 2004 further reinforced both the regionalization and the Europeanization of development planning in Poland. This document provided the legal basis for the preparation of the National Development Plan 2007–13 – later renamed *National Development Strategy 2007–15* – which constitutes the central and most important instrument of development planning in Poland today.[18] The strategy has a distinct spatial and regional focus, since the disparities between regions and developmental gaps in Poland are regarded as one of the central contemporary political challenges. Consequently, regional development policy is considered as one of the central means of solving the country's major development problems and future challenges.

The overall allocation of funds provided to Poland within the framework of the EU Cohesion Policy between 2007 and 2013 is outlined in Table 6.3. Apart from the marked increase of financial contributions, the most fundamental change in the allocation of financial resources between the former programming period 2004–6 and the new programming period 2007–13 is that there is no longer an Integrated Operational Programme (IROP) managed by the central government. In fact, for the first time in the short history of the Polish regions the voivodships have their own regional operational programmes (ROPs) in the new programming period, which are drafted, managed and implemented independently of the central government directly by the voivodships themselves. Another fundamental change is that the expenditures for the Cohesion Policy have to be focused more strictly on 'Lisbon goals' requiring a stronger emphasis on expenditures promoting information technology, the knowledge-based economy as well as research and development (see also Chapter 4 above).

However, as Table 6.3 also shows, by far the largest share of funds – more than 40 per cent of all financial resources provided by the EU Structural Funds and the Cohesion Fund between 2007 and 2013 – is allocated to the 'development' and 'modernization' of technical and transport infrastructure as well as measures of environmental protection (mainly promoting the establishment of new sewage systems, waste management systems and energy-efficient energy supplies). This is due to the fact that the former OP Transport and the financial contribution provided by the Cohesion Fund have been merged into one huge OP in the current programming period. Another remarkable change that was initiated in the new programming period was the establishment of the OP 'Development of Eastern Poland' – a programme that is specifically dedicated to the restructuring of eastern Poland in basic infrastructure and in economic terms. This programme was introduced because the eastern part of the country belongs to the least developed areas of the European Union. Thus, with the introduction of the new programming period, structural imbalances within Poland, which

Table 6.3 Implementation of EU Cohesion Policy in Poland 2007–13

	EU funding in EUR (billion)	Share of total SF+CF (%)
OP infrastructure and environment	27.9 (ERDF and CF)	41.5
OP innovative economy	8.25 (ERDF)	12.25
OP human capital	9.7 (ESF)	14.40
OP European territorial cooperation	0.69 (ERDF)	1.0
OP development of Eastern Poland	2.3 (ERDF)	3.4
OP technical assistance	0.5 (ERDF)	0.7
16 individual regional operational programmes	16.6 (ERDF)	24.65
Reserves	1.3	1.9
+ national contribution	approximately 17 (20 of total)	

Source: Ministry of Regional Development, Poland 2009.

were disregarded by Polish politics for so long, are being actively tackled. These structural imbalances and other patterns of spatial inequality will be depicted in the following sections in more detail.

4 Patterns of spatial inequality in Poland then and now

Although the initiatives of local an regional development arose during the 1990s, even more so in the past few years, and although there has been an increasing political awareness for the extraordinary spatial and regional inequalities in the territory of Poland, Poland has experienced an enormous spatial polarization of economic activities and socio-economic well-being over the past two decades (Kozak 2000; Błazyca *et al.* 2002; Gorzelak 2006). However, this is not a complete new phenomenon in Poland that has just emerged over recent years. In fact, it is an old and well-known problem in Poland's history and development discourse. It has just reinforced with the enforcement of the economic reform and the introduction of neo-liberal strategies of economic activation after the regime change.

Leading Polish geographers like Antoni Kuklinski (1981) or Grzegorz Gorzelak (2000) have pointed out that huge urban-rural divides and marked gaps in territorial development were always prevalent throughout the troublesome history of Poland. During the course of radical political and economic transformation after 1989, however, the historical urban-rural divisions were considerably reinforced. Moreover, there is one major structural imbalance in Poland which seems to constitute the most persistent and complex – and definitely the most discussed – territorial imbalance in Polish history: the structural gap between the western part of Poland which is traditionally more prosperous and more dynamic in economic terms and the area to the East of the Vistula river where subsistence agricultural production has been prevalent most of the time.[19] The West–East divide in socio-economic development is considered to be so strong that it is often seen in both public and academic discourses as a divide between 'Poland A' and 'Poland B'; and sometimes the areas which are directly located at the eastern border of the country are even regarded as 'Poland C' (cf. Błazyca *et al.* 2002; Gorzelak 2006). Thus, there is a strong spatial distinction between centre and periphery in the collective memory of the Polish people.

To some extent this historical West–East divide is still evident in structural data and key socio-economic statistics. It shows up in various socio-economic indicators as well as in depictions of the density of transport infrastructure (cf. Topolski 1997; Błazcka *et al.* 2002; Głebocki and Rogacki 2002). This is often associated with the long period of partition between 1795 and 1918, but it is also linked to more general socio-cultural patterns of economic development and waves of industrialization in Europe (cf. Zukowski 2004). The western part of contemporary Poland was more industrialized during the nineteenth century and witnessed higher degrees of urbanization and a slightly denser web of infrastructure of roads and train connections.[20] During communist times the road and train infrastructure was not systematically modernized, and in particular the rural population in the eastern part of the country was able to resist the socialization of agricultural production and to remain on low-productive subsistence agriculture. In this way, structures of *longue durée* still seem to have a huge impact on spatial development of contemporary Poland (Gorzelak 2006; Herbst 2007; Zarycki 2008).

In fact, since the beginning of regime change in Poland at the end of the 1980s the western territories have done better economically then the eastern parts: 'The historically higher developed regions display better adaptability to the competitive open economy. Their richer and more modern economic structure, better qualifications of the labour force, better equipment with high-quality institutional and material infrastructure make them more attractive to domestic and foreign investors.' (Gorzelak 2000: 136). On the other hand, it is evident that some of the country's major cities and larger agglomerations have been able to profit most from integration into the world economy. Indeed, the pre-eminent core of economic development is Warsaw (Warszawa), the Polish capital and the most important political and economic centre of the country. However, in contrast to other post-socialist countries in Central and Eastern Europe, the Polish economic territory is relatively polycentric and the capital city is not the only dynamic pole of economic growth. Apart from Warsaw there are other dynamic centres of development as well, and they are spread all over Poland, for example in the cities of Poznań, Wrocław and Gdańsk, in the first instance, followed by some slower developing cities such as Kraków in the south of Poland, and Szczecin, Gdańsk and Bydgoszcz in the north.

Certainly, these few major urban areas display the highest rates of economic output and growth as well as the largest concentration of investments and highly productive businesses. In many other areas of Poland, in turn – above all in the areas which are mainly shaped by agriculture and low levels of industrial production – the socio-economic situation is problematic (cf. Krasnodębski 2006; Tarkowska 2008). There are some stagnating areas in the northern and the eastern part of Poland with weaker capacities for future economic development, and at the same time relatively high levels of unemployment, poverty and outward migration of people of working age (Czerny and Czerny 2002). These are, above all, some rural areas in the northern and north-eastern part of Poland where agriculture was dominated by state administration for decades, and old industrial districts where socialist industries were closed down following structural changes during the 1990s. In these areas people have tended to move away to the few booming urban areas within the country or abroad – a trend has reinforced since EU accession in 2004 (see also: Mau and Büttner 2010: 542f.).

Last but not least, it must be noted as well that not all urban areas developed favourably during the process of transformation. Indeed, there are some larger cities and agglomerations with huge socio-economic problems due to difficulties in adapting their economic structures to the new conditions of post-industrial production and in restructuring the main sectors of the economy. Thus, the general trend of a growing urban–rural polarization in contemporary Poland is also accompanied by a sectoral divide between 'old-industrial' areas and new industrial districts and has been radically reinforced after 1989 with the introduction of the market economy. Since then it has been the dominant pattern of uneven spatial development (cf. Błazyca *et al.* 2002). During communist times the key industries used to be heavy industries like metal production, engineering and shipbuilding. These industries were privileged by the communist party and accordingly the prosperous regions at that time were regions where such activities were located. This fundamentally changed with the beginning of economic transformation in 1989. Areas and cities with favourable conditions for post-industrial production have experienced an upswing of economic dynamism and the situation in regions with less favourable conditions has become accordingly more complicated. These were, above all, the larger industrial agglomerations around Katowice in (Upper) Silesia, the former industrial engine of communist Poland, which were facing huge difficulties in restructuring the coal and steel sectors and dealing with corresponding environmental pressures (cf. Dornisch 2002); or the city of Lódz, the second largest Polish city by population famous for its tradition of textile production and for its film academy located at the centre of the country. Although other regions faced similar challenges, the consequences of radical economic transformation seemed to be the most severe in Upper Silesia in the early 1990s. This region contained almost all the country's heavy industries, 64 out of 66 deep coal mines and one of the two major steelworks – the second of which is located in Wałbrzych located in the southern part of Lower Silesia (Dolnośląskie). The restructuring of heavy industries was one of the most sensitive issues in the course of huge reforms during the 1990s, indeed. But there are also many examples of successful restructuring of heavy industries, such as the privatization of the copper mines around Lubin, which is also located in Lower Silesia and still constitutes one of the most important and potent companies of Poland these days.[21]

Differences in socio-economic performance amongst the 16 Polish voivodships

Once the newly created Polish voivodships were established a huge amount of statistical material has produced on the situation and the development of the newly created Polish regions over the past ten years. Hence, they have been the subject of massive scientific research and assessment, and they are assessed and ranked according to their socio-economic performance and future potential for economic development. The assessments and rankings of socio-economic development vary significantly depending on what kind of factors have been taken into account and included in the measurement. Indeed, the most common indicator of spatial disparities is the measurement of economic productivity per inhabitant measured in terms of GDP per capita. It is commonly used by economists, sociologists and geographers to measure the inequalities of economic productivity and developmental gaps amongst regions (cf. Barro and Sala-i-Martin 1992; Dunford 1996; Heidenreich 1998; Duro 2001; Martin 2001; Castro 2003; Heidenreich and Wunder 2008). And it is also used by the European Commission to determine the allocation of EU structural funds and to distinguish 'competitive areas' from so-called 'convergence areas' (formerly labelled as 'objective-1'-regions).

On the basis of the measurement of 'development' in terms of GDP per capita the territory of Poland – and most of the other new EU member states from Central and Eastern Europe – is regarded as 'lagging behind'.[22] Accordingly, we can see in the following overview of structural indicators of the 16 Polish voivodships that there is only one region which is above the 75 per cent threshold of the EU average; namely, the Voivodship of Mazowieckie where the booming capital city Warsaw is located. The rest of the regions are either equal to the national average (54 per cent of the EU average) or lower (see Table 6.4). Moreover, not surprisingly, it can be noted that the ranking of Polish regions according to levels of GDP per capita outlined in Table 6.4 largely reflects the general patterns of inequalities in the Polish territory that have been described just above. Almost all regions containing the biggest cities in Poland are at the top of Table 6.4 – they are regarded as the 'stronger' and 'more prosperous' areas of Poland. Furthermore, all regions that are located in the eastern part of Poland (to the East of the Vistula River) are among the five lowest ranking regions differentiated in Table 6.4 by the black line. Accordingly, Dolnośląskie, the western region of our sample, belongs to the group of Polish regions with the highest economic output; though still much lower than Mazowieckie. And, in fact, the two eastern regions that were selected for this case study occupy the lowest positions, with a GDP per capita of about 7,900 euros per capita (in PPS), amounting to about 35 per cent of the EU-27 average (as of 2005).

Table 6.4 also provides information on the economic structure of all 16 Polish voivodships and their basic employment and unemployment indicators, which gives an impression of the socio-economic situation in the three selected regions. As can be seen, Dolnośląskie has one of the lowest levels of agriculture and one of the highest levels of employment both in the service sector and in more traditional industries. In the two eastern regions this is exactly the other way round, with Lubelskie having the highest share of the working population in the agricultural sector and the lowest level of employment of all Polish regions. However, even though the productivity of the agricultural sector as such is relatively low, we can assume that it still constitutes a reasonable source of income and the major employment opportunity for a huge amount of people in these regions (Czerny and Czerny 2002). In fact, the hidden unemployment in the East of Poland is still considered to be substantial. It is estimated that the level of unemployment in Lubelskie and Podkarpackie would be much higher than official statistics indicate if all long-term unemployed people who carry out some sort of subsistence-farming also registered officially (Gorzelak 2006).

Conclusions

It was demonstrated in the preceding sections that there are huge disparities and structural imbalances in present-day Poland. The country is marked by distinct urban–rural divisions, a sectoral divide between degraded old-industrial areas and new post-industrial business locations and by a more general, more structural gap between the western and the eastern part of the country. Most of these disparities have a strong historical dimension reflecting long-lasting structural continuities. However, the historical geographical disparities have been reinforced significantly since the beginning of societal transformation in 1989. And despite – or maybe even because of – the huge efforts of *economic* revitalization at the local and regional level, the multitudinous establishment of special economic zones (SEZs), technology parks (TPs) and other initiatives of local and regional development over the past 15 years, spatial polarization has increased in recent times.

On the basis of this short depiction of major differences in socio-economic indicators amongst the 16 Polish voivodships, the major rationale of the selection of the three regions for the case study should have become clear conclusively: while Dolnośląskie belongs to the group of Polish regions with the best economic performance, the two eastern regions are the lowest ranking. Indeed, while Dolnośląskie is one of the most 'urbanized' regions with one of the highest population densities in Poland and the city of Wroclaw as one of the most vital economic centres in Poland, Lubelskie and Podkarpackie are the most 'agricultural' regions with relatively low population densities. These marked differences also show up in other indicators, such as levels of private income (in terms of average monthly gross wages), urbanization, population density, transport

Table 6.4 Main socio-economic indicators of all Polish voivodships, Poland and EU-27

	Economic productivity			Employment structure by sector (in % of total)*			Rates of employment and unemployment			
	GDP per capita (PPS) 2005	GDP per capita (PPS 2005, EU25=100)	GDP growth (annual average % change), 1995–2004*	Agriculture	Industry	Services	Total, 2006	Long-term unemployed (% of total unemployed), 2006	Youth unemployment (15–24 years), 2005*	Employment rate (as % of pop. aged 15–64), 2006
EU (27 Countries)	**22,400**	**100**	**2.3**	**6.2**	**27.7**	**66.1**	**8.2**	**45.8**	**18.8**	**64.3**
Polska	**10,532**	**54.0**	**4.3**	**17.4**	**29.2**	**53.4**	**13.9**	**56.3**	**36.9**	**54.3**
Mazowieckie (*Warszawa*)	18,184	81.2	6.2	15.9	21.7	62.4	12.3	52.0	31.9	58.8
Śląskie (*Kattowice aggl.*)	12,386	55.3	3.5	4.3	38.8	56.8	14.2	57.1	38.8	51.1
Wielkopolskie (*Poznań*)	12,278	54.8	5.9	16.5	34.8	48.8	12.7	62.6	34.9	55.2
Dolnośląskie (*Wrocław*)	**11,862**	**53.0**	**3.7**	**8.5**	**33.0**	**58.4**	**17.3**	**55.7**	**45.0**	**52.5**
Pomorskie (*Gdańsk*)	11,281	50.4	4.0	11.7	30.5	57.8	13.8	49.3	36.3	53.2
Zachodniopomorskie	10,660	47.6	2.8	10.2	28.2	61.7	17.2	55.4	41.7	49.4
Łódzkie (*Łódź*)	10,545	47.1	4.3	16.8	31.0	52.2	13.4	61.9	33.1	56.2
Lubuskie	10,357	46.2	3.5	11.4	31.9	56.7	14.0	36.4	35.3	52.7
Kujawsko-Pomorskie	10,013	44.7	3.2	17.2	32.4	50.5	16.2	64.3	39.1	51.2
Małopolskie (*Kraków*)	9,799	43.7	4.2	23.1	27.9	49.0	12.6	59.9	36.7	55.8
Opolskie	9,514	42.5	2.8	18.2	31.6	50.3	13.5	43.6	36.1	54.3
Warmińsko-Mazurskie	8,782	39.2	4.0	16.4	30.4	53.2	16.0	65.4	39.9	50.7
Świętokrzyskie	8,586	38.3	4.0	33.2	22.5	44.2	15.5	64.6	43.6	54.7
Podlaskie	8,501	37.9	3.9	34.4	20.7	44.9	11.3	53.8	30.6	57.0
Podkarpackie	**7,927**	**35.4**	**3.5**	**25.6**	**28.3**	**46.0**	**13.7**	**50.3**	**43.3**	**53.7**
Lubelskie	**7,839**	**35.0**	**2.7**	**35.9**	**19.3**	**44.8**	**12.8**	**50.4**	**30.3**	**56.9**

Source: Eurostat Database: General and Regional Indicators.

Notes

* Source: CEC (2007d).

The table shows major socio-economic indicators for all Polish voivodships at the time when the three regional cases were selected for the qualitative case study and the qualitative interviews were conducted, namely the first half of 2007. Over the meantime newer data and indicators are available, of course. The Eurostat Database, for instance, shows the levels of GDP/capita for the year 2008. Moreover, it also indicates employment and unemployment statistics of all EU regions (NUTS II) for the year 2009. These statistics reflect a slight increase of GDP-levels since 2005 and a marked decrease of unemployment levels in all Polish voivodships during the past four years. Yet the overall picture of a marked distinction between the eastern regions and economically better-off regions, such as Mazowieckie, Wielkopolskie and Dolnośląskie, has not changed much and has rather further intensified. (see: Eurostat Database. Online. Available at: http://epp.eurostat.ec.europa.eu/portal/page/portal/statistics/search_database (accessed March 2011).

infrastructure, accessibility and connectivity to larger economic centres, as well as the inflow of foreign direct investments (FDI) and so forth. Hence, the differences of living conditions between eastern and western Poland and the differences amongst the three selected regions are structural, and this structural gap has huge implications for the future prospects of these regions (see also Figure 6.2 below).[23] Against this backdrop it is interesting to explore on a comparative basis, how all three regions fit into the contemporary 'regional world' and in which way the available world-cultural definitions of the situation are adopted by each of the different regions?

However, the example of Dolnośląskie also strikingly shows that favourable economic development does not necessarily mean that employment levels will rise or that social problems would automatically disappear. Though Dolnośląskie is considered to be one of the most promising regions in Poland, not least due to the huge dynamism of Wrocław, its prospering capital city, it turns out that the new economic dynamics have failed to show up in employment statistics (at least until the beginning of 2007, since then it dropped substantially due to huge flows of out-migration). In fact, the official rate of unemployment in Dolnośląskie is one the highest in Poland (see Table 6.4). One must therefore be careful in drawing premature conclusions on the direct correlation between economic performance (measured in terms of GDP) and over 'development' or 'underdevelopment', 'prosperity' or 'poverty', and 'modernity' or 'backwardness' of the population in different geographical regions.

Moreover, every measurement or assessment of spatial inequalities or other regional characteristics is aggregated – it gives some information on the region and its population as a whole, but does not say anything about the 'real' dispersion of inequalities amongst the population. And every aggregated measurement of development at the regional level does not say anything about the developmental gaps and imbalances *within* the regions. Yet analyses on the county-level (NUTS-3) clearly reveal that while the economic performance in larger Polish cities such as Warsaw, Wrocław or Poznań is comparable to Western European cities, the hinterland of these cities is often largely characterized by low levels of economic productivity and agriculture, which is similar to the situation in eastern regions of Poland (cf. Gorzelak 2006).[24] Hence, there are different ways to apply the centre–periphery metaphor in geographic analyses. Each evaluation of centre–periphery distinctions always depends on the cognitive interests of the respective researchers and on what is regarded as the standard of development at a certain period of time. And therefore an exploration of the prevailing standards and the underlying constitutive assumptions, which is in the centre of this analysis, is indispensable.[25]

Thus, each region has its own characteristic internal disparities and imbalances which may or may not be considered to be development problems. Low levels of economic performance, low levels of population densities, or higher rates of unemployment are not problematic per se. They only become problematic against the backdrop of prevailing evaluative standards of success and failure, or notions of development and underdevelopment. This is an act of interpretation which must be explored more carefully and in greater depth by way of qualitative phenomenological analyses and cannot just be deduced from aggre-gated quantitative statistics. This is the major subject of the following chapter in which the self-presentation of the selected regions and expert assessments of the development situation and a status of the three selected regions are explored in more detail. This analysis will reveal prevailing (world-cultural) standards of development and underdevelopment with which the development of regions are generally assessed and examined in contemporary Europe.

Lubelskie (2008)	Podkarpackie (2008)	Dolnośląskie (2008)
Lubelskie is located in the eastern part of Poland next to the Mazowieckie Voivodship (which is home to Warsaw, Poland's booming capital) and north of Podkarpackie. Hence, Lubelskie lies at the external border of the European Union, sharing about 470 km of border with Belarus and Ukraine. It is one of the larger voivodships of Poland but is sparsely populated, showing one of the lowest population densities and a relatively low level of urbanization. The capital city Lublin is the region's most important urban area. It is also the largest city in eastern Poland.	Podkarpackie is located in the south-east of Poland bordering Slovakia in the south (about 140 km of border), and Ukraine in the east constituting 235 km of EU external border. Though the density of population is much higher than in the Lubelskie Voivodship, Podkarpackie is the least urbanized region of Poland. The largest city of the region is Rzeszów with 165,000 inhabitants. The southern part of the region is mainly shaped by the Carpathian Mountains with one of Poland's most attractive National Parks: the Bieszczady Mountains.	Dolnośląskie is located in the south-west of Poland, sharing a border with two other EU member states – Germany and the Czech Republic. It is one of the most populated and urbanized regions of Poland. The geo-economic structure of the region is quite diverse. It contains huge rural areas, mountains and natural reserves, but also larger industrial areas. Wrocław, the region's capital, is regarded as Poland's most vital growth pole of Poland these days, a dynamic centre with huge tourist attractiveness and highly productive and innovative industries.
Lubelskie is the 'poorest' region of Poland and one of the 'poorest' ten regions of the European Union (in terms of GDP/capita). The region is not very industrialized and still has a large agricultural sector (about 40 per cent of the working population work in agriculture, mainly on small farms). Though Lubelskie is relatively close to Warsaw, it is quite weakly connected with the Polish capital and other cities.	Podkarpackie is also amongst the 'poorest' regions both of Poland and the European Union (in terms of GDP/capita). It is quite remote from important economic centres and also relatively weakly connected in terms of railways and motorways. The most important economic sectors are agriculture and tourism. It also has a certain tradition of engineering, especially in the aviation industry.	Dolnośląskie is regarded as one of the up-and-coming regions of Poland with quite well-established connections to other economic centres, both domestic ones and international (esp. in east-west direction). It has become an attractive location for foreign direct investment and hosts different kinds of industries, both manufacturing industries and highly innovative businesses.
Surface: 25,114 km² (8% of total area of Poland) – about 60% of land area is agricultural; 22.7% forests – almost 25% of the total territory is legally protected: (2 National Parks and 17 Landscape Parks)	Surface: 17,844 km² (5.7% of total area of Poland) – about 40% of total area agricultural land; 36.9% forests – more than 40% of the territory is legally protected (2 National Parks and 11 Landscape Parks)	Surface: 19,948 km² (6.4% of total area of Poland) – about 50% of land area is agricultural, 29.5% forests – about 18% of the territory is legally protected (2 National Parks and 12 Landscape Parks)
Population (by end of 2007): 2,167,200 inhabitants – density: 87 persons per km² (national average: 122) – 46.6% living in urban areas and towns: – decline since 2000: approx. –40,000 (official)	Population (2007): 2,097,300 inhabitants – density: 118 persons per km² – 40.5% living in urban areas and towns – decline since 2000: approx. –4,000	Population (2007): 2,878,900 inhabitants – density: 145 persons per km² – 71% living in urban areas and towns – decline since 2000: approx. –33,000
Largest cities: Lublin (360,000 inhabitants); Chełm (71,000); Zamość (68,000); Biała Podlaska (58,000); Puławy (55,000); Świdnik (40,000).	Largest cities: Rzeszów (165,000); Przemyśi (70,000); Stalowa Wola (70,000); Mielec (65,000); Tarnobrzeg (51,000); Krosno (50,000).	Largest cities: Wrocław (635,000); Wałbrzych (126,000); Legnica (106,000); Jelenia Góra (87,000); Lubin (76,000); Głogów (68,000); Świdnica (60,000)
GDP per capita (in PPS) 2005: EUR7,839 (35% of EU27)	GDP per capita (in PPS) 2005: EUR7,927 (35% of EU-27)	GDP per capita (in PPS) 2005: EUR11,862 (53% of EU27)
Avr. monthly gross wage (2004): 2,290 PLN (87%/PL av.)	Avr. monthly gross wage (2004): PLN 2,180 (83%/PL av.)	Avr. monthly gross wage (2004): PLN 2,617 (99%/PL av.)

Figure 6.2 Major characteristics of the three selected Polish regions (2008).

7 The world-cultural make-up of Polish regions

Introduction

This chapter exhibits key assessments of both major developmental problems and opportunities of the three selected regions and shows how regions are reconceptualized under contemporary world-polity conditions. This provides us with more in-depth insights and much more detailed information on the current situations in *each* of the three selected regions than the previous sketch of aggregated data in Table 6.4 above. In addition to that, the subsequent sections inform us much deeper about major internal development challenges, and outline what aspects and characteristics of the various regions are considered as favourable or problematic by official authorities, policy-makers and professionals in the field of regional development. Against the backdrop of the information on the marked structural differences between the Western and Eastern regions provided thus far, we can assume that prevailing (world-cultural) assessments directly affect regional identity-formation in the newly created regions. Yet the question is *how* world-cultural standards affect the identity-formation of regions and *what kind of* interpretative frames and expectations are most significant and relevant in this regard.

Hence, the following analysis provides an overview of most common and prevailing 'world-cultural' assessments and interpretations of development and underdevelopment in a comparative way and shows how this affects identity-formation in the three selected regions. The analysis starts with a short comparative overview and summary of the most common and widespread expert assessments of major 'weaknesses' and 'strengths' of the three selected regions as outlined in expert evaluations, official publications and reports from other 'authoritative' sources. This gives us a relatively detailed impression of the major problems and opportunities of development in the three selected regions against the backdrop of prevailing evaluative standards of 'good' and 'favourable' regional development in contemporary times. The data derive from official SWOT-analyses; thus, official assessments of strengths, weakness, opportunities and threats of the regions – a standard practice of strategic development planning (see Chapter 5). It is argued here that these kinds of evaluations have a direct effect on the self-conception of regions, or rather of regional actors, and thus directly affect the constitution of regional actor-identities (1). Further on, we will have a look at how the three regions are presented to the outside world on official websites. This gives us an impression of the regions' self-presentation and 'impression-management' (Goffman) against the backdrop of prevailing evaluative standards of regional development (2). Finally, 'local' and 'subject-ive' expert assessments and evaluative statements on the current situation in each of the three regions are outlined in more detail. This discussion is based on a comparative analysis of qualitative interviews with experts, practitioners and state officials, which were conducted during a field study between April and July 2007 (3). Thus, each of the following sections increasingly adds more qualitative insights on each of the three regions, starting from relatively general world-cultural evaluations of problems and opportunities and ending in a comparative depiction of local insider opinions. By the end of this chapter we should have a relatively 'dense' picture of each of the three regions and be able to see to what extent sub-national territories are fundamentally shaped by common assumptions and conceptions of 'development' and 'underdevelopment'.

1 'Strengths' and 'weaknesses' of the three selected regions

The following depiction of the prevailing assessments of development problems and opportunities in the three selected regions is based on the analysis of pub-licly available material. These assessments are 'world-cultural' in the literal sense in that they mainly derive from expert assessments and expert circles and provide relatively authoritative interpretations of the situation in the respective regions. The data derives from the following sources: first, a scientific analysis of all Polish regions undertaken in 2006 by experts from the EUROREG Insti-tute (Gorzelak *et al.* 2006), one of the major university-based, but independent, institutes in Poland which particularly focuses on spatial development; second, presentations of the major characteristics of the three regions outlined in an offi-cial brochure published by the Polish Ministry of Regional Development in 2007 (Polish Ministry of Regional Development 2007a, 2007b, 2007c); and, third, a short description of regional assets provided by the Polish Information and Foreign Investment Agency (PAIiIZ) in autumn 2008.[1] In addition, the SWOT analyses and socio-economic diagnoses published in the official development strategies of the regions were also examined for this analysis. Since all the aspects outlined in all these various documents and data sources are so over-whelmingly detailed, only major characteristics and interpretations were taken up and integrated into Figure 7.1.

Not surprisingly, this comparative overview of the major world-cultural assessments of the developmental problems and opportunities of the three selected regions mirrors the major structural divergences in contemporary Polish territory which were briefly described in the previous chapter. Accord-ingly, the two eastern regions have a relatively low rating concerning their current developmental situation and their potential for favourable development in the future. Both regions are alleged to have a variety of serious shortcom-ings, such as huge infrastructural problems ranging from poorly developed

Assessment of Lubelskie (2008)	Assessment of Podkarpackie (2008)	Assessment of Dolnośląskie (2008)
Development problems:	Development problems:	Development problems:
– highly underdeveloped and outdated infrastructure	– highly underdeveloped and outdated infrastructure	– good road connection to the west, less with Polish cities
– almost no connection to major transport routes	– weak connection to major transport routes	– low level of national and international air connections
– unfavourable border location (esp. with Belarus)	– most south-easterly and least urbanized Polish region	– high urban–rural divide, low level of education in rural areas
– low level of industrialization, ineffective agriculture	– low level of economic development, ineffective agriculture	– still relatively low level of services compared to EU
– low level of competitiveness of the regional economy	– low level of innovativeness, weak SME development	– still low level of R&D (compared to EU)
– lowest investment rate of the country	– low investment rate, still weak preparation for investments	– outlays in R&D lower than national average
– high level of out-migration (esp. younger people)	– high level of out-migration (esp. younger people)	– declining population and high emigration from rural areas
– high share of non-working population/ unskilled farmers	– high level (hidden) unemployment (esp. rural population)	– good economic prospects, but still huge unemployment
– prevalence of poverty and rising risks of social exclusion	– prevalence of poverty/ lowest average income in Poland	– growing number of elderly people requiring social services
– low level of social services and environmental policies	– low level of sport and recreation facilities	– drastic social problems + pollution in old-industrial areas
– weak/ low metropolitan function of Lublin	– weak/ low metropolitan function of Rzeszów	– foreign investments concentrated mainly around Wrocław
– poor development of areas with high tourist attractiveness	– poor development of areas with high tourist attractiveness (Slovakia, Ukraine)	– poor conditions of many historical buildings/ attractions
– serious deterioration of historical buildings	– small level of trans-border cooperation (Slovakia, Ukraine)	– lack of investment in social infrastructure (esp. health)
Development opportunities:	Development opportunities:	Development opportunities:
+ favourable conditions for agriculture (esp. eco-farming):	+ long tradition of engineering (esp. aviation industries)	+ great potential for dynamic (business) development:
• production of high-quality food (esp. fruits)	→ most important location for aviation in Poland	• diverse multi-sectoral economy
• renewable energy (esp. bio-mass/ bio-fuel)	+ rich mining deposits and minerals (also: mineral waters)	• high investment outlays + entrepreneurship
+ high potential for tourism (culture-, agro-, eco-tourism)	+ good development of Special Economic Zone (Mielec)	• huge academic and R&D potential
• one of the ecologically cleanest regions in Poland	+ great potential for tourism and recreation businesses	• Wrocław an outstanding metropolitan area
• rich and diverse cultural heritage/ history	• one of ecologically cleanest regions in PL	• motorways/ high railway and road density
• various spas and health resorts	• rich cultural heritage and potential for tourism	• rich mining deposits and mineral resources
+ growing potential of certain scientific research centres: agriculture, environmental protection, biotechnology etc.	• great tourist attractions (nature), many spas	• border location and good cooperation
+ relatively young population – huge educational potential and low labour costs	• Carpathian mountains and Bieszczady natural resort	• congress-, spa-, cultural-, & eco-tourism
	+ relatively young population and low labour costs	+ Strong cultural heritage: huge diversity and open culture
Sources: Polish Ministry of Regional Development 2007b, PAIiIZ, Gorzelak et al. 2006	Sources: Polish Ministry of Regional Development 2007c, PAIiIZ, Gorzelak et al. 2006	Source: Polish Ministry of Regional Development 2007a, PAIiIZ, Gorzelak et al. 2006

Figure 7.1 Official assessments of 'weaknesses' and 'strengths' of the three selected regions (2008).

roads and other major transport connections (i.e. no motorways and very poor railway connections) to weak and problematic economic structures, not to mention endemic social problems. The assessments of the development opportunities of Dolnośląskie are, in contrast, strikingly positive and optimistic. Nonetheless, the overview also indicates a number of developmental problems and shortcomings in this voivodship as well. Hence, the expert assessments show that in one way or the other all three regions have their own internal problems which are in need of 'resolution'.

Indeed the overview of common expert assessments of problems and opportunities of the three selected Polish regions in Figure 7.1 also provides a good summary of the most common and contemporary evaluative standards of 'good' regional development. For example, a 'dense', 'comprehensive' and 'up-to-date' provision of *transport infrastructure*, as well as other types of *modern technical infrastructure*, is regarded as a fundamental requirement of favourable regional development. The same applies to the basic economic structure of the respective regions. In turn, the prevalence of a 'largely out-dated' infrastructure and an 'ineffective' or 'unproductive' agricultural sector is generally seen as a clear obstacle to development in the eastern regions, accordingly. Moreover, apart from the overall economic structure, the opportunities and competitiveness of a region are mainly measured by the amount of *(foreign) investments*, the availability of 'young' and 'skilled' workers – so-called *human resources* – and the *existence of larger urban agglomerations* – so-called 'metropolitan lighthouses' – which have the ability to concentrate financial, human, and cultural capital. These are favourable for development and function as the 'developmental core' and 'engines' of a region.

Against this backdrop, in turn, the 'still relatively high level of unskilled agricultural workers', 'low rate of urbanization' and 'low level of industrialization' in the two eastern regions are clearly seen as indisputable deficiencies. Beyond that, the peculiar *geographic location* of the regions is also perceived as an 'unfavourable precondition for development', since international cooperation with people of Belarus and Ukraine will supposedly not act as a significant stimulator of future development of the two eastern regions – at least not as much as cross-border exchanges in the western areas of the country. Moreover, apart from listing purely economic factors, the reports also assert that the eastern regions suffer from 'rising risks of poverty and social exclusion'. Relatively 'high levels of (hidden) unemployment' and 'low standards of living in the rural areas' are identified, in particular, as major development challenges in the two eastern regions.

On the other hand, as we can also see in the three boxes of Figure 7.1, some of the alleged burdens of development are rated positively as well, and they are reinterpreted as assets for prospective future development. In fact, the extraordinarily low degree of urbanization and industrialization in the two eastern regions means that they are amongst the 'least polluted' and 'ecologically least devastated' regions in Poland and the whole European Union. This is put forward and turned into favourable conditions for the *development of tourism* and *ecological agricultural production* in official expert assessments and publications. Even the remaining *folk traditions* and the existing *historical heritage* of the regions are put forward as favourable conditions for future development; especially with respect to the potential of tourism development. Moreover, the world-cultural assessments also suggest some new sources of economic value-creation under post-industrial conditions. In Lubelskie these include the *expansion of the existing food industry* and the *development of 'modern' agro-businesses*, such as the expansion of ecological farming, biotechnology, and technologies of environmental protection. In Podkarpackie they include the *development of cultural and ecological tourism* as well as the *expansion of engineering industries and engineering sciences*, especially the aviation industry which has a long tradition in this area and thus constitutes a real characteristic of this region, indeed.

These are the major directions which are suggested by numerous expert evaluations and assessments for the future of regions in eastern Poland. However, according to the expert assessments, the development of these aforementioned sectors and areas would strongly depend on future efforts on the part of the regional authorities to develop these areas. As we can also see in the diagnoses of problems in the two eastern regions, the touristic attractiveness of the regions is still considered to be relatively low for much of the regions' infrastructure and potential tourist spots (historical buildings, spas, hiking trails etc.) are still relatively run-down and in need for refurbishment. Moreover, policies and measures on environmental protection have also been criticized as being insufficient (cf. Gorzelak *et al.* 2006).

In marked contrast to the world-cultural evaluations of the two eastern regions discussed above, the expert assessments of Dolnośląskie suggest that the region seems to offer all the ingredients necessary for successful regional development: not only a 'huge potential' for the development of 'multi-faceted innovative businesses' and 'tourism', but also a 'diverse' and 'multi-sectoral economy' that would offer assets for the development of both more traditional industries, such as mining, as well as manufacturing industries. In this context, the role of Wrocław as the 'development engine' of the region is also highlighted as a crucial element for future wealth in the region. It is regarded as the 'outstanding metropolitan centre' of the region, offering a 'wide range of research institutes' and 'qualified human resources'. However, the official expert assessments also point out the existing problems of the region: a 'marked urban-rural divide', 'huge social and environmental problems in old-industrial areas', 'many old buildings in need of refurbishment', and still 'weak transport connections with other Polish centres'. Moreover, the socio-economic diagnosis outlined in the official development strategy of Dolnośląskie even highlights 'alcoholism' and 'drug addiction' as a particular challenge to regional policy-makers, and also mentions the problem of 'out-migration' and 'population ageing'. Thus, given the overall favourable and promising position of the region, the diagnosis of problems in official documents seems extraordinarily relentless. However, there are deficiencies in all regions. And it is suggested by the reports that there is always a reason to improve and do better, even in regions with relatively favourable economic conditions. Moreover, this also shows that every diagnosis of problems is always based on certain standards and points of view (cf. The 2020 Development Strategy for the Lower Silesia Province, p. 7ff.).

After this short review of the major world-cultural interpretations of problems and opportunities concerning development in the three selected regions, it should be clear that expert assessments directly contribute to the mobilization of efforts to overcome the identified shortcomings. The regions are carefully analyzed and some of the standard recipes of economic mobilization and value-creation are proposed on the basis of this assessment. In this sense, expert assessments can execute a strong force of social mobilization. As long as experts 'reveal' the problems and challenges of development, and as long as resources or assets for favourable future development are identified, efforts of active intervention and improving society are mobilized (cf. Meyer *et al.* 1997: 170ff.). – In the following section we will explore how regions present themselves to the outside world. This gives us a first impression of how regions are reconfigured and presented as 'modern' and 'up-to-date' areas where it is worth travelling to and investing money. It also shows in what way the assessments and interpretations that were just presented play a role in regional development practice.

2 The world-cultural self-presentations of the regions

If one wants to study and comprehend the world-cultural reconfiguration of European regions an analysis of the official websites of these regions can be quite telling, indeed. All professional organizations and governmental bodies, and ever more increasingly modern individuals as well, present themselves to the outside world through official internet domains. These days there is almost no 'modern' or 'professional' social entity without an individual web-presentation. This also applies to regions, cities and smaller municipalities all across Europe and to the three Polish regions which are examined here as well.[2] A short query with any usual search engine and a brief look at the respective websites of the three regions provides a huge amount of information on the current social, economic and political structure of the regions in just a few seconds. There is so much and it is so overwhelming that it is difficult to comprehend and digest all at once.

There are, for instance, links to the various governmental bodies, to important facts and figures on the regions, and to the most important events that are planned to take place within the regions throughout the year. Moreover, there are links to the most important economic institutions that might be relevant for potential investors, and there are links to cultural institutions, to various non-governmental bodies and other social institutions. A visitor to the websites is also informed about important tourist spots. One can download all the information that is relevant and helpful for an actual visit. Thus, in short, the websites of the regions contain all the relevant data that are standard and obligatory in most contemporary public relations management of regional authorities.

What is striking from the very first glance at the main pages of the web portals of three Polish regions, indeed, is the availability of numerous buttons, banners and links to issues that represent 'world culture' in classical and most typical sense. There are banners and labels of international certifying institutes, such as ISO 9001 quality certificates, as well as web-links referring to the regional umbrella organizations of eco-farming, tourism organizations and to the major regional innovation centres, business incubators and research institutes. The three regions have also put direct links to their official development strategies – sometimes even available in English. And there are various buttons and links that directly refer to available EU funds, EU funding guidelines, and managing authorities of particular EU programmes where potential beneficiaries can apply for receiving support from the EU structural funds in one way or the way.

If one starts to browse through the web portals, one can furthermore also find short presentations and short descriptions of the regions in English and some other languages. These short descriptions are directed at potential tourists, potential investors and all other people who are interested in the region in question and would like to get more information. Certainly, these short presentations are mainly of a promotional character, aimed at creating a positive image of the regions. Nonetheless, for an exploration of the prevailing standards of regional development, they are quite informative and telling. In loose reference to Ervin Goffman's theory of dramaturgical action and the performance of self in everyday interactive processes (Goffman 1959 and 1967), we can interpret these short promotional self-presentations of the regions as a central element of the 'impression management' of the regions – as the presentation of the regions' 'self' and 'identity' under world-cultural conditions. Although the websites – and, in particular, the short descriptions of the regions – are mainly promotional, the regions cannot simply invent something which is not true. In one way or the other the 'impression management' of the regions must be based on some sort of substance, otherwise their credibility would be undermined. However, more than ever before, modern actors are being forced to present themselves as individual and unique. Therefore we can expect all regions to vigorously try to 'stage-manage' their uniqueness and particular identity, presenting themselves both as modern and distinctive social entities. In fact, these texts can be read as a vital part of the enactment of modern world-cultural actorhood (cf. Meyer and Jepperson 2000). In explicit reference to Goffman, John Meyer and his colleagues even consider the symbolic dimension of modern and professional actorhood as the central and most important dimension of 'world-cultural diffusion' (cf. Meyer *et al.* 1997: 150f.).

Yet, when the self-descriptions of the three selected regions are looked at and analysed in comparison to one another, differences in the style and attitude of the presentations become apparent. Thus, different structural conditions of development between western and eastern Poland are also visible in the way the regions present themselves to the outside world. We can observe marked differences in the regions' confidence in their perceived 'strengths' and 'assets' they present to the outside world. In fact, the presentation of Dolnośląskie's position and future prospect is vigorous and highly confident. The difficult 'peripheral' location of the two eastern regions, in turn, is also mentioned in the self-presentations. Nonetheless, they mainly try to promote themselves in a positive way, i.e. as attractive tourist destinations with 'unique cultural heritage' and 'beautiful landscapes'.

Lubelskie – a 'beautiful' and 'exotic' cultural region in Europe's East

The difficulties and ambiguities faced by the regions in eastern Poland in putting a positive spin on their unfavourable geographical position already becomes apparent in the very first sentence of the English self-description of the Lubel-skie Voivodship. On the one hand, the region presents itself as a region that is located in the 'centre of Europe', and at the same time it also highlights its par-ticular historical and geographic 'peripherity'. This peculiar simultaneity of being both 'centre' and 'periphery' at the same time is presented as an old his-torical fact that accounts for the uniqueness and for the particular traditional cul-tural richness of the region:

> There is a beautiful and exotic region in Europe, right in the centre of the continent, and at the same time on its periphery. This is the Lublin Region, an area for centuries at the cultural cross-roads of East and West, combining traditions of Catholicism, Orthodoxy, Judaism, as well much more oriental ones: Greek, Armenian, Tartar (…).[3]

This kind of self-description is idiomatic for all areas and regions which are con-sidered to be located in Central *and* Eastern Europe, since the ambiguity between the centre and the periphery is already inherent to the notion of 'Central and Eastern Europe' in general. Presenting itself as 'exotic' due to its particular geo-graphical position, historical experience and historical location 'at the cultural cross-roads of east and west' is therefore an interesting rhetoric twist. Moreover, in light of the discussion on contemporary world-cultural standards and frames of regional development it is even more intriguing that Lubelskie puts forward its multi-ethnic and multi-religious past with such vigour. 'The Lublin Province, already 530 years old, is a region of clean, unpolluted nature (protected in two national parks and 17 landscape parks), vivid country traditions and crafts, as well as magnificent monuments of the past not to be found elsewhere.'[4]

As pointed out in the previous chapter, it is a historical fact that the territory of contemporary Lubelskie used to be highly multi-ethnic and multi-religious in former times. It was located at the border of Christianity and Orthodoxy. More-over, during the so-called 'Lublin–Lithuanian Union' (Unia Lubelska) between 1569 and 1791, the former Kingdom of Poland used to be one of the most open and most liberal states in Europe. Therefore, many ethnic minorities that were persecuted and excluded in other countries were allowed to settle in Poland (cf. Davies 1981a). Consequently, until the beginning of Nazi-German Occupation in 1939 various religious groups and ethnicities had been present in the area around Lublin; in fact, the Jewish community even constituted half of the population in cities like Lublin and in many other places in Poland. After the end of the Nazi occupation in 1945, however, the multi-ethnic and multi-religious tradition of Poland and Lubelskie in particular was destroyed. Almost no Jewish people and communities were left and the subsequent communist government of Poland continued with the strategy of 'ethnic cleansing' and 'ethnic homogenization' – though in a more subtle way than the unprecedentedly cruel Nazi German occupiers did before. Yet, since the 1960s, Poland has been (and still is) one of the most ethnically homogenous countries in Europe. To this day, more than 95 per cent of the population of Poland is both Polish and Catholic (Therborn 1995).

Given this background information it is intriguing, indeed, to see that contemporary Lubelskie has started to re-discover and revive its multi-ethnic past and explicitly refers to its former multi-cultural traits which ceased to exist decades ago. Beyond this, the new emphasis on Lubelskie's local and regional traditions is accompanied by a general increase in emphasis of local and regional cultures and traditions in general, especially in official rhetorics and policy programmes – not least those promoted by European funds (see Buzalka 2007: 133ff.). In Western conceptions of successful social integration, 'multiculturalism' is today commonly considered as an asset for favourable development rather than a burden. This definitely distinguishes the 'excessive nationalism' that was prevalent in Europe during the first half of the twentieth century from the era of reconciliation and international cooperation that began after the Second World War in Western Europe. In Poland, however, these particularly 'Western' conceptions and models of 'multi-culturalism' only began to diffuse into the country after the fall of communism in 1990, as the country underwent a period of world-cultural transformation (cf. Buzalka 2007). These new world-cultural conditions have brought about new self-conceptions and self-interpretations of regional histories during the process of region-building.

Thus, it must be noted that – as in other regions and cities all over the world – the revival of the multi-ethnic and multi-cultural past has been discovered as an important resource of regional mobilization and a catalyst of international tourism within the newly created Polish regions. In the absence of strong industries and other resources that could be used for economic mobilization, the Lubelskie Voivodship explicitly intends to promote tourism. Hence, the extraordinary cultural and natural 'heritage' of the region is explicitly highlighted as the second big asset of the region, and the short self-description of the Lubelskie Voivodship ends with a detailed listing of various extraordinary tourist attractions in the region, such as the city of Zamość, a well-preserved and newly refurbished Renaissance settlement that can also be found on the list of UNESCO World heritage sites, the city of Lublin, and many other unique places and centres of recreation all over the region. This also shows in which way the institutional imperative of preserving traditional cultures, historical buildings, and natural landscapes, that is impelled nowadays by authoritative international political actors such as UNESCO, the EU and other international agencies, constitutes an important basis for regional development in contemporary eastern Poland.

Podkarpackie – a region of high 'cultural' and 'natural' quality

The English version of the self-description of Podkarpackie starts with an equally ambivalent reference to its particular geographic location in the most south-eastern area of Poland, and also enthusiastically points out the rich cultural and natural assets of the country:

> The Podkarpackie Province is worth paying attention to, because although it is the most south eastern region of Poland, it has a very rich offer for anyone who may wish to come here. Natural and cultural qualities make it immensely attractive for tourists. The Podkarpackie region already has excellent tourist infrastructure, ready to meet even the highest expectations, but we assure you, it is only the beginning of future things to come, which will surprise all our guests surely and positively (...).
>
> Centuries-old frontier of culture has left many valuable remains, like the material culture relics, both laic and sacral, also immaterial culture relics, apparent in preserved traditions and customs of the ethnic groups, which lived here before and do live here now. What is more, the Podkarpackie nature will amaze many lovers of the natural world, and its diversity might cause vertigo![5]

This quote again mainly highlights the touristic value of regional traditions and nature. And, indeed, the Podkarpackie Voivodship has a huge potential for hiking and other types of nature tourism. It is in fact one of the least populated and least industrialized areas in Poland with a high rate of legally protected natural landscape (40 per cent of the whole territory) mainly in the Carpathian Mountains in the southern part of the country.[6] The mountain areas are increasingly mobilized as attractive tourist spots. This has led to the development of hiking paths and other types of basic tourist infrastructures, as well as the popular revival of some archaic ethnic traditions which have been preserved in some villages (cf. Buzalka 2007: 185ff.).

Hence, the revival of old cultural traditions and the exploitation of the region's most exciting landscapes are motivated by market-based notions, namely by the need to open up new sources of income. However, we should note that the world-cultural reinvention of regions is multi-dimensional and not solely limited to the economic realm. As for instance, Laurent Thevènot (2002) and others have convincingly shown in an ethnographic study on development projects in the French Pyrenees, objects of development are not confined to one particular 'order of worth' (see also: Boltanski and Thevènot 1991; Lamont and Thevènot 2000). Hence, the strong efforts to preserve and promote regional cultures and the regional countryside that we find in the newly created regions should not only be considered to be motivated by market-based or efficiency-based rationales. They can also be motivated and supported by strong communitarian efforts or a commitment to preserving the cultural and natural heritage of a certain region ('green worth'). But one thing is sure: in a region which is increasingly mobilized around highly generalized and rationalized (world-cultural) claims of progress and future development, development policies can no longer be justified solely on the basis of distinctly local, or rather 'parochial', sentiments. Accordingly, as the following quote taken from the same text as the above excerpt shows, the development of Polish regions is mainly justified in highly modernist progress- and future-oriented terms:

> It is doubtless that our province has multiqualified staff, ready to undertake challenges in all areas of social and economic life. Huge potential of young people, studying and gaining experience in the Podkarpackie universities is the great chance for the region to further develop and fight the growing competition. One might say that after Poland joined the European Union, our province took the responsibility of maintaining contact with our partners from Ukraine and helping our Eastern neighbour in joining the EU structure. We are involved, because we are determined to develop our province and improve the quality of local life. We are pro-social, and we express our love of fighting the problems of everyday life in many non-governmental organizations. We are open for any good idea, which might help our little Homeland and us. We are simply gnarly![7]

Dolnośląskie – one of Poland's 'fastest developing' regions

The self-description of Dolnośląskie is markedly different from the presentations of the two eastern regions in style and attitude. It starts with the following headline: 'According to analysts worldwide, Lower Silesia ranks among Poland's fastest-developing regions.'[8] The text continues with a detailed listing of all strengths and assets of the region ranging from its particular border position, the favourable structure and conditions of its regional economy, especially with regard to the huge future development potential. Subsequently, the text continues with an enthusiastic reference to the centrepiece of the region's development, the city of Wrocław. This is the capital of the region and by far the most metropolitan and most dynamic centre of the whole area:

> Wrocław, the capital of Lower Silesia, is considered by EU spatial planning institutions as one of the most significant centres of development and innovation in the nascent new European space. The prospect of Poland's integration with the European Union makes the region all the more economically attractive, a good testimony to which are numerous investments made in the region by renowned international companies.

> (ibid.)

Most interestingly, the self-description continues with a positive reference to the strongly ambiguous history of the area where the region is located. Above all, the region's location on the border and its chequered political history is highlighted and framed in a positive way. Although – or perhaps because – Dolnośląskie was often annexed to different states and ruled by different empires over the past centuries, the region itself is presented as a shelter of continuity and wealth: 'For the most part of its history Lower Silesia was a frontier land, and at the same time one of the richest regions of whichever country it happened to belong to' (ibid.). Moreover, though the area of contemporary Dolnośląskie was one of the regions in Europe that was most dramatically affected by World War II and by the negative consequences of detached and arbitrary elite politics, the particular historical experience of the region is now presented and re-framed as one of its major assets. In fact, right after 1945 a huge part of the region's population was simply exchanged due to the overall westward territorial shift of the Polish state. The Polish speaking population of contemporary western Ukraine was mainly resettled to Wrocław and the German-speaking inhabitants were expelled. Thus, since a reasonable part of the population is constituted by 'newcomers' and 'outsiders', the region is presented as an 'enterprising' community, a 'melting pot' of various nations with open-minded people and attitudes. This is seen as a clear asset and a resource for innovative economic development:

> For the past 50 years, Lower Silesians have been perceived as an exceptional 'melting pot' of different nations, whose mixing led to the creation of a completely new culture. This is due to the fact that the region was settled between 1945 and 1947 by completely new inhabitants. Immigrants came to Lower Silesia from different regions of pre-war Poland, mostly from its eastern territories, which after the new political division of Europe after World War II became part of the Soviet Union (nowadays Lithuania, Belarus and Ukraine). Thus, the present-day Lower Silesians form a relatively young, well-educated, open and enterprising community.
>
> (ibid.)

Furthermore, the assets and the current development level of the region are presented using the highest and most emphatic superlatives. It is vigorously pointed out that

> In terms of economy, the Lower Silesia Province is one of Poland's best developed regions. (...) Lower Silesian Province is among Poland's leading regions in terms of the number of companies with foreign capital and the amount of the foreign capital invested.
>
> (ibid.)

And reference is made to the extraordinarily favourable social and institutional underpinnings of the regional economy which are considered as crucial conditions for the favourable economic development in contemporary theories of economic mobilization (cf. Chapter 5): 'The dynamic development of the Lower Silesian economy is accompanied by an ever faster development of institutions fostering entrepreneurship, companies providing services for businesses and government and non-governmental business agencies and organizations' (ibid.). Finally, the authors of the region's self-presentation do not forget to highlight its potential for agricultural production. And the huge tourist attractiveness based on extraordinary diversity both in terms of its rich cultural heritage and nature:

> Although not a typical agricultural area, Lower Silesia has a climate condu- cive [to] farming. (…) The Sudeten and their foothills, the Kłodzko Valley, numerous castles, Cistercian monasteries, historical churches, many places of worship, spas, relics of technology, Gothic and Baroque treasures of Wrocław and other Lower Silesian towns are a real magnet for both Polish and foreign tourists; it is estimated that Lower Silesia hosts an average 4 million tourists a year. The diversity of the region's relief (ranging from mountainous areas in the south to lowland, densely forested areas with plenty of ponds in the north), numerous tourist trails, picturesque land- scapes, historical treasures and the climate make Lower Silesia a place where even the most demanding tastes will be satisfied.
>
> (ibid.)

So much for the depiction and comparison of self-presentations of the three regions. In the next and final section of this chapter we will focus in more detail on the prevailing interpretations and evaluative statements of practitioners and experts from the three regions with regard to the current developmental status of those regions. This discussion complements the above depiction of the broader and more general assessments 'strengths' and 'weaknesses' of the three regions. These interpretations are certainly more subjective and local than those state- ments given in official reports and external assessments. Nevertheless, we will see that they mostly reflect prevailing world-cultural interpretations of 'develop- ment' and 'backwardness'.

3 Reasons for concern and future optimism: assessments of local experts

The subsequent depiction of local assessments and interpretations of the devel- opment situation and opportunities of the respective regions is based on a comparative analysis of qualitative interviews with experts and practitioners who are directly involved in regional development in Poland. More precisely, these are public officials employed in Poland's Ministry of Regional Develop- ment, regional authorities dealing with regional development as well as repre- sentatives of regional development agencies (RDAs) and other non-governmental actors from the three selected regions. This comparative analysis of interview statements exhibits a double function: On the one hand, it provides insider information and 'local' interpretations of the current situation in the three selected regions. On the other hand, all experts are part of a larger process of social mobilization which is explored here in more detail. The statements show relatively common expert interpretations of development and underdevelopment.

An in this sense they are more than just 'local' assessments, but represent interpretations which is quite common and widespread in contemporary modernity, both in expert circles and in everyday life.

In principle, more or less the same amount and types of 'experts' were interviewed in each region, and all interviewees were asked the same core questions of how they see and evaluate the development situation in their region. In this way, the various statements of the interviews with experts from different regions could be compared and analyzed in relation to one another.[9] This comparison reveals a clear difference in the way regional experts talked about the development of their respective region, in particular between Dolnośląskie and the two eastern regions of Lubelskie and Podkarpackie. Therefore, the following portrayal of expert assessments and interpretations is structured along the line of this East–West imbalance. It starts with a depiction of predominant interpretations of the 'backwardness' in eastern Poland, and moves on to the characterization of the particular optimism and confidence expressed by interviewees and policy-makers in Dolnośląskie. However, we will see that dominant interpretative patterns mainly used to describe 'eastern backwardness' are also used to describe internal problems and structural imbalances within Dolnośląskie. Thus, the predominant characteristics of the 'eastern backwardness' represent more general interpretative patterns of backwardness which are not necessarily limited to eastern Poland.

Local interpretations of 'eastern backwardness'

'Far-reaching backwardness', 'lagging-behind' in multiple terms, and gradually 'catching-up'. These were the terms used by experts in Lubelskie and Podkarpackie involved in the implementation of EU structural policies and other projects of development when asked to characterize the development status of their regions. While in interviews with experts and policy-makers in Dolnośląskie a certain proud and confidence about the current status and future prospects of their region was perceivable, interviewees from Lubelskie and Podkarpackie did not attempt to negate or embellish the problems of their regions. In fact, they were very blunt and realistic – and sometimes even sarcastic – when they were asked to describe the current situation in their region and in the area of eastern Poland in general. This becomes apparent in particular in the following excerpt of an interview with two relatively young representatives of a non-governmental organization (NGO) in Lublin that is specialized in the training and education of unemployed people and farmers in the countryside. The two interviewees characterized the 'backwardness' of their region quite straightforwardly:

Respondent 1: Good aspects? – Do we have good aspects? [laughing]

Respondent 2: We are not in the West, and we are not in the East, where Russia is, right? So we are between the hammer and the anvil... [laughing]

R1: Okay, but speaking about our weaknesses: first and foremost, this is our horrible backwardness, not only in relation to countries like Germany or France, but to all other European countries and also to Western Poland. There is simply a huge gap. The Vistula river divides the country into Poland A and Poland B – and we are even Poland C.

Interviewer: But is this really true? I mean, I thought this is merely an old stereotype?

R2: Thank you for the compliment [laughing]. –

R1: I mean in the bigger cities one just might not recognize it so much, but you can also see it. However, as you know, the majority of our voivodship is rural – there is Lublin, Zamość and Biała Podlaska and that's it – and the situation in the rural areas is simply a catastrophe: There is no internet, the roads are... – in fact, there are none, since one cannot call them roads – and the worst thing is the mentality of the people. I know, I'm strongly generalizing now, but it is a catastrophe: the people in these areas still don't have a sense for the necessity of life-long learning. The people just think they finish school, find a job and that's it.

(Int. 17, 166 – translated from Polish by S.B.)

The two respondents certainly exaggerate in their assessments of the 'backwardness' of rural areas in eastern Poland. In fact, there are paved roads in most of the rural areas in Poland – though not always in the best condition – and the provision of rural communities with basic infrastructure such as electricity, telecommunication etc. is widely assured. However, the peculiar severity in the above statements stems from comparisons and certain standards of development in mind: first of all by comparing the situation in rural Poland with urban Poland, and, second, even more importantly, by comparing eastern Poland with good examples from western areas and with more affluent areas in Western Europe. In relation to urban Europe, the situation in rural Poland appears to be a 'catastrophe'. In this way comparisons with external references and models of 'best practice' fundamentally shape assessments of development and underdevelopment.

Even more interestingly, furthermore, the 'horrible backwardness' of rural Poland is not only described as a question of out-dated infrastructure, but is particularly addressed as a 'problem of mentality'. Hence, a problem of 'attitudes' and of 'thinking'. Consequently, the rural population is characterized as being locked-in mentally which makes them to stick to 'old' and 'out-dated' patterns of behaviour and thinking. This is a common and widespread interpretative frame of structural backwardness. In an interview with a representative of a regional development agency (RDA) in Rzeszów, the capital city of Podkarpackie, similar aspects were mentioned to characterize the existing barriers of development in the outermost and most backward area of the region, the

Bieszczady mountains in the most south-eastern part of Poland. The interviewee highlighted that this terrain was one of Poland's most beautiful areas and the most popular natural resort of Poland with a huge tourist potential. But at the same time it still was one of the most 'backward' and 'underdeveloped' areas of Poland.[10] According to the interviewee the people were particularly poor in this area and whole families were unemployed. The major problem was, the interviewee said, that people still were '*not very active and creative*', and they still were '*not willing enough to qualify for the new employment opportunities*'. Therefore, the interviewee further explained, it was very difficult to promote tourism in this area despite its great tourist potential. But since tourism was the only alternative for the inhabitants of the Bieszczady mountains, the interviewee noted dryly, the people finally had to choose this path anyway (Memory Protocol of an Interview with Int. 6).

Development and underdevelopment as a problem of 'culture' and 'mentality'

As mentioned earlier already, it is an old and fairly popular notion in the Polish discourse, both in academia and everyday life, to associate the 'problem of mentality' of eastern Poland with historical factors, such as above all the strong influence of 'Russia' or 'eastern culture' in the eastern part of Poland both during the long nineteenth century and during communism in the post-war period. Generally speaking, 'Russia' or 'eastern culture' is associated with *parochialism*, *deadlock* and *backwardness*; 'western culture', in turn, is usually associated with cultural imperatives which are generally regarded as indicators of favourable development, such as *activity*, *progress*, and reasonable *material prosperity*. This also became apparent during the interviews with various experts on regional development in Poland. The following statement of a representative of the ministry of regional development in response to a question about the major differences between western and eastern regions in contemporary Poland is a good example of this widespread opinion:

> There are many factors that actually account for the differences between western and eastern Poland. And of course, there are big historical factors, such as the influence of different cultures. If one part of the country is under the influence of another country, like Russia in the eastern part, Germany in the western part, and Austria in the south, of course, then the culture in terms of what these countries represent is different. Therefore, it is not so strange that after 200 years people in these different parts also acquire some of the behaviours and attitudes [of these neighbouring countries]. – So, this historical background has a big influence on what is happening, of course.
>
> (Int. 25)

Similarly, in interviews with experts in Dolnośląskie, the culture was always highlighted as a positive aspect and a particular asset of the region. Due to the historical experience of industrialization and various massive shifts of population and resettlements in the area the 'culture' and 'mentality' of people in Dolnośląskie was described as particularly 'open-minded', 'flexible', and 'mobile'. And this was deliberately set against the alleged cultural mindset predominating in eastern Poland, which has been characterized as a 'culture of immobility' (Int. 11 and Int. 13).[11] However, this distinction of 'mobility' vs. 'immobility' was also used by interviewees from Podkarpackie, when they were asked to distinguish their region from other regions in eastern Poland. The historical demarcation between Podkarpackie (Habsburg-Hungarian occupation) and Lubelskie (Russian occupation) was put forward as a major signifier of possible cultural differences of contemporary Podkarpackie in comparison to the other regions in eastern Poland. It was pointed out that the territory of contemporary Podkarpackie used to be one of the areas where many people left to go overseas at the beginning of the twentieth century.[12] And it was also highlighted that people from this area were amongst the first to leave the country to work in the West at the beginning 1990s right after the fall of communism.

It is striking that structural out-migration, which is usually considered as a clear sign of underdevelopment and an indication of social decay, was put forward here as an indicator of the particular 'activity' and 'mobility' of the inhabitants of Podkarpackie. And, even more remarkably, that the long-lasting history of emigration is nowadays considered as a factor of favourable future development of the region. The fact that many people from Podkarpackie have a lot of international contacts with people from all over the world and that people with Polish origin are coming back to invest in the region and start their own businesses, even from overseas, is therefore seen as an outstanding stimulus of favourable development:

> This region is very mobile in the sense that it has one of the highest shares of people who went overseas. This was due to the characteristic poverty of Galicia – this is a proverbial term: the 'Galician poverty'. The people had to leave for bread, but this also intensified the mobility in general. Today, there are such intensive contacts with people from abroad that in this month [June 2007, S.B.] we even opened our first direct air connection with New York. It was opened, because here there is just such a high demand for overseas flights. In Lubelskie, in turn, this is totally different. They don't have anything like that. The difference is also visible in that a lot of people from this region are working in Western Europe today – because they are mobile. And these are people who are able to help themselves – one can say. And this is not visible in official statistics on unemployment or on GDP.
>
> (Int. 9, translated from Polish by S.B.)

It is not easy to assess, in fact, whether this is truly unique for Podkarpackie, or whether people from all other Polish regions could tell the same story. But it is a matter of fact that the old historical region of Galicia, the former 'poor house' of the Austro-Hungarian Empire, has had a long history of out-migration (cf. Hann and Magocsi 2005). Yet, this statement shows that both mental and physical 'mobility' has attained such a high status in contemporary times that even an aspect that is usually seen as a problematic in terms of development is re-interpreted positively, or even as a 'competitive advantage' in comparison to other regions.[13] This underlines that 'activity', 'mobility', and the ethos that 'people are able to help themselves' were highlighted as positive attitudes in contrast to cultural patterns of 'ritualism' or 'passivism' which are associated with 'eastern culture'. But apart from that we can conclude this paragraph that there was a strong consensus among all interviewees that there is no big difference between regions in eastern Poland apart from these different socio-cultural factors. Indeed, it was pointed out by all interviewees that there are not so many differences amongst the regions in eastern Poland and that differences are not so 'visible'. The regions are considered as, more or less, similarly 'lagging behind in economic terms, due to similar structural shortfalls.

Local assessments of the current situation in the two eastern regions

All interviewees generally pointed to the same characteristics of 'eastern backwardness'. Most of them were already mentioned in the previous overview of more general and official assessments of regional development in Poland. Thus, there is a huge consensus among Polish experts of the still existing and far-reaching structural gaps in regional development. All eastern regions were 'not very industrialized' and 'strongly shaped by agriculture'; they had 'outdated infrastructure' that had not been renewed during times of communism. And the rural areas, and especially the most eastward border areas in the regions, were suffering from huge levels of poverty and out-migration these days.

Nonetheless, the interviewees in Lubelskie and Podkarpackie also pointed out numerous examples and indications of favourable economic development in their regions. First and foremost, it was highlighted by representatives of regional development agencies (RDAs) that the rate of entrepreneurship and the interest in doing business was quite high in their regions. There were many people who would visit them and ask for ways of starting their own business. Furthermore, interviewees in the eastern regions pointed out some of the showpieces of their regional economies which could be the basis of favourable economic development in the future. In Lubelskie, for example, experts highlighted the strong agricultural tradition of the region, which would provide excellent conditions for food production in accordance with most contemporary standards of ecological farming and food processing. Moreover, there are also some larger companies, especially chemistry plants that used to be state-owned and have since been transformed into competitive private companies during the process of transformation in the 1990s, i.e. the *Puławy S.A.* and the *PZL-Świdnik*, formerly state-owned producers of helicopters. However, as already mentioned, the most important and significant aviation industries in Poland are traditionally found in the area of contemporary Podkarpackie. It was stressed that nowadays more and more important foreign investors from the aviation sector were coming to the region to invest in the existing special economic zones (SEZs).

Last but not least, the experts in Podkarpackie and Lubelskie also referred to the 'huge reservoir of young and well-educated people' in their regions, especially in the capital cities of the two eastern regions, Lublin and Rzeszów, where the research institutes and institutions of higher education are located. Thus, not all young people are moving away from the regions, with many young people moving from rural areas to the cities for their studies and work. A representative of a regional development agency (RDA) in Podkarpackie mentioned in this regard: *'In the whole area of Rzeszów there are about 50,000 students. This is in fact quite exceptional for a city which has 169,000 inhabitants in total, isn't it?'* (Int. 6, translated from Polish by S.B.).[14] Similarly, a young representative of an RDA in Lublin also pointed out that the out-migration of younger people was not the largest problem of the region. On the contrary, he expressed huge optimism that most of the well-educated people who moved away for education would come back one day and start their own businesses in Lubelskie:

> So, you see. I'm here, and I'm not going anywhere – to work in a pub in London or something like that ... [laughing]. Of course, there are a lot of young people moving to the western countries of the European Union, but to be honest, most of them were not as well educated as those who are staying in Lublin. So, if they have a job for a few years, they saw the only chance besides staying in Lublin in moving to other countries. So I don't want to say that all people who moved to other countries are not well educated – of course, there are also a lot of well-educated people moving to Western Europe, but not for work in general, but mainly for education – to increase their skill competitiveness. And I think that these people will return to this region and invest here.
>
> (Int. 18)

In fact, the city of Lublin accommodates four universities and one technical university: first, the Maria-Curie-Skłodowa University of Lublin with about 36,000 students, second, the Catholic University of Lublin which is one of the most famous universities of Poland, since the former pope John Paul II. used to lecture there during his university career (about 18,000 students); third, the University of Medicine (about 6,500 students); fourth, the University of Natural Studies with about 13,000 students); and, fifth, the Technical University [*Politechnika*] with about 1,000 students. This accounts for almost 90,000 students in a city of 360,000 inhabitants, plus a number of private universities and research institutes. Therefore, Lublin is considered to be the Polish city with the highest proportion of students in relation to the total number of inhabitants (last update 2009).

Nonetheless, despite these indications of optimism, there was a huge consensus amongst interviewees from the eastern regions that the existing 'structural shortcomings' would constitute a huge burden for the future development of the regions. And the interviewed experts and policy-makers in the eastern regions are aware of the fact that counties and municipalities in eastern Poland will remain 'much poorer' than counties and municipalities in western Poland in the near future, since they were simply 'less competitive'.

Implications of the structural disadvantage of the eastern regions

In fact, interviewees in the two eastern regions have vigorously pointed out some systematic disadvantageous for the future development of their regions that directly result from existing structural shortcomings. First of all, it was highlighted that as long as the transport infrastructure will not be changed and developed substantially the eastern regions will always have lower chances of getting foreign investors. 'We don't have any express roads in our region, so when potential investors come to Poland and think of where to invest their money, they will think of investing in a city which has an airport and good roads' (Int. 18).[15] Therefore, it was unanimously declared by all interviewees from the eastern regions, both policy-makers and practitioners alike, that the most important priority for the development of eastern Poland must be the upgrading of transport infrastructure and the construction of both west-east motorway connections that transcend the borders with Belarus and Ukraine, and a north-south connection through eastern Poland. Besides this, investment in the construction and expansion of airports were also recommended in order to foster tourism and to enable logistics independent of cumbersome transport via roads and trains.

Secondly, some interviewees have pointed out that the structural disadvantage of the eastern regions also as an effect on the allocation of public money from the national government and from EU funds. Thus, it was pointed out that the eastern regions are not just disadvantaged structurally in terms of infrastructure development, overall social well-being and economic dynamism, but also in terms of public investment decisions. This is articulated exemplarily in the following statement of a representative of an RDA in Lubelskie:

> When I compare our regions Podlaskie, Lubelskie, and Podkarpackie, I think we are more or less the same – when we talk about wealth, when we talk about our competitiveness, and when we talk about innovativeness. [This is] because we are all in the Eastern part of Poland, and the money from the national government was always transferred in greater sums to the Western part than to eastern Poland.
>
> (Int. 18)

This impression is confirmed, in fact, by assessments of the spatial distribution of EU structural funds in Poland between 2004 and 2006. A more recent study reveals that the biggest receivers of EU funds within this particular operational programme were the Mazowieckie region – the most prosperous Polish region where Warsaw is located – as well as the two western regions of Zachodniopomorskie and Wielkopolskie (cf. Płaziak and Trzepacz 2008: 40).

Moreover, apart from complaints about systematic disadvantages in receiving EU funding, public officials mentioned two other systematic disadvantages faced by eastern regions in the current system of allocating EU funds in Poland. In fact, a representative of the administrative office of the regional government in Lubelskie, who is involved in the planning of EU policies in the regions, explained that just because of the strict requirement of co-financing on the part of the recipient of the EU funds or the respective local and regional authorities the room for manoeuvre of eastern regions and communes was much more limited than for their western Polish counterparts. This would leave no space for other alternative initiatives apart from co-financing EU-related projects as a person involved in the implementation of EU regional policy in Lubelskie stated:

> The Western regions – the Western *gminy* – are richer. They have more in the budget. So, for example, of this investment money in their own budget, they can allocate 50 per cent for the co-financing of EU funds, and they still have 50 per cent for their own investment plans – for what they want to do, for what they decide to implement. And in the Eastern regions, if we want to absorb all the EU money that is allocated to us, we have to use all the money which is in our budget to co-finance the EU money, because otherwise we will not absorb all the money.
>
> (Int. 23)[16]

Last but not least, the policy-makers in eastern Poland also mentioned that it was very hard for the eastern regions to comply with new standards and requirements of contemporary EU development policy visions. When asked about the new regulations in EU regional development policy with an emphasis on the 'Lisbon goals', such as the promotion of the knowledge society, innovativeness and entrepreneurship and so forth, the same interviewee stated quite sceptically:

> Yes, indeed, it is not easy to implement. And you have to remember, the Lubelskie region is not very rich and many of these issues are outside of our competence. This is because all or most of the things that are linked with innovation are dependent on what the Ministry of Science decides – i.e. which university will get more or less money etc. But the region actually doesn't have any influence on the universities. On how they cooperate, on how they get their resources for their day-to-day running etc. (...) And it also depends on the profile of the programmes. In our new Regional Operational Programmes it's really hard, because you have to cope with people who want to have more money for roads, because these are the needs of the people. And in our rural areas, for example, we have just 9% of households with access to water treatments. So, they still just put their waste water into the rivers, into the ground, or somewhere else.
>
> These are the real problems of the people, and people in the *gminy* want these problems to be solved first. They don't want to think about business

incubators, they don't want to think about spending on innovation and things like that. So, that's the problem, you know, on the one hand we have to see what the Lisbon agenda says and what the government demands from us, and on the other hand we are still combating the demands from the bottom, you know, from the *gminy*, that they want to tackle their own problems with basic infrastructure. And that's hard – that's really hard ...

(Int. 23)[17]

Distinct urban-rural divides, but overall future optimism in Dolnośląskie

When representatives of the administrative office of the self-government of Dolnośląskie were asked the same questions regarding potential problems or contradictions between the long-term developmental goals of the region and the requirement to comply with new 'Lisbon goals' as their eastern counterparts, the answers were strikingly different and unambiguous. Unlike public officials in the two eastern regions the interviewees did not see any problem or contradiction at all. They were convinced that Dolnośląskie is able to meet all standards of the 'Lisbon agenda', since the region had 'extraordinarily excellent conditions' for the development of 'innovative businesses'. As the following excerpt shows, the region is simply considered to be able to fulfil all demands, standards and requirements of development practice:

I: Do you see difficulties in integrating the new requirements of innovation, such as the Lisbon goals, into your overall regional development strategy?

R: No, no – there aren't any. It's true that we have to include the Lisbon Strategy in our new Regional Operational Programmes. However, in the past we already prepared our Innovation Strategy, and this fits perfectly well with the Lisbon agenda. It fits because we have formulated about three priorities or activities that have to be realized both according to the Lisbon Strategy and according to our Innovation Strategy. And there is no discrepancy. On the contrary, there is even a strong correlation (...).

I: So, you don't see any problems in achieving both things at the same time: your own long-term development goals and the Lisbon goals?

R: No, there are no problems.

I: That's interesting, because in other interviews, such as those with some of your counterparts in other regional ministries – especially in eastern Poland – the people pointed out that it is rather difficult to promote things like the knowledge economy, innovative businesses and so forth, when you have to invest in basic infrastructure at the same time ...

R: And this is different in our region. We have about 30 schools of higher education in the whole area of Dolnośląskie. We have very strong academic institutions, very strong research institutes that not only belong to the strongest in the country or in Europe, but in the whole world. In Lublin, in eastern Poland, there is one, or maybe two higher schools of education in total. In contrast, we have more than 150,000 students in Wrocław, and it is a big city!

(Int. 11)

The huge difference in the assessment of the difficulties in implementing new European policies of regional development amongst public officials of regions in eastern and western Poland is striking, indeed. And this small excerpt is typical for the overall certainty and optimism about the future prospects of Dolnośląskie expressed in almost all interviews with practitioners in the region. Obviously, this is due to the different developmental situations of the regions and the different perceptions of future prospects in western Poland. Experts in Dolnośląskie simply feel that the situation in their region is relatively favourable compared to other regions; not only in relation their counterparts in the eastern part of Poland, but, as mentioned, in fact, even in comparison to some of the stagnating neighbouring regions in eastern Germany. They are convinced that Dolnośląskie has certain important 'competitive advantages' compared to other regions. That the region can offer excellent conditions for both more traditional industries and new post-industrial businesses. And they are aware of their favourable geographical location in direct proximity to the big markets in Western Europe.[18]

However, to be fair and well-balanced, it must be mentioned as well that the interviews with various experts in Dolnośląskie also revealed a number of structural shortcomings and problems within the region which are less obvious and less expected in light of the favourable 'objective' development prospects and the enthusiastic expert assessments. Some experts and practitioners interviewed in Dolnośląskie stated that there also was a *marked urban-rural distinction* within the region: the gap between Wrocław and the other areas and cities of the region. This would become apparent, first and foremost, in terms of a huge dispersal of structural unemployment within the region. It was mentioned that there are cities and regions in Dolnośląskie where the official unemployment rate is about 30 per cent and higher, whereas in Wrocław the unemployment rate was quite low (according to Int. 13). But it was also mentioned that the problem of unemployment has been increasingly replaced by the problem of out-migration. Over the past decades many people have simply left the region's deprived rural and old-industrial areas and migrated to Wrocław, to other prospering cities in Poland, and – since EU accession in 2004 ever more frequently and rapidly – abroad. This often left municipalities and areas suffering from high levels of out-migration with cumulating developmental problems (Int. 27).

Moreover, similar to the interpretations that were already put forward in assessments of major development problems in eastern Poland, the urban–rural divide in Dolnośląskie is also described as a 'problem of mentality'. When asked

for an explanation for the difficult social situation in smaller and poorer municipalities in Dolnośląskie, an interviewee from a non-governmental organization
that is specialized in the further education and training of students and younger
people in Wrocław also referred to the problem of 'mental' or 'attitudinal immobility' and resistance to change:

> However, these elements of mentality, which are – generally speaking –
> very typical for people in the East, are of course prevalent in our region as
> well. If we speak, for example with people who work in community centres
> and social services, who have direct contact with unemployed people or
> with farmers living in small villages, they tell you exactly the same: that
> there are people who don't want to work, even if there is work, who don't
> want to depend on anything or anybody, who want to survive on a very low
> social level, or who just work from time to time in illicit employment. All
> these problems are also in our region, but on a lower scale than in eastern
> Poland, at least as far as I can say.
>
> (Int. 13, translated from Polish by S.B.)

And in an interview with a representative of a regional development agency
(RDA) in Wałbrzych, a smaller city located in the southern part of the region
which was suffering from huge levels of unemployment and massive social
problems after the fall of communism, the rising gap between Wrocław and the
rest of the region was highlighted as a major problem. It was pointed out that the
road and train connections between Wrocław and other cities were not yet sufficiently developed or upgraded. In his opinion, fast train and motorway connections between the other smaller cities in the region and Wrocław would be one
of the best measures to foster a more balanced development. Then people could
simply commute to Wrocław for work on a daily basis if they wanted to, and
would not be forced to move away for a job. Vice versa, the respondent further
explained, it would also raise the opportunities for business development in the
area. However, from his point of view, this was still not acknowledged and
tackled enough by the regional authorities. On the contrary, since they would
mainly aim at promoting the metropolitan functions of the prospering capital city
of the region, public investments were more directed to Wrocław and its direct
surroundings rather than to other cities and areas:

> In my opinion, Wrocław is not fully open to the rest of the region. This is
> what I think. Wrocław is not able to share its success with the rest of the
> region. Okay, we can say: 'Wrocław is the capital of Dolnośląskie and it is
> important to develop it'. But the people who develop this region on the part
> of the state, the people in the regional government, they should care more
> about the development of the whole region, not only in Wrocław. But until
> now the situation is that everything goes to Wroclaw and the other cities are
> not valued enough.
>
> (Int. 27, translated from Polish by S.B.)

Conclusions

The comparative analysis of assessments and descriptions of the developmental situation given by experts and practitioners in the three selected regions has clearly shown that many interpretations of a particular 'eastern backwardness' and the overall world-cultural assessments of development prospects of the regions are widely shared. Thus, the existing structural imbalances of spatial development are widely acknowledged – even among practitioners in the different regions. The future opportunities of the eastern regions are rated as relatively low, and experts from the regions can highlight a number of structural disadvantages of their regions in comparison to the western area of the country, which might contribute to a further widening of the existing gap between Eastern and Western Poland. In this way, we can say in fact that the two eastern regions are truly 'peripheral'. This is definitely different in Dolnośląskie, the western counterpart, where policy-makers and practitioners are unanimously optimistic about their future development. However, we have also seen that Dolnośląskie has certain internal development problems as well, which are quite similar to some of the diagnosed shortcomings of the eastern regions. In this sense, all three regions share similar development problems and challenges. Yet they show up in different ways and might require different solutions. Nonetheless, despite the huge level of consistency in the assessment of development problems and opportunities among various experts, we have also seen that assessments of the situation are always strongly dependent on respective standpoints and reference points. Looking at Dolnośląskie's self-description one might get the impression that the region has everything that is regarded as favourable for successful regional development these days. All the important world-cultural attributes and signifiers are mentioned and highlighted. And while the two eastern regions that are mainly shaped by agriculture try to avoid the 'stigma' (Goffman) of backward agricultural regions, Dolnośląskie confidently points out its agricultural potential.

We have noticed as well that the standard frames of development thinking, such as *centre* vs. *periphery*, *innovativeness* vs. *backwardness*, *openness* vs. *cultural lock-in* and *mobility* vs. *immobility* play a major role in the discourse on regional development in Poland, and especially in the 'impression-management' (Goffman) of the regions themselves. It could be seen that standard conceptions of contemporary regional development, expert evaluations, and the constant assessments of regions with standard measures are highly relevant for the constitution of regional 'selves'. All regions point to those 'assets' which have been determined on the basis of highly reflexive and evaluative processes (SWOT-analysis). In fact, it is one of the characteristics of current efforts of regional mobilization that particular regional culture(s) and tradition(s) and even their natural habitats are promoted strategically by regional policy-makers. Nonetheless, it also turned out that there are striking differences in the way regions with different development levels and future prospects present themselves to the outside world. We can see, in this context, that policy-makers in Dolnośląskie are able to present the future prospects of their region so self-confidently, since they can refer to expert evaluations, assessments and rankings of the Polish regions that prove the top rank of their region. In fact, these days regional authorities, policy-makers and other actors concerned with development of regions are constantly shown by external expert evaluations and rankings where they stand in the relation to other regions. This is an important element in the constitution of social entities in our contemporary 'global ecumene' (Tenbruck 1990). This strongly contributes to the creation of identity and fundamentally shapes the way social actors perceive themselves. If social actors know where they are located on the respective scale, they know better where they are in relation to their counterparts.

In the subsequent chapter, we will further explore the diffusion of world-cultural standards and principles on the basis of a comparison of the development strategies of the three selected regions. These strategies constitute the 'formal structure' (Meyer *et al.* 1997) of the world-cultural make-up of the new regions, the blueprints of development. And accordingly, they should also be considered as a central part of the 'impression-management' of the regions. But strategies also lead to concrete decisions and largely determine the scope of development interventions within the regions. Some of the projects and activities the three regions have pursued and implemented in recent years are also presented subsequently.

8 Strategizing all the way down

Traces of 'standardized diversification'

Introduction

In the following the all-embracing strategizing of regional development practice in contemporary Poland will be depicted in more detail. The chapter explores how the existing development strategies of the three selected Polish regions came into being and how they affect development activities in the regions today. According to official statements, the regional development strategies (RDS) are the major documents of development planning of the 16 Polish voivodships and thus the most important policy documents drawn up by the regional governments. They specify the major goals, objectives and priorities of development policy of the regions. And they are supposed to serve as focal points of future development and as guidelines for all operational development activities:

> A strategy of the development of a province is the policy tool of the province's self-government, enabling it to support developmental processes. It expresses aspirations of a regional community and its will to achieve common objectives included in a vision of the development that determines priorities and ways of the realisation of planned activities. (...) **It is the most important manifesto document of self-government in the province.** Without the strategy it would be very difficult to effectively manage the development of the region and to organize partnership co-operation with the main actors of the regional scene.
> (Podkarpackie Development Strategy 2000–6, English version: 7, emphasis as original)

It has been obligatory for the regions since their creation in January 1999 to prepare distinct development strategies. This obligation was prescribed by legislation that enforced the large-scale administrative reform of the country. The respective legislative acts determined the major principles as well as the major rules and procedures for preparing these documents, and they specified the role of individual administrative bodies of regional government in this process. More concrete principles and schedules for drawing up the strategies were specified by supplementary resolutions of the regional authorities themselves.

Both the process of strategy-building and the quality of the first strategic documents that were adopted by the 16 Polish regional governments between 1999 and 2001 were strongly criticized by scientific analysts of regional policy in Poland. In fact, an expert in Polish regional politics who has assessed the system of regional policy-making that was implemented in Poland over the past decade, strongly doubted that the existing regional development strategies have been functional and effective. From his perspective, most of the documents simply failed to pin down the most crucial and significant challenges of development: 'It appears that regional strategies do not help identify development aims, but merely serve as demonstration documents' (Grosse 2006: 156f.). The strategies that were put in place, he pointed out articulately, '(...) not only waste[d] scarce financial resources, but turned the documents into a wish list instead of concrete actions' (ibid.). Yet, from a macro-phenomenological research perspective that aims to capture the rapid and massive diffusion of world-cultural models in European regional development, the existing regional development strategies are not just regarded as 'empty bottles' and 'ineffective collections of nice intentions'. Rather, these documents are seen as an expression of the current rationales of development practice in the Polish regions, reflecting the normative principles, obligations and standard routines which shape regional development practice in contemporary Europe.

Hence, one of the specific features of this study is to interpret the strategic decision-making behind regional development policies as a central element of the world-cultural make-up of Polish regions. And this concerns both the preparation of regional development strategies (RDS) and the implementation of development policies according to strategic principles. In fact, the development strategies are mainly prepared by experts and scientists with expertise in issues of regional development and regional politics (i.e. geographers, economists, political scientists, and sociologists) and promote the latest and most contemporary standards of scientific planning (practice). Moreover, the strategies have received official political approval from the regional parliaments, and therefore constitute relatively manifest and explicit 'social facts' (Durkheim) and development imperatives. Hence, independent of their effectiveness, an exploration of the regional development strategies of Polish regions is a good approach to capture the distinctive world-cultural nature of social mobilization in contemporary Polish regions.

The following analysis starts with a short reconstruction of the preparatory process of the first regional development strategies in Poland in 1999 and 2000. This will give us an impression of the major procedures behind the strategy-building in Polish regions and show the role of scientific experts from the very beginning of the process (1). Subsequently, the major aims, objectives and priorities of the newly revised development strategies of Dolnośląskie, Lubelskie and Podkarpackie will be depicted in more detail. The revision process coincided with the introduction of a new national development strategy for 2007–15 and the preparation of regional authorities for the current programming period 2007–13 (2). The explorative part of this chapter ends with a short comparative summary of concrete development projects and activities that are implemented in the regions (3). This gives us some hints to traces of 'regional specialization' and individual paths of regionalization, what we can understand as the 'standardized diversification' of contemporary Polish regions (4).

1 Strategy-building as a funnel of world-cultural diffusion

From the very beginning the process of strategy-building in the newly created Polish voivodships has been accompanied and assessed by scientific expertise. Though the whole process was politically steered and coordinated, the documents were mainly drafted and created by scientists and other scientifically trained 'professionals'. The proceedings for the first round of strategy building that took place in the 16 voivodships between 1999 and 2000 are well documented, since the process was accompanied by a larger scientific debate amongst leading scientists (geographers, economists, sociologists) who were involved in the process in one way or the other. This debate was published in the leading Polish journal of regional sciences in 2000.[1] It gives us a good insight into the major debates in Poland at that time and some background information on some of major parameters and conditions of this process. However, in the context of an exploration of policy-diffusion within the framework of the EU Cohesion Policy, this debate represents even more: It is a major manifestation of the *transfer* and *translation* of 'abstract' (world-cultural) models of regional development and strategic planning into Polish politics. Therefore, it constitutes the starting point of a more detailed exploration of the world-cultural make-up of regional development strategies in this chapter.

The expert debate on the process of strategy development

The preparation of individual and distinct regional development strategies (RDS) was considered by experts and policy-makers in Poland as a milestone in the history of spatial development and planning of the country. The need to prepare the RDS was proclaimed in scientific debates that had ambitious aspirations for far-reaching social change and development, and was promoted with a strong modernist impetus. Andrzej Klasik, one of the leading figures of the debate on the preparation of the RDSs in 1999/2000 describes the necessity of strategy-building in the introductory chapter of his contribution to the abovementioned special issue of *Studia Regionalne i Lokalne* as following:

> The restructuring and globalization of regions requires a holistic development approach. This entails, in fact, the development of regions in terms of international competitiveness and in all their general structural aspects. **The restructuring of Polish regions is finally leading to their cultural transformation**.
> (Klasik 2000: 7, translated from Polish by S.B., emphasis in original)

This statement ideally expresses the prevailing modernist spirit and optimism that was associated with the new era of regional mobilization in Poland by the end of the 1990s. Klasik highlighted the importance of the new RDS as a tool to stipulate a far-reaching 'cultural transformation' of the country. Not only a superficial modifications to economic or political structures, but an all-encompassing change in existing orientations, attitudes, and identities. Accordingly, Klasik further noted that

> *[t]he result will be the change in the identities of the regions which will entirely focus on new specializations of production and services, new qualifications and competences, and new lifestyles of local societies. **The process of restructuring leads to a change in the regional leadership and governing elite.***

(ibid, translated by S.B., emphasis in original)

This envisaged 'change of regional leadership', and in particular the envisaged change in the 'governing elite', is put forward as one of crucial factors for successful regional development in contemporary models of regional governance (cf. Benz and Fürst 2002; Cooke 2003). And accordingly it was also highlighted so vigorously by Klasik as a fundamental aspect of regional development planning in Poland. In line with new standards of *strategic* regional planning and the mobilization of *regional agency* (see Chapter 5 above) the whole process of strategy-building in the new voivodships is promoted as an opportunity to change the existing 'planning culture' in Poland. It is therefore not surprising that Klasik also claimed that 'public consultation' was one of the most important preconditions of strategic regional development planning, and that he considers the strategy as an expression of 'good governance' per se. Without a decent development strategy, Klasik pointed out, it would not be possible to organize cooperation amongst the major actors in the regions and to govern the regions' further development effectively (Klasik 2000).

A brief look at the preparatory process of the first regional development strategies in Poland shows that the whole process was certainly this combined 'political' *and* 'intellectual' process as it was envisaged by the scientific advisors and advocates of strategic regional development planning in Poland. Moreover, given the fact that the timing and the specific procedures of strategy development were entirely left up to the newly created regional governments, and neither specified nor prescribed by law, the whole process proceeded remarkably smooth and quick, indeed. Though the regional governments had only been officially established in January 1999, by the end of 2000 all 16 newly created Polish voivodships had their own official regional development strategies – approved by regional politicians and officially adopted by the regional parliaments.[2]

Certainly, this relative 'efficiency' in the process of strategy development in the newly created voivodships was largely driven by external factors and constraints, and especially by the strict timeline scheduled to prepare for the EU's Pre-Accession and Structural Funds that were allocated between 2000 and 2004 (cf. Żuber 2000; Garsztecki 2001, 2005; Gorzelak 2000b; Grosse 2006). Hence, the individual governments were not really free to choose and decide on the structure, content and procedural regulations of their development strategies. In light of the expected inflow of EU funding, the regional governments were by and large forced to comply with the official standards, goals, regulations and requirements of EU funding, and they had to comply with the principle of partnership not only in relation to the local governments and other key actors in the region, but also in relation to the national government (Klasik 2000). Beyond that, apart from official institutional constraints and formal obligations, the informal cooperation of national and regional authorities also contributed to the relative smoothness and efficiency of this process. Since the regional administrations had just been newly established, the public officials of the 'Department of Coordination' for the EU Pre-Accession and Structural Funds in the former Ministry of Economy and Labour – which was later transferred to the Ministry of Regional Development – served as natural and frequently-consulted advisers from the very beginning of the process (Int. 18 and Int. 25). In fact, the employees in the Department of Coordination had the greatest level of competence with regard to EU funding regulations at that time due their experience with the Pre-Accession Fund. And, in addition, knowledge and expertise concerning strategy development were concentrated in the Department of Coordination, since this department was also responsible for the creation of the National Development Plan 2000–6 (NDP) and the National Regional Development Strategy 2000–06 – a sub-strategy of the NDP 2000–6 that outlined the indicative allocation of EU pre-accession funds across Poland. Thus, in sum, both the prospect of EU funding and the whole process of preparing the National Regional Development Strategy served as major reference points for the process of strategic development planning in the Polish regions in 1999 and 2000 (cf. Żuber 2000).

The preparation of the first regional development strategies 1999 to 2000

The first regional development strategies (RDS) in the Polish voivodships were drafted in parallel to the preparation process of the National Strategy for Regional Development 2000–06 outlined by the Department of Coordination. And during the whole process of strategy-building there was a constant exchange amongst public officials in the regional administrations and the central government through various training sessions, educational activities, and other types of professional exchange between the two levels of government. Activities funded under the heading of 'technical assistance' promoted the intense involvement of 'knowledgeable experts' from both academia and from public administrations, tapping into their particular knowledge and competences. According to official statements, the Department of Coordination allocated roughly EUR200,000 for technical support in the strategic development process, which was spent on training sessions, publications, expert consultations and so forth (Żuber 2000). In fact, the standard procedures and methods of strategy-building in Poland are fundamentally shaped by scientific principles and practices. This becomes apparent first and foremost in the structure of the documents itself and in the general procedure of the process of strategy development. Hence, apart from some minor procedural differences, the first process of strategy-building in Poland was organized in the following way (see also Figure 8.1):

(a) The strategy-building process in the newly created voivodships started with a comprehensive, scientifically-based diagnosis of the situation in the regions, an exploration of the particular development problems and challenges as well as the strategic assets and options for future development. This culminated in the compilation of a detailed SWOT-analysis and a discussion of the future strategic options taking account of the given assets and resources available for development. This is supposed to provide the regional authorities and other important development actors in the regions with an overview of the basic facts and conditions of the region's situation which can be used as a basis for 'rational' or 'strategic' decisions. Therefore, the diagnoses of the regions which are included in the documents constitute comprehensive descriptions of the regions' socio-economic situation and development, and they largely contain the most up-to-date socio-economic data and the most contemporary scientific knowledge pertaining to regional planning.

(b) Following the evaluation of the socio-economic and strategic situation of the regional territories, their major strategic aims and the special strategic objectives were formulated in reference to the previously diagnosed problems, assets, and options for future development. This process was accompanied by consultations with experts and key actors in the given region, in order to involve as many groups and people as possible in the process and to give them the opportunity to exchange opinions.

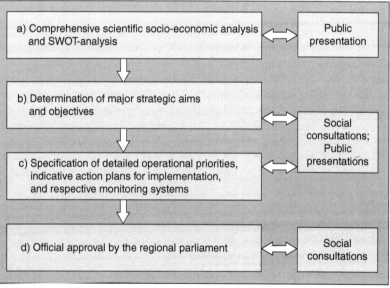

Figure 8.1 The basic organizational procedure of strategy-building in Poland.

(c) The general strategic goals and priorities were subsequently specified in more concrete 'operational priorities' and 'action plans'. In accordance with the funding guidelines of the draft version of the National Strategy for Regional Development, financial tables were prepared which outlined the indicative allocation of public funds (both national and external) for various fields of activity, and a detailed action plan was set out which specified the implementation procedures and monitoring system for the whole planning system according to standard methods of development planning and implementation.

(d) After the overall preparatory processes of strategy-building were finished, the documents also underwent a process of official political approval by the regional authorities. They were discussed and evaluated by the relevant committees of the respective regional parliaments. During these sessions, various political actors had the opportunity to criticise elements of the strategy and to ask for corrections and clarifications. Following official approval by all parliamentary committees in a given region, each strategy was then brought to the general assembly of the regional parliament. And after a final public debate it was finally officially adopted by the regional parliament in question.

The strong interplay between scientific expertise and political practice also becomes apparent in the organizational process of strategy development. The process was officially steered and represented by the most important political actors, but it was mainly executed by practitioners and knowledgeable experts from regional administrations, universities and relevant development actors. Again, the particular organization of the process slightly varied from region to region – e.g. the extent of consultations and the number of people involved in the process varied significantly between the regions.[3] However, in principle, the organizational processes were mainly structured as follows:

The major executive tasks and the major procedural functions were conducted by coordinating groups and various issue-specific working groups. The *coordinating groups* that consisted of a small number of public officials from the regional governments and some experienced practitioners governed and coordinated and whole executive process of strategy development. They worked closely with *consultants* and *(external) experts* who gave their input on the major methodological and organizational aspects of the process, and also cooperated with experts and practitioners in the *working groups* who had been asked to give their professional input regarding various fields of development, ranging from the economy, infrastructural issues, environmental issues and various social aspects. Officially, however, the process was governed and coordinated by regional steering committees and programming committees. The main function of the *steering committees* was to present the process to the public and to bring all important regional authorities together. They were in charge of the process of reaching a consensus on the most important strategic decisions at the highest level from the very beginning of the process. The steering committees consisted of the main representatives of regional the governments, the Marshall or Vice-Marshalls of the voivodships, the Chairmen and Vice-Chairmen of the voivode-ships' parliaments (*sejmik*), the Voivods as the official representatives of the central government in the regions and selected 'important' and 'influential' actors and opinion leaders such as representatives of the largest banks, the mayors of the larger cities, or highly renowned citizens. The relatively small and selective group of people in the steering committee was complemented by the *programming committee*, a much larger circle of representatives from the regional parliament and all local governments [*powiaty*] as well as various other important regional actors, such as representatives of regional development agencies, business organizations, academic institutions, and other important organizations. Figure 8.2 shows a schematic division of tasks amongst the different actors involved in the preparation process.

Hence, in principle, the whole process of strategy preparation at the regional level constituted the 'concerted' and 'cooperative' exercises suggested in how-to handbooks of development planning and adhered to the official procedural standards of 'European' regional development planning. The process brought together a variety of different actors, and a huge amount of people were directly involved in the process of strategy development at one stage of the process or another. During and after the preparation process, the documents were published on official websites so that all citizens were given the opportunity to look at the documents during the preparation process, and there were

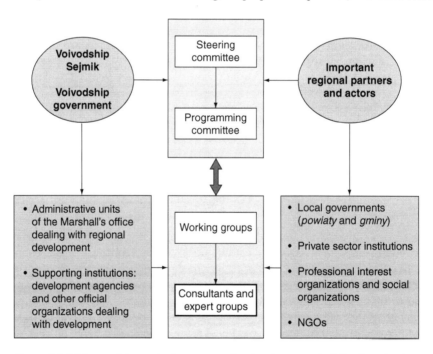

Figure 8.2 Major participants in the process of regional strategy-building in Poland.

also numerous presentations and consultations at local level in order to inform the regional population about the strategies. In this sense, a huge amount of people were able to contribute their input and opinions on the strategies, and the strategies underwent both a professional process of strategy-building as well as a political process of debate and bargaining. Finally, the documents were discussed in official political fora and received official approval by the regional parliaments.

In practice, however, we can observe that the main body of the strategies was developed by a small number of experts and working groups. The public influence on the character of the strategies was therefore not very high. The social consultations and the official political process did not usually lead to intricate ideological debates about the major direction of development or the substance of the strategies. Indeed, most of the political struggles and political 'hard talk' was connected to the territorial allocation of prospective funds (Żuber 2000). All representatives of regional governments tried to get as much funding as possible for their own regions, and in accordance with 'good' political practice they kept a watchful eye on the process to ensure that other regions were not disproportionately or unjustifiably privileged. Nevertheless, in general the major assumptions of the strategies and major strategic goals were widely shared and mainly taken for granted. We can conclude, therefore, that the huge emphasis on consultations and broad political participation in the process of strategy-building did not stimulate a huge politicization of the process of strategy-building. On the contrary, it is the major aim of this procedure to integrate as many (important) regional actors around the table in order to share opinions and find compromises before things get too much 'political'. In fact, the development strategies are not supposed to be influenced by 'particularistic' interests or narrow-minded short-term thinking. This was also expressed during interviews with people who were involved in the process of strategy-building. One example is the statement of a public official from Dolnośląskie who was part of the team that managed and administered the process of strategy-building in the region:

> The strategy does not have a political character. It is apolitical. All political representatives, in principle in the Sejmik, where the different representatives of different parties are [brought together], had the opportunity to say what they like, what they don't like, and what should be added. In this way a consensus is worked out. Therefore this strategy went through discussions in all Sejmik committees, since before it goes to the plenary discussion in the Sejmik, it must be reviewed properly by the Sejmik committees. (...) and when the Sejmik has the positive approval of all committees, the strategy becomes officially adopted. And that's it.
>
> (Int. 11)

Moreover, a public official of the central government who was strongly involved in the process of preparing the National Development Strategy (NDS) 2007–15, acknowledge the importance of 'social consultations' in development planning in contemporary Poland. He pointed out that the consultations were open to everyone, everybody was supposed to give his or her opinion – either at public meetings or via the internet – and that these opinions were seriously taken into account. On the other hand, however, he said that it was the nature of all kinds of consultation processes to have as many different opinions as people around the table. All participants would represent their particular interest in the first place, and all think that their input is the most important and most valuable. Therefore, the interviewee conceded, at the end policy-makers – and in this case: strategy-makers – always had to make decisions on what to include and what not to. And they always had to keep in mind what is realistic and justified by scientific expertise and supported by expert opinions (according to a memory protocol from Int. 2).

Hence, in sum, it is the very nature of the process of strategy-building that it is open to various interests and absorbs a whole range of different opinions. Various political actors give their point of view and openly express their opinions and criticism. Some criticism is taken into consideration, and some of it might be diminished by other, better, or 'more rational' arguments. Thanks to the discursive processes that are institutionalized in consultations, a certain compromise and consensus among participating parties is achieved that is more or less shared by everyone. At the end of the day, however, all the strategies are based on relatively fixed and clear-cut standards and principles of regional development which are vigorously promoted by professionals and experts as the essence of contemporary development practice. In this way, the process of strategy-building functions as a kind of 'funnel' for institutional diffusion that integrates as many (important) regional actors as possible into the world-cultural project of 'prudent' and 'rational' development planning and fosters the *translation* of relatively general and standardized knowledge of regional development in a particular regional context.

From a critical viewpoint this predominance of scientific expertise in political practice is considered to be problematic because it diminishes open political dialogue and silences potential critical voices that are not based on justified, highly rationalized, and 'legitimate' claims. This seems to be a principal dilemma of development planning: the most rational and diligent process of decision-making is not necessarily the most democratic one – even though one of the explicit aims of contemporary concepts of strategic planning is to raise 'participation'. However, here we are entering the domain of policy analyses and political philosophy which will not be further elaborated here (cf. Mannheim 1936; Ranciere 1995; Cuttler 2003: 13f.; Crouch 2004). Yet, in light of our discussion of the world-cultural underpinnings of region-building in Poland, it is just interesting to note that the new strategic approach of regional mobilization in Poland has fostered the expansion of rationalized planning structures, encourages local actors, and mobilizes ever more actors to participate in highly structured and professionalized processes of development planning. But one thing is clear: it only includes those who are able to speak a certain professional language and enact patterns of behaviour which are commonly shared in expert circles.

2 The new 2020 strategies of the three regions

In this section the major strategic visions, objectives and fields of activity contained in the current official development strategies of Dolnośląskie, Lubelskie and Podkarpackie are presented more extensively. These strategies were put in place in 2005 and 2006 based on a revision of the first strategic document from 2000. For the purpose of clarity I have foregone a detailed exploration of major differences between old and new strategies, since the principal orientations, the major strategic objectives, goals and priorities have not fundamentally changed between the old and new strategies. The main change is that the whole planning process was more structured and coordinated from the very beginning and that the main focus of the strategies was even more re-focused in accordance with the strategic objectives and guidelines of the current programming period of the Cohesion Policy 2007–13. Some interviewees have considered this as a stronger 'centralization' of regional planning, although the regions have been given more competences than ever before in the short history of their existence. This paradox will be briefly outlined in the following paragraph, before we look more closely at the major strategic goals and objectives of Dolnośląskie, Lubelskie and Podkarpackie.

Stronger unification of regional development planning between 2004 and 2006

The former official regional development strategies (RDS) of the 16 Polish voivodships were revised and re-structured between 2004 and 2006 in a collective and cooperative process involving representatives from all regions and advisors from the Ministry of Regional Development. The process was initiated and coordinated by the Department of Structural Policy Coordination of the ministry and some of their professional advisors. But the major roadmap and objectives for updating the regional strategies were worked out in cooperation with representatives of the regional governments in various operational workshops and expert meetings. Obviously, the expert circle around the Department of Structural Policy Coordination did have a lead in the process as they were the initiators, moderators and driving forces of the revision of the major regional planning document (Int. 18).

One reason for the revision of the first RDS from 2000 was to improve development planning at the local and regional level, and to prepare regional planning for the new programming period of EU funding between 2007 and 2013, which required a stronger orientation to the principles and goals of the renewed Lisbon agenda. It has also been said that the major reason for the revision of the first RDS was caused by the fact that for the first time in the history of EU funding in Poland the regions were allowed to outline their own and distinct regional operational programmes (ROPs) (cf. Żuber 2007). These are operational programmes with a financial volume of about EUR3 billion for each of the 16 Polish voivodships, and are being managed and implemented between 2007 and 2013 in direct cooperation with the EU Commission and the regional government, fully independent of control by the national administration. Hence, the EU accession of Poland in 2004 and the full integration of the country into the funding structures of EU structural policies brought about a new level of Europeanization in domestic spatial development planning. The revision of the existing RDS was put forward in light of the preparation of the new overarching strategic planning document of the Polish government that was required by the EU Commission to be eligible for EU regional development funding in the new programming period 2007 to 2013, the so-called 'National Strategic Reference Framework' (NSRF). Accordingly, this also entailed a revision of the formerly existing RDS with reference to the new national planning documents and the new European guidelines and regulations. This is also highlighted in the introductory chapter of the current development strategy of Dolnośląskie:

> According to the decisions made, the concentration of the updated Strategy on the goals and priorities identified in the key European Union documents (including, first and foremost, the Lisbon Strategy and the Gothenburg Strategy) is to be an important novelty. It does not, however, limit the autonomy of self-government authorities in the scope of specifying its own regional goals and priorities that are the quintessence of the Strategy. On the contrary, in spite of the countrywide integration of the expectations related to the creation of formal strategies, their contents should increasingly depend on regional communities.
>
> (The 2020 Development Strategy of Dolnośląskie, English version, p. 5)

The revision of the regional development strategies of all 16 voivodships between 2004 and 2006 has clearly brought about a more structured and unified system of multi-level development planning in Poland. Whilst the link between the former RDS and the previous National Development Plan (NDP) 2000–6 was rather informal and unspecific, this link between regional and national planning and the substitution of the regional strategies under the umbrella of national spatial planning is more explicit. Therefore, some of the Polish experts on regional policy who were interviewed in spring 2007 considered the revision as a clear indication of an increasing re-centralization of regional development planning and regional development policy. However, from the perspective of experts that were directly involved in the process, this was seen as an integral element of the 'modernization' of the Polish regional planning system and a 'necessity' for the 'effective' absorption of prospective EU structural funds between 2007 and 2013.[4]

Consequently, the whole system of regional planning from the local to the national level was intended to be unified and restructured in order to be prepared for the new funding procedures of EU structural funds between 2007 and 2013. The process of strategy-building was carefully supervized and accompanied by experts and advisors from the ministry of regional development. The reference points and design parameters were determined during collaborative workshops among representatives of the regional governments and representatives of the central government. The overarching reference point for development planning in the regions was the National Development Strategy (NDS) 2007–15, it is the basis for all the planning activities of public administrations in Poland, both on a territorial and sectoral basis. The revised regional development strategies, in turn, constitute the major planning documents for all planning activities in the regions. They are meant to constitute the major reference for the concrete executive planning of the regional operational programmes (ROPs), development strategies of the local communities, and other financial instruments and strategic documents, such as the Regional Innovation Strategies (RISs) which were also outlined in some regions in accordance with the European Lisbon agenda.

Symbolic re-nationalization of Europeanized development planning: the National Development Strategy 2007–15

The National Development Strategy (NDS) 2007–15 constitutes the overarching blueprint of spatial development planning in contemporary Poland. It is supposed to integrate all other approaches and strategies of development planning at various level of government, while taking into account the requirements and suggestions of European funding guidelines that are relevant for Poland these days. Thus, the NDS 2007–15 bundles all national reports, planning documents, strategies and programmes that are directly related to European structural policies into a common national vision of future development. This includes the aims and objectives of the National Reform Programme and the National Report on Social Security and Social Integration that had to be prepared by all EU member states in accordance with the Lisbon agenda, the six national 'operational programmes' (OPs) and the 16 regional operational programmes (ROPs) that were prepared to absorb the funds provided in the framework of the EU Cohesion Policy between 2007 and 2013, as well as all the other OPs relating to the Common Agricultural Policy and Common Fisheries Policy and so forth. Accordingly, the overarching 'European context' that decisively influenced the preparation of the NDS 2007–15 in Poland were the renewed Lisbon agenda and the Sustainable Development Strategy – a sub-strategy of the Lisbon agenda – the New Financial Perspective 2007–13, the Integrated Guidelines for EU Structural Policies, and in particular the EU Cohesion Policy, the Common Agricultural Policy and the Common Fisheries Policy.[5]

However, it must be noted that the preparation of the NDS 2007–15 constituted a completely voluntary act on the part of the previous Polish government and respective ministries, since it is not prescribed by any EU directive or regulation. In contrast to documents that are required under EU law, such as the NSRF, the OPs and the other obligatory reports and strategic plans mentioned above, this document goes beyond the a fulfilment of 'European' obligations. In fact, it constituted an additional effort on the part of the Polish government to modernize the national system of development planning and regional governance. Accordingly, it is stated in the strategy that it should serve as '(...) a foundation for an effective usage by Poland of the development funds, both national ones and the ones from the European Union, for the achievement of the social and economic goals' (Ministry of Regional Development of Poland 2006a: 7). Hence, the NDS should not just be considered as an indication of the strong 'Europeanization' of domestic development planning in Poland, but as a symbolic act of re-framing development agendas that are largely driven from outside by EU standards, regulations and funding guidelines in 'domestic' terms. The strategy is supposed to show that the Polish government takes a long-term and rational view of development planning, that it has its own agenda that even exceeds the limited scope of EU programming, and that it is not just driven by European regulations imposed from outside. In Figure 8.3 below an excerpt of the NDS 2007–15 is depicted. It shows the major strategic vision and the priorities of the strategy. Beyond that, this excerpt also gives an impression of the overall scientific outlook and rhetorics of the strategy.

The 2020 development strategies of Dolnośląskie, Lubelskie and Podkarpackie

Given all background information on the Europeanization of regional governance in Poland, and on the preparation and revision of the Polish regional development strategies (RDSs) it certainly comes without surprise that the current development strategies of the three selected regions Dolnośląskie, Lubelskie and Podkarpackie are relatively similar in scope, structure and major fields of activities. Even though the levels of development is markedly different (at least amongst regions in western and eastern Poland). In fact, all strategies are built upon the same standards and principles of regional development. All three regions proclaim similarly high and ambitious aims in terms of development. They all place an emphasis on 'raising the level of living conditions and the wealth of citizens', 'improving the competitiveness of the regional economy' and 'achieving sustainable and multi-faceted growth'. All three regions aim to 'increase the competitiveness and innovativeness of their economy'. they all want to develop their capacities to 'develop into knowledge societies'. they all want to 'improve the internal territorial cohesion' of their regional populations and to bring transport and technical infrastructure up to 'European standards'. Moreover, they all want to 'improve the social cohesion', 'social activity' and 'social participation' of their citizens. And all three strategies have an outlook up to the year 2020, when the socio-economic prospects of the three regions are expected to have significantly improved. This was one of the most significant changes between the old and new strategies.

Hence, in short, the official development strategies of the regions are more or less completely determined by priorities, principles and standards of European regional development policy (see Chapter 5). There is almost no difference or deliberate differentiation of strategic aims and objectives visible among the major planning documents of the regions. In this sense, the various strategic documents could indeed be considered as mere representations of the 'formal structure' (Meyer *et al.* 1997) of regional mobilization in Europe of today. The

Excerpt of the strategic core of the Polish National Development Strategy 2007–15:

The main aim of the National Development Strategy *'is to raise the level and quality of lives of Poland's residents: individual citizens and families.'* (23)

'By raising the level of life we mean the growth of incomes in the sector of households, facilitating access to education and trainings, which leads to raising the level of education of the society and raising the qualifications of the citizens, growth of employment and labour productivity, resulting in both reducing unemployment, as well as increasing the level of professional activity and improvement of health of residents of Poland.

By raising the quality of life we mean an essential improvement of the state and growth of the feeling of safety among the citizens, possibility of using the functional and easily accessible technical and social infrastructure, life in a clean and healthy and favourable natural environment, participation in a democratic life, participation in culture and tourism, membership in integrated, helpful local community, enabling a better harmonization of family and professional life and activity within civic society.

Raising the level and quality of life is to be effected by the state's policy that allows for fast, constant economic development in a long-term perspective, based on the development of the human capital increasing the innovativeness and competitiveness of the economy and regions, including on investments in the sphere of research and development, and on receiving stable economic, social and environmental conditions ensuring a European level and quality of life of citizens and families in the country and local communities. Functioning of the community and its safety should be based on the subsidiary principle. (...)

The above goal can be reached only in conditions of realizing the rules of balanced development and caring for and keeping the cultural heritage of Poland. This goal can be reached in circumstances of significant differentiations of the level of development of regions, marginalization of rural areas and lack of respect for the spatial organization of Poland' (23f., original emphasis)

→This leads to the following five development priorities of the Polish Development Strategy 2007–15:
1. Growth of competitiveness and innovativeness of the economy
2. Improvement of the condition of the technical and social infrastructure
3. Growth of employment and raising its quality
4. Building an integrated social community and its safety
5. Development of rural areas
6. Regional development and raising the territorial cohesion

Source: Ministry of Regional Development (2006a: 23–5).

Figure 8.3 Major strategic aims and priorities of development in Poland 2007–15.

preparation and implementation of distinct regional development strategies would then appear as a relatively superficial and unmotivated execution of pre-vailing formal and normative standards of contemporary development planning.

In Tables 8.1 and 8.2 the major strategic aims and objectives, as well as the major priorities and some of the envisaged measures of development

Table 8.1 Strategic visions, objectives and priorities of Dolnośląskie

The 2020 Development Strategy of Dolnośląskie Adopted in November 2005

Major development objective:
Increasing the level of living conditions for the inhabitants of Lower Silesia and improving the region's competitiveness while respecting the principles of sustainability.

The future vision of the region:
The region aims at becoming a hub region on the European map of hub regions.

The 'economic' objective: Creating a competitive and innovative economy.	The 'spatial' objective: Increasing spatial and infrastructural cohesion of the region and its integration with European growth areas.	The 'social' objective: Developing social solidarity and creative and open citizen attitudes.
Priorities and measures: 1) Increasing the investment attractiveness Supporting promotion and marketing of the region via training and information projects, creation of internet platforms, conference and trade fair participation etc. Supporting agglomerations and areas of intensive accumulation of economic activities; Fostering cooperation with the most innovative and most competitive centres in Europe, and all sectoral actions to develop an innovative economy; Supporting development of business environment institutions 2) Creation of knowledge-based economy Development of modern technologies and a service sector (both tangible and intangible), i.e. through supporting R&D activities of	*Priorities and measures:* 1) Improving spatial cohesion Fostering polycentric development; region-wide spreading of development effects of the Wroclaw Metropolitan Area; shaping communication systems and development and improvement of pan-regional infrastructure, esp. in the European transport corridors; supporting infrastructure investments at the local level 2) Sustainable development of rural areas Investments in infrastructure; promoting conditions for large production farms and creating non-agricultural workplaces and agro-tourism; increasing the potential of forest production; creating an incentive system for economic and social activation of rural areas	*Priorities and measures:* 1) Social integration and counteracting social exclusion Supporting disabled and other vulnerable groups; enhancing child-care systems; social activation of the elderly including the establishment of care systems; equalizing opportunities for women and men; reducing poverty, esp. in areas subject to structural unemployment; drug prevention; promoting innovative social policy approaches and problem prevention etc. 2) Strengthening civil society and culture Increasing social activity in the area of culture; protection of cultural heritage; promotion of regional identity; supporting and promoting pro-social attitudes and partnership; activation

enterprises and the use of modern technologies by entrepreneurs, or implementing a system of information on the latest service products; supporting the creation of new innovative companies, the promotion of innovative attitudes, the absorption and diffusion of innovation and supporting technology transfer between enterprises

3) Supporting economic activity
Supporting SME development; promoting regional products through common marketing strategies; supporting economic cooperation in the region, esp. by creating network structures and clusters and broadening interregional and international cooperation; promoting economic education of the inhabitants and entrepreneurial attitudes; supporting the process of privatization of public enterprises; supporting the development of export activities of regional enterprises; supporting the creation of a region-wide network of relations of tourist enterprises and esp. projects improving and enhancing the spa tourist potential

3) Improving spatial order and the harmony of spatial structures
Regeneration of degraded areas; enhancing international cooperation in the scope of spatial planning; protection of the region's cultural heritage

4) Ensuring ecological safety for society and the economy
Implementation of a system for monitoring air quality; improving ground water supplies and waste management (recycling and segregation systems and waste sites meeting the most important European Union standards); improving quality of degraded and reclaimed soil; ecological education, protection of areas of high natural value; improving biological and landscape diversity; ensuring anti-flood protection and increasing water retention; creation of a comprehensive system for monitoring the quality of the environment

5) Ensuring energy safety
Enhancing and modernizing national systems of energy transmission as well as distribution networks; diversification of energy sources, with particular attention to renewable energy sources (above all: hydroelectric power plants; successive provision of access to natural gas and ensuring a strategic reserve; enhancing and modernizing heating systems etc.

of local communities, esp. in rural areas and small towns; strengthening and developing the cooperation between public administration and NGOs etc.

3) Improving the quality and efficiency of the education and scientific research system
Development of teaching personnel; access to IT technologies; increasing the number of persons majoring in mathematical, natural and technical sciences; creating conditions and institutions for life-long education; promoting exchanges; increasing the scope of information regarding vocational training and the quality of counselling etc.

4) Improving public safety and health
Equipping police with adequate technical means; supporting effective forms of cooperation between citizens and the police; promoting active and healthy lifestyles, esp. through education, supporting sports tournaments such as city marathons; increasing the effectiveness of health care facilities and disease prevention

5) Active labour market policy and strengthening human resource development
Skill development (i.e. vocational training for persons in danger of losing jobs; training and counselling for farmers leaving the agricultural sector); promotion of employment and entrepreneurship etc.

Source: Lower Silesian Parliament (2005), dense summary of the original content of the RDS; own depiction.

Table 8.2 Strategic visions, objectives and priorities of Lubelskie and Podkarpackie

Lubelskie Development Strategy 2006–2020
Adopted by the regional parliament in July 2005

<u>Mission statement:</u>

Stimulating multifaceted processes of regional development that facilitate a sustainable and balanced development of the region and contributing to the improvement of the quality of life and a growth of wealth for the inhabitants of Lubelskie.

<u>Major strategic objective:</u>

Achieving sustainable and balanced socio-economic development in Lubelskie by increasing the competitiveness of the region and optimal utilization of its developmental potential.

1) Increasing regional economic competitiveness and the capacity for the creation of jobs	*2) Development of a modern society and of resources necessary for adaptation to the knowledge economy*	*3) Improving the attractiveness and cohesion of the territory in the Lubelskie region*	*4) Developing inter-national cooperation and improving the effectiveness of regional development policy*
1.1 Restructuring of traditional sectors of the regional economy and adaptation to the rules of the Common Market	2.1 Shaping population policies that are favourable for the development of the region	3.1 Improvement of transport infrastructure and accessibility of the voivodship	4.1 Developing the interregional cooperation of the voivodship within international, national and trans-border frameworks
1.2 Development and stipulation of the competitiveness of the regional agro-business	2.2 Increasing the level of skills and knowledge of inhabitants	3.2 Preservation and strengthening of the natural, territorial and cultural variety of Lubelskie	4.2 Increasing institutional capacity of the region to carry out effective regional policies (through monitoring, training, technical improvements, certifications, improvement in planning etc.)
1.3 Specializing in selected sectors of production	2.3 Growth of employment through better mobilization of the resources of inhabitants	3.3 Development of urban centres and the metropolitan functions of Lublin	4.3 Improving the effectiveness of regional marketing and the capacity to attract foreign investments
1.4 Development of SMEs and their innovative potential	2.4 Supporting social integration and reducing poverty	3.4 Improving the quality of life of the rural population and multifunctional development of rural areas (i.e. development of infrastructure and agro-tourism)	
1.5 Support R&D activities and their utilization by businesses	2.5 Fostering and utilization of the social and cultural capital of the region		
1.6 Development of information society and IT infrastructure	2.6 Improvement of public safety and order		

Podkarpackie Development Strategy 2007–2020
Adopted by the Regional Parliament in October 2006

<u>Major strategic objective:</u>

Increasing the national and international competitiveness of the regional economy by boosting its innovativeness, having an effect on the creation of favourable employment conditions as well as a rise of incomes and living-standards for the inhabitants.

Areas of activity:	*Objectives, priorities and measures:*
Regional economy	Creating conditions for an increase in economic competitiveness through the development of entrepreneurship and conditions of innovativeness as well as increasing investment attractiveness
Technical infrastructure	Improving the technical infrastructure and the accessibility of the region by supporting investments in motorways, railways and a regional airport (Rzeszow-Jasionka), supporting investments in modern water supplies and sewage systems, improving the energy supply and IT infrastructure
Rural areas and agriculture	Multifunctional development of rural areas that aids the development of profitable agricultural production and the creation of non-agricultural sources of income, i.e. through the renewal and modernization of rural areas and agricultural infrastructure, promotion of markets for agriculture
Environmental protection	Improving the environmental quality as well as the preservation and protection of natural resources and the landscape, through protection of water resources and rationalization of water management, preventing expansion of waste and improving waste management etc.
Social capital	Multifaceted development of social capital enabling a comprehensive utilization of the potential and possibilities of personal development of the inhabitants of the region, i.e. through improving the quality of the educational system and vocational training, promoting culture and civil society
International cooperation	Supporting the development of regional development, utilizing the tourist potential and cultural heritage as well as protecting the natural environment
Health care	Ensuring health care of inhabitants: reduction of morbidity rates and mortality of inhabitants through improvement in health care, coordination of activities to minimize risks to health through information campaigns, education, improvements in health care infrastructure
Social security	Integration activities in the field of social services, esp. activities fighting marginalization and social exclusion (activation, integration), supporting families and childcare, modernization and establishment of social services, promotion of civil society and voluntary work etc.

Source: Zarząd Województwa Lubelskiego (2005) and Zarząd Województwa Podkarpackiego (2006), summary, transl. from Polish by S.B.

intervention as outlined in the official development strategies (RDSs) of the three regions are depicted one after another. These tables just present a small selection and a rough sketch of the major goals and aims of the regions in order to provide an opportunity for looking at the major strategic objectives of the three regions in a comparative way. The first table, 8.1, shows the 2020 development strategy of the Dolnośląskie Voivodships. It is the most detailed and most differentiated depiction of the three strategies and also shows a number of measures envisaged under each of the priorities. In order to avoid overwhelming complexity and repetition the depiction of the strategies from the two eastern regions in Table 8.2 is less detailed and only indicates major objectives, areas of activity and major priorities of funding. However, this should not imply that the strategies of the two eastern regions were less detailed and less differentiated than the strategy of Dolnośląskie. In principle, the concrete measures envisaged by the two eastern regions do not differ much from the measures put forward by the western region.

It is striking to see how wide-ranging and encompassing envisaged development interventions are determined in the strategic documents. In fact, the strategic documents do not just outline the approaches of economic mobilization (such as investments in technical infrastructure, innovation policies, human capital development, etc.) and sustainable development (improving energy efficiency, environmental protection, effective waste management etc.) but also very far-reaching and sophisticated measures of social and cultural 'mobilization' which roughly have been identified as new techniques of social government in late modernity (cf. Burchell *et al.* 1991; Rose 1999; Rose and Miller 2008). This results in a bundle of different and largely idiosyncratic measures that range from the 'improvement' and 'rationalization of social services' – especially by improving health care, education and training schemes, public safety, civil society and the inclusion of marginalized groups – to the 'preservation of cultural heritage' as well as the 'promotion' of both 'regional identity' and 'international cooperation'. A brief look at some measures outlined in the 'social objective' of the current development strategy of Dolnośląskie (Table 8.1) contains some of the principles and techniques of 'social activation' that are nowadays widely discussed as 'neo-liberal' social policy interventions in Europe of today. This impressively shows the extent to which policies and policy priorities that are proposed and propagated by the European Union have entered municipal and sub-national levels in the post-socialist EU member states and the way in which they fundamentally determine the definition of policy interventions at these levels of government. Indeed, many of the measures of cultural and social governance are supported by the funding structure of the European Social Fund (ESF) and vigorously promoted by the European Union as a new policy tools to 'combat exclusion' (Rumford 2000; Bernhard 2006, 2010; Münch 2010) or new strategies of cultural mobilization (cf. Shore 2000). These include such diverse strategies as 'increasing social activity in the area of culture', 'supporting and promoting pro-social attitudes', 'activating elderly people', 'promoting self-employment and entrepreneurship', 'creating conditions and institutions for life-long learning', or measures to improve 'public safety' and 'health' among the regional population, e.g. by supporting 'effective forms of co-operation between the citizens and the police' or even 'promoting active and healthy life-styles through public campaigns and the funding of sports events'.

3 Effective strategies? – major development projects in the three regions

Finally, we will have a look at what is actually implemented in the regions. Hence, the aim is to look beyond the strategies, the 'formal structure' of regional mobilization, and see what regions actually do and how the strategic objectives are implemented. However, this analysis does not represent a classical policy-analysis that aims to measure both the efficiency and efficacy of development interventions – this is and has already been done massively by numerous policy-analysts.[6] In contrast, the following sections simply impart a few impressions of some concrete measures and projects implemented in the regions and in what way these measures might potentially affect the development of the three selected regions. We start with a short description of some measures which are entirely planned and governed at the national level, but which also have a great impact and influence on the development of the three regions. We will subsequently have a look at the priorities and the financial allocations in the regional operational programmes (ROPs) 2007–13 of the three regions, since the ROPs are the major operative instruments of regional development in the regions. Most of the financial resources that are at the regions' disposal are allocated to the regions through this programme or are spent on measures outlined in this programme. Finally, we will have a look at major projects which are financed and envisaged by the regions. This should give us some hints to major paths of development within the three regions.

Programs and projects governed and implemented nation-wide since 2004

Although all Polish voivodships have had their own distinct RDSs since 2000, most of the measures and policies of regional development have not been planned and governed by the regional governments themselves, but by the central government. This applies to the implementation of the pre-accession funds allocated before 2004, and even more to the implementation of the five sectoral operational programmes (SOPs), the two community initiatives, the Cohesion Fund (CF) and the Integrated Operational Programme for Regional Development (IROP) funded by the EU Cohesion Policy between 2004 and 2006 (see also Table 6.2 above). Nonetheless, all measures and projects funded by these programmes have affected development in the individual Voivodships in one or the other way. They were implemented in all voivodships, or rather in municipalities, business organizations, public institutions and non-governmental organizations located in the different voivodships.

It is estimated that in the period between 2004 and 2007 nearly 85,000 projects co-funded by EU Structural Funds and the Cohesion Fund were implemented all over Poland. Priority was given to the improvement of basic infrastructure (more than 50 per cent of all projects, i.e. establishment of more than 100 sewage treatment plants and 49 programmes related to waste recycling) and transport routes (by the end of 2007 3,700 km of roads and over 200 km of motorways had been built or modernized, and 350 km of railway tracks had been upgraded). Moreover, about 15,000 of these projects focused on business support, in particular SME development. And the funding provided by the EU Cohesion Policy 2004–6 also stimulated the development or modernization of 78 research laboratories as well as the establishment of 19 technology incubators, 27 business parks, and 17 research and technology parks. In fact, the major part of the funding and reimbursement of project expenditures was complete by the end of 2008. However, in some programmes (such as the IROP) the process of reimbursement has lasted until 2010.[7]

It was already mentioned during the discussion of expert opinions on the development of the three selected regions in the previous chapter that the projects funded by the different programmes and initiatives between 2004 and 2006 were not allocated equally among all 16 voivodships. In fact, it was the major urban areas of Poland as well as the western regions that profited most from initiatives of regional development and EU funding over the past few years (cf. Płaziak and Trzepacz 2008). In the former programming period the most important programme of the voivodships, a programme that was partly managed by the regional governments and which directly transferred resources for the development of basic infrastructure was the Integrated Operational Programme for Regional Development (IROP). It distributed about EUR200 million to each of the 16 voivodships (in the period 2004 and 2006), and this money was mainly spent on the construction of roads, sewage and waste management systems, or the reconstruction of public infrastructure and historical buildings in municipalities and local communes in all three regions.[8]

The current programming period for the EU Cohesion Policy and the Common Agricultural Policy from 2007 to 2013 is providing Poland with more than EUR 80 billion to be spent on initiatives of local and regional development by 2013 and beyond. By far the largest operational programme in Poland under the current programming period of the Cohesion Policy 2007 to 2013 is the OP 'Infrastructure and Environment'. It integrates resources provided by the ERDF and the cf. and amounts to EUR27.9 billion (at 2007 prices). This programme entails ambitious goals in boosting the development and country-wide provision of basic infrastructure, including in particular a significant expansion of motorways, express roads and railway connections, but also the further expansion of sewage systems, waste management plants and so-called 'environmental management systems'.[9]

Without doubt, the development and expansion of motorways, express roads and railroads would have tremendous effects on the overall development of the Polish voivodships. This was vigorously highlighted during interviews with experts and policy-makers in Poland (see Chapter 7 above). However, the currently envisaged expansion of motorways, express roads and railways in Poland affects the Polish regions to an unequal extent.[10] This can be well illustrated at the example of our three selected regional cases: In fact, the only motorway connections which actually exist at present already are two motorways that connect the western border areas with Kraków in the south and Łódź in the middle of the country. Beyond that, there are no other motorways or express roads in the rest of Poland at present (as of 2009). Yet, the motorways and express roads that are envisaged to be built by beginning of June 2012, which is the start of the European Football Championships in Poland and Ukraine, include the completion of the west-east motorway connections through Podkarpackie to the Ukrainian border and the development of a north-south connection from Gdańsk via Łódź to Katowice. Thus, the overall accessibility of Lublin and Rzeszów, and especially the connections from Lubelskie and Podkarpackie to Warsaw, the booming capital city of the country, will remain relatively low in the foreseeable future.[11]

A similar outlook for the eastern regions is foreseeable when we look at major express railroad connections that are planned to be built in Poland by 2020. In fact, in the near future only the central part of Poland and the larger agglomerations in this central area of Poland – namely, Poznań, Warsaw, Łódź and Wrocław – will soon be connected with one another through high-speed railroad connections.[12] This will markedly increase the speed and frequency of travels between western regions and Poland's core areas, but until today the inclusion of the eastern areas into the web of high-speed connections, or overcoming the historical imbalances in the dispersion of railway lines between Eastern and Western Poland, is neither planned nor envisaged, yet. Certainly, the eastern part of Poland is not completely disregarded in the current modernization and expansion of road and railroad connections. Many train connections are also remodelled and refurbished in the eastern part of Poland. Nonetheless, the historical gap in the development of infrastructure, a Poland of 'two speeds', will remain. And it can be doubted that the special operational programme 'Development of Eastern Poland' which was particularly set up to provide extra money for the development of the eastern regions can compensate for this.

The Operational Programme 'Development of Eastern Poland'

Despite aforementioned inequalities in the future expansion of transport infrastructure, it must be highlighted that the huge structural differences between eastern and western Poland are generally acknowledged by Polish policy-makers. And plans are afoot to tackle these in the current programming period via an operational programme that is dedicated in particular to the five regions in eastern Poland that are most 'lagging behind' (in terms of GDP). The OP 'Development of Eastern Poland' allocates a total of EUR2.3 billion to fund particular development projects exclusively to the five most disadvantaged voivodships in eastern Poland: Lubelskie, Podkarpackie, Podlaskie, Świętokrzyskie and

Warmińsko-Mazurskie (see Table 8.3) Accordingly, our two exemplary cases Lubelskie and Podkarpackie should profit from this OP in the following ways: Under priority axis 1, financial support is provided for improvements to the infrastructure of universities, for measures promoting the innovativeness of the regional economy, or for promotional activities in the regions and projects enhancing international cooperation. Under priority axis 2, about EUR300 million is provided to improve the provision of broadband in all five regions. Under priority axis 3, public transport systems are to be improved in all five regions, including the development of an integrated municipal transport system in and around Lublin (with about EUR90 million of EU funds) and in Rzeszów (with about EUR50 million). Under priority axis 4, regional roads and by-passes will be constructed in Lubelskie (approximately EUR66 million) and in Podkar-packie (EUR102 million) for carefully determined projects. Furthermore, under priority axis 5, plans are afoot to improve sustainable tourism by creating cycle routes to connect all five voivodships in eastern Poland and to build the corre-sponding tourism infrastructure. Construction has already started and it is esti-mated to cost about EUR50 million.

All these projects and many more are planned to be implemented by 2015 at the latest. They are supposed to be tailored to the special situation in the eastern regions and the particular needs of the local population. However, this OP is neither managed nor implemented by the regional governments of the voivod-ships concerned. In fact, the overall managing authority of this OP is the Minis-try of Regional Development, and the intermediate body managing and supervising the process is the so-called 'Polish Agency for Enterprise Develop-ment' (PAED), a governmental organization located in Warsaw.

Table 8.3 OP 'Development of Eastern Poland' 2007–13

OP: Development of Eastern Poland	*EU Funding: EUR2.3 billion (ERDF)*

This programme is an additional element of support with the framework of EU structural funds deliberately dedicated to 'hastening the pace' of social and economic development in the five most disadvantaged regions in Eastern Poland: *Lubelskie, Podkarpackie, Podlaskie, Świętokrzyskie* and *Warmińsko-Mazurskie.*

The six funding priorities of Operational Programme Development of Eastern Poland are:
(1) Stimulating development of knowledge based competitive economy,
(2) Improving access to broadband Internet in Eastern Poland,
(3) Development of selected metropolitan functions of voivodship cities,
(4) Improving accessibility and standard of transport links in voivodships of Eastern Poland,
(5) Enhancing the role of sustainable tourism in the economic development of the area,
(6) Optimizing the implementation process of the OP Development of Eastern Poland.

Source: Polish Ministry of Regional Development and European Commission 2009.

Seeds of regional self-determination: the regional operational programmes 2007–13

The current regional operational programmes (ROPs) 2007–13 are by now the most important operational programmes funded by the EU in the short history of the new Polish voivodships. The ROPs were prepared by the regional governments of the voivodships themselves, based on the revised regional development strategies (RDS), and they are managed and implemented independently of interference of the central government. The Ministry of Regional Development merely supervized the process of preparation and lead the negotiations with the EU Commission in 2007. Now that the programmes are running, the central government only monitors the efficiency of the implementation in the regions and ensures it matches with the overall goals and aims outlined in the National Strategic Reference Framework (NSRF) 2007–13 and the National Development Strategy (NDS) 2007–15.

The preparation and introduction of the independently managed regional operational programmes has been a highly debated issue in the past years, indeed. While this slight step of regionalization in the planning and management of OPs was already agreed upon between the 16 regional governments and the central state in order to compensate for the relative low influence the regions had between 2000 and 2006, the realization of this agreement was not assured anymore when the preparations for the new programming period actually started. However, the hesitation was less on the part of the Polish central government than on the part of the EU Commission, which simply doubted that all Polish voivodships had the capacity to efficiently manage and implement an OP with an allocation of more than one billion euros of Structural Funds. Moreover, the Commission was also afraid of increasing the complexity of the management system for the Cohesion Policy. Instead of corresponding and negotiating with just one party (i.e. the Polish Ministry of Regional Development), the EU Commission would have to increase its regular contacts, exchanges and respective monitoring structures to accommodate the introduction of 16 independent ROPs in Poland from 2007 onwards. Hence, the stimulation of regional mobilization in Poland through the EU Cohesion Policy has certain limits. For example, the concern about the overall efficiency and manageability of the planning and implementation structure potentially limits the forces of regional mobilization that are awakened by the procedures of European regional development policies.

Nonetheless, at the end of this debate, the Polish government was successful in negotiating a parallel structure of six national OPs and 16 ROPs. Consequently, a total amount of EUR16.6 billion was allocated to the 16 ROPs (for an overview of all OPs in the period 2007–13 see Table 6.3 above). This money has been allocated among the 16 Polish voivodships according to an 80–10–10 algorithm which determines that all voivodships participate in the distribution of 80 per cent of total funds allocated for the ROPs according to their share of the population. The remaining 20 per cent of funds is distributed only among those voivodships with a GDP per capita of less than 80 per cent of the national average and in which the unemployment rate is higher than 150 per cent of the national average.[13] Hence, this brought about EUR1,213 million for Dolnośląskie, EUR1,156 million for Lubelskie, and EUR1,136 million for Podkarpackie of total ERDF in the period 2007–13. And this is complemented by another EUR200 to 300 million of co-funding from the national budget for each of the voivodships (see Appendix 1). Thus, the overall allocation of funds for each ROP of the Polish voivodships between 2007 and 2013 amounts to EUR1.5 billion, accounting for an annual budget of about EUR200 million for each of the voivodships to carry out their own regional development policies. These financial resources allocated to the individual ROPs constitute the major contribution to the current annual budgets of the 16 Polish voivodships, and this annual contribution is determined by the 'voivodship contracts' negotiated between the regional governments and the central state.[14]

In fact, the current ROPs can be considered as small versions of the national operational programmes funded by EU Cohesion policy. They mainly co-fund projects that are determined by the funding priorities of the EU Cohesion Policy between 2007 and 2013, such as transport infrastructure, tourism, culture, education, the infrastructure of environmental protection, information society, healthcare as well as innovation, entrepreneurship and SME development. As shown in Appendix 1, the major priority areas and respective allocation of funds per priority area do not differ much among the three voivodships. In all three regions about half of the budget allocated to the ROPs goes to the promotion of economic competitiveness and innovation as well as the development of transport infrastructure. In Dolnośląskie the financial contributions earmarked for economic mobilization are certainly significantly higher than in the two eastern regions. In general, health facilities and measures for environmental protection receive the least amount in all three voivodships, since measures in these areas are mainly provided by national health policies and other OPs managed at the national level. Thus, although the regional budgets have never been as high as they are today, the room of manoeuvre of the Polish voivodships in conducting their own regional policies is still relatively limited.

Key projects in Lubelskie, Podkarpackie, and Dolnośląskie

Despite the relative similarity of official development strategies and the weak independence of regional governments, we can observe huge dynamism in regional development and countless projects and initiatives implemented in the regions which are co-funded in one way or the other using EU funds. In fact, it is not possible to outline all these projects in detail, and it would be by far an exhausting outline of numerous standard projects and measures. As already shown in the previous sections, most of the projects are very basic initiatives of infrastructure development in the regions, such as roads and motorway constructions, the establishment of sewage systems or water treatment plants, or the refurbishment of historical buildings and monuments. Moreover, all regions make huge efforts in promoting entrepreneurship and new innovative businesses.

Nonetheless, with regard to our more general exploration of the contribution of EU Structural Funds and the Cohesion Fund to a new world-cultural make-up of regions and the emergence of new regional 'identities', it is useful to look beyond the standard procedures of Structural Fund implementation and explore potential traits and traces regional specialization. Consequently, some of the key projects and most distinctive activities in each of the three regional cases are briefly outlined below.

Lubelskie: promotion of organic food production, culture and new business dynamics

A short glance at some of the outstanding projects and activities conducted by regional authorities, development agencies, and citizens in the Lubelskie Voivodship reveals that the strengths and potentials identified and discussed in the analysis of expert reflections on regional development in Poland are actively developed and promoted. Due to the long tradition of agricultural production and the relatively favourable opportunities for food processing and production in the region, one of the outstanding projects of the region is the establishment of the so-called 'Organic Food Valley' (in Polish: *Dolina Ekologicznej Żywności*). It is a joint venture between producers of organic food and other ecological products and services, organic shops, organizations of agricultural consulting and certification, and adjoining research institutes which aim to foster cooperation between all of these actors and increase their visibility under a common label. The Organic Food Valley and its respective support organization, the *EkoLubelszczyzna* association, are based on the concepts of clustering and regional cooperation which are so prominent in expert discourses on regional development these days. This initiative was started in 2004 as a pilot project of the regional innovation strategy (RIS).[15]

Based on similar principles, a so-called 'Cluster of Culture of the Lubelskie Region' (*Klaster Kultury Lubelszczyzny*) was founded by the end of 2007 with the support of various EU programmes and funds. It constitutes a cooperative network of local and regional NGOs and cultural organizations, local and regional authorities and related research institutes which aims to promote traditional, regional folk art and cuisine as well as all other types of 'cultural experiences' and 'events', while strengthening the cultural potential, the cultural offering and the tourist potential of the region. A major project of the Cluster of Culture is the operation of an internet platform and database for all cultural institutions in the region.[16] The Cluster of Culture project certainly supports the region's major emphasis on re-vitalizing its multi-faceted cultural traditions and traits. In light of this strategy, many historical monuments and buildings have already been refurbished during the past decade, such as the historical centre of Zamość, the renaissance city that is a UNESCO World Heritage site located in the eastern border area of the region, or the former Nazi concentration camp Majdanek.[17] Furthermore, plans are also afoot to strengthen the cultural potential of the region by promoting the city of Lublin in the campaign for 'European city of Culture 2016'. In this context, cultural institutions and initiatives play a major role for the success of the campaign.[18]

Apart from all these projects focused on the cultural and social development of the region the major project – and certainly one of the most cost-intensive projects co-funded by the ERDF in Lubelskie over the past years – is the construction of a new regional airport next to the industrial park in Świdnic, an area to the south of Lublin. This airport should help to decrease the generally relatively low level of accessibility in the region and enable potential tourists, business people and all other people who are interested in visiting the region to reach it directly and without being forced to make a detour via Warsaw or other Polish airports.[19]

Podkarpackie: a new centre of aviation in an unspoiled natural surrounding

Certainly, the authorities in the voivodship of Podkarpackie do not need to build a new regional airport, since there is already an airport in the region with a reasonable amount of international destinations – even a direct connection to New York. Beyond that, the area has a long tradition of aviation. Thus, the problem of accessibility by air has not been as big as for other areas in eastern Poland. In fact, the special role of aviation in the region – as manifested by the remnants of the Polish aviation industry from communist times and by the study programmes focusing on aviation and engineering that have long been offered at local schools and universities – presented an opportunity to regional authorities to follow this path and further promote this special element of the regional economy. Consequently, the settlement of new businesses from the aviation sector and other engineering sectors in local special economic zones (SEZs) has been vigorously promoted over the past decade. Moreover, since April 2003 the regional aviation industry has been marketed under the label of 'Aviation Valley' (*Dolina Lotnicza*), the major industrial cluster of the Podkarpackie Voivodship. The Aviation Valley project was established as a means to support cooperation amongst all actors in the regional aviation industry, support their business environment, and promote the Polish aviation industry to potential investors and customers. During the former programming period of Cohesion Policy, promotional activities and efforts to strengthen the international recognition of this cluster were also co-funded by the INTERREG-III-programme of the European Union. Today, the Aviation Valley represents almost 80 companies within the regions (as of the end of 2009).[20] It is recognized internationally, and it is also promoted by the EU Commission as a 'success story', as an example of 'good' and 'innovative' regional development within the current framework of European regional development policy (see Figure 8.4).

Furthermore, similar to the Lubelskie Voivodship, Podkarpackie aims to promote its tourism attractiveness. Accordingly, old towns, small villages, old monuments, old spas and buildings are being refurbished with the support of EU funds throughout the whole region. And many new initiatives and cultural

---

'When an entire region takes off'

'In South-East Poland, "Aviation Valley" suits its name. Proud of its hundred-year-old history in aeronautics, it is home to most of the companies in this sector and training centres for pilots and scientific research organisations. The majority of these companies are situated in the voivodship of Podkarpackie (Low Carpates), the capital city of which is Rzeszów. It notably has a Polytechnic College, which offers a specialist course in aeronautics construction. Although the region is disadvantaged (nearly 18 per cent unemployment) and essentially rural, it has many advantages: low labour costs, nearly 16,000 highly qualified employees, proximity to an international airport and a planned motorway which will connect the South-West and West of Poland.'

(Excerpt from an official presentation of 'success stories' taken from the webpage of the DG Regio of the European Commission in September 2009).

Figure 8.4 'When an entire region takes off' – EU information on the Aviation Valley.

organizations are trying to revive and promote local traditions and special regional cultures, exploring new ways of supporting and promoting regional identity and culture. Yet, in slight contrast to the Lubelskie region, which aims to promote the richness and diversity of its historical culture, Podkarpackie emphasizes the particular 'purity' and 'authenticity' of the regional environment and culture. The region is already the area in Poland with the highest rate of legally protected natural land, and it aims to extend environmental protection and facilities of sustainable tourism in its mountain areas in the South.

Dolnośląskie: continuous development of existing industries and structures

A brief glance at major activities in Dolnośląskie shows that the regional and local authorities of the Dolnośląskie Voivodship are trying to build upon and further develop the region's multi-faceted potential for value-creation, ranging from is traditional industries to the good conditions for creating post-industrial businesses, as well as the relatively high level of 'tourist attractiveness'. There are not just a few major or distinctive key projects in the region, such as the Aviation Valley in Podkarpackie, or the Cluster of Cultures in Lubelskie. However, this does not mean that the regional authorities do not actively promote the particular 'strengths' and 'development potential' of the region. In the contrary, it can be observed that major development actors from all around the region are very active in promoting social and economic development in their particular local environment and aim to fully enhance the region's economic potential. Thus, the various regional development agencies (RDAs) have established industrial parks (IPs) at different places in the region, and in some places new science and technology parks (STPs) have been established and are currently being further developed at the moment. One outstanding example is the so-called 'Lower Silesian Technology Park' (T-Park), which was opened in spring 2009 to

encourage innovative businesses from the automotive industry, information technology sector, telecommunications sector, and health resort sector to invest in
the Szczwano Zdrój and Wałbrzych areas. The T-Park is mainly run by the local
regional development agency and supported by local governments, and it is co-
financed by the ERDF with more than EUR10.[21]

Another outstanding example of the numerous activities that aim to stimulate
the development of new innovative and knowledge-intensive businesses in the
region is the establishment of a so-called 'Incubator Technology Centre' in
Wrocław. The project, which is aimed at 'minimizing the gap between the strong
scientific potential of the Lower Silesia region and relatively low level of innovative enterprises (...)', is also co-financed by the ERDF (more than 80 per cent
of the total costs of EUR5.6 million).[22] In addition to this, the 'metropolitan
functions' of Wrocław are being further strengthened through the restoration of
many roads, squares and buildings in and around Wrocław, as well as the expansion of university institutes, and new facilities for tourism, conferences and trade
fairs. In this way, the regional authority is aiming to make the city – and with it
the whole region – an attractive and vibrant magnet for tourists and business
people from all over the world.

4 All-embracing mobilization and standardized diversification of Polish regions – a brief summary

In the preceding sections we have extensively discussed a whole range of inci-
dences and indications of all embracing world-cultural mobilization of the new
Polish regions. The regional authorities are mobilized as purposeful, methodi-
cally and strategically acting development agents which are supposed to plan,
manage and implement development projects as 'effectively' and 'rationally' as
possible on the basis of the most contemporary techniques of planning and governance (cf. Bradley *et al.* 2003). Accordingly, an increasing number of 'compe-
tent' and 'knowledgeable' experts are involved in the process of regional
mobilization in the various regions, contributing to the implementation of development initiatives which aim to transform the existing 'underdeveloped' or 'low
performing' regional structures into new, more 'up-to-date' spatial entities which
should ensure a 'substantial improvement in living conditions and the quality of
life'. This is both required and extensively promoted by EU structural policies.
Indeed, the EU Cohesion Policy and other policies financed by EU Structural
Funds clearly foster a massive expansion of rationalized structures of development and intervention and the diffusion of modernist world-cultural standards,
principles and practices of development. Consequently, regions are promoted by
regional authorities and key regional actors as locations with 'unique' and
'attractive' conditions for living and visiting, and they outline ambitious regional
development strategies and documents for development planning that set out
goals and measures which are to be used to improve living conditions. In fact,
carrying out detailed development and investment plans is also a key requirement of the EU Cohesion Policy. In this sense, the strategies constitute the

'formal structure' (Meyer) of regional development policy in contemporary Europe, and they symbolically support the performance of the newly created Polish voivodships as modern sights and agents of change.

However, as we have seen in the preceding sections, the transformation is far from limited to a mere symbolic make-up of regional actor-identities that does not affect social behaviour and institutional structures within the regions. In fact, the regions are given considerable financial resources to implement the whole panoply of contemporary development practices outlined in their strategies. This fosters a quite substantial transformation in existing social and economic structures in accordance with prevailing standards, models and standard practices of regional development. Accordingly, the regional authorities and other major agents of development of the three Polish voivodships examined also aim to introduce numerous projects and measures which are now widely considered as standard practices of regional economic mobilization. They are implementing the most up-to-date innovation policies and human development policies, and are creating science and technology parks, entrepreneurship incubators, business clusters and regional umbrella organizations which are sometimes even called 'valleys' in reference to the Silicon Valley, the iconic prototype of successful post-industrial value creation in Northern California. The regions also rediscover their particular history and unique regional settings in relation to other areas and regions and re-interpret them as important conditions and resources for favourable future development. Based on deliberate analyses and assessments of regional particularities, different regional self-conceptions are created and promoted. This is a highly reflexive expert-driven process of region-making, which we can conceive in loose reference to social-scientific theories of modernity and individualization (cf. Elias 1978; Wagner 1994; Beck *et al.* 1994) as a process 'standardized diversification' of regions. This notion should capture the paradoxical situation that all over Europe distinctive regional histories, particularities, and identities are pronounced and promoted as never before. But at the same time they are structured on the basis of the same world-cultural principles and practices of development and become ever more similar. Accordingly, Table 8.4 outlines some traces facets of regional specialization among the three regions of Dolnośląskie, Lubelskie and Podkarpackie that were more intensively studied and introduced here, and summarizes some elements which were discussed in the preceding chapters:

However, in light of the relatively weak independent decision-making authority of the newly created Polish voivodships – and in particular in light of the still relatively weak provision of the voivodships with their own financial resources on a fully *un*conditional basis – doubts regarding the voivodships' capacities to pursue their ambitious development strategies can be raised. In fact, it can be clearly noted that the emergence of gradually different regional actor-identities in the course of world-cultural mobilization of sub-national regions has so far not contributed to any upsurge of new forms of intra-regional solidarity or even new regionalist particularisms. Although regional structures are increasingly emphasized these days as new refuges of social identification and social stability

Table 8.4 Traces of the standardized diversification of the three selected regions

Dolnośląskie	Lubelskie	Podkarpackie
*Self-conceptions** '(Post-)Industrial Allrounder' and 'European hub region'	'Exotic cultural region' with a modern food-processing industry	'An unspoiled mountain area' with a solid aviation industry
Major foci: Expansion of the. metropolitan functions of Wrocław (cultural and academic centre, conference and exhibition centre); promotion of automotive and knowledge- intensive industries as well as tourism (city tourism as well as spa and nature tourism)	Modern food production, esp. expansion of organic farming and biotechnology: promotion of agro-tourism, cultural tourism, as well as spa and leisure tourism; further development of Lublin as the cultural and urban centre of the region	Development of existing and new aviation industries and engineering; promotion of agro-tourism, green tourism and 'active recreation' tourism (esp. in the mountain area)
Key projects: Incubator Technology Centre in Wrocław and technology parks at other places (such as the 'T-Park' in Szczwano Zdrój); restoration of Wrocław and other towns; expansion of motorways and high-speed railway connections; expansion of tourist infrastructure; restoration of devastated and degraded areas	Organic Food Valley; Cluster of Culture; Construction of regional airports; restoration of basic infrastructure, cultural heritage, major tourist sights, and spas; development of tourist infrastructure and 'new industrial districts' in Swidnic and Puławy); expansion of IT infrastructure (e.g. broadband internet) and agro-research	Aviation Valley; Development of tourist infrastructure (esp. in the Carpathian mountains) and 'new industrial districts', esp. in Mielec); restoration of basic infrastructure, major tourist sights, and spas; construction of West– East railway and motor- way connections; expansion of IT infrastructure and university

Source: Own depiction, based on preceding analyses.

Note
* The self-conceptions have been extracted from the analysis. Thus, they constitute interpretations of the researcher in the first place, but sometimes they have been explicitly put forward in the development strategies and other regional self-descriptions.

in an age in which the capacity of nation-state integration is decreasing, in none of the three studied Polish regions was regional identity put forward as a resource for the mobilization of new forms of collective identifications or separatism. On the contrary, the current phase of all-embracing social mobilization in the regions of Poland has even brought about a significant devaluation of older, collectivist mechanisms of social integration that were typical of well-established welfare states in Western Europe or of the former communist societies (at least according to official political doctrines), such as the provision of social security (cf. Münch and Büttner 2006; Münch 2010). In the new Polish voivodships, nonetheless, 'regional identity' and 'cohesion' are promoted to unite key regional actors and institutions, local and regional authorities under a common project of future development, but not to limit the pace of social change or as a means of social protection. In the name of future development and wealth creation, the local and regional population as well as local and regional organizations and institutions are mobilized as active, self-determined, entrepreneurial 'actors'.

Thus, the world-cultural mobilization of the regions stimulates, first and foremost, the spirit of 'instrumental activism' and liberal measures of social inclusion – namely, economic activation and labour market integration – instead of pronounced solidary and collectivistic attitudes towards those who fail to development and 'lag behind'. This has become manifest in numerous policy documents studied in the previous analysis, and this was also expressed in interviews with people who are involved in the projects, the 'social carriers' of the world-cultural project of social change:

> There was a very good programme in 2004–6, I think, a programme promoting very small businesses and entrepreneurship where the young people who wanted to start businesses had to fill in only a document and prepare their business plan, and then the EU, or rather our institution which was implementing this programme, was giving them the money to start their own businesses. Of course, this money also could have been transferred to social security, or something like that... – but no way! This money was transferred to the people who don't need social security, but just need a small amount of money to buy some machines or equipment to start their own business.
>
> (Int. 18)

This opinion, and similar attitudes of social mobilization, were widely shared and supported by development agents in the three regions, even in the two regions which are alleged to have unfavourable conditions and huge difficulties in complying with the most contemporary standards of development and the pace of social change. Despite all the problems and weaknesses, representatives of regional authorities and development agencies in the three regions proudly described the positive changes, improvements and developments that have taken place over the past decade. All interviewees were positive about the huge developmental opportunities linked to the inflow of EU structural funds that are being invested in the regions, especially for the period 2007 to 2013. This upholds the belief in a better future. And this belief is an important basis for the success and legitimacy of the current phase of an all embracing economic and social mobilization in Polish regions.

9 Conclusions

The spirit and the limits of world-cultural mobilization

The starting point of this book was the somewhat astonishing observation that old modernist beliefs in progress and in the governability of human development are alive as always, although we are constantly enlightened and informed about the problems of 'active intervention', i.e. its remainders, dark sides, repercussions and unintended consequences. It seems, in fact, that the spirit of 'active intervention' is even more vivid than ever, and we have seen that it now reaches areas and dimensions of social life that have been widely untapped and unexplored until recently. As we have seen in the previous study the spirit of all-embracing social, economic and cultural mobilization has seized social spaces and regions in the literal sense. The previous pages have provided rich evidence of an all embracing world-cultural mobilization of sub-national areas in contemporary Europe. It has been shown that a 'new regionalism' that has spread in Western Europe during the past three decades has also expanded to post-socialist countries in Central and Eastern Europe and fostered a dynamism of structural change, even in areas of Poland which were until today widely considered to be 'peripheral' and 'backward'.

In fact, the regionally-targeted efforts of development, and the structural policy interventions financed by the European Union in particular, have stimulated development initiatives and investments on contemporary Poland which had been disregarded or postponed both during times of communism *and* during the first decade of radical neo-liberal state reform. This includes, above all, the building of roads, refurbishment of historical buildings, investment in environmental protection or simply the financing of water treatment and sewage systems at the municipal level. The case studies of region-building and regional mobilization in three selected Polish regions have revealed the strong – if not predominant – role that the principles, practices and, in particular, financial resources of EU Structural Funds have played since the very beginning of political transformation, notably since the start of accession negotiations in the mid-1990s. As in many other post-socialist EU member states in Central and Eastern Europe, the historical basis for bottom-up region-building in Poland was relatively low. Nevertheless, in the course of European integration, 'functional' administrative regions with some capacities for self-government and self-administration had to be established in order to meet the qualifying criteria for EU funds. In this sense, we can see that EU funds have had and still have a strong impact on structural changes in regions and municipalities all over Poland. Due to the conditional allocation of EU funds EU structural policy interventions can reach far into the domestic affairs of the EU member states. Certainly, the EU Cohesion Policy stimulates a greater consideration of the regional dimension in national policy interventions, a stronger level of concern for measures which potentially help to overcome structural imbalances amongst different sub-national areas and a stronger participation of sub-national regional actors in the planning and implementation of development interventions.

After more than ten years of regionalization, we can concede that the administrative regions put in place in Poland in 1999 have managed to take the role expected of them in the concert of so-called 'convergence' and 'competitiveness and employment' regions. They have introduced their own regional rituals, symbols and structures of policy-making. They have (re-)invented distinct regional histories and cultural traditions. Although we have to admit that the new Polish voivodships are relatively weak both economically and politically – in particular in their financial rooms of manoeuvre – the regional authorities have acquired some degree of autonomy and assertiveness in deciding upon paths and directions of future development. And in the current programming period of the EU Cohesion Policy, all voivodships have their own regional operational programme (ROP) that they can manage relatively independently of the central government. This has definitely contributed to a strengthening of the organizing capacities of regional authorities as well as major actors and stakeholders in terms of planning, managing and implementing European regional policy. On the other hand, nonetheless, it has also fostered a stronger standardization and homogenization of development activities of all 16 Polish regions.

Regional mobilization in Europe from a macro-phenomenological perspective

Based on a distinctive macro-phenomenological research perspective that stands in the tradition of the 'world-polity approach', this study has focused on the current phase of regional mobilization in the enlarged Europe against the backdrop of the worldwide diffusion and expansion of rationalized structures. One of the major advantages of this research perspective is that it grasps both the cultural and institutional logics of diffusion without essentializing the expansion of rational structures as a self-evident, triumphal procession of ever more 'functional', instrumental rationality, or even a self-evident coming into being of 'western civilization' (Elias) in all of its allegedly 'reasonable', 'prudent', 'right-minded' dimensions. In fact, it is a radical phenomenological account of modernization that conceptualizes 'rationalization' as a cultural project which is ceremonially evoked and promoted by authoritative, scientifically grounded agents of change and inscribed in relatively authoritative (world-cultural) models. Thus, it is the account of a world in which scientific principles and practices, scientific arguments, and all other types of 'scientized' knowledge has become a significant part of our daily life – a 'knowledge society' in which scientific knowledge, practice and expertise have attained strong cultural significance in all areas of social life and certainly not only in economic terms.

In the introductory chapter, four major implications of the increasing 'rationalization' (or rather: 'scientization') of social life in light of this particular research endeavour were briefly sketched out. These were: 1) an increasing generalization and institutionalization of 'reflexive mechanisms' in structures of political planning and social government; 2) a shift in the prevailing modes of societal government from hierarchical and mechanical top-down modelling or social organization towards 'societal self-regulation'; 3) a significant reorganization of the relations between government and social space; and 4) an increasing 'self-application' of the scientific conceptions of the 'knowledge-based society' by the emerging 'knowledge society' itself, intensifying and accelerating social change in certain prioritized areas and dimensions of social life. In light of the numerous empirical accounts of an all-embracing world-cultural mobilization of regions in Europe today that were presented in the previous chapters these four analytical assumptions can be specified with more empirical depth:

Ad 1) It was shown in the preceding analysis of the emergence of Polish regions as pro-active development actors in the course of European integration that the institutionalization and generalization of the mechanisms of planning, reflection, scrutiny, control and re-adaptation is a standard practice of European regional development policy. One of the first official acts of the newly constituted regional authorities in Poland was the preparation and adoption of distinct regional development strategies in accordance with standard models of the strategic management cycle of development planning, ranging from scientific SWOT-analyses and the determination of strategic goals up to the institutionalization of more or less sophisticated systems of evaluation, monitoring and control. In this context, the legally prescribed obligation to constantly monitor and audit EU-funded projects as set out by the regulations of the EU Cohesion Policy as eligibility criteria for receiving EU funding, or the requirement to carry out *ex-ante*, *mid-term* and *ex-post* evaluations of the efficiency and effects of EU spending play a major role. This is supposed to ensure – and above all document – the efficient and effective use of EU funds and guarantee the overall acceptance and legitimacy of EU structural policy interventions. And it certainly should help to increase the overall 'functionality' of planning and the availability of information on problems, pitfalls, or 'inefficiencies' which is necessary for further rational decision-making.

The other side of the coin is, however, a perpetuation and unwarranted expansion of rationalized systems 'in their own right'. In fact, ever more experts, rational agents and external consultants are included in planning processes and occupied with 'monitoring' and 'evaluating' the effects of development interventions. Yet the major problem of the increasing 'rationalization' of development interventions is not just the danger of and expansion of expert-driven structures of planning, monitoring and control beyond what is necessary, functional or efficient, or the fact that the EU Cohesion Policy is largely expert-driven. The major problem is, in fact, that it seems to be the only way to do 'development' and that alternative ways of approaching 'development', alternative initiatives outside the broad realm of scientifically explored and modelled options become less possible – and, even more strikingly: less conceivable. Nonetheless, one has to keep in mind that the opportunity cost of increasing 'forecasting', 'transparency' and 'controlling' can be the hindrance and elimination of exactly those social and cultural resources of development that are anxiously desired these days. Never before has the old criticism of technocratic and expert-driven rationalization been so stark as it is today, since it is precisely those vivid 'human activities', such as creativity, spontaneity or trust that are hard to model, standardize and reproduce. But they are most highly rated in contemporary conceptions of 'good development' (cf. Boltanski and Chiapello 2006).

Ad 2) The reinforcement of world-cultural mobilization in European society at the sub-national level, which has been described in the previous chapters, can certainly be considered as an indication of the shift from hierarchical top-down models of organizing society to increasing societal (and above all individual) self-regulation. This has been emphasized by numerous and quite diverse analysts of contemporary modernity and modern politics (cf. Foucault 1991; Wagner 1994; Rose and Miller 2008). In the context of the discussion on regional mobilization, it must be pointed out that this process is not appropriately or sufficiently understood as an increasing 'autonomization' of sub-national areas – in our case regions – from the rule and control of higher levels of government. Using the example of the three Polish regions in this study, it can even be questioned, indeed, whether the regions enjoy much autonomy and political self-determination within the European multi-level system of policy-making and planning at all. Hence, as we have seen in this empirical case study, the major characteristic of the current wave of regional mobilization in contemporary Europe seems to be the integration of more and more professionals, professional non-governmental organizations and 'active citizens' in the planning and implementation of development projects at the local and regional level.

Consequently, the process which has been described on the preceding pages is not only an expression of an increasing expansion of expert authority and the rule of 'disinterested cultural others' (Meyer and Jepperson 2000) over the whole territory of the European Union; it rather constitutes a more fundamental process of mobilizing society around certain standards of 'professional' social action and interaction which could be conceived as a projected 'professionalization of everyone' (Willensky 1964). Thus, the major effect of increasing the world-cultural mobilization of sub-national regions is, above all, an intended transformation of 'passive' citizens into people who professionally manage their own lives ('entrepreneurs', if you will) and the mobilization of individuals to actively influence the course of their own lives. However, in light of the huge standardization and global significance of some world-cultural scripts of appropriate professional behaviour and world-cultural models of development, the fundamental sociological question of whether people are able to *make* their own history, or whether they largely act upon standards and rules which are determined outside their personal reach, remains hotly debated – even in the new era of advanced self-determination.

Ad 3) It is one of the major arguments of this study that during the past three decades we have witnessed the consolidation of a relatively widely shared common sense on necessities and required ingredients of successful regional development practice on a global scale. In fact, by the beginning of the 1980s 'new industrial districts' which became productive sources of economic value-creation had been 'discovered' by economists and economic geographers. This was the starting point of a new wave of regionalism during the 1980s and 1990s, both in scientific research and political practice. Consequently, the 'region' has become a focal point of many sentiments of social and economic renewal. Indeed, both scientists and scientifically grounded agents of change have produced numerous scientific accounts of successful region-building and regional mobilization. These accounts have been vigorously promoted as new imperatives and 'myths' of development in transnational expert fora. At the level of European policy-making we have even witnessed the emergence of a relatively comprehensive and 'mature' *script* of regional mobilization with the introduction of the EU Cohesion Policy about two decades ago. This script neither prescribes one particular model of regionalization, nor one particular type of regional policy. But it mobilizes regions – or rather regional authorities, regional institutions and key development actors – to participate in development planning and actively promote the development of their home region (*regional agency*). It also mobilizes efforts of development around four world-cultural 'myths' of regional development: *innovation, competition, cohesion* and *sustainability*. And it has materialized in a whole array of standard organizing principles and standard procedures that have to be complied with, but which are often adopted routinely and without questioning.

It was shown in Chapter 5 that all four myths often evoke diverse claims of 'good' development and that they are often brought forward in highly stylized and idiosyncratic ways. However, they all share the same impetus of active intervention and the aim of mobilizing local and regional professionals and professional groups from different functional realms of society to interrelate and work together in order to enhance the developmental opportunities of the population in the given sub-national spaces. In light of this conceptual and discursive shift, the relation between government and space has changed decisively: The proactive usage and (re-)shaping of local and regional space – and in particular local and regional *institutions, culture* and *knowledge* – has become the main focus of development interventions. This brings about an all-embracing mobilization of both tangible *and* intangible resources which are identified as being favourable for the stimulation of 'good' development, i.e. regionally specific economic sectors and 'competences', productive social milieus and organizational clusters, or even particular cultural traditions, natural landscapes and sceneries, and socio-cultural histories).

Ad 4) The current wave of world-cultural mobilization in regions of contemporary Europe is certainly also an expression of the reinforcing political efforts to expand the structure of the post-industrial knowledge society across the territory of the European Union. Thus, the thesis of the rise of a 'knowledge society' is not simply a neutral description of social changes in contemporary modernity. With the 'discovery' of a fundamental break between society and the economy in late-industrial society by economists and social scientists during the 1960s and 1970s, it immediately became a political imperative. Since then, it increasingly guides the policy agendas of both national governments and international development agents. This strong entanglement between the social-scientific descriptions of contemporary society and the application of these models in social and political practice reinforces and accelerates the expansion of knowledge-based structures, while the supposition of the 'rise of the knowledge society' constitutes a self-fulfilling prophecy.

In the European context the phase of experimentation with new concepts of economic and social mobilization at the local and regional level as well as new measures of top-down development planning during the 1980s – often initiated and funded by the European Commission – can be identified as a major political stimulus for the rise of regional mobilization in Europe. At the end of the 1980s the spatial and, in particular, regional dimension of policy-making attained stronger recognition in European politics with the introduction of the European Cohesion Policy. It was pointed out in Chapter 4 that the EU Cohesion Policy was initially invented and introduced to complement the creation of a common European market and counter-balance potential risks of exclusion for the most peripheral areas. However, it was also highlighted that after more than 20 years of existence, the Cohesion Policy is still far from achieving this goal. Nevertheless, to this day the major guiding aims, procedures and areas of policy intervention under the Cohesion Policy have neither been given up nor substantially changed. Next to agricultural policy, 'regional policy' (as the essential part of the Cohesion Policy) has become the most important policy area of the European Union in terms of annual spending. The overall spending on measures funded under the heading of the Cohesion Policy has now exceeded the spending carried out under the European Recovery Plan after the Second World War, the famous 'Marshall Plan', and over time average spending has increased rather than decreased.

This apparent contradiction between 'expenditures' and 'output' can be understood, in my opinion, if we consider the emergence and expansion of the Cohesion Policy within the wider framework of the 'projected' transformation of European modernity towards the expansion of the 'knowledge society'. Since the first attempts at regional experimentation during the 1980s and in particular since the introduction of the Cohesion Policy, regional policy has become the central means of enhancing 'future progress' and at the same time strengthening the territorial cohesion of the European Union. Since 2007 at the latest, after the renewal and reaffirmation of the Lisbon agenda in 2005, the Cohesion Policy has become the central means of implementing the ambitious Lisbon goals in all local areas across Europe. In this way, the EU Cohesion Policy constitutes a vital element in the new 'politics of inclusion' which has begun to take shape during the past two decades of European integration (cf. Rumford 2000; Münch 2010; Bernhard 2010). It strengthens the transnational dimension of policy-making and especially the spatial differentiation of policy interventions. However, the irony of the Cohesion Policy, it would seem, is that the more it mobilizes regions, or rather regional actors and institutions, the more it fosters the diversification of sub-national spaces both in symbolic terms as well as with regard to structural socio-economic dimensions.

The unequal performance of regional identities in contemporary world-polity

The macro-phenomenological study of region-building that was outlined in this book conceives processes of regionalization not merely as 'endogenous' bottom-up processes, or the other way round: as an entirely enforced top-down process that largely remains alien to local and regional actors and institutions. In fact, from the perspective of macro-phenomenological institutionalism, we can consider the process of region-building and regional mobilization as an emergence of 'modern' regional actor identities against the backdrop of largely global structures and principles of contemporary world-polity.

It has become widespread in contemporary sociology to refer to the increasing significance of 'modern' world polity when one wants to explain that sports events, educational systems, airport-buildings and hotels, the laws of environmental protection and human rights are becoming ever more similar on a world-scale (Baecker 2009: 21). The current rise of regions, the marked pronunciation of local and regional uniqueness and long-lasting traditions, however, are usually regard as attempts of pronouncing 'difference' and 'distinctiveness' in the world-polity: 'Whoever wants to play a role in contemporary world society – or just wants to exist – has to have an address and – in association with this address – a certain place and responsibility' (ibid.: 22ff., translated from German by S.B.). Hence, regional cultural differentiation – and not world-cultural approximation – is usually regarded as the driving forces of regionalization in contemporary times. And regional differentiation is seen as the fundamental mechanism which produces 'diversity' in contemporary society.

I can certainly agree with some aspects of this interpretation and point of view. Nonetheless, in light of my own research experience I would add that this interpretation still underestimates the highly projected nature of regionalization in the contemporary times. Just as it holds for airports, hotels, legal principles or standard practices of modern organizations, we have to acknowledge that regions (or rather regional idioms, traditions and cultures) are to a larger and ever increasing extent produced and reproduced on the basis of world-cultural practices and principles. In our globally connected and loosely integrated world-polity, 'regional identities' do not just emerge out of thin air or out of emergent and contingent historical processes, but have to be produced and put forward in terms of relevant and legitimate world-cultural justifications and accounts of modern regional agency. This is at least the case if regional authorities want their regions to be recognized as 'modern' and 'relevant' areas ('where it is worth paying attention to' as it is stated e.g. in the self-presentations of Podkarpackie) and as legitimate participants in the games 'modern' actors play (Scharpf 1999).

As we have seen from the example of the preceding macro-phenomenological study of region-building in contemporary Poland, contemporary projects of regionalization are indeed strongly influenced by world-cultural standards and expectations. In the course of region-building, distinct regional histories, traditions, cultures and regionally specific sceneries or even competences have been explored, discovered and vigorously pronounced by regional authorities and other agents of development in the regions. The 'world-cultural' perception of strengths and weakness, opportunities and threats and the strategic outline of projects and paths of regional re-creation and social mobilization determine to a large extent the self-understanding of regional actors. This distinctive re-invention of particular local and regional histories and traditions, i.e. the mobilization of active and entrepreneurial citizens and organizations, the multi-faceted 'self-culturalization' (Reckwitz 2009) of regions in terms of post-industrial usability and productivity, are hallmarks of regional mobilization in contemporary 'post-traditional' Europe (cf. Matthiesen 2006: 156ff.). And, as shown above, not only in major city-regions but in fact also in the most 'backward' and 'outermost' regions of the European Union. Thus, the new culture-based attempts at regional mobilization seem to open up new and previously unknown opportunities of development, especially in those areas which are detached from major European transport routes and which do not at first glance seem to have the most favourable conditions for post-industrial value-creation (i.e. being urban, having larger 'innovative' and 'creative' social strata, having 'highly productive' service industries, having good 'transnational accessibility' and 'connectivity', having 'young, skilled and dedicated human captial', and having 'good opportunities' for the expansion of the leisure and recreation industries, etc.). And it is one of the major promises of the new attempts and approaches of reflexive regional 'self-culturalization' that favourable development and future progress is possible everywhere, if only people, institutions and organizations would get active, start to acknowledge and recognize the richness and uniqueness of their cultural, historical and natural heritage and promote it in the most favourable ways possible.

At the same time, however, we have also noticed that the constant perception and assessment of strengths, weakness, opportunities and threats also limits the possibilities of regional renewal and reinvention. It has been shown that the ingrained 'structural' differences between regions also determined the projection and 'impression-management' of the examined Polish regions. While the people interviewed in Dolnośląskie – the more prosperous region at the western border – were extraordinarily confident and optimistic about the future prospects of the region, and the region's self-conception is that of a 'post-industrial all-rounder' and 'future European hub region', the regional self-understanding in the two eastern regions is markedly different. Regional actors in eastern Poland are fully aware of their 'backwardness'. The policy-makers in the two eastern regions are also optimistic about current changes, and they put forward countless projects of regional renewal. But the awareness of huge structural imbalances and dis-advantages, as well as the awareness of an 'eastern wall' is strongly inscribed in the perception of both Polish policy-makers and 'ordinary' citizens alike and its confirmed and reproduced by numerous and expert assessments of economic, social and cultural imbalances amongst the newly created Polish regions.

In this way, 'given' structural conditions determine conceptions and per-ceptions of unequal regional development. And they also determine the self-understandings of regions and the performance of their projected world-cultural actor identities. In this way, a macro-phenomenological study of region-building and regional mobilization as it is outlined in this book could connect with existing anthropological and ethnologic attempts to capture the 'ethos' of regions, or the 'habitus' of places (cf. Lindner 2003), in the tradition of Pierre Bourdieu's conception of social distinction and lived social space (cf. Bourdieu 1984 and 1985). However, instead of emphasizing regional 'biographies', the historical or genealogical development of a certain region or place, macro-phe-nomenological perspectives emphasize the importance and decisive role of the *current* world-cultural context in which the formation of a regional 'ethos' or 'identity' is being shaped. In fact, regional histories and identities are always essentially produced and reproduced in reference to existing standards of devel-opment, and they are even constantly measured, assessed and ranked according to both numerous quantitative *and* qualitative indicators.

Some remarks and qualifications on the flipsides of world-cultural diffusion

Throughout almost all of this study the importance of scientific knowledge and expert involvement for the planning and projection of social change and devel-opment in contemporary Europe and its regions has been emphasized. Extensive references to the 'flipside' of this project of world-cultural regional mobilization, i.e. its limits, its failures or impasses, have been largely omitted throughout this study. Yet it was pointed out in the introduction to world-polity research that – though phenomenological sociology is a distinctly non-evaluative research approach – the major proponents of macro-phenomenological world-polity have put forward some evaluative statements, indeed. Namely, they alleged a high degree of *decoupling* between formal models – the official façades of world-cultural performance – and lived social practice in everyday-life. And, in fact, on the basis of the multi-faceted literature that extensively described and assessed the process of post-socialist transformation in Central and Eastern Europe during the past two decades, we would expect a high degree of decoupling. In this context, even the notion of a characteristic 'civilizational incompetence' (Sztompka 1993) was put forward in the early 1990s in order to stress the legacy of communism and the shortcomings of post-socialist society that allegedly hinder the 'full' realization of 'modernity'. And the current context of post-socialism is widely described as a medium of massive 'hybridity' and asynchro-nicity, where Western models have been transferred and often imposed quite rapidly, but never 'fully' realized and enacted due to lack of cultural, financial and political resources as well as historical legacies (cf. Offe 1994; Delhey 2000; Hann 2002; Outhwaite and Ray 2005; Merkel 1999; Schimmelfennig and Sedel-meier 2005).

Without doubt, there is certainly a huge amount of phenomena and negative developments in Poland today that could be seen as clear signs of 'decoupling': i.e. there is a huge amount of hidden unemployment and poverty and a certain amount of discontent of a large section of the population with the rapid and far-reaching social transformations of the past 20 years. Moreover, a huge amount of economic activity in contemporary Poland still does not appear in official stat-istics, since many people (especially in the rural areas) have just withdrawn from 'official' public life, and a huge amount of personal incomes are produced in grey markets and other types of 'informal' economic networks (cf. Mróz 2005).[1] Consequently, it must appear as a major limitation or shortcoming of this study that these aspects of decoupling have not been deliberately and systematically studied and explored. In the previous case study the current process of regionali-zation was largely described as a relatively dynamic and all-embracing force of cultural change that has far-reaching consequences for the local lives of people and transforms local and regional areas. Against this backdrop I want to empha-size clearly at this point that I have deliberately shied away from systematically searching for and elaborating indications of 'decoupling'. The major intent of this study was to illuminate the strong world-cultural drive of social changes in contemporary Europe and its member states, not the evaluation of problems. I believe, nevertheless, that many aspects and indications of the negative repercus-sions have become apparent in this study – sometimes explicitly, and sometimes between the lines. But I would like to leave the assessment of the flipsides and limits of change in contemporary Poland to the readers themselves and to other studies which deliberately focus on the problems of current changes and transformations.[2]

However, before one focuses on the phenomenon of 'decoupling' I want to point out three caveats with regard to the assessment of pitfalls and problems of development in the 'new west' (Reiter 2007) that I have drawn from my own macro-phenomenological analysis. First, world-cultural diffusion cannot and should not be understood as a one-way street to disseminate some allegedly 'Western' models of social organization, and therefore it cannot simply be meas-ured against the backdrop of certain clearly pre-defined standards of 'Western' modernity or as deviations from a certain Western standard or model. Second, the standards of evaluating 'good' or 'bad' development, social cohesion or decay, inclusion or exclusion, are highly relative and they are largely dependent on the changing world-cultural understandings of what constitutes good and bad devel-opment. One must just imagine that many problems that are found in contempor-ary SWOT analyses – such as environmental problems, gender inequality, or having regional 'human capital' with the 'wrong' age structure or skills-set – would not have been highlighted 30 years ago. In this sense, every study on the negative consequences of world-cultural diffusion is highly dependent on prevailing world-cultural standards of development. Third, the diffusion of 'world culture' should be understood as a process that is largely carried out and promoted by 'knowledgeable experts' and embedded in 'epistemic communities' (Haas) of the contemporary world polity. And in the example of the EU Cohesion Policy it can be seen that regional mobilization also requires a great deal of financial resources to be effective. Thus, the diffusion of world-cultural models largely depends on the anchoring and translation of world-cultural models by experts, professionals, policy-makers and active citizens to suit local contexts. The more local and regional actors believe in these standards and models, the more diffusion we can expect. In the case of regional mobilization in contemporary Poland, polemically speaking, this belief is also 'bought' to some extent since a huge part of the current activism and dynamism derives from the EU funds available to professionals and active citizens. The crucial question, however, is what happens after 2013 when the level of EU funds might substantially decrease.

The spirit and the limits of the current project of social mobilization

Last but not least, it should be mentioned again that the structural change in subnational Polish regions that was described in this study is a highly conditional process, which is both highly exclusive *and* expansive at the same time. The preceding analysis of the opinions of Polish experts has shown that many assessments and interpretations of the situation are widely shared, regardless of the interviewees' regional or occupational backgrounds. Though there are huge differences in development levels and in the future prospects between eastern and western regions, the belief in a better future is prevalent in all three regions – at least amongst the agents who are driving forward these changes. They have pointed out quite straightforwardly the many 'pitfalls' and 'burdens' of development, and we have also learnt that the experts have a relatively clear vision of the recipes of development and the principles of how to achieve future progress. From these expert assessments we have also learnt, however, that there is (still) a reasonable number of people who are 'resistant to change', who are 'resistant' to the 'new requirements of life', and we have learnt that this is especially true for the rural parts of *both* eastern and western Poland alike. In turn, the strong persistence and expansion of 'informal' business activities are a clear indication that many people are very active, entrepreneurial and creative in the literal sense – but not in the way predominating world-cultural standards and expectations would require them to be.[3]

This gives us an indication of the distinctive limits and limitations of current projects of modernization. The project of regional mobilization that we have explored in contemporary Poland is highly dependent on the 'cultural fit' of all people involved in this project. Obviously, the world-cultural project of social mobilization works best in urban or somewhat 'urbanized' areas, where young and well-educated people are found in abundance, since it is deeply embedded in networks of professionals and professional organizations. In this sense, the current phase of regional development is a highly *exclusive* project. It is a project of 'knowledgeable experts' that favours certain 'rationalized' standards, attitudes, habits and symbolic principles and disregards others. It is a *conditional* project that requires a certain level of 'professionalism' on the part of all beneficiaries and all agents of change that are involved, i.e. of preparedness and willingness to obey certain cultural rules and to speak a certain language. Consequently, we can expect a huge amount of decoupling between the 'carriers' of world-cultural diffusion and rural, less educated, less open or less eloquent people who are not able to meet these standards of 'professionalism'.

At the same time, the world-cultural project of modernization is a very *expansive* and *inclusive* project that aims to integrate as many people as possible to participate in projects of development. As we have seen, the current wave of regional mobilization is strongly based on the assumption that individuals, organizations, social relations and even inter-organizational relations can be changed via constant learning and education. Similarly, in a more recent OECD report on regional development in Poland, 'regional disparities' and the 'gap' between urban and rural areas are mainly explained by the differences in human capital development: 'Human capital development is a key explanatory variable for regional competitiveness and disparities in Poland. Lower educational levels in rural populations limit labour mobility and contribute to inadequate economic diversification.' (OECD 2008: 23). Since education and human capital development, as well as the competences and habits required to deal with and apply knowledge, are seen as the major prerequisites of contemporary knowledge society, education and learning are crucially important for the expansion of world culture. Statements made by interviewees about there being a lot of training sessions and courses 'for people who want to change their job, who want to develop their employees', or remarks that refer to the importance of the promotion of entrepreneurship and self-responsibility – i.e. 'that money is better transferred to people who start their own business than wasted on generous social security' – are strong expressions of this new 'spirit' of social mobilization that is about to take shape. Accordingly, both the willingness and the preparedness for constant learning and further education, and the willingness to comply with the given standards are fundamental preconditions for the success and the wider social acceptance of this project, but at the same time it is also an indication of its limitations. Yet, as long as the agents of change who are in charge of this project – the 'professionals', the 'knowledgeable experts' and 'active citizens' – have a strong belief in that and in what they are doing, one can expect that the current wave of all-embracing social mobilization will further expand.

Appendix

Appendix 1 The regional operational programmes (ROPs) of the three selected regions

ROP of the Dolnośląskie Voivodship	EU Funding: 1,213 million (ERDF) + national contribution: 348 million

Strategic Goal: *Improving the quality of life of the inhabitants of Dolnośląskie and increasing the region's competitiveness while respecting principles of sustainable development.*

	Million EUR	Share of total (%)
Priority 1: Growth of competitiveness of Dolnośląskie enterprises ('Enterprises and innovation')	461.0	29.5
Priority 2: Development of the information society ('Information Society')	119.9	7.7
Priority 3: Development of transport infrastructure ('Transport')	273.5	17.5
Priority 4: Improvement of Environment and Ecological Safety	152.0	9.7
Priority 5: Environmentally friendly energy infrastructure ('Energy')	48.0	3.1
Priority 6: Exploitation and promotion of tourism and cultural spa potential ('Tourism and Culture')	135.0	8.6
Priority 7: Development and modernization of education infrastructure ('Education')	120.1	7.7
Priority 8: Modernization of health infrastructure ('Health')	64.6	4.1
Priority 9: Rehabilitation of degraded urban areas ('Towns')	132.7	8.5
Priority 10: Technical Assistance	54.1	3.5

Appendix 1 Continued

ROP of the Lubelskie Voivodship	*EU Funding: 1,156 million (ERDF) + national contribution: 204 million*

Strategic Goal: *Increasing the competitiveness of the region leading to faster economic growth, and an increase in employment taking into consideration natural and cultural qualities of the Region*

	Million EUR	*Share of total (%)*
Priority 1: Enterprises and innovation	285.5	21.0
Priority 2: Economic Infrastructure	88.4	6.5
Priority 3: Attractiveness of urban areas and investment areas	81.6	6.0
Priority 4: Information Society	68.0	5.0
Priority 5: Transport	305.9	22.5
Priority 6: Environment and clean energy	183.6	13.5
Priority 7: Culture, tourism and inter-regional cooperation	129.2	9.5
Priority 8: Social Infrastructure	179.5	13.2
Priority 9: Technical Assistance	38.1	2.8

ROP of the Podkarpackie Voivodship	*EU Funding: 1,136 million (ERDF) + national contribution: 208 million*

Strategic Goal: *To increase domestic and international economic competitiveness and to improve the accessibility of the Podkarpackie region.*

	Million EUR	*Share of total (%)*
Priority 1: Creating conditions for the development of knowledge-based entrepreneurship	352.8	26.2
Priority 2: Improving the region's accessibility and investment attractiveness (transport and energy)	401.3	29.8
Priority 3: Creating the conditions for the development of information society	80.0	5.9
Priority 4: Preventing environmental degradation/ counterbalancing ecological threats etc.	200.5	14.9
Priority 5: Developing social capital (education, health protection, social welfare, sport + recreation)	141.7	10.5
Priority 6: Promoting tourism, protecting cultural heritage and developing cultural institutions	43.6	3.2
Priority 7: Promoting intra-regional cohesion in order to diminish intra-regional disparities	93.6	7
Priority 8: Technical Assistance	31.1	2.3

Source: Polish Ministry of Regional Development, 2009. Own depiction.

Appendix 2 List of expert interviews and other analysed primary sources[#]

Atlas.ti-Nr.	Type of interview or material/and type of archiving	Date of interview
Int. 1	Interview with a representative of the Ministry of Regional Development (Dept. IROP), Warsaw [Transcript in English]	7 March 2007
Int. 2	Interviews with employees at the Ministry of Regional Development (Dept. of SF Coord.), Warsaw [Memory Protocol]; Complemented by an excerpt of an official publication of the head of the department on the preparation of the National Development Plan 2007–13. Published in Sartorius (2005: 33–8)	27 April 2007
Int. 3	Interviews with employees at the EUREG Institute, Warsaw [Memory Protocol in English]	2 March 2007/ 6 March 2007
Int. 4	Statement of a Polish expert on regional development. Officially published in Sartorius (2005: 51–8) with the title: 'Lisbon 2000' and 'Brussels 2005'. [Excerpt in English]	–
Int. 5	Statement of an expert from the German team of the German-Polish Twinning. Officially published in Sartorius (2005: 81–100) with the title: 'The management of Structural Funds – a complex system requiring further development'.	–
Int. 6	Interviews with two representatives of a Regional Development Agency in Rzeszów (Podkarpackie) [Transcript in Polish and Memory Protocol in English of one session]	7 May 2007
Int. 7	Interview with three employees at the Marshall Office of the Voivodship of Podkarpackie (Dept. Regional Development), Rzeszow [Transcript in Polish]	1 June 2007
Int. 8	Interview with an employee at the Voivode Office of the Voivodship of Podkarpackie (Dept. IROP Monitoring and Control), Rzeszow [Transcript in Polish]	12 June 2007
Int. 9	Interview with a major representative of the Voivode Office of the Voivodship of Podkarpackie (Dept. IROP Monitoring and Control), Rzeszow [Transcript in Polish]	12 June 2007
Int. 10	Interview with a representative of the Regional Development Agency in Mielec (Podkarpackie) [Transcript in Polish]	20 June 2007
Int. 11	Interview with a representative of the Marshall Office of the Voivodship of Dolnośląskie (Dept. Regional Development), Wrocław [Transcript in Polish]	24 May 2007
Int. 12	Interview with a representative of the Voivode Office of the Voivodship of Dolnośląskie (Dept. IROP Monitoring and Control), Wrocław [Transcript in Polish]	14 June 2007
Int. 13	Interview with two representatives of a non-profit organization in Wrocław (Dolnośląskie) [Transcript in Polish]	14 June 2007

Int. 14	Excerpts of an expert report on 'Institutions, mechanism and processes of supporting innovation' in Lower Silesia produced by Prof. Krystyna Moszkowicz and Dr. Leszek Kwieciński (2006), University of Wrocław .	—
Int. 16*	Interview with two representatives of the Marshall Office of the Voivodship of Lubelskie (Dept. Regional Development), Lublin [Memory Protocol]	11 May 2007
Int. 17	Interview with two representatives of a non-profit organisation in Lublin (Lubelskie) [Transcript in Polish]	6 June 2007
Int. 18	Interview with a representative of a Regional Development Agency in Lublin (Lubelskie) [Transcript in Polish]	5 June 2007
Int. 19	Interview with two representatives of the Voivode Office of the Voivodship of Lubelskie (Dept. IROP Monitoring and Control), Lublin [Transcript in Polish]	19 June 2007
Int. 20	Interview with a scientific expert and consultant on regional development in Poland, Akademia Economiczna, Kraków [Transcript in Polish]	29 May 2007
Int. 23**	Interview with a representative of the Marshall Office of the Voivodship of Lubelskie (Dept. Regional Development), Lublin [Transcript in English]	6 June 2007
Int. 24	Excerpt of the introductory remarks of the Development Strategy of the Voivodship of Dolnośląskie 2020	
Int. 25	Interview with a representative of the Ministry of Regional Development (Dept. Regional affairs), Warsaw [Transcript in English]	16 May 2007
Int. 26	Interview with a representative of a Regional Development Agency in Lublin (Lubelskie) [Transcript in English]	10 May 2007
Int. 27	Interview with a representative of a Regional Development Agency in Wałbrzych (Dolnośląskie) [Transcript in English]	15 June 2007

Notes

\# This list contains 24 analytical units in the order of appearance as they are stored and archived with ATLAS.ti (3 Int.-units undefined). It consists of 20 face-to-face interviews with various Polish experts in the field of regional development and 4 excerpts of information relating to and complementing the information provided in the interviews. In all three selected regions about four to five interviews with people from similar institutions, offices and organizations were conducted in the period between March and June 2007. In addition, about five interviews were conducted in Warsaw with public officials from the Polish Ministry of Regional Development and independent experts. The interviews were either conducted in Polish or in English (depending on the choice of the interviewees). The interviews conducted in Polish language were transcribed by a native-speaking student assistant in Kraków, the interviews conducted in English were transcribed by the author in English language. All material depicted above was put together, filtered and analysed according to a coding scheme created by the author.

* Int. 15 not defined in this Atlas.ti-file.

** Int. 21 and 22 also not defined

Notes

1 Introduction

1 Note that I will mainly use the notion of 'mobilization' instead of 'modernization' throughout this book to underline the strong 'mobilizing', or rather 'activating', force of modernization in loose reference to Karl Deutsch's (1961) notion of 'social mobilization'.

2 In Germany, for example, a federalist system was introduced at the very beginning of state formation, reflecting the fragmented territorial structure during nation-building. In centralist France, in turn, the management of various provinces has traditionally been a task of central state administration rather than strong regional governments. For an example of the southern European experience see Ulrike Liebert's (1986) study on the political mobilization in Andalusia in the south of Spain against the central state during the 1970s.

3 These two strands are strongly interwoven, in fact. Political economy also usually rests on a conception of the multilevel structure of government. The multilevel governance perspective also often rests on politico-economic accounts: Marks *et al.* (1996), Cox (1997), Boyer and Hollingsworth (1997), Brenner *et al.* (2003). However, all these different perspectives rest on an 'absolute' conception of geographic space. On the various conceptions of space in sociology and contemporary human geography, see: Agnew and Duncan (1989), Soja (1989), Massey *et al.* (1999), Gieryn (2000), Hubbard (2002).

4 Yet in German sociology there have been attempts to overcome this deficit since the early 1990s. See for example: Kaelble (1987), Lepsius (1991), Münch (1994), Bach (2000, 2008), Vobruba (2001, 2007). However, these approaches were not much received in the international context. For a concise discussion of more recent sociological accounts of European integration see also: Trenz (2008).

5 For a similar attempt, but from a completely different theoretical angle, see also: Rumford (2000).

6 Hence, the macro-phenomenological world-polity approach can certainly be grouped to the diverse array of 'new culturalist approaches' to modernity and social government that have flourished since the breakthrough of a new 'cultural turn' both in humanities and the social sciences alike (cf. Alexander and Seidman 1990; Foucault 1991; Boltanski and Thevenot 1991; Wagner 1994, 2001b; Rose 1999; Reckwitz 2002; Boltanski and Chiapello 2006; Miller and Rose 2008). According to Reckwitz (2004), it was the common concern of these new culturalist approaches to shed light on the implicit normative, cultural and pre-political assumptions that are usually taken for granted or even obscured in prevailing 'liberal' self-descriptions of society and especially in mainstream policy research of Western social sciences.

7 Accordingly, the world-polity approach certainly has some commonalities with some approaches developed in the political sciences, especially those approaches which deliberately focus on the role of ideas, culture and discourse in politics (cf. Steinmetz

1999; Goldstein and Keohane 1993; Ruggie 1998; Acharya 2004; Blyth 2003; Schmidt 2008), the diffusion and cultural construction of certain standards, norms and policies (Finnemore 1998; Simmons *et al.* 2006) as well as policy translation (cf. Haas 1992; Radaelli 1995; Sabatier 1998; Knill 2001; Kohler-Koch 2002). However, it is not confined to the exploration of 'political' or 'bureaucratic' change in transnational political fora.

8 Note that I use the term 'constructionism' in classical phenomenological tradition (cf. Berger and Luckmann 1966; Schütz 1973) rather than 'constructivism'.

9 This trend becomes apparent most explicitly at the example of the 'Lisbon agenda' of the European Union which proclaims a massive expansion of 'knowledge society' and 'knowledge-based industries' as the most appropriate way of obtaining future progress and wealth in Europe of today: See http://ec.europa.eu/growthandjobs/index_en.htm (accessed 14 February 2011).

2 A critical introduction to world-polity research

1 In political science, institutions are often considered as highly standardized collective actors, or rather aggregates of individuals with distinct collective identities and purposes, such as political parties or concrete bureaucratic organizations (cf. Scharpf 1997; Weingast 2002). Sometimes institutions are conceptualized as formal standards and official organizational principles, codified, for example, in legal documents and other types of regulatory systems (cf. Stone Sweet *et al.* 2001; Hall and Soskice 2001). More 'sociological' approaches in political science, however, stress the importance of 'informal', implicit or less specified types of institutions (cf. Steinmo *et al.* 1992; Hall and Taylor 1996; Hollingsworth and Boyer 1997; Rothstein 1998; Pierson 2004). For concise overviews of the numerous approaches to institutionalist analysis in the political sciences, see: Douglas (1986), Thelen (1999) and Schmidt (2008).

2 See, for instance, the huge difference between one of the first loose and tentative conceptions of the world-polity perspective, namely Boli-Bennett and Meyer (1980), and the more recent comprehensive reader *World Culture: Origins and Consequences* by Lechner and Boli (2005).

3 This does not mean, however, that world-polity research neglects the existence of individual human beings. On the contrary, 'culture' is not conceived as a free-floating set of ideas and values, as in classical idealist philosophy, but in continuous contact and exchange with 'practice': 'Culture has the strikingly tautological habit of becoming incorporated into the very "stuff" that it defines, into the things that owe their existence and meaning to the cultural complex that constitutes them. Reversing the common observation that individuals, groups, and organizations are "embedded" in their surrounding cultural environments, we should also think of culture as embedded in the objects, actors, scenes, and structures whose nature and operations are culturally organized.' (Boli and Lechner 2005: 16f.). – For an overview of the classic debate on the micro-macro-problem in social sciences, see: Alexander *et al.* (1987).

4 The notion *sacred canopy* was initially put forward by Peter L. Berger (1967). However, the theoretical reflection on the distinction of the 'sacred' and the 'profane' has a much longer tradition in modern social thought. It has been one of the fundamental analytical categories of cultural sociology (cf. James 1902; Durkheim 1915; Eliade 1949; Levi-Strauss 1966, 1970; Bellah 1970; Alexander 1988). According to this tradition of social thought, the 'sacred' constitutes a moral sphere of human nature which is principally outside of everyday life; it is transcendent, immutable and gives meaning and value to human action (Boli 2006: 100). Accordingly, even in distinctly non-religious societies acts of 'sacralization' are seen to be central to the creation and maintenance of value commitments (cf. Joas 2001).

5 In fact, the proponents of the world-polity approach have observed that the expansion of modern sciences was much more restricted by political structures of modern

nation-states during the nineteenth century and until the middle of the twentieth century than it is today, and accordingly the scope of sciences was relatively limited in itself. However, with the exponential worldwide expansion of modern science, science-related structures, and, in particular, institutions of higher education since the beginning of 1960s, this has fundamentally changed (Schofer 2004; Drori and Meyer 2006: 42f.).

6   A good illustration of 'authoritative scientization' and an example of an extraordinarily successful 'word-cultural model' with an almost universal status is Milton Friedman's neo-classic models and his plea for a 'slim state' (cf. Friedman 1962). In fact, since the early successes with state reform in Chile in 1973, the legendary 'Chicago Boys' became the paradigmatic figureheads of neo-liberal state reform during the 1980s and 1990s. Their model has diffused globally with and without their direct involvement as policy advisors (cf. Sachs 1992a; Chossudovsky 1997; Stiglitz 2003).

7   On the methodological foundations of world-polity research see, above all: Ramirez (1987) and Schofer and McEneaney (2003).

8   I have borrowed the distinction of 'technical' vs. 'existential' knowledge from the German sociologist Gerhard Schulze. In his phenomenological study of major types of expressive individual lifestyles in contemporary German society, called the 'Experience Society' (*Die Erlebnisgesellschaft*) (Schulze 2000: 223ff.), he defines 'technical knowledge' similar to what Weber (1980) called 'instrumental rationality', namely: all knowledge which is necessary to attain goals in most efficient ways. 'Existential knowledge', in contrast, is much less specific and instrumental than technical knowledge, since it determines the constitution of things in all various dimensions. Thus, existential knowledge is the knowledge which constitutes the cultural frames of interpretation. And this encompasses different kinds of 'cognitive frames' – or rather 'apriorities' (Kant) – such as existential definitions of the situation, constitutive models of reality, primary perspectives on the relation between the self and the world and so forth, not just instrumental orientations.

9   In this regard, Lechner and Boli (2005) particularly refer to the example of sports associations and new global events like the Olympic Games (since the end of the nineteenth century), soccer or cricket championships (since the first half of the twentieth century) to account for more mundane dimensions of 'standardization'.

10   For a look at one attempt to specify the 'moral substance' of world culture see John Boli's 'tentative sketch' of the 'global moral order', as he calls it, which he has drawn from a qualitative analysis of constructions of 'virtue' and 'evil' in documents of international organizations, non-governmental organizations and companies as well as in global public discourses (see Boli 2006).

11   In fact, in the first famous passage of their *Manifesto of the Communist* party Karl Marx and Friedrich Engels described the expansionist and all-encompassing character of 'Western bourgeois culture' as following: 'The bourgeoisie has, through its exploitation of the world market, given a cosmopolitan character to production and consumption in every country. (...) It compels all nations, on pain of extinction, to adopt the bourgeois mode of production; it compels them to introduce what it calls civilization into their midst, i.e., to become bourgeois themselves. In one word, it creates a world after its own image.' (Marx and Engels 1969/1848).

12   Similarly, the concept of world culture should by no means be understood as a mere 'product' or 'instrument' of hegemonic economic interests, or what nowadays is often referred to as hegemonic expansion of the 'American way of life'. Certainly, the rise of modern society cannot be understood without taking into account the development of market society as well as the emergence of a new primary class, the 'capitalist class' or the 'Western bourgeoisie' (cf. Sklair 1991; Lash and Urry 1994; Jessop 2002b; Hirst and Thomas 2006). One should also not neglect the coercive and destructive forces the expansion of modern capitalism and the hegemonic status Western societies throughout of modernity, and not only in times of colonialism and imperialism (cf. Polanyi 1944; Wallerstein 1974a, 1980, 1989; Offe 2006). However, as

pointed out before, the rationalizing thrust of world cultural diffusion is not just limited to the economic realm and instrumental rationalization (cf. Meyer 1987).

3 Outline of a phenomenology of late modernity

1 According to John Meyer and his colleagues, 'institutions' are rules deriving from a broad cultural background; they are '(…) a set of cultural rules that give generalized meaning to social activity and regulate it in a patterned way.' (Thomas *et al.* 1987: 32). Hence, the world-polity perspective applies a conception of institutions which is as broad as their notion of culture; in fact, both notions are often used interchangeably.

2 On the role of engineering and technical scientific rationality in modern state-formation see: Carroll (2006).

3 See in this context the distinction of 'reflexivity as a quality of human action as whole' and 'institutional reflexivity' as a historical phenomenon that Anthony Giddens highlighted in his classic book *New Rules of Sociological Method* (Giddens 1993: 6f.).

4 Kellner and Berger borrowed this characterization of the new reflective elite from Helmut Schelsky's polemic description of a new 'theocracy of intellectuals' (*Priester-herrschaft der Intellektuellen*) published in 1975. It was especially the joining together of 'instruction', 'mentoring' and 'planning' (*Belehrung, Betreuung und Beplanung*), Schelsky argued, on which the authority of the new professionals was based (Schel-sky 1975: 367ff.).

5 Note that Karin Knorr-Cetina (1999) proposes to distinguish between different 'epis-temic cultures', since there are fundamental differences in the internal structures and logics of various scientific communities. However, when we speak of the 'scientific approach' or 'scientific attitude' in this study, we refer to the universe of all various epistemic cultures and a particular kind of methodical and reflexive approach to reality as well as the production of a particular kind of knowledge. On the 'division' of professions and expert labour, see also: Abbott (1988).

6 Evers and Gerke (2005) stress that since the 1970s the reinforced spread and institu-tionalization of sciences all over the world has contributed to the increasing impor-tance of scientists, even in developing countries. Here, even more than in advanced industrial societies, (former) scientists serve as government advisors, ambassadors or private entrepreneurs and constitute a vital part of the 'strategic group' of develop-ment experts.

7 What Polanyi forcefully described in the first chapters of *The Great Transformation* is nothing less than the emergence of the modern social sciences, and modern economic theory in particular. With the rise of the industrial mode of production, Polanyi (2001: 40f.) points out, society was 'discovered' as the major 'problem' of societal develop-ment, which was accompanied by the emergence of massive scientific reflection on development problems and questions of social change. Thus, in contrast to conven-tional wisdom, Polanyi claims that industrialization was not just shaped by new inno-vations in physics and other natural sciences, but mainly by the emergence of social scientific thinking. See Polanyi (2001: 124).

8 This does not mean, however, that macro-phenomenologists only focus on ideas and knowledge. Similar to Polanyi (2001), Strang and Meyer explicitly stress the impor-tance of social forces and political conflict, cf.: 'In some way, models must make the transition from theoretical formulation to social movement to institutional impera-tive.' (Strang and Meyer 1993: 495). Yet, phenomenological institutionalism does not mainly and primarily focus on concrete social actors and political conflict.

9 The so called 'neo-liberal' paradigm postulates a return to neo-classical economics and growth theories, but without the interventionist impetus of Keynesian kind (cf. Keynes 1997 [1936]). Instead of state intervention, neo-liberalism praises the market

as the one and only instrument that guarantees future prosperity, stability and socio-economic well-being (for an overview, see Lee Mudge 2008). Hence, the neo-liberal paradigm simply abandons the major foundations of Keynesian development economics, namely that developing economics represent a special case and that governments are able to influence development (cf. Myrdal 1957; Hirschman 1958, 1994; Amin 1976). This revival of *laissez-fair* economics has become a powerful (if not the most powerful) notion of development of contemporary times, even though it is distinctly anti-interventionist.

10 In fact, in the past decade the concept of 'human development' and the fight against extreme poverty and social exclusion has gained huge prominence, not least due to the adoption of the Millennium Development Goals (MDGs) by the United Nations (U.N.) and the successive implementation of the UN Millennium Development Project. See www.un.org/millenniumgoals/ (accessed 6 March 2011). Besides that, the promotion of democratic principles and standards of 'good governance', the protection of local traditions, cultures and ecological systems, the promotion of civil society participation, the promotion of gender equality, human rights and individual self-determination have become commonly shared goals of current development practice. In light of these changes, some authors even celebrated the advent of new 'global social policies' (Deacon 2007) that rapidly diffuse beyond former geographical and ideological barriers.

4   A phenomenology of the rise of a 'new regionalism'

1 On the epistemological and methodological problems and specifics of sociological research in general, and the major assumptions of phenomenological sociology in particular, see above all: Schütz (1973: 3ff.) and Giddens (1984: 334ff. and 1993). On the epistemic foundations of modernity and the relation between scientific concepts and social reality, see also: Foucault (1965 and 1989) and Latour (1993).

2 In fact, one of the first who intensively studied the political and territorial implications of the paradigmatic shift from Fordism to new post-Fordist modes of production was a group of (mostly French) scientists who are loosely grouped under the heading of *régulation* theory (cf. Aglietta 1982; Lipietz 1986; Jessop 1990; Benko and Liepietz 1995; Saillard 1995).

3 For an overview of this wide field of interdisciplinary research see the comprehensive collection of path-breaking articles and texts edited by Michael Keating (2004). For a comprehensive and differentiated discussion on the emergence and the major paradigmatic trends of new regional research, see: Storper (1995).

4 This branch of research in fact also intensively fuelled the renaissance of economic sociology which emphasizes the decisive role of culture, social relations, localized practices and conventions on market-building and economic value-creation (cf. Smelser and Swedberg 1994; Storper and Salais 1997; Beckert and Zafirovski 2006).

5 For a more detailed review of the literature on innovation and space see also: Simmie (2004). For a 'sympathetic critique' of the new research on regional innovation and learning, see Hudson (1999).

6 The UNDP, for example, mainly focuses on the promotion of local development in less developed countries and transition economies, see www.undp.org/governance/sl-dlgud.htm (accessed 16 June 2009). At the World Bank and other loan-giving institutions, regional devolution is proposed as a means of strengthening public administration capacity (see the section 'decentralization & sub-national regional economies' at http://web.worldbank.org/, accessed 16 June 2009), while the Council of Europe promotes local and regional self-government in accordance with their overall aim of establishing and strengthening democratic institutions all around the European continent, see www.coe.int/T/Congress/Default_en.asp (accessed 16 June 2009).

7   At the example of the OECD the role of international organizations as diffusers of world-cultural models becomes most evident and most striking. With an annual budget of about 340 million EUR (2008), the OECD does not and cannot implement its own policy programmes. However, this organization has become one of the world's largest producers and disseminators of scientifically grounded expertise in the fields of economics and public policy, publishing huge amounts of statistical material, surveys, country reports, and evaluations of more prescriptive policy proposals (about 250 new publications per year according to official OECD information given at www.oecd.org as of 22 July 2008). See also: Rose (1999: 36f.); Münch (2009); Martens and Leibfried (2008); Martens and Jacobi (2010).

8   In fact, in the Preamble of the *Treaty of Rome*, the founding script of the European economic integration signed in May 1957, the aim of reducing existing differences between regions and the 'backwardness' of less favoured regions is already highlighted as one of the major policy objectives of the European Community.

9   The NUTS classification subdivided territorial units of the European Union in three more or less comparable categories: NUTS-1 (the level of member states or larger subdivisions of larger member states territories), NUTS-2 (functional sub-national regions or regions with up to 3 million inhabitants) and NUTS-3 smaller regions or counties. See http://ec.europa.eu/eurostat/ramon/nuts/basicnuts_regions_en.html (accessed June 2009).

10 The first programming period started in 1989 and lasted until the end of 1993. Currently, we are witnessing the fourth programming period from 2007 to 2013. For a concise overview of the past two decades of Cohesion Policy implementation, see CEC (2008b). Moreover, there are numerous textbooks and compendia available; see amongst others: Leonardi (2005), Evans (2004) and Molle (2007). See also the information provided online by the EU Commission at http://ec.europa.eu/regional_policy/index_en.htm (11 July 2009).

11 While total spending has increased substantially in the past decade, annual spending for Cohesion Policy has more or less remained the same since the end of the 1990s. After the doubling of annual spending for Cohesion Policy between 1989 and 1993, from less than EUR10 billion in 1989 to more than EUR 20 billion in 1993, annual spending was again almost doubled between 1994 and 1999 to EUR39 billion (in July 2008 prices). Today, the annual spending for Cohesion Policy amounts to EUR47 billion. With this significant share of spending, Cohesion Policy occupies the second largest position in the overall EU budget – amounting to more than one third of the EU budget – after expenditure for the Common Agricultural Policy (CAP), which amounts to roughly EUR55 billion of annual spending in 2009. Data taken from CEC (2008b).

12 In fact, between 1948 and 1952 within the framework of the so-called *European Recovery Programme* (ERP), which is publicly regarded as the 'Marshall plan', loans and grants of about 13 billion US-Dollars (more than USD130 billion at current prices) were provided by the U.S. government to 16 Western European countries for the reconstruction of infrastructure and industries destroyed during the Second World War. For more information, see Agnew and Entrikin (2004) and Behrman (2007). See also http://harvardmagazine.com/1997/05/marshall.plan.html (17 July 2009).

13 For more information visit the official website of the Council of European Regions at www.cor.europa.eu/ (accessed 17 July 2009).

14 For more information on ESPON see the official webpage at www.espon.eu (accessed 16 June 2009). And for a general overview on the 'Europeanization' of Spatial Research and Planning in recent years, see: Faludi (2008).

15 The European Commission has concluded official memoranda of cooperation in the field of regional policy with China, Russia, and Brazil. Moreover, a number of other countries and inter-governmental regional organizations, such as South Africa,

Ukraine, MERCOSUR, and the Western African Economic and Monetary Union, 'expressed interest' in closer expert cooperation (cf. CEC 2008b: 4f.).

16 There are clear indications that regional inequalities within Europe have increased rather than decreased over the past two decades (cf. Martin 2001; Heidenreich and Wunder 2008). Even the European Commission's Directorate General for Regional Policy admitted a rather ambiguous or even weak impact of the Cohesion Policy in their regular Reports on Economic and Social Cohesion (CEC 2004, 2007 and 2010). However, an overall 'impact' of the EU Cohesion Policy and its direct 'effects' on regional development is hard to assess. And therefore it is a highly contested matter (cf. Martin 2001; Armstrong 1995; Armstrong and Taylor 2000; Martin 2000; Bachtler and Wren 2006; Batterbury 2006; Bradley 2006; Molle 2007).

17 The new regulations of Cohesion Policy require 60 per cent of all measures in the 'least developed' regions and 70 per cent of measures in all other regions to be dedicated to priorities of the Lisbon agenda, such as promoting research and innovation, developing human capital and entrepreneurship, etc. – only some regions in Central and Eastern Europe are exempted from this provision. For more detailed information on the current programming period: see CEC (2007a, 2008a, 2008b) and http://ec. europa.eu/regional_policy/index_ en.htm (accessed 17 July 2009).

18 For a detailed listing and depiction of so called 'Lisbon priorities' in the EU Cohesion Policy 2007–13, see also: CEC (2007: 91ff.).

19 In fact, from a neo-Marxist perspective the extension of regional development agendas is seen as an expression of a major 'discursive shift' in contemporary capitalism (cf. Storper and Walker 1989; Tickell and Peck 1992; Hudson 2001; Brenner *et al.* 2003; Paasi 2009). This has been summarized by the geographer Arnoud Lagendijk as following: 'From a historical perspective, the region presented an available window to experiment with new regulatory forms and "fixes". This has been aimed, in particular, at improving economic performance through its embedding in the non-economic, and on accommodating non-economic targets (cohesion, sustainability).' (Lagendijk 2007: 1204).

20 Thus, the world-cultural approach has commonalities with contemporary governmentality studies, especially the type of analyses put forward by Nikolas Rose and colleagues (cf. Rose 1999; Rose and Miller 2008). See in this context also: Drori *et al.* (2003: 265–79).

21 For a similar observation, but markedly different interpretation, see: Jessop (2002a). In this article Jessop identifies the upswing of three alternative discourses apart from prevailing economic neo-liberalism, namely: neo-corporatism, neo-statism, and neo-communitarianism. See Jessop (2002a: 459ff.).

22 This is certainly true for all types of technical advances deriving from sciences. But is also and particularly true for models and interpretations produced in social sciences – see on this issue: Polanyi (2001: 124f.), Foucault (1965 and 1972), Giddens (1984: 334ff.), Carroll (2006), Illouz (2008), or Rose and Miller (2008). On the close link between scientific discourse of a 'new regionalism' and political practice see also, amongst others: Lovering (1999) as well as Röttger and Wissen (2004).

5 The European script of regional mobilization

1 Exemptions might be existing neo-Marxist analyses of the development discourse or studies based on Foucaultian governmentality perspectives (cf. Lagendijk and Cornford 2000; Painter 2002; Lagendijk 2006, 2007; Varro and Lagendijk 2006; Paasi 2009).

2 The empirical material on which this analysis is based mainly derives from official policy papers, publications and public statements of the most influential political actor in the field: the European Union. All documents were publicly accessible. Often they can be found in the internet and just downloaded from the relevant web pages. All

sources are indicated and quoted in the text. Familiar terms and idiomatic quotations taken from primary sources are often set italics.

3 See on the problem of future-orientation and the role of uncertainty and belief in human agency, above all: Schütz (1973: 19ff.) and Giddens (1993: 77ff.).

4 This distinction of different types of norms – *fundamental norms, organizing principles*, and *standard procedures* – is adapted from Antje Wiener (2008: 65ff.) who distinguishes between these three types of norms in international politics according to their different degrees of generalization, specification and contestation.

5 See also a more recent special report on 'Innovation in Europe' in the Business Week that maps some of the most innovative industries and places in Europe, see: Fishbein (2008).

6 A more recent book by Kenichi Ohmae (2005), a former business consultant, who has become a prominent advocate of regionalism and regional economies, maps a few empirical examples, such as Silicon Valley and northern Italy, but also Hong Kong, Shanghai or Singapore, as 'role models' of successful business development. See also Ohmae (1995).

7 Yet the creation of new academic concepts and terms never ends. Cooke and Schwartz (2007) recently proposed the concept of 'creative regions', another more recent proposal is the model of the 'intelligent region', or rather 'intelligent city' (cf. Komninos 2008).

8 One only has to look at the numerous titles of OECD publications on regional development during the past few years, such as *Building Competitive Regions: Strategies and Governance* (OECD 2005a), *Business Clusters: Promoting Enterprise in Central and Eastern Europe* (OECD 2005b), *Competitive Regional Clusters: National Policy Approaches* (OECD 2007). Other more recent publications such as *Globalization and Regional Economies* (OECD 2007) and *Specialization, Regional Clusters and Competitiveness* provide detailed descriptions of the adoption of models of best practice in OECD member states. See also www.oecd.org (accessed 22 July 2009).

9 For more information on the LEED Programme and the OECD's policy proposals to promote economic development in rural areas see www.oecd.org (accessed 22 July 2009).

10 Taken from the official introduction to the policy programme 'regional development' at the webpage of the OECD, available www.oecd.org, subject 'regional development' (accessed 22 March 2011).

11 Taken from the official introduction to the innovation policy of the European Union at the webpage of the Directorate General of 'Regional Policy' of the European Commission. Available at: http://ec.europa.eu/regional_policy/innovation/intro_en.htm (accessed 22 March 2011).

12 For more information on EU support of innovative actions co-financed by the European Regional Development Fund (ERDF) between 1994 and 2002 visit the EU website at: http://ec.europa.eu/regional_policy/innovation/innovating/index_en.htm (22 July 2009).

13 See: www.consilium.europa.eu/uedocs/cms_Data/docs/pressdata/en/intm/91989.pdf (accessed 22 July 2009).

14 SERN stands for 'Sustainable European Regions Network' (SERN), a common project of 12 European regions that was co-funded by the Regional Policy's Innovative Actions programme between 2003–5.

15 It is alleged that the huge increase in the status of cohesion, and especially the strong territorial focus of cohesion, in EU regional governance goes back directly to French initiatives and the strong influence of French policy-makers between the mid-1980s and the mid-1990s during the presidency of Jacque Delors. In fact, the rationale of the EU Cohesion Policy has huge similarities with the French tradition of *aménagment du territoire* which was introduced in France in the aftermath of the Second World War as a means of overcoming the huge imbalances between Paris and the rest of the country (cf. Faludi 2004).

16 As anchored in the consolidated version the Treaty of the European Union published in the *Official Journal C 325* on 24 December 2002.

17 Ibid.

18 This impression is also confirmed by the various 'Cohesion reports' published by the European Commission on a regular basis, in which regional (socio-economic) disparities within and amongst EU member states are measured extensively, but almost no links to issues of trans-European solidarity or European social integration are made (CEC 1996, 2001, 2004, 2007, 2010). See on this issue also: Delhey (2004).

19 On the contradictions of EU cohesion see also the extensive discussion of Rumford (2000).

20 As published by the European Union in the *Official Journal C115* on 9.5.2008.

21 Territorial cohesion is proposed as a means of fostering 'density' of economic activities and social interactions, reducing 'distance' between growth poles and 'division' between people and policy areas (cf. CEC 2008c). These three challenges to territorial cohesion were identified by the World Development Report 2009, published by the World Bank as the three major factors influencing the pace of economic and social development, see: http://econ.worldbank.org/wdr/ (accessed 22 March 2011).

22 Available at: www.un-documents.net/wced-ocf.htm (accessed 15 July 2009).

23 See for an overview: www.un.org/esa/desa/aboutus/dsd.html (accessed 15 July 2009).

24 Accordingly, we can also find alternative, distinctly non-industrial notions in European regional development practice. In Austria, for instance, the concept of a 'slow region' was brought up based on ideas and concepts of the 'slow food' movement. As many other projects of regional development all around Europe this project has been co-financed and supported by EU Structural Funds. For more information see: www.raumplanung.steiermark.at/cms/beitrag/10025342/690211/ (accessed 22 March 2011).

25 Though this document has remained non-binding, it outlined for the first time a common long-term vision of 'balanced' and 'sustainable' territorial development in the European Union. In the conceptual part of the ESDP there is also direct reference to and a depiction of the sustainable development triangle depicted in Fig. 5.2, see CEC (1999: 10).

26 The official EU legal document of Cohesion Policy for the new programming period 2007 to 2013 is Council Regulation (EC) No. 1083/2006 of 11 July 2006.

27 For more information on the European Sustainable Development Network see: www.sd-network.eu/ (accessed 15 July 2009).

28 Taken from the official webpage of the EU Sustainable Development Strategy. See: http://ec.europa.eu/environment/eussd/ (accessed 15 July 2009).

29 Ibid.

30 One of the pioneers of regional sciences and modern regional development models was the economist Walter Isard, who created the U.S. American Regional Science Association in 1954 and made the *Central Place Theory* of the German geographer Christaller (1933) popular to a wider scientific audience in the post-war period (cf. Isard 1956, 1960). Isard, who was employed at Harvard University and M.I.T. during the 1950s, also inspired other scholars at M.I.T. to focus on issues of regional development and to develop theories and scientific methods of regional planning (cf. Friedmann and Alonso 1964). Consequently, in the 1950s and 1960s, Harvard University and M.I.T. became one of the centres of modern regional development sciences offering the first theories, textbooks, and educational programmes of regional planning. For a concise overview, see: Friedmann (2001).

31 At the beginning of the 1990s the European Union funded some pilot projects in sustainable urban regeneration and strategy-oriented planning in some larger European conurbations such as Vienna, Berlin, London and Barcelona as well as some smaller cities such as Zurich, Marseille and Halle/Leipzig. For more information on the URBAN Community Initiative programmes: see CEC (2009).

32 See the official EC regulation determining the rules and procedures of Cohesion Policy as published in the Official Journal. Also published in the legal annex of CEC (2007: 39ff.).

33 See: http://ec.europa.eu/regional_policy/sources/docoffic/working/sf2000_en.htm (accessed 14 July 2009).

34 For more info see: http://ec.europa.eu/regional_policy/interreg3/index_en.htm and http://ec.europa.eu/regional_policy/cooperation/index_en.htm (accessed 14 July 2009).

35 In fact, planning cultures and practices of evaluation still differ substantially across Europe due to different schools and traditions of evaluation (cf. Bachtler/Wren 2006). However, the Europeanization of spatial and regional planning and the elaboration and spread of standardized models and practices of programming, monitoring and evaluation also foster isomorphic tendencies (cf. Faludi 2008).

36 See: http://ec.europa.eu/regional_policy/sources/docgener/evaluation/evalsed/index_en.htm (accessed 15 July 2009).

37 See Adams *et al.* (2006) and www.interreg3c.net/sixcms/detail.php?id=10958 (accessed 14 July 2009).

6 Region-building and regional mobilization in Poland

1 I will mainly use the original Polish terms in the following.

2 Certainly, this is nothing special and unique for Poland. There are similar distinctions in many other European countries as well, such as the distinction between northern Italy and the *miseria* of the *Mezzogiorno* in southern Italy (cf. Lepsius 1990c; Putnam 1993), or the distinctions between the west and east, and even north and south in Germany. The same is true for the role and importance of the EU Cohesion Policy in other EU member states, such as Ireland, Spain, Portugal and many others. However, in contrast to regional development and regional mobilization in Western Europe the structural imbalance in Poland has thus far not been discussed extensively in European studies.

3 The analytical distinction of 'centre' and 'periphery' usually characterizes large-scale patterns of inequality and asymmetries amongst larger territories, such as continents or the whole globe (Wallerstein 1974, 1980, 1989; Rokkan *et al.* 1987; for a concise overview, see: Strassoldo 1981). The area of Central and Eastern Europe is a considered as a periphery of the European continent for ages, since it is historically located at the cross-roads of Roman-Catholicism and Greek Orthodoxy (cf. Panther 1997; Hann 2002; Vobruba 2005).

4 These included Estonia, Latvia, Lithuania, Poland, the Czech Republic, Slovakia, Slovenia and Hungary, which joined the European Union in 2004, as well as Romania and Bulgaria, which joined in 2007. In 1990 the German Democratic Republic was already integrated into the structures of Western Germany in October 1990 and thus underwent a very peculiar path of transformation.

5 This relative absence of a pronounced political mobilization of regionalization in Central and Eastern Europe is explained by a characteristic 'incongruence of ethnic and historic regionalisms' (Brusis 2002: 549ff.). After centuries of numerous territorial changes, after two world wars with massive forced resettlement in the first half of the twentieth century, and after some decades of centralism under communist rule, the historical basis for the articulation of regional traditions was relatively weak (cf. Gorzelak and Kukliński 1992; Rykiel 1997; Kłoczowski 1997).

6 For the official version of this law see: www.mswia.gov.pl/portal/pl/53/1661/ (accessed 22 August 2009).

7 According to information provided by the Office of the Committee for European Integration (OCEI) Poland has received about EUR3.9 billion of PHARE assistance between 1990 and 2003, and it is estimated that Poland received about EUR5.7 billion of EU pre-accession assistance altogether, including the two new instruments that

were introduced in 2000, the ISPA and the SAPARD programmes. For more information on all external pre-accession funds (see: OCEI 2004).

8 From the very beginning of PHARE funding in Poland during the early 1990s, expert advice played a major role in the implementation and management of PHARE assistance (cf. Gurbiel 2005). For more information on the role and structure of external advice in pre-accession assistance in Poland and in particular the Franco-German twinning project between 2003 and 2005 see, amongst others: Sartorius (2005).

9 This has also been repeatedly pointed out in interviews with Polish experts of regional development.

10 On the role of regional development agencies (RDAs) in Western European countries see amongst others: Yuill (1982) and Halkier *et al.* (2002).

11 It is in fact one of the particularities of the Polish SEZs that they are all run privately and for profit. For more a general overview on SEZs in Poland, see: KPMG (2006).

12 The number of SEZs in Poland has been limited to 14 since EU accession in 2004, and their existence is only guaranteed until 2020 because the major principle of SEZs, i.e. providing tax exemptions and direct subsidies to companies and investors located within them, violates the rules of EU competition law. However, it is still possible for the 14 Polish SEZs to increase in size and even open up new sub-zones in new areas in accordance with legally determined ceilings. See also: Blauberger (2009).

13 SEZs and their sub-zones are mainly concentrated in Northern Poland as well as in and around previous major industrial areas in central and southern Poland. In regions such as Lubelskie, Mazowieckie and Warminsko-Mazurskie the dispersion of SEZs and TPs is relatively low. See for an overview and for more information: KPMG (2006). In Table 6.1 the RDAs, SEZs, and STPs of the three regional representatives are depicted.

14 This becomes apparent, first and foremost, in low levels of financial endowment of the regions and strong limitations in sovereignty (cf. Grosse (2006: 152f.).

15 During the age of the Holy Roman Empire, for instance, Silesia was part of the Bohemian crown and in 1526 was annexed to the Habsburg Monarchy of Austria. In 1742 after the war of the Austrian succession it fell under Prussian hegemony (cf. Davies 1981a, 1981b).

16 The historical area of Silesia also slightly transcends the borders of the Polish territory. Some smaller parts of the Sudeten in the North of the Czech Republic are called the 'Czech Silesia'. A small area along the eastern border of Germany, the Silesian-Lusatian Region (*Schlesische Oberlausitz* in German), is also attributed as the historical core of Silesia.

17 For more information on the EEA and Norwegian Financial Mechanisms 2004–9 and the Swiss–Polish Co-operation Programme 2007–12 see the respective website of the Polish Ministry of Regional Development at: www.mrr.gov.pl/english/strategies/ (accessed 22 August 2009).

18 Available at: www.mrr.gov.pl/english/strategies/ (accessed 22 August 2009). The official title of the document was changed from 'plan' into 'strategy' in 2005 during the change from the former SLD to the PiS/PSL government, since, for the new government, the term 'plan' had too strong connotations with communist planning.

19 The Vistula river (*wisła* in Polish) is the longest river in Poland, crossing the country from the Carpathian mountains and Kraków in the south, to the Baltic Sea in the north of Poland via Warsaw.

20 Until recently, there were almost no express roads and motorways (less than 1,000 km in total), and the only existing motorways can be found in the western part of the country. See for more information a presentation of the Polish Ministry of Infrastructure and Transport on road construction in Poland at: www.en.mi.gov.pl/files/2/46f38651bb49e/MinisterstwoInfrastruktury.pdf (accessed 12 March 2011).

21 See: www.kghm.pl (accessed 12 March 2011).

22 The determination of the 'wealth' of a region and the measurement of a territory by its economic productivity measured in terms of GDP per capita constitutes a widespread standard both in sciences and political practice. It is also proposed in how-to handbooks on EU regional policy-making as a standard technique for getting a picture of current developmental trends (cf. Molle 2007: 13ff.). According to EU standards a region with a GDP per capita of less than 75 per cent of the average of all EU areas is regarded as a 'convergence region' and as 'lagging behind', and is therefore eligible for extra-funding and special treatment. However, it must be noted that the EU average is not fixed. It decreases as much as more 'poor', or rather economically less productive, areas join the European Union.

23 In fact, the structural differences also have a political dimension, since the regions in eastern Poland are also regarded as the most traditional and conservative areas of Poland (cf. Zarycki and Nowak 2000; Hann 1998; Buzalka 2007). The population in eastern Poland is generally speaking more sceptical with regard to European influence and European integration (cf. Gorzelak 2006: 52ff.).

24 A striking example in this context is the region of Mazowieckie which contains Warsaw, the Polish capital: The 'hinterland' of the Polish capital in fact is very sparsely populated and mainly consists of forests, agricultural land and national parks, and is therefore in a sense quite similar to many areas in the eastern part of Poland. Nonetheless, the whole area is rated very positively due to the extraordinary economic dynamism of the capital city. But this does not say anything about whether the economic performance of the city has 'spill-over' effects on the other parts of the same statistical unit.

25 It was already pointed out that the analytical distinction between centre and periphery usually characterizes large-scale patterns of inequality and power asymmetries within larger territories (cf. Wallerstein 1974, 1980, 1989; Rokkan *et al.* 1987). In recent times, however, static centre–periphery distinctions are strongly challenged. Accordingly, the 'peripherity' of certain places is measured in terms of 'accessibility' and 'connectivity' to account for new conditions of the global network-capitalism (cf. Schürmann and Talaat 2000).

7 The world-cultural make-up of Polish regions

1 See: www.paiz.gov.pl (accessed 22 October 2008).

2 See: www.lubelskie.pl (Government of the Lublin Voivodship), www.si.podkarckie.pl (Government of the Sub-Carpathian Voivodship), and www.dolnyslask.pl (Government of the Lower Silesia Voivodship) (accessed 12 November 2009).

3 Excerpt taken from: www.turystyka.lubelskie.pl/index.php/lrt/page/135/ (accessed 21 March 2011).

4 Ibid.

5 Excerpts taken from: www.wrota.podkarpackie.pl/en/about_reg (accessed 21 March 2011). It is a website called 'Gate to Podkarpackie' which is co-financed by EU funds and officially authorized by the Marshal's Office of the Podkarpackie Voivodship.

6 For more information on this particular area in the most south eastern part of Poland see: www.bieszczady.pl/ (accessed 22 March 2011).

7 Excerpt taken from: www.wrota.podkarpackie.pl/en/about_reg (accessed 21 September 2009).

8 Taken from: www.umwd.dolnyslask.pl/ (last access: 03 March 2009). Not available anymore. The content of this webpage was replaced in 2009.

9 The interviews were undertaken in Polish or in English depending on the wish and language skills of respective interviewees. They were undertaken discursively, but along the lines of a prepared catalogue of subjects and questions that was prepared by the interviewer. All interviews lasted for about one to two hours. Most of the interviews were recorded and transcribed, some interviews were summarized in memory

protocols. The interviews in Polish language were transcribed by a Polish-speaking student assistant. All other interviews were transcribed by me. Finally, all texts (both Polish and English ones) were put together in ATLAS.ti and analyzed according to various analytical categories. The material is listed as archived in ATLAS.ti. An overview of the interviews and a list of the interview partners can be found in Appendix 2.

10 For more information on this particular area in the most south-easterly part of Poland see: www.bieszczady.pl/ (22 March 2011).

11 The distinction of attitudinal mobility vs. immobility constitutes a popular distinction in discourses on modernity and modernization (cf. Lepsius 1990c).

12 The huge wave of Polish emigration at the beginning of the twentieth century was famously described and analyzed by Thomas and Znaniecki (1984) in their classical masterpiece *The Polish Peasant in Europe and America*.

13 On the importance and centrality of 'mobility' in contemporary modernity, see, above all: Urry (2007).

14 In fact, it is only slightly exaggerated by the interviewee that 'one third' of the inhabitants of Rzeszów are students or members of research institutes and universities. According to official information outlined on the websites of the major institutions of higher education in Rzeszów, the University of Rzeszów has over 25,000 full-time and part-time students and the Rzeszów University of Technology has another 13,000 enrolled students. This accounts for almost 40,000 students in a city of about 170,000 inhabitants (according to the author's own inquiries in autumn 2008).

15 The structural disadvantage in the 'investment attractiveness' of the eastern regions highlighted by the interviewees can be confirmed by other observations. For example, in the brochure *Investing in Poland 2008* published by the Polish Information and Foreign Investment Agency (PAIiIZ) to inform potential foreign investors about investment opportunities in Poland, the eastern regions are hardly mentioned at all. In fact, the brochure mainly highlights the bigger cities, such as Warsaw, Wrocław, Lódź, Gdańsk, Poznań, Katowice and Kraków, as the most attractive spots for business investments as well as the 14 existing special economic zones (SEZs) in Western Poland. See also: http://investing-in-poland.pl/index-2.html (accessed 29 August 2009).

16 This is fully confirmed by the assessment of Płaziak and Trzepacz (2008). Their study indicates that in Lubelskie almost 100 per cent of infrastructure investments between 2004 and 2006 were financed by EU funds; in Podkarpackie the rate of EU funding is higher than 70 per cent, whereas in Dolnośląskie the EU-dependency in infrastructure investment is one of the lowest of all Polish regions with a share of about 55 per cent.

17 It is important to note in this context that the Polish regions were not required to implement the Lisbon goals in the current programming period 2007–13 on the part of the European Union. In fact, all 'poorer' areas and regions were exempted from this new requirement of the EU Cohesion Policy. However, the Polish government decided to comply with the Lisbon requirements in the new programming period as much as possible and integrated the Lisbon agenda into their National Development Strategy 2007–15. Consequently, all Polish regions have to comply with Lisbon goals as well. But, as the quote shows, the regional governments in the eastern regions are struggling to keep pace with the new imperatives of European regional development policy and with the creation of favourable conditions for the emergence of a 'knowledge society'.

18 Over the past two decades Dolnośląskie and all the other regions along the western border of Poland have indeed attracted a huge amount of foreign investors for the purposes of opening up shop floors close to the huge consumer markets in Western Europe – not only companies from the European Union, but also American and Asian companies. On the assessment of the innovation and economic development of Dolnośląskie see, amongst others: Hardy (2004), Moszkowicz and Kwieciński (2006), and Heidenreich (2008).

8 Strategizing all the way down: traces of 'standardized diversification'

1 See *Studia Regionalne i Lokalne* No. 3/2000. Available at: www.studreg.uw.edu.pl/ (accessed 25 November 2008).
2 Since the law on administrative reform did not make any prescriptions regarding the timing and the major procedural aspects of the process, the preparation procedures were slightly different from voivodship to voivodship. Some regional authorities largely relied on external consultants, who were in the main scientists from Poland with expertise in the field of (regional) geography or (regional) economics; others, in turn, mainly resorted to experts from their own regional departments and professors from local universities. In principle, however, the procedural and organizational arrangements of the process were quite similar among all Polish regions. Most of the regions adopted their first strategies in June and July 2000, some already in spring 2000 (such as our representative cases from eastern Poland: Lubelskie and Podkarpackie) and some waited until autumn 2000 (Mazowieckie and Zachodnio-Pomorksie) (cf. Żuber 2000).
3 In some regions there were fewer than 100 participants. But in Lubelskie, for example, about 200 people were directly involved in the process of strategy development and gave their opinion through workshops, consultations and so forth (Żuber 2000).
4 There were concerns raised by experts and scientists that the first regional development strategies of the 16 voivodships had been too heterogeneous and not sufficiently structured in accordance with each other (cf. Grosse 2006; Gorzelak *et al.* 2006; Żuber 2007). Moreover, the revision of regional planning in Poland was also seen as an opportunity to consolidate the epidemic spread of strategic plans and planning documents in municipalities and regions since 1999. This was pointed out by a former under-secretary of state of the Ministry of Regional Development, see: Jerzy Kwiecinski: 'Development strategy as a tool for increasing competitiveness'. Plenary session 1 of the conference 'Regional Development in Central and Eastern Europe' held in Warsaw on 20 September 2007. Download at: www.euroreg.uw.edu.pl/index.php/ wydarzenia/7-konferencje/95-plenary-session-1.html (accessed 22 March 2011).
5 This is explicitly pointed out and explained in the National Development Strategy 2007–15. On page 79 of the English version of the official document an overview of the institutional context of development planning in Poland and the relation between domestic development planning and European standards, requirements and guidelines is depicted (cf. Ministry of Regional Development of Poland 2006a: 79).
6 Definitely, the effects of spatial development planning and in particular the implementation of the EU Cohesion Policy in Poland have been excessively studied by numerous scientists and research institutes (cf. Gorzelak 2006; Grosse 2006 and 2007b). Beyond that, both the EU Commission and the Polish government have contracted 'independent' scientific research institutes and private consulting companies to evaluate the implementation of structural funds. One example of a private study contracted by the Commission is the analysis of Blomeyer Consulting (2007).
7 Source: European Commission 2009. Available at: http://ec.europa.eu/regional_ policy/sources/ docgener/informat/country2009/pl_en.pdf (accessed 27 August 2009).
8 According to information provided by the Ministry of Regional Development this brought about EUR 223.6 million of EU funds from IROP to Dolnośląskie, EUR 201 million to Lubelskie, and EUR 192.2 million to Podkarpackie (at 2007 prices). For more information see: Ministry of Regional Development of Poland (2007a, 2007b, 2007c) and: www.zporr.gov.pl/ (accessed 22 September 2009).
9 See: www.pois.mi.gov.pl/ (accessed 22 March 2011).
10 For a view on maps showing present and envisaged roads and motorways, see the presentation 'Drogi na Euro 2012' of the Polish Ministry of Infrastructure, Warsaw, 2008. Available at: www.mi.gov.pl/files/2/46f38651bb49e/MinisterstwoInfrastruktury.pdf (accessed 22 March 2011).

11 For a detailed overview of the current state of road construction in Poland as of spring 2011, see the National Road Report of the Polish Ministry of Infrastructure, 3 March 2011. Available at: www.en.mi.gov.pl/files/0/1793122/detailedroadreport0303.pdf (accessed 22 March 2011).

12 See: www.mi.gov.pl/files/0/1788236/2008084ProgramKDPdokonsultacji.pdf (accessed 22 March 2011).

13 Obviously, the determination of the distribution of funds was a highly disputed issue in numerous meetings between representatives of the voivodships. This 80–10–10 algorithm constitutes a compromise which should take into consideration both the various sizes of the voivodships (in terms of population) and the diverging socio-economic situations in terms of unemployment and economic performance (according to information gathered in interviews with policy-makers in 2007).

14 On the current structure and role of the voivodship contracts in the regional policy of Poland see: www.mrr.gov.pl/rozwoj_regionalny/polityka_regionalna/kontrakty_ wojewodzkie/ (accessed 22 September 2009).

15 For more information on the Organic Food Valley see: www.dolinaeko.wspa.lublin. pl/ and for information on the major supporting institution see: www.ekolubelszc-zyzna.pl (accessed 22 September 2009).

16 For more information on this project: www.klasterkultury.lublin.pl/ (accessed 22 September 2009) and for an overview of the background and motives in establishing the new clusters in Lubelskie see the presentation by Barbara Szymoniuk (2007): 'Partnership of clusters: an opportunity for European peripheries. The Case of the Lubelskie Region in Eastern Poland' at the Conference 'Regional Development in Central and Eastern Europe', Warsaw 2007. Available at: www.euroreg.uw.edu.pl/index.php/ en/events/7-konferencje/95-plenary-session-1.html (accessed 22 September 2009).

17 See: www.zamosc.pl/ and http://majdanek.pl/ (accessed 22 September 2009).

18 In October 2010 Lublin was in fact shortlisted for the final competition on the title 'European Capital of Culture 2016'. See: http://kultura.lublin.eu/ (accessed 22 March 2011).

19 For an overview of existing and planned airports in Poland see a report of PMR Consulting. Available at: www.paiz.gov.pl/files/?id_plik=8435 (accessed 22 March 2011).

20 See: www.dolinalotnicza.pl (accessed 22.09.2009).

21 See: http://t-park.eu (accessed 22 September 2009).

22 According to information provided on the website of the EU Commission's DG Regio. Available at: http://ec.europa.eu/regional_policy/projects/ (accessed 22 September 2009). And for more information on the incubator visit the website of the Wrocław Technology Park see: www.technologpark.pl (accessed 22 September 2009).

9 Conclusions: the spirit and the limits of world-cultural mobilization

1 According to a newsletter of *Business Monitor International* on 'The looming shadow economy' published in April 2009 (Available at: www.riskwatchdog.com/pdf/makepdf. php?pid=725, accessed October 2009) the revenues of shadow economy in Poland are estimated to be growing in 2009 by PLN25 billion (more than 14 per cent) up to PLN200 billion (US$53billion).

2 It has been highlighted already that many facets and aspects of 'decoupling' are constantly being analyzed and addressed by policy-analysts. The effectiveness of Cohesion Policy as well as the efficient and democratic absorption of EU funds are constantly measured and evaluated. Policy analysts have monitored potential gateways of corruption within the system as well as possible misallocations of funds (cf. Grosse 2006, 2007). Beyond that, ethnographers have pointed to cultural and psycho-sociological

categories of resistance to the current changes and transformations, and especially the emergence of new types of populism in rural Poland (cf. Hann 1998; Buzalka 2007).

3 Often economists are undecided, in fact, whether informal business activities are dysfunctional to development or not. On the one hand, it is widely acknowledged that informal economic activities would foster moral hazard and destroy the functioning of (modern) markets in the long run. On the other hand, however, it is also highlighted sometimes that for short periods, such as in transition and fast structural changes, employment in grey markets and information economic activities might help to reduce the expansion of social problems and apathy. There is even the notion of a 'good shadow economy' which might help to foster activism, creativity, innovation and flexibility and also solidarity of social actors. See, for example, Kozłowski (2005) or the following webpage at: http://wikipreneurship.eu/index.php5?title=The_good_shadow_ economy (accessed October 2009).

Bibliography

Abbott, A. (1988) *The system of professions. An Essay on the Division of Expert Labor*, Chicago: University of Chicago Press.

Acharya, A. (2004) 'How Ideas Spread: Whose Norms Matter? Norm Localization and Institutional Change in Asian Regionalism', *International Organization* 58: 239–75.

Adams, N., Alden, J. and Harris, N. (eds) (2006) *Regional and Development and Spatial Planning in an Enlarged European Union*, Aldershot: Ashgate.

Adams, N., Harris, N. (2005): *GRIDS – best practice guidelines for regional development strategies*, Wales: Cardiff University. Available at: www.interreg3c.net/sixcms/detail.php?id=10958 (accessed 22 July 2008).

Adamski, W., Machonin, P., Zapf, W. (2002) (eds) *Structural Change and Modernization in Post-Socialist Societies*, Hamburg: Krämer Verlag.

Aglietta, M. (1982) *Regulation and Crisis of Capitalism*, New York: Monthly Review Press.

Agnew, J.A. and Duncan, J.S. (1989) *The Power of Place: Bringing together geographical and sociological imaginations*, Boston: Unwin Hyman.

Agnew, J. and Entrikin, J.N. (eds) (2004) *The Marshall Plan Today: Model and Metaphor*, London: Routledge.

Alexander, J.C. (1988) *Durkheimian Sociology: Cultural Studies*, Cambridge: Cambridge University Press.

Alexander, J.C. (2003) 'Modern, Anti, Post, and Neo: How Intellectuals Explain "Our Time"', in J.C. Alexander (ed.) *The Meaning of Social Life. A Cultural Sociology*, Oxford: Oxford University Press, pp. 193–228.

Alexander, J.C., Giesen, B., Münch, R. and Smelser, N.J. (eds) (1987) *The Micro–Macro Link*, Berkeley: University of California Press.

Alexander, J.C. and Seidman, S. (eds) (1990) *Culture and Society: Contemporary Debates*, Cambridge: Cambridge University Press.

Amin, A. (1989) 'Flexible Specialization and Small Firms in Italy: Myths and Realities', *Antipode*, 21(1): 13–34.

Amin, A. (1999) 'An Institutionalist Perspective on Regional Economic Development', *International Journal of Urban and Regional Research* 23(2): 365–78.

Amin, A. (ed.) (1994) *Post-Fordism: A Reader*, Oxford: Oxford University Press.

Amin, A. and Thrift N. (eds) (1994) *Globalization, Institutions, and Regional Development in Europe*, Oxford: Oxford University Press.

Amin, A. and Thrift, N. (1995) 'Institutional issues for the European regions: from market and plans to socioeconomics and powers of association', *Economy and Society*, 24(1): 41–66.

Amin, A. and Tomaney, J. (eds) (1995) *Behind the Myth of European Union: Prospects for Cohesion*, London: Routledge.

Amin, S. (1976) *Unequal Development. An Essay on the Social Formations of Peripheral Capitalism*, New York: Monthly Review Press.

Anderson, B. (1983) *Imagined Communities. Reflections on the Origin and Spread of Nationalism*, London: Verso.

Appadurai, A. (1997) *Modernity at Large. Cultural Dimensions of Globalization*, 2nd edn, Minneapolis: University of Minnesota Press.

Armstrong, H.W. (1995) 'Convergence among Regions of the European Union, 1950–1990', *Papers in Regional Science*, 74(1): 143–52.

Armstrong, H.W. and Taylor, P. (2000) *Regional Economics and Policy*, Oxford: Blackwell.

Arnason, J. (1993) *The Future that Failed: The Collapse of Communism in Eastern Europe*, London: Taylor and Francis.

Asheim, B. (1997) ' "Learning regions" in a globalised economy: towards a new competitive advantage of industrial districts?', in S. Conti and M. Taylor (eds) *Interdependent and uneven development: global-local perspectives*, London: Avebury, pp. 143–76.

Bach, M. (2008) *Europa ohne Gesellschaft. Politische Soziologie der Europäischen Integration*, Wiesbaden: VS Verlag.

Bach, M. (ed.) (2000) *Die Europäisierung nationaler Gesellschaften. Kölner Zeitschrift für Soziologie und Sozialpsychologie, Sonderheft 40*, Wiesbaden: Westdeutscher Verlag.

Bache, I. (2008) *Europeanization and Multi-level Governance: Cohesion Policy in the European Union and Britain*, Lanham: Rowman and Littlefield.

Bachtler, J. and Downes, R. (2000) 'The Spatial Coverage of Regional Policy in Central and Eastern Europe', *European Urban and Regional Studies* 7(2): 159–74.

Bachtler, J. and Wren, C. (2006) 'Evaluation of European Union Cohesion policy: Research questions and policy challenges' *Regional Studies* 40(2): 143–53.

Bachtler, J., Downes, R., Helinska-Hughes, E. and Macquarrie, J. (1999) 'Regional Development Policy in the Transition Countries', *Regional and Industrial Policy Research Papers* No. 36, Glasgow: University of Strathclyde.

Bachtler, J., Downes, R. and Gorzelak, G. (eds) (2000) *Transition, Cohesion and Regional Policy in Central and Eastern Europe*, Aldershot: Ashgate Publishing.

Baecker, D. (2009) 'Das Projekt der Regionalisierung', in M. Hey & K. Engert (eds) *Komplexe Regionen – Regionenkomplexe: Multiperspektivische Ansätze zur Beschreibung regionaler und urbaner Dynamiken*, Wiesbaden: VS Verlag, pp. 21–6.

Bagnasco, A. (1977) *Tre Italie*, Bologna: Il Mulino.

Baker, S. (2006) *Sustainable Development*, London: Routledge.

Balcerowicz, L. (1999) *Socialism, Capitalism, Transformation*, Budapest: Central University Press.

Baldersheim, H., Illner, M., Offerdal, A., Rose, L. and Swianiewicz, P. (eds) (1996) *Local Democracy and the Process of Transformation in East-Central Europe*, Colorado: Westview Press.

Baldersheim, H., Illner, M. and Wollmann, H. (2003) *Local Democracy in Post-Communist Europe*, Opladen: Leske + Budrich.

Barro, R.J. and Sala-i-Martin, X. (1992) 'Convergence.', *Journal of Political* Economy 100: 223–51.

Barro, R.J. and Sala-i-Martin, X. (1995): *Economic Growth*. Cambridge, MA: The MIT Press.

Barry, A. (1993) 'The European Community and European government: harmonization, mobility and space', *Economy and Society* 22(3): 314–26.

Barry, A., Osborne, T. and Rose, N. (eds) (1996) *Foucault and Political Reason*. London: UCL Press.

Barthes, R. (1957) *Mythologies*, Paris: Éditions du Seuil.

Bartlett, C.A. and Goshal, S. (1989) *Managing Across Borders: The Transnational Solution*, 2nd edn, Boston, MA: Harvard Business School Press.

Bartlett, C.A. and Goshal, S. (1999) *The Individualized Corporation. A Fundamentally New Approach to Management*, New York: Collins.

Bartolini, S. (2005) *Restructuring Europe. Centre formation, system building, and political structuring between the nation state and the European Union*, Oxford: Oxford University Press.

Batterbury, S.C.E. (2006) 'Principles and purposes of European Union Cohesion policy evaluation', *Regional Studies* 40(2): 179–88.

Bauman, Z. (1991) *Modernity and Ambivalence*, Cambridge: Polity Press.

Bauman, Z. (1998) *Globalization: The Human Consequences*, Cambridge: Polity Press.

Bauman, Z. (2000) *Liquid Modernity*, Cambridge: Polity Press.

Bayly, C.A. (2004) *The Birth of the Modern World 1780–1914: Global Connections and Comparisons*, Malden, MA: Blackwell Publishing.

Beck, U. (2000) *What is Globalization?* Cambridge: Polity Press.

Beck, U. and Bonß, W. (eds) (1989) *Weder Sozialtechnologie noch Aufklärung? Analysen zur Verwendung sozialwissenschaftlichen Wissens*, Frankfurt/M.: Suhrkamp.

Beck, U. and Grande, E. (2007) *Cosmopolitan Europe*, Cambridge: Polity Press.

Beck, U., Giddens, A. and Lash, S. (1994) *Reflexive Modernization: Politics, Tradition and Aesthetics in the Modern Social Order*, Stanford: Stanford University Press.

Becker, G.S. (1993) *Human Capital: A Theoretical and Empirical Analysis with Special Reference to Education*, 3rd edn, Chicago: University of Chicago Press.

Beckert, J. and Zafirovski, M. (eds) (2006) *International Encyclopedia of Economic Sociology*, London: Routledge.

Behrman, G. (2007) *The Most Noble Adventure: The Marshall Plan and the Time When America Helped Save Europe*, New York: The Free Press.

Bell, D. (1973) *The Coming of the Post-Industrial Society. A Venture in Social Forecasting*, New York: Penguin Books.

Bell, D. 'The New Class: A Muddled Concept', in B. Bruce-Briggs (ed.) *The New Class?* New Brunswick, NJ: Transaction Books, pp. 169–90.

Bellah, R.N. (1970) *Beyond Belief: Essays on Religion in a Post-Traditional World*, New York: Harper & Row.

Bennett, R.J. (ed.) (1990) *Decentralization Local Governments, and Markets. Towards a Post-Welfare Agenda*, Oxford: Clarendon Press.

Benz, A. and Eberlein, B. (1999) 'The Europeanization of regional policies: patterns of multi-level governance', *Journal of European Public Policy* 6(2): 329–48.

Benz, A. and Fürst, D. (2002) 'Policy Learning in Regional Networks', *European Urban and Regional Studies* 9(1): 21–35.

Berger, P.L. (1967) *The Sacred Canopy*, Garden City, NY: Doubleday.

Berger, P.L. and Luckmann, T. (1966) *The Social Construction of Reality: A Treatise in the Sociology of Knowledge*, Garden City, NY: Anchor Books.

Bernhard, S. (2006) 'The European Paradigm of Social Exclusion', *Journal of Contemporary European Research* 2: 41–57.

Bernhard, S. (2009) 'Die Symbolische Inszenierung als „kultureller Anderer" – Zur

Auslegung weltkultureller Skripte im Feld der europäischen Inklusionspolitik', *Berliner Journal für Soziologie* 19: 29–54.

Bernhard, S. (2010) *Die Konstruktion von Inklusion. Europäische Sozialpolitik aus soziologischer Perspektive*, Frankfurt/M.: Campus.

Beyme, von K. (1994) *Systemwechsel in Osteuropa*, Frankfurt/M.: Suhrkamp.

Bianchini, F. (2002) 'Cultural Planning for urban sustainability', *Diagoog – webtijdschrift voor (een) agogiek in dialog* 2(1): 1–16.

Blauberger, M. (2009) 'Compliance with Rules of Negative Integration. European State Aid Control in the New Member States', *Journal of European Public Policy* 16(7): 1030–46

Blazyca, G., Heffner, K. and Helińska-Hughes, E. (2002): 'Poland – Can regional policy meet the challenge of regional problems?', *European Urban and Regional Studies* 9(3): 263–76.

Blomeyer Consulting (2007) *The Structural Funds' Implementation in Poland – Challenges for 2007–2013. Study requested by the European Parliament's Committee on Budgetary Control*, Brussels: European Parliament.

Blyth, M. (2002) *Great Transformations: Economic Ideas and Institutional Change in the Twentieth Century*, Cambridge: Cambridge University Press.

Blyth, M. (2003) 'Structures do not come with an Instruction Sheet: Interests, Ideas, and Progress in Political Sciences', *Perspectives on Politics* 1(4): 695–706.

Boje, T., Van Steenbergen, B. and Walby, S. (eds) (2007) European Societies: Fusion or Fission? London: Routledge.

Bohle, D. (2000) 'Internationalisation: An Issue Neglected in the Path-Dependency Approach to Post-Communist Transformation', in M. Dobry (ed.), *Democratic and Capitalist Transitions in Eastern Europe: Lessons for the Social Sciences*, Dordrecht: Kluwer Academic Publishers, pp. 235–61.

Boli, J. (2006) 'The rationalization of virtue and virtuosity in world society', in M.-L. Djelic and K. Sahlin-Andersson (eds), *Transnational Governance: Institutional Dynamics of Regulation*, Cambridge: Cambridge University Press, pp. 95–118.

Boli, J. and Thomas, G.M. (1997) 'World Culture in the World Polity: A Century of International Non-Governmental Organization', *American Sociological Review* 62(2): 171–90.

Boli, J. and Thomas, G.M. (eds) (1999) *Constructing World Culture: International Nongovernmental Organizations since 1875*, Stanford: Stanford University Press.

Boli-Bennett, J. and Meyer, J.W. (1980) 'Constitutions as Ideology' *American Sociological Review* 45(3): 525–7.

Bollman, N.P. (2004) 'The Regional Civic Movement in California', *National Civic Review* (Spring 2004): 3–15.

Boltanski, L. and Chiapello, E. (2006) *The New Spirit of Capitalism*, London: Verso Books.

Boltanski, L. and Thevenot, L. (1991) *De la justification. Les économies de la grandeur*, Paris: Édition Gallimard.

Bönker, F., Müller, K. and Pickel, A. (eds) (2002) *Postcommunist Transformation and the Social Sciences. Cross-Disciplinary Approaches*, Lanham: Rowman and Littlefield.

Börzel, T.A. (2001). *Shaping States and Regions. The Domestic Impact of Europe*, Cambridge: Cambridge Univeristy Press.

Börzel, T.A. (2002) *States and Regions in the European Union. Institutional Adaptation in Germany and Spain*, Cambridge: Cambridge University Press.

Bourdieu, P. (1984) *Distinction: A Social Critique of the Judgement of Taste*, London: Routledge.

Bourdieu, P. (1985) 'The Social Space and the Genesis of Groups', *Social Science Information* 24(2): 195–220.

Boyer, R. and Hollingsworth, J.R. (1997) 'From National Embeddedness to Spatial and Institutional Nestedness', in J.R. Hollingsworth and R. Boyer (eds), *Contemporary Capitalism: The Embeddedness of Institutions*, Cambridge: Cambridge University Press, pp. 433–84.

Bradley, J. (2006) 'Evaluating the impact of European Union Cohesion policy in less-developed countries and regions', *Regional Studies* 40(2): 189–200.

Bradley, J., Załeski, J. and Żuber, P. (2003) 'The role of ex-ante evaluation in CEE National Development Planning: A case study based on Polish administrative experience with NDP 2004–2006', paper presented at the Fifth European Conference on Evaluation of the Structural Funds on Challenges for evaluation in an Enlarged Europe (Workshop 5: Capacity for Evaluation), Budapest, June 2003.

Braudel, F. (1996, 1st edn 1945) *The Mediterranean and the Mediterranean World in the Age of Philip II,* Berkely: University of California Press.

Brenner, N., Jessop, B., Jones, M. and MacLeod, G. (eds) (2003) *State/Space: A Reader*, Malden: Blackwell Publishing.

Bruce-Briggs, B. (ed.) (1979) *The New Class?* New Brunswick, NJ: Transaction Books.

Brunsson, N. and Jacobsson, B. (2000) *A World of Standards*, Oxford: Oxford University Press.

Brusis, M. (2002) 'Between EU Requirements, Competitive Politics, and National Traditions: Re-creating Regions in the Accession Countries of Central and Eastern Europe', *Governance: International Journal of Policy, Administration, and Institutions* 15(4): 531–59.

Brusis, M. (2005) 'The Instrumental Use of European Union Conditionality: Regionalization in the Czech Republic and Slovakia', *East European Politics & Societies* 19: 291–310.

Brusis, M. (ed.) (1999) 'Central and Eastern Europe on the Way into the European Union: Regional Policy-Making in Bulgaria, the Czech Republic, Estonia, Hungary, Poland and Slovakia', *CAP Working Paper* (December 1999), Munich. Available at: www.cap-lmu.de/publikationen/1999/cap_regional_policy_making.php (accessed 10 September 2008).

Bruszt, L. (2005) 'Governing subnational/regional institutional change: The evolution of regional (sub-national) development regimes – challenges for institution building in the CEE countries and sub-national institutional experimentation', *NewGov Working paper*, Florence. Available at: www.eu-newgov.org/datalists/deliverables_detail.asp?Project_ID=15 (accessed 15 March 2007).

Bunce, V. (1999) *Subversive Institutions: The Design and the Destruction of Socialism and the State*, Cambridge: Cambridge University Press.

Burawoy, M. and Verdery, K. (eds) (1999) *Uncertain Transition: Ethnographies of Change in the Postsocialist World*, Lanham: Rowman and Littlefield.

Burchell, G., Gordon, C. and Miller, P. (eds) (1991) *The Foucault-Effect: Studies in Governmentality*, London: Harvester Wheatsheaf.

Buzalka, J. (2007) *Nation and Religion: The Politics of Commemoration in South-East Poland*, Halle Studies in the Anthropology of Eurasia, Münster: LIT Verlag.

Camagni, R. (1991) *Innovation networks: spatial perspectives*, London: Belhaven Press.

Carroll, P. (2006) *Science, Culture, and Modern State Formation*, Berkeley: University of California Press.

Castells, M. (1996) *The Information Age: Economy, Society, and Culture. Volume 1: The Rise of the Network Society*, Oxford: Blackwell Publishers.

Castells, M. (1997) *The Information Age: Economy, Society, and Culture. Volume 2: The Power of Identity*, Oxford: Blackwell Publishers.

Castells, M. (1998) *The Information Age: Economy, Society, and Culture. Volume 3: End of Millennium,* Oxford: Blackwell Publishers.

Castells, M. (2002) 'Local and global: cities in the network society', *Tijdschrift voor Economische en Sociale Geografie* 93(5): 548–58.

Castro, J.V. (2003) 'Regional Convergence, Polarization and Mobility in the European Union, 1980–1996.' *European Integration* 25(1): 73–86.

CEC [Commission of European Communities] (1996) *Report on Economic and Social Cohesion,* Brussels. Online. Available: http://ec.europa.eu/regional_policy/sources/docoffic/official/repor_en.htm (accessed 15 March 2011).

CEC (1999) *ESDP – European Spatial Development Perspective. Towards Balanced and Sustainable Development of the Territory of the European Union,* Luxembourg: Office for Official Publications of the European Communities. Available: http://ec.europa.eu/regional_policy/sources/docoffic/official/reports/pdf/sum_en.pdf (accessed 15 July 2009).

CEC (2001a) *Unity, solidarity, diversity for Europe, its people and its territory. Second Report on Economic and Social Cohesion.* Online. Available: http://ec.europa.eu/regional_policy/sources/docoffic/official/repor_en.htm (accessed 15 March 2011).

CEC (2001b) *A Sustainable Europe for a Better World: A European Union Strategy for Sustainable Development,* Commission's proposal to the Gothenburg European Council. COM(2001) 264 final. Brussels.

CEC (2004) *A new partnership for cohesion: convergence competitiveness cooperation. Third report on economic and social cohesion,* Brussels: Commission of the European Communities.

CEC (2005a) *Relaunching the Lisbon Strategy: A Partnership for Growth and Employment.* COM(2005) 330 final, Brussels: Commission of the European Communities.

CEC (2005b) *Cohesion Policy in Support of Growth and Jobs: Community Strategic Guidelines, 2007–2013.* COM(2005) 0299, Brussels: Commission of the European Communities.

CEC (2006a) *Putting knowledge into practice: A broad-based innovation strategy for the EU.* COM(2006) 502 final, Brussels: Commission of the European Communities.

CEC (2006b) *Innovative strategies and actions: Results from 15 years of Regional Experimentation,* European Commission Working Document, Brussels: DG Regio.

CEC (2007a) *Cohesion policy 2007–13. Commentaries and official texts,* Luxembourg: Office for Official Publications of the European Communities.

CEC (2007b) 'Regions as partners: The European Territorial Cooperation Objective', *Inforegio Panorama* 24, Luxembourg: Office for Official Publications of the European Communities.

CEC (2007c) 'Gender mainstreaming and regional development', *Inforegio Panorama* 22, Luxembourg: Office for Official Publications of the European Communities.

CEC (2007d) *Growing Regions, Growing Europe. Fourth report on economic and social cohesion,* Brussels: Commission of the European Communities.

CEC (2008a) *Working for the regions: EU Regional Policy 2007–2013,* Brussels: Commission of the European Communities.

CEC (2008c) *Turning Territorial Diversity into Strength: Green Paper on Territorial Cohesion.* COM(2008) 616, Luxembourg: Office for Official Publications of the European Communities.

CEC (2008d) 'Regional Policy and enlargement: Moving up a gear through pre-accession funding', *Inforegio Panorama* 27, Luxembourg: Office for Official Publications of the European Communities.

CEC (2008e) 'Regional Policy, sustainable development and climate change', *Inforegio Panorama* 25, Luxembourg: Office for Official Publications of the European Communities.

CEC (2009) *Promoting Sustainable Urban Development in Europe. Achievements and Opportunities*, Luxembourg: Office for Official Publications of the European Communities.

CEC (2010) *Investing in Europe's future. Fith report on economic, social and territorial cohesion*, Brussels: Commission of the European Communities.

Chakrabarty, D. (2000) *Provincializing Europe: Postcolonial Thought and Historical Difference*, Princeton: Princeton University Press.

Chandler, A.D. (1962) *Strategy and Structure: Chapters in the History of the Industrial Enterprise*, Cambridge, MA: M.I.T. Press.

Chase-Dunn, C. (1989) *Global Formation: Structures of the World Economy*, Cambridge: Basil Blackwell.

Checkel, J.T. (2005) 'International Institutions and Socialization in Europe: Introduction and Framework', *International Organization* 59: 801–26.

Chossudovsky, M. (1997) *The Globalization of Poverty: Impacts of IMF and World Bank Reforms*, London: Zed Books.

Christaller, W. (1933) *Die zentralen Orte in Süddeutschland*, Jena: Gustav Fischer.

Christiansen, T., Jørgensen, K.E. and Wiener, A. (eds) (2001) *The Social Construction of Europe*, London: Sage Publications.

Coase, R. (1937) 'The Nature of the Firm', *Economica* (4): 386–405.

Cohen, R. and Kennedy, P. (2007) *Global Sociology*, 2nd edn, Houndmills: Palgrave MacMillan.

Coleman, J.S. (1990) *Foundations of Social Theory*, Cambridge, MA: Harvard University Press.

Comte, A. (2003, 1st edn 1855): *The Positive Philosophy* (transl. by Harriet Martineau), Whitefish: Kessinger Publishing.

Conzelmann, T. and Knodt, M. (eds) (2002) *Regionales Europa – Europäisierte Regionen*. Mannheimer Jahrbuch für Europäische Sozialforschung, Band 6, Frankfurt/M.: Campus.

Cooke, P. (1983*) Theories of Planning and Spatial Development*, London: Hutchinson.

Cooke, P. (2003) *Strategies for Regional Innovation Systems: Learning Transfer and Applications*, United Nations Industrial Development Organization (UNIDO) Policy Paper, Vienna. Available at: www.unido.org/fileadmin/import/11898_June2003_CookePaperRegional_Innovation_Systems.3.pdf (accessed 14 March 2011).

Cooke P. and Morgan, K. (1998) *The Assotiational Economy. Firms, Regions, and Innovation*, Oxford: Oxford University Press.

Cooke, P., Heidenreich, M. and Braczyk, H.-J. (eds) (2004) *Regional Innovation Systems: The role of governance in a globalized world*, 2nd edn, London: Routledge.

Cooke, P. and Schwartz, D. (eds) (2007) *Creative Regions: Technology, Culture and Knowledge Entrepreneurship*, London: Routledge.

Cox, K.R. (ed.) (1997) *Spaces of Globalization: Reasserting the Power of the Local*, New York: The Guilford Press.

Crouch, C. (2004) Post-Democracy, Oxford: Oxford University Press.

Crouch, C., Le Galès, P., Trigilia, C. and Voelzkow, H. (eds) (2004) *Changing Governance of Local Economies: Responses of European Local Production Systems*, Oxford: Oxford University Press.

Czarniawska, B. and Sevón, G. (eds) (1996) *Translating Organizational Change*, Berlin: Walter de Gruyter.

Czerny, M. and Czerny, A. (2002) 'The Challenge of Spatial Reorganisation in a peripheral Polish region', *European Urban and Regional Studies* 9(1): 60–72.

Davies, N. (1981a) *God's Playground. A History of Poland, Vol. 1: The origins to 1795*, Oxford: Clarendon Press.

Davies, N. (1981b) *God's Playground. A History of Poland, Vol. 2: 1795 to the present*, Oxford: Clarendon Press.

Dawkins, C.J. (2003) 'Regional Development Theory: Conceptual Foundations, Classic Works, and Recent Developments', *Journal of Planning Literature* 18: 131–72.

De Bruijn, P.J.M. and Lagendijk, A. (2005) 'Regional innovation systems in the Lisbon strategy', *European Planning Studies* 13(8): 1153–72.

Deacon, B. (1998) 'Global and Regional Agencies and the Making of Post-Communist Social Policy in Eastern Europe' in M. Rhodes and Y. Mény (eds), *The future of European welfare: a new social contract?* Houndsmille: Macmillan Press, pp. 204–26.

Deacon, B. (2007) *Global Social Policy & Governance*, London: Sage Publications.

Delanty, G. (2000) *Modernity and Postmodernity*, London: Sage Publications.

Delanty, G. and Rumford, C. (2005) *Rethinking Europe: Social theory and the implications of Europeanization*, London: Routledge.

Delhey, J. (2000) 'Korruption in Bewerberländern zur Europäischen Union. Institutionenqualität und Korruption in vergleichender Perspektive', *Soziale Welt* 53: 345–66.

Delhey, J. (2004) 'European social integration. From convergence of countries to transnational relations between peoples', *WZB Discussion Papers* SP I 2004–201. Berlin.

Delhey, J. (2007) 'Do Enlargements Make the European Union Less Cohesive? An Analysis of Trust Between EU Nationalities, *Journal of Common Market Studies* 45: 253–279.

Delhey, J., Böhnke, P., Habich, R. and Zapf, W. (2002) 'Quality of Life in a European Perspective. The Euromodule as a New Instrument for Comparative Welfare Research', *Social Indicators Research* 58(1): 161–176.

Deutsch, K.W. (1961) 'Social Mobilization and Political Development', *American Political Science Review* 55 (September): 634–47.

Dicken, P. (2003) *Global Shift: The Internationalization of Economic Activity*. London: Routledge.

Diener, E. and Suh, E. (1997) 'Measuring Quality of Life: Economic, Social and Subjective Indicators', *Social Indicators Research* 40(1–2): 189–216.

Dimitriou, H.T. and Thompson, R. (eds) (2007) *Strategic Planning for Regional Development in the UK: A Review of Principles and Practice*, London: Routledge.

Djelic, M.-L. (2008) 'Sociological studies of diffusion: is history relevant?', *Socio-Economic Review* 6: 538–57.

Djelic, M.-L. and Quack, S. (2007) 'Overcoming path dependency: path generation in open systems', *Theory and Society* 36: 161–86.

Djelic, M.-L. and Sahlin-Andersson, K. (eds) (2006) *Transnational Governance: Institutional Dynamics of Regulation*, Cambridge: Cambridge University Press.

Dobbin, F., Simmons, B. and Garrett, G. (2007) 'The Global Diffusion of Public Policies: Social Construction, Coercion, Competition, or Learning?', *Annual Review of Sociology*, Vol. 33: 449–72.

Dornisch, D. (2002) 'The Evolution of Post-socialist Projects: Trajectory Shift and Transitional Capacity in a Polish Region', *Regional Studies* 36(3): 307–21.

Douglas, M. (1986) *How Institutions Think*, Syracuse, NY: Syracuse University Press.

Drori, G.S. (2006) 'Governed by Governance: The New Prism for Organizational Change', in G.S. Drori, J.W. Meyer and H. Hwang (eds), *Globalization and Organization: World Society and Organizational Change*, Oxford: Oxford University Press, pp. 91–118.

Drori, G.S. and Meyer J.W. (2006) 'Scientization: Making a world safe for organizing', in M.-L. Djelic and K. Sahlin-Andersson (eds) *Transnational Governance: Institutional Dynamics of Regulation*. Cambridge: Cambridge University Press, pp. 31–52.

Drori, G.S., Meyer J.W., Hwang, H. (eds) (2006) *Globalization and Organization: World Society and Organizational Change*, Oxford: Oxford University Press.

Drori, G.S., Meyer J.W., Ramirez, F.O. and Schofer, E. (eds) (2003) *Science in the Modern World Polity: Institutionalization and Globalization*, Stanford: Stanford University Press.

Dunford, M. (1996) 'Disparities in Employment, Productivity and Output in the EU: The Roles of Labour Market Governance and Welfare Regimes', *Regional Studies* 30: 339–57.

Durkheim, E. (1915) *The Elementary Forms of the Religious Life*. Translated by Joseph Ward Swain. London: George Allen & Unwin Ltd.

Durkheim, E. (1960, 1st edn. 1893): *The Division of Social Labour in Society*. Glencoe: Free Press.

Duro, J. A. (2001) *Regional Income Inequalities in Europe: An updated Measurement and some Decomposition Results*, Instituto de Análisis Económico CSIC, Barcelona.

Edquist, C. (1997) *Systems of Innovation: Technologies, Institutions and Organizations*, London: Pinter.

Eisenstadt, S.N. (2000) 'Multiple Modernities', *Daedalus* 129(1): 1–29.

Eisenstadt, S.N. (ed.) (2002a) *Multiple Modernities*, New Brunswick, NJ: Transaction Publishers.

Eisenstadt, S.N. (2002b) 'Some Oberservations on Multiple Modernities', in D. Sachsenmaier, S.N. Eisenstadt and J. Riedel (eds), *Reflections on Multiple Modernities. European, Chinese and Other Interpretations*. Leiden: Brill, pp. 27–40.

Eliade, M. (1949) *Traité d'histoire des religions*, Paris: Edition Payot.

Elias, N. (1969) *The Civilizing Process, Vol.I. The History of Manners*, Oxford: Blackwell.

Elias, N. (1982) *The Civilizing Process, Vol.II. State Formation and Civilization*, Oxford: Blackwell.

Elias, N. (1978) *What is Sociology?* London: Hutchinson of London.

Elster, J., Offe, C. and Preuss, U.K. (1998) *Institutional Design in Post-Communist Societies: Rebuilding the Ship at Sea*, Cambridge: Cambridge University Press.

Eriksson, J., Karlsson, B.O. and Tarschys, D. (eds) (2005) *From Policy Takers to Policy Makers. Adapting EU Cohesion Policy to the Needs of the New Member States*, Report No. 5, Stockholm: Swedish Institute for European Policy Studies.

Escobar, A. (1995) *Encountering Development: The Making and Unmaking of the Third World*, Princeton: Princeton University Press.

Esteva, G. (1985) 'Development: Metaphor, Myth, Threat', *Development: Seeds of Change* 3: 78–79.

Etzioni, A. (1993) *The Spirit of Community. Rights, Responsibilities, and the Communitarian Agenda*, New York: Crown Publishers.

Evans, A. (2004) *EU Regional Policy*, Oxford: Richmond Law and Tax.

Evers, H.-D. and Gerke, S. (2005) *Knowledge is Power: Experts as a Strategic Group*, Working Paper No. 8a, Centre for Development Research: Department of Political and Cultural Change, Bonn: University of Bonn.

Falkner, G., Treib, O.; Hartlapp, M. and Leiber, S. (2005) *Complying with Europe: EU Harmonisation of Soft Law in the Member States*, Cambridge: Cambridge University Press.

Faludi, A. (2004) 'Territorial Cohesion: Old (French) Wine in New Bottles?', *Urban Studies* 41(7): 1349–65.

Faludi, A. (ed.) (2008) *European Spatial Research and Planning*, Cambridge, MA: Lincoln Institute of Land Policy.

Favell, A. (2006) 'The Sociology of EU Politics', in K.E. Jørgensen, M.A. Pollack and B. Rosamond (eds), *The Handbook of EU Politics*, London: Sage Publications, pp. 122–38.

Favell, A. and Guiraudon, V. (2009) 'The Sociology of the European Union: An Agenda', *European Union Politics* 4: 550–76.

Featherstone, K. and Radaelli, C. (eds) (2003) *The politics of Europeanization*, Oxford: Oxford University Press.

Featherstone, M. and Lash, S. (1995) 'Globalization, Modernity and the Spatialization of Social Theory: An Introduction', in M. Featherstone, S. Lash and R. Robertson (eds), *Global Modernities*, London: Sage Publications, pp. 1–24.

Feldman, M.P. (1994) *The Geography of Innovation*, Dordrecht: Kluwer Academic Publishers.

Ferry, M. (2003) 'The EU and recent regional reform in Poland', *Europe-Asia Studies* 55(7): 1097–1116.

Ferry, M. (2007) 'From Government to Governance: Polish Regional Development Agencies in a Changing Regional Context', *East European Politics and Societies* 21: 447–74.

Ferry, M., Gross, F., Bachtler, J. and McMaster, I. (2007) *Turning Strategies into Projects: The Implementation of 2007–13 Structural Funds Programmes*, IQ-Net Thematic Paper No. 20(2), Glasgow: European Policies Research Centre.

Finnemore, M. (1996a) *National Interests in International Society*, Ithaca: Cornell University Press.

Finnemore, M. (1996b) 'Review: Norms, Culture, and World Politics: Insights from Sociology's Institutionalism' *International Organization* 50(2): 325–47.

Finnemore, M. and Sikkink, K. (1998) 'International Norm Dynamics and Political Change', *International Organization* 52(4): 887–917.

Fishbein, J. (2008) 'Europe's Innovation Hot Spots', in *Business Week*, 28 April 2008. Available at: www.businessweek.com/globalbiz/europe/special_reports/20080428 europeaninn.htm (accessed 22 July 2008).

Fligstein, N. (2001) *The Architecture of Markets: An Economic Sociology of Capitalist Societies*, Princeton, NJ: Princeton University Press.

Fligstein, N. (2008) *Euroclash. The EU, European Identity and the Future of Europe*, Oxford: Oxford University Press.

Fligstein, N. and Stone Sweet, A. (2002) 'Constructing Polities and Markets: An Institutionalist Account of European Integration', *American Journal of Sociology* 107(5): 1206–43.

Florida, R. (2002) *The Rise of the Creative Class. And How It's Transforming Work, Leisure, Community, and Everyday Life*, New York: Basic Books.

Foucault, M. (1965) *Madness and Civilisation: A History of Insanity in the Age of Reason*, New York: Random House.

Foucault, M. (1972) *The Archaeology of Knowledge*, London: Routledge.

Foucault, M. (1989) *Résumés des cours*, Paris: Collège de France.

Foucault, M. (1991) 'Govenmentality', in G. Burchell, C. Gordon and P. Miller (eds) *The Foucault-Effect. Studies in Governmentality*, London: Harvester Wheatsheaf, pp. 87–104.

Fourcade, M. (2006) 'The Construction of a Global Profession: The Transnationalization of Economics', *American Journal of Sociology* 112(1): 145–94.

Fourcade-Gourinchas, M. (2002) 'The Rebirth of the Liberal Creed: Paths to Neoliberalism in Four Countries', *American Journal of Sociology* 108(3): 533–79.

Freeman, C. (1982) *The Economics of Industrial Innovation*, London: Pinter.

Freidson, E. (1986) *Professional Powers. A Study of the Institutionalization of Formal Knowledge*, Chicago: University of Chicago Press.

Friedkin, N. (2004) 'Social Cohesion', *Annual Review of Sociology* 30: 409–25.

Friedman, J. and Weaver, C. (1979) *Territory and function: The evolution of regional planning*, Berkeley: University of California Press.

Friedman, M. (1962) *Capitalism and Liberty*, Chicago: Chicago University Press.

Friedmann J. (2001) 'Regional Development and Planning: The Story of a Collaboration', *International Regional Science Review* 24(3): 386–95.

Friedmann, J. and Alonso, W. (eds) (1964) *Regional planning and development: A reader*, Cambridge, MA: MIT Press.

Friese, H. and Wagner, P. (2002) 'The Nascent Political Philosophy of the European Polity', *Journal of Political Philosophy* 10(3): 342–64.

Fukuyama, F. (1992) *The End of History and the Last Man*, New York: Penguin Books.

Fürst, D. (2004) 'Regional Governance', in A. Benz (ed.) *Governance – Regieren in komplexen Regelsystemen*, Wiesbaden: VS Verlag, pp. 45–64.

Gambetta, D. (ed.) (1988) *Trust: Making and Breaking Cooperative Relations*, Oxford: Oxford University Press.

Gardiner, B., Martin, R. and Tyler, P. (2005) 'Regional Dimensions of Europe's Growth Problem: Some Brief Reflections on the Sapir Report', *Regional Studies* 39(7): 979–86.

Garsztecki, S. (2001) 'Regionalisierung in Polen – Die Verwaltungsreform im zweiten Jahr ihrer Umsetzung', in Europäisches Zentrum für Förderalismus-Forschung (ed.), *Jahrbuch Förderalismus 2001: Förderalismus, Subsidiarität und Regionen in Europa*, Baden-Baden: Nomos, pp. 306–18.

Garsztecki, S. (2005) 'Regionen und Denzentralisierung in Polen: neue Entwicklungen', in Europäisches Zentrum für Förderalismus-Forschung (ed.), *Jahrbuch Förderalismus 2005: Förderalismus, Subsidiarität und Regionen in Europa*, Baden-Baden: Nomos, pp. 427–40.

Geertz, C. (1973) *The Interpretation of Cultures*, New York: Basic Books.

George, A.L. and Bennett, A. (2005) *Case Studies and Theory Development in the Social Sciences*, Cambridge, MA: MIT Press.

Gerhards, J. (2007) *Cultural Overstretch? Differences Between Old and New Member States of the EU and Turkey*, London: Routledge.

Gerring, J. (2004) 'What Is a Case Study and What Is It Good for?', *American Political Science Review* 98(2): 341–54.

Gerschenkron, A. (1962) *Economic Backwardness in Historical Perspective: A Book of Essays*, Cambridge, MA: Harvard University Press.

Gibbons, M., Limoges, C., Nowotny, H., Schwartzman, S., Scott, P. and Trow, M. (1995) *New Production of Knowledge: Dynamics of Science and Research in Contemporary Society*, London: Sage Publications.

Giddens, A. (1984) *The Constitution of Society. Outline of the Theory of Structuration*, Berkeley: University of California Press.

Giddens, A. (1990) *The Consequences of Modernity*, Stanford: Stanford University Press.

Giddens, A. (1993) *New Rules of Sociological Method. A Positive Critique of Interpretative Sociologies*, 2nd edn, Stanford: Stanford University Press.

Giddens, A. (1999) *Runaway World: How Globalization is Reshaping Our Lives*, London: Profile.

Gieryn, T.F. (2000) 'A Space for Place in Sociology', *Annual Review of Sociology* 26: 463–96.

Gladwin, T.N., Kennelly, J.J. and Krause, T.-S. (1995) 'Shifting Paradigms for Sustainable Development: Implications for Management Theory and Research', *The Academy of Management Review* 20(4): 874–907.

Goffman, E. (1959): *The Presentation of Self in Everyday Life*, Garden City: Doubleday.

Goffman, E. (1967): *Interaction Ritual*, New York: Pantheon.

Goldstein, J. and Keohane, R.O. (eds) (1993) *Ideas and Foreign Policy: Beliefs, Institutions, and Political Change*, Ithaca: Cornell University Press.

Goodman, E. and Bamford, J. (eds) (1989) *Small Firms and Industrial Districts in Italy*. London: Routledge.

Gordon, C. (1991) 'Governmental Rationality: An Introduction', in G. Burchell, C. Gordon and P. Miller (eds), *The Foucault-Effect. Studies in Governmentality*, London: Harvester Wheatsheaf, pp. 1–52.

Gorzelak, G. (1996) *The Regional Dimension of Transformation in Central Europe*. Regional Studies Association, London: Jessica Kingsley.

Gorzelak, G. (2000) 'Poland', in J. Bachtler, R. Downes and G. Gorzelak (eds): *Transition, Cohesion and Regional Policy in Central and Eastern Europe*, Aldershot: Ashgate, 125–54.

Gorzelak, G. (2006) 'Poland's Regional Policy and Disparities in the Polish Space', *Studia Regionalne i Lokalne*, Special Issue 2006: 39–74.

Gorzelak, G. and Kukliński, A. (eds) (1992) *Dilemmas of Regional Policies in Eastern and Central Europe*, Warsaw: European Institute for Regional and Local Development.

Gorzelak, G. and Jałowiecki, B. (2000) 'Metodologiczne podstawy strategii rozwoju regionu na przykładzie województwa lubuskiego', *Studia Regionalne i Lokalne* Nr. 3(3)/2000: 41–56.

Gorzelak, G., Kozak, M., Płoszaj, A. and Smętkowski, M. (2006) *Charakterystyka Polskich Wojwództw 1999–2004*, Warszawa: Ministerstwo Rozwoju Regionalnego.

Gouldner, A. (1979) *The Future of Intellectuals and the Rise of the New Class*, New York: Seabury.

Grabbe, H. (2001) 'How does Europeanization Affect CEE Governance? Conditionality, Diffusion and Diversity', *Journal of European Public Policy* 8(6): 1013–31.

Grabher, G. (1993) 'The weakness of strong ties. The lock-in of regional development in the Ruhr area', in G. Grabher (ed.) *The embedded firm. On the socioeconomics of industrial networks*, London: Routledge, pp. 255–77.

Grabher, G. and Stark, D. (1997) *Restructuring Networks in Post-Socialism. Legacies, Linkages, and Localities*, Oxford: Oxford University Press.

Grant, R.M. (2008) *Contemporary strategy analysis*, 6th edn, Malden, MA: Blackwell Publishing.

Green Cowles, M., Caporaso, J. and Risse, T. (2001) *Transforming Europe – Europeanization and Domestic Change*, Ithaca: Cornell University Press.

Grosse, T.G. (2006) 'An Evaluation of the Regional Policy System in Poland: Challenges and Threats emerging from Participation in the EU's Cohesion Policy' *European Urban and Regional Studies* 13(2): 151–65.

Grosse, T.G. (2007a) 'Die EU-Kohäsionspolitik in Polen', *Polen-Analysen* 24: 2–11.

Grosse, T.G. (2007b) *Save public assets: Monitoring Corruption Threats in the Distribution of Structural Funds. The Case of Integrated Regional Programmes (IROP) in Poland. Research Report*, Warsaw: Institute of Public Affairs.

Gualini, E. (2004) *Multi-level Governance and Institutional Change. The Europeanization of Regional Policy in Italy*, Aldershot: Ashgate.

Gurbiel, K. (2005) 'Some Remarks on Twinning Projects', in W. Sartorius (ed.), *Implementation of European Regional Development Fund in Poland. Results of the German-French Twinning Project in the Polish Ministry of Economy and Labour*, Warsaw, pp. 17–22. Available at: www.erdf.edu.pl (accessed 17 May 2007).

Haas, E. (1990) *When Knowledge Is Power*, Berkeley: University of California Press.

Haas, P.M. (1992) 'Introduction: Epistemic Communities and International Policy Coordination', *International Organization* 46 (1): 1–36.

Habermas, J. (1975) *Legitimation Crisis*, Boston: Beacon Press.

Habermas, J. (1985) *Reason and the Rationalization of Society. The Theory of Communicative Action, Vol. 1*, Cambridge: Polity Press.

Habermas, J. (1990) *The Philosophical Discourse of Modernity*, Boston, MA: The MIT Press.

Hadjimichalis, C., Hudson, R. (2007) 'Rethinking Local and Regional Development: Implications for Radical Political Practice in Europe', *European Urban and Regional Studies* 14(2): 99–113.

Halkier, H., Danson, M. and Damborg, C. (eds) (2002) *Regional Development Agencies in Europe*, London: Routledge.

Hall, P. (1970) *The Theory and Practice of Regional Planning*, London: Pemberton Publishing.

Hall, P. (1982) *Urban and Regional Planning*, 2nd edn, London: George Allen and Unwin.

Hall, P.A. and Soskice, D. (2001) 'An Introduction to Varieties of Capitalism', in P.A. Hall & D. Soskice (eds), *Varieties of Capitalism: The Institutional Foundations of Comparative Advantage*. New York: Oxford University Press, pp. 1–68.

Hall, P.A. and Taylor, R.C. (1996): 'Political Science and the Three New Institutionalisms', *Political Studies*, Vol. 44, 936–957.

Hall, P.G. and Markusen, A.R. (eds) (1985) *Silicon Landscapes*, Boston: Allen and Unwin.

Hann, C. (2000) 'Discovering Social Anthropology in Galicia.', Supplementary materials to Chris Hann: *Teach Yourself Social Anthropology*, London: Routledge. Available: http://era.anthropology.ac.uk/Teach-Yourself/hann3.pdf (accessed October 2008).

Hann, C. (1998) 'Postsocialist Nationalism: Rediscovering the Past in Southeast Poland', *Slavic Review* 57(4): 840–63.

Hann, C. (2003) 'Is Balkan Civil Society an Oxymoron? From Königsberg to Sarajevo, via Przemyśl', *Ethnologia Balkanica* (07/2003): 63–78.

Hann, C. (ed.) (2002) *Postsocialism: Ideals, Ideologies and Practices in Eurasia*, London: Routledge.

Hann, C. and Magocsi, P.R. (eds) (2005) *Galicia: A Multicultured Land*, Toronto: University of Toronto Press.

Hannerz, U. (1992) *Cultural Complexity. Studies in the Social Organization of Meaning*, New York: Columbia University Press.

Hannerz, U. (1996) *Transnational Connections: Culture people, places*, London: Routledge.

Hardy, J. (2004) 'Rebuilding Local Governance in Post-Communist Economies. The Case of Wrocław, Poland', *European Urban and Regional Studies* 11(4): 303–20.

Harvey, D. (1989): *The Condition of Postmodernity*, Oxford: Blackwell Publishing.

Hasse, R. (2003) *Wohlfahrtspolitik und Globalisierung. Zur Diffusion der World Polity durch Organisationswandel und Wettbewerbsorientierung*, Opladen: Leske+Budrich.

Hasse, R. and Krücken, G. (2005) *Neo-Institutionalismus*, 2nd edn, Bielefeld: transcript Verlag.

Hausner, J., Kudłacz, T. and Szlachta, J. (1997) 'Regional and Local Factors in the Restructuring of Poland's Economy: The Case of Southeastern Poland', in G. Grabher and D. Stark (eds), *Restructuring Networks: Legacies, Linkages, and Localities in Postsocialism*, Oxford: Oxford University, pp. 190–208.

Healey, P., Khakee, A., Motte, A. and Needham, B. (eds) (1997) *Making Strategic Spatial Plans: Innovation in Europe*, London: Routledge.

Heidenreich, M. (1998) 'The Changing System of European Cities and Regions', *European Planning Studies* 6(3): 315–32.

Heidenreich, M. (ed.) (2006) *Die Europäisierung sozialer Ungleichheit. Zur transnationalen Klassen- und Sozialstrukturanalyse*, Frankfurt/M.: Campus.

Heidenreich, M. (2008) 'The Reinvention of Economic Regions in Poland. The Examples of Lower Silesia and Małopolska', *Oldenburger Studien zur Europäisierung und zur transnationalen Regulierung*, Nr. 19/2008. Oldenburg. Available at: www.uni-oldenburg.de/cetro/download/Nr._19_jm.pdf (accessed September 2008).

Heidenreich, M. and Wunder, C. (2008) 'Patterns of Regional Inequality in the Enlarged European Union', in: *European Sociological Review* 24(1): 19–36.

Heintel, M. (2001) ‚Mainstream-Regionalentwicklung', *Landnutzung und Landentwicklung* 42: 193–200.

Heintz, B., Münch, R. and Tyrell, H. (eds) (2005) *Weltgesellschaft. Theoretische Zugänge und empirische Problemlagen*. Sonderheft der Zeitschrift für Soziologie, Stuttgart: Lucius&Lucius.

Held, D., McGrew, A. and Goldblatt, D. (1999): *Global Transformations*, Stanford: Stanford University Press.

Hellman, J.S. (1998) ‚Winners Take All. The Politics of Partial Reform in Postcommunist Transitions', *World Politics* 50(1): 203–34.

Herbst, M. (2007) *Kapitał ludzki i kapitał społeczny a rozwój regionalny*. Centrum Europejskich Studiów Regionalnych i Lokalnych UW, Warszawa: Scholar.

Heuberger, F.W. (1992) 'The New Class: On the Theory of a No Longer Entirely New Phonomenon', in H. Kellner and F.W. Heuberger (eds), *Hidden Technocrats. The New Class and New Capitalism*, New Brunswick: Transaction Publishers, pp. 23–48.

Hironaka, A. (2003) 'Science and the Environment', in G.S. Drori, J.W. Meyer, F.O. Ramirez and E. Schofer (eds), *Science in the Modern World Polity: Institutionalization and Globalization*, Stanford: Stanford University Press, pp. 249–64.

Hirschman, A.O. (1958) *The Strategy of Economic Development*, New Haven: Yale University Press.

Hirschman, A.O. (1994) 'The Rise and Decline of Development Ecnomics', in R. Kanth (ed.), *Paradigms in Economic Development. Classic Perspectives, Critiques, and Reflections*, Armonk, NY: M.E. Sharpe, pp. 191–210.

Hirschman, A.O. (1977) *The Passions and the Interests: Political Arguments for Capitalism Before Its Triumph*, Princeton: Princeton University Press.

Hirst, P. and Thomas, G. (2004) *Globalization in Question*, 2nd edn, Malden, MA: Polity Press.

Hirst, P. and Zeitlin, J. (1998) 'Flexible Specialization: Theory and Evidence in the

Analysis of Industrial Change', in J.R. Hollingsworth and R. Boyer (eds), *Contemporary Capitalism: The Embeddedness of Institutions*, Cambridge: Cambridge University Press, pp. 220–39.

Hiß, S. (2006) *Warum übernehmen Unternehmen gesellschaftliche Verantwortung? Ein soziologischer Erklärungsversuch*, Frankfurt/M.: Campus.

Hollingsworth, J.R. and Boyer, R. (eds) (1997) *Contemporary Capitalism. The Embeddedness of Institutions*, Cambridge: Cambridge University Press.

Hooghe, L. (ed.) (1996) *Cohesion Policy and European Integration: Building Multi-level Governance*, Oxford: Clarendon Press.

Hooghe, L. and Keating, M. (1994) 'The politics of EU regional policy', *Journal of European Public Policy* 1(3): 368–93.

Hooghe, L. and Marks, G. (2001) *Multi-level Governance and European Integration*, Lanham: Rowman and Littlefield.

Hoover, E.M. and Fisher, J. (1949) *Research in regional economic growth. Problems in the study of economic growth*, New York: National Bureau of Economic Research.

Hopgood, S. (2006) *Keepers of the Flame: Understanding Amnesty International*, Ithaca: Cornell University Press.

Hubbard, P., Kitchin, R., Bartley, B. and Fuller, D. (2002) *Thinking Geographically: Space, Theory and Contemporary Human Geography*, London: Continuum.

Hudson, R. (1999) ' "The Learning Economy, the Learning Firm and the Learning Region": A Sympathetic Critique of the Limits to Learning', *European Urban and Regional Studies* 6(1): 59–72.

Hudson, R. (2001) *Producing Places*, New York: The Guilford Press.

Hughes, J., Sasse, G. and Gordon, C. (eds) (2005) *Europeanization and regionalization in the EU's enlargement to Central and Eastern Europe: the myth of conditionality*, Basingstoke: Palgrave Macmillan.

Huntington, E. (1915) *Civilization and Climate*, New Haven: Yale University Press.

Hwang, H. (2006) 'Planning Development: Globalization and the Shifting Locus of Planning', in G.S. Drori, J.W. Meyer and H. Hwang (eds), *Globalization and Organization: World Society and Organizational Change*, Oxford: Oxford University Press, pp. 69–90.

Illouz, E. (1997) *Consuming the Romantic Utopia. Love and the Cultural Contradictions of Capitalism*, Berkeley: University of California Press.

Illouz, E. (2008) *Saving the Modern Soul: Therapy, Emotions, and the Culture of Self-Help*, Berkeley: University of California Press.

Immerfall, S. and Therborn, G. (eds) (2009) *Handbook of European Societies*, New York: Springer.

Isard, W. (1956) *Location and space economy: A general theory relating to industrial location, market areas, land use, trade, and urban structure*, Boston: Technology Press of MIT.

Isard, W. (1960) *Methods of regional analysis: An introduction to regional science*, Boston: Technology Press of MIT.

James, W. (1902) *The Varieties of Religious Experience*, New York: Longmans.

Jessop, B. (1990) *State theory: Putting the Capitalist state in its place*, Pennsylvania: Pennsylvania State University Press.

Jessop, B. (2002a) 'Liberalism, Neoliberalism and Urban Governance: A State-Theoretical Perspective' *Antipode* 34: 452–72.

Jessop, B. (2002b) *The Future of the Capitalist State*, Cambridge: Polity Press.

Jessop, B. (2007) *State Power: A Strategic-Relational Approach*, Cambridge: Polity Press.

Jessop, B. and Sum N.-L. (2006) *Beyond the Regulation Approach: Putting Capitalist Economies in their Place*, Cheltenham: Edward Elgar.

Joas, H. (2001) *The Genesis of Values*, Chicago: The University of Chicago Press.

Joas, H. and Knöbl, W. (2009) *Social Theory. Twenty Introductory Lectures*, Cambridge: Cambridge University Press.

Kaelble, H. (1987) *Auf dem Weg zu einer europäischen Gesellschaft. Eine Sozialgeschichte Westeuropas 1880–1980*, München: C.H. Beck.

Karmack, A.M. (1976) *The Tropics and Economic Development. A Provocative Inquiry into the Poverty of Nations*, Baltimore: The Johns Hopkins University Press.

Katz, B. (ed.) (2000) *Reflections on Regionalism*. Washington, D. C.: Brookings Press.

Katzenstein, P.J. (2005) *A World of Regions: Asia and Europe in the American Imperium*, Ithaca: Cornell University Press.

Keating, M. (1998a) *The New Regionalism in Western Europe. Territorial Restructuring and Political Change*, Aldershot: Edward Elgar.

Keating, M. (1998b) 'Is there a Regional Level of Government in Europe?', in P. Le Galès and C. Lequesne (eds), *Regions in Europe*, London: Routledge, pp. 11–29.

Keating, M. (2001) 'Rethinking the Region: Culture, Institutions and Economic Development in Catalonia and Galicia', *European Urban and Regional Studies* 8(3): 217–34.

Keating, M. (2003) 'The Invention of Regions: Political Restructuring and Territorial Government in Western Europe', in N. Brenner, B. Jessop, M. Jones and G. MacLeod (eds), *State/Space: A* Reader, Oxford: Blackwell Publishing, pp. 256–77.

Keating, M. (ed.) (2004) *Regions and Regionalism in Europe*. Cheltenham: Edward Elgar.

Keating, M. and Hughes, J. (eds) (2003) *The Regional Challenge in Central and Eastern Europe. Territorial Restructuring and European Integration*, Brussels: P.I.E. – Peter Lang.

Keating, M. and Loughlin, J. (eds) (1997) *The Political Economy of Regionalism*, London: Frank Cass.

Keating, M., Loughlin, J. and Deschouwer, K. (2003) *Culture, Institutions and Economic Development. A Study of Eight European Regions*, Cheltenham: Edward Elgar.

Kellner, H. and Berger, P.L. (1992) 'Life-style Engineering: So Theoretical Reflections', in H. Kellner and F.W. Heuberger (eds), *Hidden Technocrats. The New Class and New Capitalism*, New Brunswick: Transaction Publishers, pp. 1–22.

Kellner, H. and Heuberger, F.W. (eds) (1992) *Hidden Technocrats. The New Class and New Capitalism*, New Brunswick: Transaction Publishers.

Keohane, R.O. (ed.) (1986) *Neorealism and Its Critics*, New York: Columbia University Press.

Keynes, J.M. (1997, 1st edn 1936) *The General Theory of Employment, Interest and Money*, Amherst, NY: Prometheus.

Klasik, A. (2000) 'Strategia rozwoju regionu', *Studia Regionalne i Lokalne* 3(3): 7–22.

Kłoczowski, J. (1997) 'East Central Europe – Historiographical Interpretations', in A. Kukliński (ed.) *European Space, Baltic Space, Polish Space – Part II*, Warsaw: European Institute for Regional and Local Development, pp. 201–12.

Knill, C. (2001) *The Europeanization of National Administrations. Patterns of Institutional Persistence and Change*, Cambridge: Cambridge University Press.

Knöbl, W. (2006) 'Of Contingencies and Breaks: The US American South as an Anomaly in the Debate on Multiple Modernities', *Archives Européennes de Sociologie*, Vol. XLVII, No. 1, pp. 125–57.

Knorr-Cetina, K. (1999) *Epistemic Cultures. How the Sciences Make Knowledge*, Cambridge: Harvard University Press.

Knorr-Cetina, K. and Preda, A. (eds) (2004) *The Sociology of Financial Markets*, Oxford and New York: Oxford University Press.

Knox, P. and Agnew, J. (1989) *The Geography of the World-Economy*, London: Edward Arnold.

Koenig, M. (2008) 'Institutional Change in the World Polity: International Human Rights and the Construction of Collective Identities', *International Sociology* 23: 95–114.

Kohler-Koch, B. (1999) 'The Evolution and Transformation of European Governance', in: B. Kohler-Koch & R. Eising (eds.) *The Transformation of Governance in the European Union*, London: Routledge, pp. 14–35.

Kohler-Koch, B. (2002) 'European Networks and Ideas: Changing National Policies?' *European Integration online Papers (EIoP)*, No. 6. Available at: www.eiop.or.at/eiop/texte/2002–006.htm (accessed 22 February 2009).

Komninos, N. (2008) *Intelligent Cities and Globalisation of Innovation Networks*. London: Routledge.

Koselleck, R. (ed.) (1977) *Studien zum Beginn der modernen Welt*. Stuttgart: Klett-Cotta.

Kozak, M. (2000) 'Regional Development Policy in Poland in the 1990s', in Bachtler, J., Downes, R. and Gorzelak, G. (eds), *Transition, Cohesion and Regional Policy in Central and Eastern Europe*, Burlington: Ashgate, pp. 319–30.

Kozak, M. (2006) 'System zarządzania europejską polityką regionalną w Polsce w pierwszym okresie po akcesji', in *Studia Regionalne i Lokalne* 24(2): 39–74.

Kozłowski, P. (2005) 'In the shadows: the grey economy's brighter side', *Research in Progress – Economic* 4(8): 28–9. Available at: www.english.pan.pl/images/stories/pliki/publikacje/academia/2005/08/kozlowski.pdf (accessed October 2009).

KPMG (2006) *The Benefits of Complementarity and Collaboration: An analysis of special economic zones, industrial parks and technology parks in Poland*. Report of KPMG Poland. Available at: www.kpmg.pl/index.thtml/en/library/raporty/index.html (accessed 11 July 2009).

Krasner, S. (ed.) (1983) *International Regimes*. Ithaca: Cornell University Press.

Krasnodębski, Z. (2003) *Demokracja Peryferii*, Gdańsk: Wydawnictwo słowo/obraz terytoria.

Krasnodębski, Z. (2006) 'Verlierer und Gewinner in Ostmitteleuropa'. In: *OST-WEST. Europäische Perspektiven* 7(2). Available at: www.owep.de/2006_2_krasnodebski.php (accessed 16 June 2009).

Krücken, G. (2005) 'Der „world-polity"-Ansatz in der Globalisierungsdiskussion', in J.W. Meyer (ed.), *Weltkultur. Wie die westlichen Prinzipien die Welt durchdringen*, Frankfurt/M.: Suhrkamp, pp. 300–18.

Krugman, P. (1991) *Geography and Trade*, Cambridge, MA: MIT Press.

Kuhn, T.S. (1962) *The Structure of Scientific Revolutions*, Chicago: Chicago University Press.

Kukliński, A. (ed.) (1981) *Polarized Development and Regional Policies. Tribute to Jacques Boudeville*, The Hague: Mouton Publishers.

Laclau, E. (1996) *Emancipation(s)*, London: Verso.

Lagendijk, A. (2006) 'Learning from conceptual flow in regional studies: Framing present debates, unbracketing past debates', *Regional Studies* 40(4): 385–99.

Lagendijk, A. (2007) 'The Accident of the Region: A Strategic Relational Perspective on the Construction of the Region's Significance', *Regional Studies* 41(9): 1193–1208.

Lagendijk, A. and Cornford, J. (2000) 'Regional institutions and knowledge – tracking new forms of regional development policy', *Geoforum* 31: 209–18.

Lakatos, I. (1976) *Proofs and Refutations,* Cambridge: Cambridge University Press.

Lamont, M. and Laurent T. (eds) (2000) *Rethinking Comparative Cultural Sociology. Repertoires of Evaluation in France and the United States*, Cambridge: Cambridge University Press.

Landes, D. (1998) *The Wealth and Poverty of Nations. Why Are Some So Rich and Others So Poor*, New York: W.W. Norton & Company.

Lane, J.-E. (2000) *New Public Management*, London: Routledge.

Lane, R.E. (1966) 'The Decline of Politics and Ideology in a Knowledgeable Society', *American Sociological Review* 31: 649–62.

Larsen, J., Urry J. and Axhausen, K. (2006) *Mobilities, Networks, Geographies*, Aldershot: Ashgate.

Lash, S. and Urry, J. (1987) *The End of Organized Capitalism*, Cambridge: Polity Press.

Lash, S. and Urry, J. (1994) *Economies of Signs and Space*, London: Sage Publications.

Latour, B. (1993) *We Have Never Been Modern*, Cambridge, MA: Harvard University Press.

Lawson, C. and Lorenz, E. (1999) 'Collective Learning, Tacit Knowledge and Regional Innovative Capicity', *Regional Studies* 33(4): 305–17.

Le Galès, P. and Lequesne, C. (eds) (1998) *Regions in Europe*, London: Routledge.

Le Galès, P. and Scott, A. (2008) 'Une révolution bureaucratique britannique? Autonomie sans contrôle ou 'freer markets, more rules', *Revue française de sociologie* 49(2): 301–30.

Leborgne, D. and Lipietz A. (1992) 'New technologies and new modes of regulation: some spatial implications', *Environment and Planning D: Society and Space* 6: 263–80.

Lechner, F.J. and Boli, J. (2005) *World Culture: Origins and Consequences*, Oxford: Blackwell Publishing.

Lee Mudge, S. (2008) 'What is neo-liberalism? The state of the art', *Socio-Economic Review* 6: 703–31.

Lee, C.K. and Strang, D. (2003) 'The International Diffusion of Public Sector Downsizing', *CSES Working Paper,* No. 18, Cornell: Center for the Study of Economy & Society.

Lefebvre, H. (1962) *Introduction à la Modernité. Préludes*, Paris: Les Editions de Minuit.

Leonardi, R. (ed.) (1993) *The regions and the European Community: The Regional Response to the Single Market in the Underdeveloped Areas*, London: Frank Cass

Leonardi, R. (1995) *Convergence, Cohesion and Integration in the European Union*, New York: St. Martin's Press.

Leonardi, R. (2005) *Cohesion Policy in the European Union: the building of Europe*, New York: Palgrave Macmillan.

Lepsius, M.R. (1990a) *Interessen, Ideen und Institutionen*, Opladen: Westdeutscher Verlag.

Lepsius, M.R. (1990b) 'Soziologische Theoreme über die Sozialstruktur der „Moderne" und die „Modernisierung"', In id. *Interessen, Ideen und Institutionen*, Opladen: Westdeutscher Verlag, pp. 211–31. (first published in: Reinhard Koselleck (ed.) (1977) *Studien zum Beginn der modernen Welt*. Stuttgart: Klett-Cotta, pp. 10–29).

Lepsius, M.R. (1990c) 'Immobilismus: das System der sozialen Stagnation in Süditalien.', in id. *Interessen, Ideen und Institutionen*, Opladen: Westdeutscher Verlag, pp. 170–210.

Lepsius, M.R. (1991) 'Die Europäische Gemeinschaft. Rationalitätskriterien der Regimebildung', in W. Zapf (ed.) *Die Modernisierung moderner Gesellschaften. Verhandlungen des 25. Deutschen Soziologentages in Frankfurt am Main 1990*, Frankfurt/M.: Campus, pp. 309–17.

Lévi-Strauss, C. (1966) *The Savage Mind*, Chicago: The University of Chicago Press.

Lévi-Strauss, C. (1970) *The Raw and the Cooked*, New York: Harper & Row.

Liebert, U. (1986) *Neue Autonomiebewegung und Dezentralisierung in Spanien. Der Fall Andalusien*. Frankfurt/M.: Campus.

Liebert, U., Falke, J. and Maurer, A. (eds) (2006) *Constitutionalization in the New Europe*, Baden-Baden: Nomos.

Lindner, R. (2003) 'Der Habitus der Stadt – ein kulturgeographischer Versuch', *Petermanns Geographische Mitteilungen* 147(2): 46–53.

Linz, J.J. and Stepan, A. (1996) *Problems of Democratic Transition and Consolidation*, Baltimore: Johns Hopkins University Press.

Lipietz, A. (1986) 'New tendencies in the international division of labor: regimes of accumulation and modes of regulation', in A.J. Scott and M. Storper (eds), *Production, work, territory. The geographical anatomy of industrial capitalism*, London: HarperCollins Publishers, pp. 16–40.

Lipietz, A. (2003) 'The National and the Regional: Their Autonomy vis-à-vis the Capitalist World Crisis', in N. Brenner, B. Jessop, M. Jones and G. MacLeod (eds) *State/Space: A Reader,* Oxford: Blackwell Publishing, pp. 239–55.

Lipset, S.M. (1959) 'Some Social Requisites of Democracy: Economic Development and Political Legitimacy', *The American Political Science Review* 53, No. 1 (March, 1959): 69–105.

Long, N. (2001) *Development Sociology. Actor Perspectives*. London: Routledge.

Long, N. and Long, A. (eds) (1992) *Battlefields of knowledge. The interlocking of theory and practice in social research and development*. London; New York: Routledge.

Lovering, J. (1999) 'Theory led by Policy: The Inadequacies of the "New Regionalism" (Illustrated from the Case of Wales', *International Journal of Urban and Regional Research* 23(2): 379–95.

Lower Silesian Parliament (2005) *The 2020 Development Strategy for the Lower Silesia Province*, Wrocław.

Luhmann, N. (1997) 'Globalization or World Society?: How to conceive of modern society', *International Review of Sociology* 7(1): 67–80.

Lundvall, B.-A. (ed.) (1992) *National Systems of Innovation: Towards a Theory of Innovation and Interactive Learning*, London: Pinter.

Maillat, D. (1995) 'Territorial dynamic, innovative *milieus* and regional policy', *Entrepreneurship & Regional Development* 7(2): 157–65.

Mairate, A. (2006) 'The 'added value' of European Union Cohesion policy', *Regional Studies* 40(2): 167–77.

Mannheim, K. (1936) *Ideology and Utopia*, London: Routledge.

March, J.G. and Olsen, J.P. (1998) 'The Institutional Dynamics of International Political Orders', *International Organization* 52(4): 943–69.

March, J.G. and Olsen, J.P. (1989) *Rediscovering Institutions*, New York: Free Press.

Marks, G., Hooghe, L. and Schakel, A.H. (2008a) 'Measuring Regional Authority', *Regional and Federal Studies* 18(2–3): 111–21.

Marks, G., Hooghe, L. and Schakel, A.H. (2008b) 'Patterns of Regional Authority', *Regional and Federal Studies* 18(2–3): 167–81.

Marks, G., Scharpf, F.W., Schmitter, P.C. and Streeck, W. (eds) (1996) *Governance in the European Union*, London: Sage Publications.

Marshall, T.H. (1981) *Citizenship and Social Class*, London: Pluto Press.

Martens, K. and Leibfried, S. (2008) 'The PISA Story. How educational policy went international: a lesson in politics beyond the nation state', *The German Times*, January 2008, p. 6.

Martens, K. and Jakobi, A.P. (2010) *Mechanisms of OECD Governance. International Incentives for National Policy-Making?*, Oxford: Oxford University Press.

Martin, P. (2000) 'The role of public policy in the process of regional convergence', *EIB Papers* 5(2): 69–79.

Martin, R. (2001) 'EMU versus the Regions? Regional Convergence and Divergence in the Euroland', *Journal of Economic Geography* (1/2001): 51–80.

Marx, K. (1976, 1st edn 1867) *The Capital*, Vol. 1, London and New York: Penguin Books.

Marx, K. and Engels, F. (1969, 1st edn 1848) *Selected Works*, Vol. 1, Moscow: Progress Publishers, pp. 98–137.

Massey, D., Allen, J. and Sarre, P. (eds) (1999) *Human Geography Today*, Cambridge: Polity Press.

Matthiesen, U. (2006) 'Raum und Wissen. Wissensmilieus und KnowledgeScapes als Inkubatoren für zukunftsfähige stadtregionale Entwicklungsdynamiken?', in D. Tänzler, H. Knoblauch and H.-G. Soeffner (eds): *Zur Kritik der Wissensgesellschaft*, Konstanz: UVK Verlag, pp. 155–88.

Mau, S. (2006) 'Grenzbildung, Homogenisierung, Strukturierung. Die politische Erzeugung einer europäischen Ungleichheitsstruktur', in M. Heidenreich (ed.) *Die Europäisierung sozialer Ungleichheit: Zur transnationalen Klassen- und Sozialstrukturanalyse*, Frankfurt/M.: Campus, pp. 109–36.

Mau, S. (2010) *Social Transnationalism. Lifeworlds beyond the Nation State*, London: Routledge.

Mau, S. and Büttner, S. (2008) 'Regionalisierung sozialer Ungleichheit im europäischen Integrationsprozess', in M. Bach and A. Sterbling (eds), *Soziale Ungleichheit in der erweiterten Europäischen Union*, Hamburg: Krämer Verlag, pp. 205–30.

Mau, S. and Büttner, S. (2010) 'Transnationality', in G. Therborn and S. Immerfall (eds) *Handbook of European Societies*, New York: Springer, pp. 531–62.

Mau, S., Mewes, J. and Zimmermann, A. (2008) 'Cosmopolitan attitudes through transnational social practices?', *Global Networks* 8(1): 1–24.

Mau, S. and Verwiebe, R. (2010) *European Societies. Mapping Structure and Social Change*, Bristol: Policy Press.

McLuhan, M. and Powers, B.R. (1992) *The Global Village: Transformations in World Life and Media in the 21st Century*, Oxford: Oxford University Press.

Meadows, D.H., Meadows, D.L., Randers, J. and Behrens, William W.III (1972) *The Limits to Growth. A Report to the Club of Rome*, New York: Universe Books.

Meadows, D.H., Meadows, D.L. and Rander, J. (1992) *Beyond the Limits*, Post Mills: Chelsea Green Publishing.

Mendel, P. (2006) 'The Making and Expansion of International Management Standards: The Global Diffusion of ISO 9000 Quality Management Certificates', in G.S. Drori, J.W. Meyer and H. Hwang (eds), *Globalization and Organization: World Society and Organizational Change*, Oxford: Oxford University Press, pp. 137–66.

Merkel, W. (1999) *Systemtransformation. Eine Einführung in die politikwissenschaftliche Transformationsforschung*, Opladen: Leske+Budrich.

Merton, R.K. (1968) *Social Theory and Social Structure*, Enlarged Edition, New York: The Free Press.

Merton, R.K. (1973) *The Sociology of Science: Theoretical and Empirical Investigations*, Chicago and New York: The University of Chicago Press.

Meyer, J.W. (1987) 'The World Polity and the Authority of the Nation-State', in G.M. Thomas, J.W. Meyer, F.O. Ramirez and J. Boli, *Institutional Structure: Constituting State, Society, and the Individual*, London: Sage Publications, pp. 41–70.

Meyer, J.W. (1999) 'The Changing Cultural Content of the Nation State: A World Society Perspective', in G. Steinmetz (ed.), *State/Culture: State-Formation after the Cultural Turn*, Ithaca: Cornell University Press, pp. 123–43.

Meyer, J.W. (2000) 'Globalization: Sources and Effects on National States and Societies', *International Sociology* 15(2): 233–48.

Meyer, J.W. (2001) 'The European Union and the Globalization of the Culture', in S.S. Andersen (ed.), *Institutional Approaches to the European Union*, ARENA report, Oslo.

Meyer, J.W. and Rowan, B. (1977) 'Institutionalized Organizations: Formal Structures as Myth and Ceremony', *The American Journal of Sociology* 82(2): 340–63.

Meyer, J.W. and Hannan, M. (eds) (1979): *National Development and the World System*. Chicago: University of Chicago Press.

Meyer, J.W. and Scott, R. (eds) (1983) *Organizational Environments: Ritual and Rationality*, London: Sage Publications.

Meyer, J.W. and Jepperson, R. (2000) 'The "Actors" of Modern Society: The Cultural Construction of Social Agency', *Sociological Theory* 18(1): 100–20.

Meyer, J.W. and Ramirez, F.O. (2005) 'Die globale Institutionalisierung der Bildung', in J.W. Meyer, *Weltkultur. Wie die westlichen Prinzipien die Welt durchdringen*, Frankfurt/M.: Suhrkamp, pp. 212–34.

Meyer, J.W., Boli, J. and Thomas, G.M. (1987) 'Ontology and Rationalization in the Western Cultural Account', in G.M. Thomas, J.W. Meyer, F.O. Ramirez and J. Boli, *Institutional Structure: Constituting State, Society, and the Individual,* London: Sage Publications, pp. 12–37.

Meyer, J.W., Boli, J., Thomas, G.M. and Ramirez, F.O. (1997) 'World Society and the Nation State', *The American Journal of Sociology* 103(1): 144–81.

Meyer, J.W., Frank, D.J., Hironaka, A., Schofer, E. and Tuma, N.B. (1997b) 'The Structuring of a World Environmental Regime, 1870–1990', *International Organization* 51(4): 623–51.

Meyer, J.W., Ramirez, F.O. and Soysal, Y.N. (1992) 'World Expansion of Mass Education, 1870–1980', *Sociology of Education* 65(2): 128–49.

Miller, D.E. (2005) *Toward a New Regionalism: Environmental Architecture in the Pacific Northwest*, Washington: University of Washington Press.

Miller, P. and Rose, N. (2008) *Governing of the Present: Administering Economic, Social and Personal Life*, Cambridge: Polity Press.

Ministry of Regional Development of Poland (2006a) *National Development Strategy 2007–2015*, Warsaw.

Ministry of Regional Development of Poland (2006b) *Narodowe Strategiczne Ramy Odniesienia 2007–2013*, Warsaw.

Ministry of Regional Development of Poland (2007a) *Polish Regions: Dolnośląskie Voivodship*. Warsaw.

Ministry of Regional Development of Poland (2007b) *Polish Regions: Lubelskie Voivodship*. Warsaw.

Ministry of Regional Development of Poland (2007c) *Polish Regions: Podkarpackie Voivodship*. Warsaw.

Mintzberg, H. (1994) *The Rise and Fall of Strategic Planning*, New York: The Free Press.

Molle, W. (2007) *European Cohesion Policy*. London: Routledge.

Montgomery, C.A. and Porter, M.E. (ed.) (1991) *Strategy: Seeking and Securing Competitive Advantage*, Boston: Harvard University Press.

Morgan, K. (2004) 'Sustainable regions: governance, innovation and scale', *European Planning Studies* 12(6): 871–89.

Mróz, B. (2005) 'The Shadow Economy in Poland and its Socio-Economic Implications'. Available at: www.wydawnictwa.wsfib.edu.pl/Polska_w_UE/mr%F3z.pdf (accessed 15 October 2009).

Münch, R. (1994) *Das Projekt Europa*, Frankfurt/M.: Suhrkamp.

Münch, R. (2001) *The Ethics of Modernity: Formation and Transformation in Britain, France, Germany, and the United States*, Lanham: Rowman and Littlefield.

Münch, R. (2009) *Globale Eliten, Lokale Autoritäten*. Frankfurt/M.: Suhrkamp.

Münch, R. (2010) *European governmentality: the liberal drift of multilevel governance*, London: Routledge.

Münch, R. (2011) *Theory of Action: Towards a New Synthesis Going Beyond Parsons*, London: Routledge.

Münch, R. and Büttner, S. (2006) 'Die europäische Teilung der Arbeit. Was können wir von Emile Durkheim lernen?', in M. Heidenreich (ed.) *Die Europäisierung sozialer Ungleichheit. Zur transnationalen Klassen- und Sozialstrukturanalyse*, Frankfurt/M.: Campus, pp. 65–107.

Myrdal, G. (1957) *Economic Theory and Underdeveloped Regions*, London: Gerald Duckworth.

Nederveen Pieterse, J. (2001) *Development Theory. Deconstructions/Reconstructions*, London: Sage Publications.

North, D.C. (1955) 'Location theory and regional economic growth', *JPE* LXIII(3): 243–58.

North, D.C. (1990) *Institutions, Institutional Change and Economic Performance*, Cambridge: Cambridge University Press.

Nowotny, H., Scott, P. and Gibbons, M. (2001) *Re-Thinking Science: Knowledge and the Public in an Age of Uncertainty*, Cambridge: Cambridge University Press.

OCEI (2004) *Pre-Accession Funds: Polish Experiences*. Warsaw: Office of the Committee for European Integration.

OECD (1997) *Sustainable Development: OECD Policy Approaches for the 21st Century*, Paris: OECD.

OECD (1999) *Boosting Innovation: The Cluster Approach*, Paris.

OECD (2005a) *Building Competitive Regions: Strategies and Governance*, Paris.

OECD (2005b) *Business Clusters: Promoting Enterprise in Central and Eastern Europe*, Paris.

OECD (2005c) *Regions at a Glance*, Paris.

OECD (2006) *OECD Rural Policy Reviews: The New Rural Paradigm: Policies and Governance*, Paris.

OECD (2007a) *Competitive Regional Clusters: National Policy Approaches*, Paris.

OECD (2007b) *Globalisation and Regional Economies. OECD Reviews of Regional Innovation*, Paris.

OECD (2007c) *Regions at a Glance 2007*, Paris.

OECD (2008) *Territorial Report on Regional development in Poland*, Paris.

Offe, C. (1994) *Der Tunnel am Ende des Lichts. Erkundungen der politischen Transformation im neuen Osten*, Frankfurt/M.: Campus.

Ohmae, K. (1995) *The End of the Nation State: the Rise of Regional Economies*, New York: The Free Press.

Ohmae, K. (2005) *The Next Global Stage. Challenges and Opportunities in our Border-less World*, New Jersey: Wharton School Publishing.

Ouchi, W.G. (1983) *Theory Z*, New York: Avon Books.

Outhwaite, W. (2008) *European Society*, Cambridge: Polity Press.

Outhwaite, W. and Ray, L. (2005): *Social Theory and Postcommunism*, Oxford: Black-well Publishing.

Paasi, A. (1986) 'The institutionalization of regions: a theoretical framework for under-standing the emergence of regions and the constitution of regional identity', *Fennia* 164(1): 105–46.

Paasi, A. (2001) 'Europe as a Social Process and Discourse: Considerations of Place, Boundaries and Identity', *European Urban and Regional Studies* 8(1): 7–28.

Paasi, A. (2003) 'Region and place: regional identity in question', *Progress in Human Geography* 27: 475–85.

Paasi, A. (2009) 'The resurgence of the "region" and "regional identity": theoretical per-spectives and empirical observations on the regional dynamics in Europe', *Review of International Studies* 35 (Supplement 1): 121–46.

Painter, J. (2002) 'Multilevel citizenship, identity and regions in contemporary Europe', in J. Anderson (ed.), *Transnational democracy: political spaces and border crossings*, London: Routledge, pp. 93–110.

Panther, S. (1997) 'Cultural Factors in the Transition Process. Latin Center, Orthodox Periphery?', J.G. Backhaus and G. Krause (eds) *Issues in Transformation Theory*, Marburg: Metropolis, pp. 95–122.

Parkin, F. (1971) *Class Inequality and Political Order: Social Stratification in Capitalist and Communist Societies*, London: Paladin.

Parsons, T. (1964) 'Evolutionary Universals in Society', *American Sociological Review* 29(3): 339–57.

Parsons, T. (1967) *Sociological Theory and Modern Society*, New York: Free Press.

Parsons, T. (1971) *The System of Modern Societies*, Englewood Cliffs: Prentice Hall.

Perloff, H.S., Dunn, E.S. Jr., Lampard, E.E. and Muth, R.F. (1960) *Regions, Resources, and Economic Growth*. Baltimore: Johns Hopkins Press.

Pieper, K. (2006) *Regionalpolitik in Ungarn und Polen. Zwei Staaten im EU-Beitrittsprozess*, Wiesbaden: VS Verlag.

Pierson, P. (2004) *Politics in Time: History, Institutions, and Social Analysis*, Princeton: Princeton University Press.

Pike, A., Rodríguez-Posé, A. and Tomaney, J. (2006) *Local and Regional Development*, London: Routledge.

Pike, A., Rodríguez-Posé, A. and Tomaney, J. (2007) 'What kind of Local and Regional Development and for Whom?', *Regional Studies* 41(9): 1253–69.

Piore, M.J. and Sabel, C.F. (1989) *The second industrial divide*, New York: Basic Books.

Plane, D.A., Mann, L.D., Button, K. and Nijkamp, P. (eds) (2007) *Regional Planning*, Cheltenham: Edward Elgar.

Płaziak, M. and Trzepacz, P. (2008) 'Spatial distribution of EU Structural Funds in Poland in 2004–2006 – Factors, Directions, and Limitations', *Bulletin of Geography/ Socio-Economic Series*, No. 9/2008: 33–45.

Polanyi, K. (2001, 1st edn 1944): *The Great Transformation. The Political and Economic Origins of Our Time*, Boston: Beacon Press.

Porter, M.E. (1990) *The Competitive Advantage of Nations*, London: The Macmillan Press.

Porter, M.E. (ed.) (1998a) *On Competition. A Havard Business Review Book*, Boston: Harvard Business School Publishing.

Porter, M.E. (1998b) 'Clusters and the New Economics of Competition', *Harvard Business Review* (Nov./Dec.): 77–90.

Porter, M.E. (2003) 'The Economic Performance of Regions', *Regional Studies* 37(6/7): 549–78.

Portes, A. (1998) 'Social Capital. Its Origins and Applications in Modern Sociology', *Annual Reviews of Sociology* 24: 1–24.

Poulantzas, N. (2003) 'The Nation', in N. Brenner, B. Jessop, M. Jones and G. MacLeod (eds), *State/Space: A Reader*, Oxford: Blackwell Publishing, pp. 65–83.

Powell, W.W. (2008) 'The New Institutionalism', in S. Clegg and J.A. Baily (eds), *The International Encyclopedia of Organization Studies*, London: Sage Publications.

Powell, W.W. and DiMaggio, P.J. (eds) (1991) *The New Institutionalism in Organizational Analysis*, Chicago: Chicago University Press.

Power, M. (1997) *The Audit Society. Rituals of Verification*, Oxford: Oxford University Press.

Pries, L. (2001) *New Transnational Social Spaces. International Migration and Transnational Companies*, London: Routledge.

Przeworski, A. (1991) *Democracy and the Market. Political and Economic Reforms in Eastern Europe and Latin America*, Cambridge: Cambridge University Press.

Putnam, R.D. (1993) *Making Democracy Work. Civic Traditions in Modern Italy*, Princeton: Princeton University Press.

Putnam, R.D. (2000) *Bowling Alone. The Collapse and Revival of American Community*, New York: Simon and Schuster.

Putnam, R.D. (2001) 'Social Capital: Measurement and Consequences', *International Symposium Report*, Chpt. 7, Toronto: HRDC and OECD. Available at: www.oecd.org/dataoecd/25/6/1825848.pdf (accessed April 2009).

Radaelli, C. (1995) 'The Role of Knowledge in the Policy Process', *Journal of European Public Policy* 2 (June): 159–83.

Ramirez, F.O. (1987) 'Institutional Analysis', in G.M. Thomas, J.W. Meyer, F.O. Ramirez and J. Boli (1987), *Institutional Structure: Constituting State, Society, and the Individual*. London: Sage Publications, pp. 316–28.

Ramirez, F.O. (2006) *From Citizen to Person? Rethinking Education as Incorporation*, CDDRL Working Paper, Nr. 53, Stanford: Center on Democracy, Development, and the Rule of Law.

Ramirez, F.O., Soysal, Y. and Shanahan, S. (1997) 'The Changing Logic of Political Citizenship: Cross-National Acquisation of Women's Suffrage Rights, 1890 to 1990', *American Soicological Review* 62: 735–45.

Rancière, J. (1995) *La Mésentente. Politique et Philosphie*, Paris: Édition Galilée.

Rapp, F. (1992) *Fortschritt: Entwicklung und Sinngehalt einer philosophischen Idee*, Darmstadt: Wissenschaftliche Buchgesellschaft.

Reckwitz, A. (2002) 'Toward a Theory of Social Practices. A Development in Culturalist Theorizing', *European Journal of Social Theory* 5(2): 243–63.

Reckwitz, A. (2004) 'Die Politik der Moderne aus kulturtheoretischer Perspektive: Vorpolitische Sinnhorizonte des Politischen, symbolische Antagonismen und das Regime der Gouvernementalität', in B. Schwelling (ed.) *Politikwissenschaft als Kulturwissenschaft. Theorien – Methoden – Forschungsperspektiven*, Wiesbaden: VS Verlag, pp. 33–56.

Reckwitz, A. (2009) 'Die Selbstkulturalisierung der Stadt', *Mittelweg* 36(2): 2–34.

Regulski, J. (2003) *Local Government Reform in Poland: An Insider's Story*, Local Government and Public Service Reform Initiative, Budapest: Open Society Institute.

Reiter, H. (2007) 'Non-solidarity and unemployment in the "New West"', in N. Karagiannis (ed.), *European Solidarity*, Liverpool: Liverpool University Press, pp. 164–85.

Ricardo, David (1996, 1st edn 1817) *On the Principles of Political Economy and Taxation*, Amherst, NY: Prometheus Books.

Richardson, H.W. (1969) *Regional Economics*, Harmondsworth: Pengiun.

Rieger, E. and Leibfried, S. (2003) *Limits to Globalization: Welfare States and the World Economy*, Cambridge: Polity Press.

Risse, T. (2010) *A Community of Europeans? Transnational Identities and Public Spheres*, Ithaca: Cornell University Press.

Ritzer, G. (1997) *The McDonaldization Thesis: Explorations and Extensions*, London: Sage Publications.

Robertson, R. (1992) *Globalization: Social Theory and Global Culture*, London: Sage Publications.

Robertson, R. (1995) 'Glocalization: Time-Space and Homogeneity-Heterogeneity', in M. Featherstone, S. Lash and R. Robertson (eds), *Global Modernities*. London: Sage Publications, pp. 25–44.

Rodríguez-Pose, A. (2000) 'Economic convergence and regional development strategies in Spain: The case of Galicia and Navarre', *EIBPapers* 5(1): 88–115.

Rodríguez-Pose, A. and Fratesi, U. (2004) 'Between Development and Social Policies: The Impact of European Structural Funds in Objective 1 Regions', *Regional Studies* 38(1): 97–113.

Rogers, E.M. (1995) *Diffusion of Innovations*, 4th edn, Detroit: The Free Press.

Rogowski, R. (ed.) (1995) *Comparative Politics and the International Political Economy: The Essential Readings*, 2 vols, Cheltenham: Edward Elgar Publishing.

Rokkan, S. (1975) 'Dimensions of State Formation and Nation-Building', in C. Tilly (ed.) *The Formation of National States in Western Europe*, Princeton: Princeton University Press: 562–600.

Rokkan, S., Urwin, D., Aarebrot, F.H., Malaba, P. and Sande, T. (1987) *Centre-Periphery Structures in Europe*, An ISSC Workbook in Comparative Analysis, Frankfurt/M.: Campus.

Romer, P. (1990) 'Human Capital and Growth: Theory and Evidence', *Carnegie-Rochester Series on Public Policy* 32: 251–86.

Rose, N. (1999) *Powers of Freedom: Reframing Political Thought*, Cambridge: Cambridge University Press.

Rosenau, J.N. and Czempiel, E.-O. (eds) (1992) *Governance without government: order and change in world politics*, Cambridge: Cambridge University Press.

Rostow, W.W. (1960) *The Stages of Economic Growth: A Non-Communistic Manifesto*, Cambridge: Cambridge University Press.

Rostow, W.W. (1994) 'The Five Stages-of-Growth. A Summary', in R. Kanth (ed.) *Paradigms in Economic Development. Classic Perspectives, Critiques, and Reflections*, Armonk, NY: M.E. Sharpe, pp. 99–106.

Rothstein, B. (1998) *Just Institutions Matter: The Moral and Political Logic of the Universal Welfare State*, Cambridge: Cambridge University Press.

Röttger, B. and Wissen, M. (2005) '(Re)Regulationen des Lokalen', in F. Kessl, C. Reutlinger, S. Maurer and O. Frey (eds) (2005) *Handbuch Sozialraum*, Wiesbaden: VS Verlag, pp. 207–25.

Ruggie, J.G. (1998) 'What Makes the World Hang Together? Neo-utilitarianism and the Social Constructivist Challenge', *International Organization* 52(4): 855–85.

Rumford, C. (2000) *European Cohesion? Contradiction in EU Integration*, London: MacMillan Press.

Rumford, C. (2002) *The European Union: A Political Sociology*, Oxford: Blackwell Publishing.

Rumford, C. (ed.) (2009) *Handbook of European Studies*, London: Sage Publications.

Rykiel, Z. (1997) 'Core and Periphery: The Economic Transformation of Polish Space', in A. Kukliński (ed.), *European Space, Baltic Space, Polish Space – Part II*, Warsaw: European Institute for Regional and Local Development, pp. 301–15.

Sabatier, P. (1998): 'The Advocacy Coalition Framework: Revisions and Relevance for Europe', *Journal of European Public Policy* 5 (March): 98–130.

Sabel, C. (1989) 'Flexible Specialisation and the Re-emergence of Regional Economies, in P. Hirst and J. Zeitlin (eds), *Reversing Industrial Decline? Industrial Structure and Policies in Britain and her Competitors*, Oxford: St. Martins, pp. 17–70.

Sachs, J.D. (1992a) 'The Economic Transformation of Eastern Europe: the Case of Poland', *Economics of Planning*, 25: 5–19.

Sachs, W. (ed.) (1992b) *The Development Dictionary. A Guide to Knowledge as Power*, London: Zed Books.

Sachsenmaier, D., Eisenstadt, S.N. and Riedel, J. (eds) (2002) *Reflections on Multiple Modernities. European, Chinese and Other Interpretations*, Leiden: Brill.

Sahlin-Andersson, K. and Engwall, L. (eds) (2002) *The Expansion of Management Knowledge: Carriers, Flows, and Sources*, Stanford: Standford University Press.

Saillard, Y. (1995) 'Globalisation, localisation and sector-based specialisation: what is the future of national *regulation*?', in R. Boyer and Y. Saillard (eds) *Regulation Theory: The state of the art*, London: Routledge, pp. 181–9.

Salais, R. and Villeneuve, R. (eds) (2005) *Europe and the Politics of Capabilities*, Cambridge: Cambridge University Press.

Salet, W. and Faludi, A. (eds) (2000) *The revival of strategic spatial planning*, Amsterdam: Royal Netherlands Academy of Arts and Sciences.

Sapir, A., Aghion, P., Bertola, G., Hellwig, M., Pisani-Ferry, J., Rosati, D., Viñals, J. and Wallace, H. (2004): *An Agenda for a Growing Europe: The Sapir Report*, Oxford: Oxford University Press.

Sartorius, W. (ed.) (2005) *Implementation of European Regional Development Fund in Poland. Results of the German–French Twinning Project in the Polish Ministry of Economy and Labour*, Warsaw. Available at: www.erdf.edu.pl (accessed 17 May 2007).

Sassen, S. (1991) *The Global City: New York, London, Tokyo*, Princeton: Princeton University Press.

Sassen, S. (2002) 'Locating cities on global circuits', *Environment & Urbanization* 14(1): 13–30.

Saxenian, A. (1994) *Regional Advantage. Culture and Competition in Silicon Valley and Route 128*, Cambridge, MA: Harvard University Press.

Senge, K. and Hellmann, K.-U. (eds) (2006) *Einführung in den Neo-Institutionalismus*, Wiesbaden: VS Verlag.

Scharpf, F.W. (1984) 'Economic and Institutional Constraints of Full-Employment Strategies: Sweden, Austria, and Western Germany, 1973–1982', in J.H. Goldthorpe (ed.), *Order and Conflict in Contemporary Capitalism*, Oxford: Clarendon Press, pp. 257–90.

Scharpf, F.W. (1997) *Games Real Actors Play. Actor-Centered Institutionalism in Policy Research*, Oxford: Westview Press.

Scharpf, F.W. (1999) *Governing Europe – Effective and Democratic?*, Oxford: Oxford University Press.

Schelsky, H. (1965) 'Der Mensch in der Wissenschaftlichen Zivilisation', in id., *Auf der Suche nach der Wirklichkeit. Gesammelte Aufsätze*, Düsseldorf-Köln: Diederichs, pp. 439–81.

Schelsky, H. (1975) *Die Arbeit tun die anderen. Klassenkampf und Priesterherrschaft der Intellektuellen*. 2. enl. edn, Opladen: Westdeutscher Verlag.

Schimank, U. (2005) *Die Entscheidungsgesellschaft: Komplexität und Rationalität der Moderne*, Wiesbaden: VS Verlag.

Schimmelfennig, F. and Sedelmeier, U. (2005) *The Europeanization of Central and Eastern Europe*, Ithaca: Cornell University Press.

Schluchter, W. (1989) *Rationalism, Religion, and Domination. A Weberian Perspective*, Berkeley: University of California Press.

Schluchter, W. (1996) *Paradoxes of Modernity. Culture and Conduct in the Theory of Max* Weber, Stanford: Stanford University Press.

Schmidt, V.A. (2008) 'Discursive Institutionalism: The Explanatory Power of Ideas and Discourse', *Annual Review of Political Sciences* 11: 303–26.

Schofer, E. and McEneaney, E. (2003) 'Methodological Strategies and Tools for the Study of Globalization', in G.S. Drori, J.W. Meyer, F.O. Ramirez and E. Schofer (eds), *Science in the Modern World Polity: Institutionalization and Globalization*, Stanford: Stanford University Press, pp. 43–74.

Schofer, E. and Meyer, J.W. (2005) 'The World-Wide Expansion of Higher Education in the Twentieth Century', *American Sociological Review* 70: 898–920.

Schofer, E. (2004) 'Cross-national Differences in the Expansion of Science, 1970–1990', *Social Forces* 83(1): pp. 215–48.

Schulze, G. (2000, 1st edn 1992), *Die Erlebnisgesellschaft. Kultursoziologie der Gegenwart*, 8th edn, Frankfurt/M.: Campus (engl. trans. The Experience Society, London: Sage Publication, 2007).

Schürmmann, C. and Talaat, A. (2000) *Towards a European Peripherality Index: Final Report for the General Directorate XVI Regional Policy of the European Commission*, Dortmund: Institut für Raumplanung.

Schütz, A. (1973) *Collected Papers I: The Problem of Social Reality*, edited by Maurice Natanson, The Hague: Martinus Nijhoff.

Schwinn, T. (2006) 'Konvergenz, Divergenz oder Hybridisierung?', *Kölner Zeitschrift für Soziologie und Sozialpsychologie* 58(2): 201–32.

Scott, A.J. (1993) *Technopolis: High-technology Industry and Regional Development in Southern California*, Berkley: University of California Press.

Scott, A.J. (1988) *New Industrial Spaces*, London: Pion.

Scott, A.J. (1996) 'Regional Motors of the Global Economy', *Futures* 28(5), 391–411.

Scott, A.J. (1998) *Regions and the World Economy: The Coming Shape of Global Production, Competition, and Political Order*, Oxford: Oxford University Press.

Scott, A.J. and Storper, M. (2003) 'Regions, Globalization, Development', *Regional Studies* 37(6/7), pp. 579–93.

Scott, W.R. (2001) *Institutions and Organizations*, 2nd edn, London: Sage Publications.

Scott, W.R. (2003) 'Institutional carriers: reviewing modes of transporting ideas over time and space and considering their consequences', *Industrial and Corporate Change* 12(4): 879–94.

Scott, W.R. (2008) 'Lords of the Dance: Professionals as Institutional Agents', *Organization Studies* 29(2): 219–38.

SERN (2004) *Cohesive thinking towards a sustainable future: report of the Sustainable European Regions network* (ISBN 0 7504 3590 S).

Shaw, M. (2003) 'The State of Globalization: Towards a Theory of State Transformation', in N. Brenner, B. Jessop, M. Jones and G. MacLeod (eds) *State/Space: A Reader*, Oxford: Blackwell Publishing, pp. 117–29.

Shore, C. (2000) *Building Europe. The Cultural Politics of European Integration*, London: Routledge.

Simmie, J. (2004) 'Innovation and Space: A Critical Review of the Literature', *Regional Studies* 39(6): 789–804.

Simmons, B.A., Dobbin, F. and Garrett, G. (2006) 'Introduction: The International Diffusion of Liberalism', *International Organization* 60: 781–810.

Sklair, L. (1991) *Sociology of the Global System*, Baltimore: Johns Hopkins University Press.

Skocpol, T. (1979) *States and Social Revolutions: A Comparative Study of France, Russia and China*, Cambridge: Cambridge University Press.

Smelser, N.J. and Swedberg, R. (eds) (1994) *The Handbook of Economic Sociology*, Princeton: Princeton University Press.

Smith, A. (2007, 1st edn 1776) *An Inquiry into the Nature and Causes of Wealth of Nations*, New York: MetaLibri.

Smith, N. (2003) 'Remaking Scale: Competition and Cooperation in Pre-National and Post-National Europe', in N. Brenner, B. Jessop, M. Jones and G. MacLeod (eds) (2003), *State/Space: A Reader*, Oxford: Blackwell Publishing, pp. 227–38.

Soja, E.W. (1989) *Postmodern Geographies: The Reassertion of Space in Critical Social Theory*, New York: Verso.

Soysal, Y.N. (1994) *Limits of Citizenship. Migrants and Postnational Membership in Europe*, Chicago: University of Chicago Press.

Spencer, H. (1851) *Social Statics: or, the conditions essential to Human Happiness specified, and the first of them developed*, London: Chapman.

Stark, D. and Bruszt, L. (1998) *Postsocialist Pathways: Transforming Politics and Property in East Central Europe*, Cambridge: Cambridge University Press.

Stehr, N. (1994) *Arbeit, Eigentum und Wissen: Zur Theorie von Wissensgesellschaften*, Frankfurt/M.: Suhrkamp.

Stehr, N. and Ericson, R.V. (eds) (1992) *The Culture and Power of Knowledge. Inquiries into Contemporary Societies*, Berlin: Walter de Gruyter.

Steinmetz, G. (ed.) (1999) *State/Culture: State-Formation after the Cultural Turn*, Ithaca: Cornell University Press.

Steinmo, S., Thelen, K. and Longstreth, F. (eds) (1992) *Structuring Politics: Historical Institutionalism in Comparative Analysis*, Cambridge: Cambridge University Press.

Stichweh, R. (2000) *Die Weltgesellschaft. Soziologische Analysen*, Frankfurt/M.: Suhrkamp.

Stiglitz, J. (2003) *Globalization and its Discontents*, New York: Norton & Company.

Stone Sweet, A., Sandholtz, W. and Fligstein, N. (eds) (2001) *The Institutionalization of Europe*, Oxford: Oxford University Press.

Storper, M. (1989) 'The transition to flexible specialization in the U.S. film industry: external economies, the division of labor, and the crossing of industrial divides', *Cambridge Journals of Economics* 13: 273–305.

Storper, M. (1995) 'The Resurgence of Regional Economies, Ten Years Later: The Region as a Nexus of Untraded Interdependencies', *European Urban and Regional Studies* 2(3): 191–221.

Storper, M. (1997) 'Territories, Flows, and Hierachies in the Global Economy', in K.R.

Cox (ed.), *Spaces of Globalization: Reasserting the Power of the Local*, New York: The Guilford Press, pp. 19–44.

Storper, M. and Salais, R. (1997) *Worlds of production. The action frameworks of the economy*, Cambridge, MA: Harvard University Press.

Storper, M. and Scott, A.J. (eds) (1992) *Pathways to Industrialization and Regional Development*, London: Routledge.

Storper, M. and Walker, R. (1984) 'The spatial division of labor: Labor and the location of industries', in L. Sawyers and W.K. Tabb (eds), *Sunbelt/Snowbelt: Urban Development and Regional Restructuring*, New York: Oxford University Press, pp. 19–47.

Storper, M. and Walker, R. (1989) *The Capitalist Imperative: Territory, Technology, and Industrial Growth*, Oxford: Basil Blackwell.

Strang, D. and Meyer, J.W. (1993) 'Institutional Conditions for Diffusion', *Theory and Society* 22(4): 487–511.

Strange, T. and Bayley, A. (2008) *Sustainable Development. Linking economy, society, environment*, Paris: OECD.

Strassoldo, R. (1981) 'Center and Periphery: Socio-Ecological Perspectives', in A. Kuklinski (ed.) *Polarized Development and Regional Policies*, New York: Mouton Publishers, pp. 71–102.

Sud de Surie, G. (2008) *Knowledge, Organizational Evolution and Market Creation. The Globalization of Indian Firms from Steel to Software*, Cheltenham: Edward Elgar.

Swianiewicz, P. (ed.) (2002) *Consolidation or Fragmentation? The Size of Local Governments in Central and Eastern Europe. Local Government and Public Service Reform Initiative*, Budapest: Open Society Institute.

Swianiewicz, P., Woodward, R., Dziemianowicz, W., Kaniewska, M., Pander, W. and Szmigiel, K. (2005): 'The Evolution of Regional Development Regimes in CEE – Poland', *NewGov Working paper*, Florence. Available at: www.eu-newgov.org/datalists/deliverables_detail.asp?Project_ID=15 (accessed March 2009).

Swidler, A. (1986) 'Culture in Action: Symbols and Strategies', *American Sociological Review* 51: 273–86.

Swyngedouw, E. (1997) 'Neither Global nor Local: "Glocalization" and the Politics of Scale', in K.R. Cox (ed.), *Spaces of Globalization: Reasserting the Power of the Local*, New York: The Guilford Press, pp. 137–66.

Sztompka, P. (1993) 'Civilisational Incompetence. The Trap of Post-Communist Societies', *Zeitschrift für Soziologie* 22(2): 85–95.

Sztompka, P. (1999) *Trust. A Sociological Inquiry*, Cambridge: Cambridge University Press.

Tarkowska, E. (2008) 'Armut in Polen', *Polen-Analysen*, No. 28: 2–10.

Tatur, M. (1991) 'Die Bedeutung der „etatistischen Gesellschaft" in Polen für die soziologische Theorie', *Leviathan* 19(2): 292–304.

Tatur, M. (1991) (ed.) (2004a) *The Making of Regions in Post-Socialist Europe – the Impact of Culture, Economic Structure and Institutions. Case Studies from Poland, Hungary, Romania and Ukraine*, Vol. 1, Wiesbaden: VS Verlag.

Tatur, M. (1991) (ed.) (2004b) *The Making of Regions in Post-Socialist Europe – the Impact of Culture, Economic Structure and Institutions. Case Studies from Poland, Hungary, Romania and Ukraine*, Vol. 2, Wiesbaden: VS Verlag.

Taylor, P.J. (1993) *Political Geography: World-Economy, Nation-State, and Locality*, Harlow: Longman.

Taylor, P.J. (2003) 'The State as Container: Territoriality in the Modern World-System', in N. Brenner, B. Jessop, M. Jones and G. MacLeod (eds) *State/Space: A Reader*, Oxford: Blackwell Publishing, pp. 101–13.

Taylor, P.J. (2004) *World City Network. A global urban analysis*, London: Routledge.

Tenbruck, F.H. (1972) *Zur Kritik der planenden Vernunft*, München: Verlag Karl Alber.

Tenbruck, F.H. (1990) 'The dream of a secular ecumene: the meaning and limits of politics of development', *Theory, Culture & Society* 7: 193–206.

Thelen, K. (1999) 'Historical Institutionalism in Comparative Politics', *Annual Reveiw of Political Science* (2): 369–404.

Therborn, G. (1995) *European Modernity and Beyond: The Trajectory of European Societies, 1945–2000*, London: Sage Publications.

Thevenot, L. (2002) 'Which road to follow? The moral complexity of an "equipped" humanity', in J. Law and A. Mol (eds), *Complexities: Social Studies of Knowledge Practices*, Durham: Duke University Press, pp. 53–87.

Thomas, G.M. and Meyer J.W., Ramirez, F.O. and Boli, J. (1987) *Institutional Structure: Constituting State, Society, and the Individual*, London: Sage Publications.

Thomas, G.M. and Meyer, J.W. (1984) 'The Expansion of the State', *Annual Review of Sociology* 10: 461–82.

Thomas, W.I. and Znaniecki, F. (1984, 1st edn 1918) *The Polish Peasant in Europe and America*. Urbana: University of Illinois Press.

Thurow, L. (1996) *The Future of Capitalism: how today's economic forces shape tomorrow's world*, New York: Morrow.

Tickell, A. and Peck, J. (1992) 'Accumulation, regulation and the geographies of post-Fordism: missing links in regulationist research', *Progress in Human Geography* 16: 190–218.

Topolski, J. (1997) 'Eastern Poland during the socialist industrialization and after. How ambitious plans fail', in H.-H. Nolte (ed.), *Europäische innere Peripherien im 20. Jahrhundert: European Internal Peripheries in the 20th Century*, Stuttgart: Steiner Verlag, pp. 226–35.

Trenz, H.-J. (2008) 'Elements of a sociology of European integration', *ARENA Working Paper*, No. 11 (2008), Oslo: Centre for European Studies. Available at: www.arena. uio.no (accessed: January 2009).

Trigilia, C. (2001) 'Social Capital and Local Development', *European Journal of Social Theory* 4: 427–42.

UNESCO (2000) *World Culture Report: Cultural Diversity, Conflict and Pluralism*, Paris: UNESCO Publishing.

Urry, J. (2003) *Global Complexity*, Oxford: Blackwell Publishing.

Urry, J. (2007) *Mobilities*, Cambridge: Polity Press.

Valente, T.W. (1995) *Network Models of the Diffusion of Innovations*, New York: Hampton Press.

Varró, K. (2008) 'Changing Narratives on EU Multi-level Space in a Globalizing Era: How Hungary as a *National* Space became Part of the Story', *European Planning Studies* 16 (7): 955–69.

Varró, K. and Lagendijk, A. (2006) 'The role of experts in CEE regionalization processes', paper presented at the RSA Conference in Leuven, Belgium, June 2006. Available at: www.ru.nl/planologie/koppeling_naar/varro/ (accessed April 2009).

Veblen, T. (1967, 1st edn 1899) *The Theory of the Leisure Class*, New York: Penguin.

Vobruba, G. (2001) *Integration + Erweiterung. Europa im Globalisierungsdilemma*, Wien: Passagen.

Vobruba, G. (2007): *Die Dynamik Europas*, 2nd edn, Wiesbaden: VS Verlag.

Voelzkow, H. (1997): 'Können Räume handeln? Die Steuerung regionaler Modernisierung', in H. Weber and B. Streich (eds), *City-Management: Städteplanung zwischen Globalisierung und Virtualität*, Opladen: Westdeutscher Verlag, pp. 177–90.

Wagner, P. (1994) *A Sociology of Modernity: Liberty and Discipline*, London: Routledge.

Wagner, P. (2001a) *A History and Theory of the Social Sciences*, London: Sage Publications.

Wagner, P. (2001b) *Theorizing Modernity. Inescapability and Attainability in Social Theory*, London: Publications.

Wagner, P., Weiss, C.H., Wittrock, B. and Wollman, H. (eds) (1991) *Social Sciences and Modern States: National Experiences and Theoretical Crossroads*, Cambridge: Cambridge University Press.

Wallerstein, I. (1974) *The Modern World System, Vol. I. Capitalist Agriculture and the Origins of the European World-Economy in the Sixteenth Century*, New York: Academic Press.

Wallerstein, I. (1979) *The Capitalist World Economy*, Cambridge: Cambridge University Press.

Wallerstein, I. (1980) *The Modern World-System, Vol. II. Mercantilism and the Consolidation of the European World-Economy, 1600–1750,* New York: Academic Press.

Wallerstein, I. (1984) *The Politics of the World-Economy. The States, the Movements and the Civilizations*, Cambridge: Cambridge University Press.

Wallerstein, I. (1989): *The Modern World-System, Vol. III. The Second Great Expansion of the Capitalist World-Economy, 1730–1840s*, San Diego: Academic Press.

Wallerstein, I. (1991) 'The national and the universal: can there be such a thing as world culture?', in A.D. King (ed.), *Culture, Globalization and the World-System. Contemporary conditions for the representation of identity*, 2nd edn, Minneapolis: University of Minnesota Press, pp. 91–105.

Wallerstein, I. (2006) *European Universalism: The Rhetoric of Power*, New York: New Press.

Waltz, K.M. (1979) *Theory of International Politics*, Reading, MA: Addison-Wesley.

Walzer, M. (1992) *What it Means to be an American: Essays on the American experience*, New York: Marsilio.

Walzer, M. (1999) *On Toleration*, Yale: Yale University Press.

Watson, W.E. (1998) *The Collapse of Communism in the Soviet Union*, London: Greenwood Press.

Weber, M. (1976, 1st edn 1920/21) *Gesammelte Aufsätze zur Religionssoziologie*, 3 vols, Tübingen: Mohr Siebeck.

Weber, M. (1980, 1st edn 1921) *Wirtschaft und Gesellschaft. Grundriss der verstehenden Soziologie. Studienausgabe*, Tübingen: Mohr Siebeck.

Weingart, P. (1983) 'Verwissenschaftlichung der Gesellschaft – Politisierung der Wissenschaft', *Zeitschrift für Soziologie* 12(3): 225–41.

Weingart, P. (2001) *Die Stunde der Wahrheit? Zum Verhältnis der Wissenschaft zu Politik, Wirtschaft und den Medien in der Wissensgesellschaft*, Weilerswist: Velbrück Wissenschaft.

Weingart, P., Carrier, M. and Krohn, W. (eds) (2007) *Nachrichten aus der Wissensgesellschaft. Analysen zur Veränderung von Wissenschaft*, Weilerswist: Velbrück Wissenschaft.

Weingast, B. (2002) 'Rational Choice Institutionalism', in I. Katznelson and H. Milner (eds), *Political Science: The State of the Discipline*, New York: Norton and Company, pp. 660–92.

Wendt, A. (1999) *Social Theory of International Politics*, Cambridge: Cambridge University Press.

Westney, D.E. (1987) *Imitation and Innovation: The Transfer of Western Organizational Patterns to Meiji Japan*, Cambridge, MA: Harvard University Press.

Wiener, A. (2008) *The Invisible Constitution of Politics: Contested Norms and International Encounters*, Cambridge: Cambridge University Press.

Wilensky, H.L. (1964) 'The Professionalization of Everyone?', *The American Journal of Sociology* 70(2): 137–58.

Williamson, O.E. (1985) *The Economic Institutions of Capitalism*, New York: Free Press.

World Bank (2005) *The World Bank's Sustainable Development Reference Guide*. Washington D.C.: ESSD Departments of the World Bank. Available: http://go.worldbank.org/A0QSVI79Q0 (15 July 2009).

Yoder, J.A. (2003) 'Decentralisation and Regionalisation after Communism: Administrative and Territorial Reform in Poland and the Czech Republic', *Europe-Asia Studies* 55(2): 263–286.

Yuill, D. (ed.) (1982) *Regional Development Agencies in Europe*, Aldershot: Gower.

Zapf, W. (ed.) (1971) *Theorien des sozialen Wandels*, Berlin: Kiepenheuer&Witsch.

Zarycki, T. (2007) 'History and regional development. A controversy over the 'right' interpretation of the role of history in the development of the Polish regions.', *GeoForum* 38(2): 485–93.

Zarycki, T. (2008) 'Polish space in the perspective of the long duration', P. Jakubowska, A. Kukliński and P. Żuber (eds), *The future of regions in the perspective of global change.* Part One, Warszawa: Ministry for Regional Development of Poland, pp. 247–98.

Zarycki, T. and Nowak, A. (2000) 'Hidden dimensions: the stability and structure of regional political cleavages in Poland', *Communist and Post-Communist Studies* 33(3): 331–54.

Zarząd Województwa Dolnośląskiego (2000) *Strategia Rozwoju Województwa Dolnośląskiego*, Lublin.

Zarząd Województwa Lubelskiego (2000) *Strategia Rozwoju Województwa Lubelskiego*, Lublin.

Zarząd Województwa Lubelskiego (2005) *Strategia Rozwoju Województwa Lubelskiego na lata 2006–2020*. Lublin.

Zarząd Województwa Podkarpackiego (2000) *Strategie Rozwoju Województwa Podkarpackiego*, Rzeszów.

Zarząd Województwa Podkarpackiego (2006) *Strategie Rozwoju Województwa Podkarpackiego na lata 2007–2020*, Rzeszów.

Zeitlin, J. (1990) *Industrial Districts and Local Economic Regeneration: Models, Institutions and Policies*, Geneva: International Institute of Labour Studies.

Ziai, A. (ed.) (2007) *Exploring Post-Development: Theory and Practice, Problems and Perspectives*, London: Routledge.

Zientara, P. (2008) 'Polish Regions in the Age of a Knowledge-based Economy', *International Journal of Urban and Regional Research* 32(1): 60–85.

Zimmer, A. and Priller, E. (2004) *Future of Civil Society: Making Central European Non-Profit Organizations Work*, Wiesbaden: VS-Verlag.

Żuber, P. (2000) 'Teoria i praktyka opracowania strategii rozwoju województwa – prace nad strategiami rozwoju województw w oewietle ankiety Ministerstwa Gospodarki', *Studia Regionalne i Lokalne* 3(3): 87–97.

Żuber, P. (2005) 'The National Development Plan 2007–2013 as a response to the challenges facing Poland in the European Union', in W. Sartorius (ed.), *Implementation of European Regional Development Fund in Poland. Results of the German-French Twinning Project in the Polish Ministry of Economy and Labour*, Warsaw, pp. 33–8.

Zucker, L.G. (1983) 'Organizations as Institutions', in S. Bacharach (ed.), *Research in the Sociology of Organizations*, vol. 2, Greenwich: JAI Press, pp. 1–47.

Zukowski, R. (2004) 'Historical path dependence, institutional persistence, and transition to market economy. The case of Poland', *International Journal of Social Economics* 31(10): 955–73.

Zürn, M. and Joerges, C. (2005) *Law and Governance in Postnational Europe*, Cambridge: Cambridge University Press.

Zürn, M. and Leibfried, S. (eds.) (2005) *Transformations of the State?*, Cambridge: Cambridge University Press.

Index